INTERNAL IMPROVEMENT

INTERNAL IMPROVEMENT

National Public Works and the Promise of Popular
Government in the Early United States

JOHN LAURITZ LARSON

THE UNIVERSITY OF NORTH CAROLINA PRESS | CHAPEL HILL AND LONDON

The paper in this book meets the guidelines for permanence
and durability of the Committee on Production Guidelines for
Book Longevity of the Council on Library Resources.

Library of Congress Cataloging-in-Publication Data
Larson, John Lauritz, 1950–
Internal improvement : national public works and the promise
of popular government in the early United States /
by John Lauritz Larson.
p. cm. Includes bibliographical references and index.
ISBN 0-8078-2595-6 (cloth: alk. paper)
ISBN 0-8078-4911-1 (pbk.: alk. paper)
1. United States—Economic policy—To 1933. 2. United
States—Economic conditions—To 1865. 3. Infrastructure
(Economics)—Government policy—United States—
History—19th century. 4. Public works—Government
policy—United States—History—19th century. I. Title.
HC105.L26 2001 338.973—dc21 00-060721

Frontispiece: Samuel F. B. Morse's "The Old House of
Representatives" was itself a tribute to the promise of popular
government in the new United States. Courtesy The Cor-
coran Gallery of Art, Museum Purchase, Gallery Fund.

05 04 03 02 01   5 4 3 2 1

For John L. Thomas and A. Hunter Dupree,
and in memory of Earl J. Leland:
three generous mentors

CONTENTS

TABLES AND MAPS

Tables

Maps

ILLUSTRATIONS

ACKNOWLEDGMENTS

INTELLECTUAL DEBTS pile up on any project, but when one takes as long as I have to finish a book the real danger lies in forgetting someone from too many years ago. Inspiration in the broadest sense began with A. Hunter Dupree, who first taught me to think about technological systems, how they come about, and how they become entangled in the process with social, economic, ideological, and even spiritual systems. For the confidence (some might say impertinence) to take on a host of "founding fathers" and other icons of American history I thank Jack Thomas, who taught me to write boldly, saying "better to hang for a sheep than a goat." For seducing me into the business of trying to understand the way the world works, I must credit an earlier mentor, the late Earl J. Leland of Luther College, whose inimitable lectures, rants, and rambles captured my imagination immediately and never let it go. To these three generous mentors this book is gratefully dedicated.

For additional courage to tackle this tangled story I am indebted to Joseph H. Harrison Jr., who in 1985 rose like a shade from the back of an OAH session at which I had just delivered an exploratory paper. This author of *the* classic 1954 dissertation on internal improvement introduced himself elegantly and placed at my disposal the insights of a lifetime pondering these issues. Andrew R. L. Cayton and Mary K. Cayton, once graduate school friends and now trusted, middle-aged colleagues, endured long conversations and reviewed drafts going back almost to the time of the Gallatin Plan itself. Likewise, A. G. Roeber urged me onward, especially during the early years of this project. At Purdue, Michael A. Morrison, James R. Farr, Harold D. Woodman, Don Parman, and other colleagues and graduate students have criticized my efforts (dare I say?) relentlessly. Away from home, I have received essential advice from Peter S. Onuf at Virginia, Harry L. Watson at North Carolina, Michael Lacey at the Woodrow Wilson Center, Robert H. Wiebe at Northwestern, Ron Hoffman at the Omohundro Institute for Early American History and Culture, Gordon S. Wood at Brown University, Mary O. Furner at Northern Illinois University, Richard John at the University of Illinois, Chicago, and Lewis Bateman, then at the University of North Carolina Press. Each of these individuals has shown me why it is we do our best work within a community of scholars and not alone in a commercial marketplace.

Money plagued early internal improvements, and it seemed about as important and hard to get to this historian of public works. For essential financial assistance and research support I am indebted to the National Endowment for the Humanities (two summers), to the American Bar Foundation, the American Association for State and Local History, the Indiana Historical Society, the North Carolina Commission for the Bicentennial of the Constitution, the Purdue Research Foundation (twice), the Purdue School of Liberal Arts Center for Humanistic Studies, the American Program at the Woodrow Wilson Center (twice), and the United States Capitol Historical Society. The National Archives made me comfortable during two forays into congressional records, for which I thank the staff in Washington, Raymond Smock (then historian of the House of Representatives), and the clerk of the House of Representatives who is custodian of petitions to the House.

In the space usually given to thanking archivists and librarians I want to notice the invaluable contribution to scholarship made by the editors and sponsors of the huge (and hugely expensive) letterpress editions of the papers of leading characters in early American history. Dozens of dependable, carefully annotated, handsomely produced volumes of the papers of Washington, Adams, Jefferson, Madison, Clay, Calhoun, Webster, and others adorn the shelves of good research libraries today. Because of them I was able to scan the whole correspondence of major players in these episodes for decades at a time. No single individual in a lifetime could possibly digest so much material in manuscript form, nor could these professional editors possibly have reproduced as many mistakes as any one pair of eyes must make deciphering a score of unfamiliar hands. Few of these publishing projects are completed, and all of them are desperate for continuing financial support. The internet alone will never relieve the expense of editorial preparation for these editions even if it someday brings down the cost of final delivery. Because of our investment in these sets, scholarship today is richer, easier, and more democratic than ever before. Everyone, please keep supporting this good work!

Three segments of this book first saw light as essays or articles, and I thank the editors and publishers for permission to incorporate material from those drafts into the final manuscript. Portions of chapter 1 appeared in "'Wisdom Enough to Improve Them': Government, Liberty, and Inland Waterways in the Rising American Empire," in *Launching the "Extended Republic,"* ed. Ronald Hoffman and Peter J. Albert (Charlottesville: University Press of Virginia for the U.S. Capitol Historical Society, 1996), 223–48. Parts of chapter 2 appeared as a 250th birthday present for Thomas Jefferson entitled "Jefferson's Union and the Problem of Internal Improvements," in *Jeffersonian Legacies,* ed. Peter S. Onuf (Charlottesville: University Press of Virginia, 1993), 340–69. Sections of chapter 4 appeared in "Liberty by Design: Freedom, Planning, and John Quincy Adams's

'American System,' " in *The State and Economic Knowledge*, ed. Mary O. Furner and Barry E. Supple (New York: Cambridge University Press for the Woodrow Wilson Center, 1990), 73–102.

Finally, my now-grown children, Anna and Olaf, and my long-suffering spouse, Suzanne, scarcely can remember a day when I was not worried about internal improvements in the nineteenth century—sometimes at the expense of immediate responsibilities in the twentieth. (I recall begging a friend one August to take my then-young son for four days so I could bang out a draft of the Jefferson essay before Peter Onuf demanded my head!) Members of my family never shared my fascination with the promise of government in the new United States, but they have not often held this obsession against me either. Jake did not live to see the work completed, but Juneau took up his job and has kept watch with extraordinary dedication. To these sturdy Norwegians (and canines) I acknowledge incalculable debts, and I offer humble thanks for your love and apparently boundless understanding. It has been a joy to know you.

INTERNAL IMPROVEMENT

An Experiment in Republicanism

WHY CREATE THE American republic? For what purpose did the inhabitants of British North America—arguably the freest and wealthiest people on earth in the middle of the eighteenth century—throw off colonial rule and establish a union of independent states? Seeking to affirm (or sometimes reform) the outcome of their Revolution, generations of Americans have supplied different answers to the question of the purpose of American republicanism: to throw off a tyrant king, to establish a continental empire, to secure the blessings of liberty, to promote equality, to release the genius of enterprise, to lead the march of "progress," to war against dictators and defend the "free world." Led by the rhetoric of the founders into believing that the republic's goals were virtuous, its truths "self-evident," Americans over two centuries have argued (and continue to argue today) that the meaning of American liberty is transparent and that all subsequent history and practical politics can be judged by the light of the creators' original intentions.

Such a reification of the founding experience badly distorts our understanding of how American republicanism took shape, how it evolved into American democracy, and how the purpose of government has changed within the framework of American constitutions. Professional historians writing about the American Revolution now place at the center of the story not a transparent mission but an experiment in republicanism. Rather than a splendid liberation (followed by inevitable decline), most historians now portray a process of innovation, driven (depending on whose account) by class conflict, localism, self-interest, or idealistic zeal, but knit together by a common vocabulary and a package of political assumptions that the revolutionaries themselves called republicanism. Of course, modern scholars disagree about the origins and influence of American revolutionary republicanism; but no serious work of history fails to acknowledge at least the widespread use of republican language in giving form to the hopes and dreams of the American founding generation.[1]

This pervasive use of the same words has encouraged explanations of the

American Revolution that attribute to the whole body of revolutionary actors the motives and reasons of an articulate few. The mistake is doubly easy to make because "gentlemen" of the eighteenth century presumed to speak for the "lower orders," while common people sometimes seized the rhetoric of republicanism as an invitation to speak for themselves. In reality, there were many different revolutions within the American revolutionary movement, and this fact profoundly influenced politics in the postrevolutionary era. Many Americans, especially property holders of elite or middling status, joined the experiment in republicanism in order to protect the liberty and happiness they already enjoyed. Others—journeymen, farm workers, laborers, women, slaves, religious dissenters—hoped through revolutionary self-creation to pry open even further the structures of a society already fluid by European standards but still hierarchical in its expectations and in danger of growing more so. Still others of all ranks resisted the revolutionary movement, fearing the chaos of experimentation or distrusting the integrity of local revolution makers—whose character they sometimes knew too well![2]

For all these citizens of the new United States, the Peace of Paris in 1783 officially marked the end of revolutionary destruction and the beginning of national creation. The work of discrediting the old order, however incomplete, was over; the work of reconstruction and innovation lay ahead. Had revolutionary republicanism projected one clear and universal meaning, this work of positive creation would have been difficult enough. But republicanism sustained all kinds of visions, rooted in different classic texts, different intellectual justifications, different personal, regional, and class aspirations. Accordingly, the work of national creation carried forward into the postrevolutionary world the work of self-definition and political imagination that had made the Revolution in the first place. Constitutional conventions first formally addressed this problem, reflecting the novel American assumption that written constitutions could radically reorganize the state, define the role of citizens in politics, and confer upon the whole extraordinary proceeding the blessing of perfect legitimacy. In practice, however, constitutional agreements proved fragile and elusive as local, class, and ideological differences emerged from under the consensus of wartime patriotism. Furthermore, for every advocate of systematic theory there were dozens of new citizens who would judge the virtue of republican government by the quality of life they enjoyed under its protection. Exercising over and over again the radical promise of self-creation that lay at the heart of republican theory, these expedient revolutionaries would revise and reinvent their governments and society until the exercise itself became imbedded in the system.[3]

This book studies one aspect of this process of national creation. My objective is to illustrate the complex interaction of different strains of revolutionary republicanism with the actual practice of politics and government under new constitutions in environments of clashing interests and rapidly changing conditions—instabilities that were exaggerated by the Revolution itself. The central issue is "internal improvement," a term used loosely in the 1780s to refer to all kinds of programs to encourage security, prosperity, and enlightenment among the people of the new United States. Gradually the first generation identified roads, canals, schools, and technological innovations as the instruments of improvement that urgently deserved public attention. Eventually the concept narrowed still further until it became synonymous with public works for improved transportation, because in the sprawling continental Union nothing threatened the mutual interests of the citizens and their states like geographical isolation. My focus, however, is not on roads and canals themselves but on government, and more specifically on the struggle by Americans at the state and federal levels to implement the promise of republican liberty by promoting designs for internal improvement.[4]

It is my contention that the positive use of government power for popular constructive purposes, such as public works of internal improvement, never was proscribed by American republicanism but lay well within the presumed legitimate authority of revolutionary governments. In fact, one of the virtues of republican government supposedly lay in its capacity to render safe and liberal the pursuit of human improvement by representative authorities. In the hands of arbitrary rulers, purposeful designs and high-handed government easily tyrannized nations, fostering the interests of corrupt favorites at the expense of the freedoms of the people. But in proper republics, designs supposedly could emanate only from the people themselves. Unless produced by dishonest intrigue, the designs of republican governors must necessarily reflect the public interest and serve the common good. Therefore, new American governments ought to have been ideally situated, not just to keep the peace and preserve order, but to foster improvement in the conditions of life.[5]

Enjoying the common rhetoric of republicanism and having carefully designed constitutions in each of the several states, postwar Americans turned with a mixture of confidence and apprehension to the problem of implementation: what should they do with their freedom and the governments they now controlled? A frankly enterprising people, Americans readily perceived their liberties in economic terms as they turned their peacetime attention once more to pursuit of private gain. They had learned their enterprising ways in a mercantilist world of bounties, restrictions, incentives, protections, and regulations, the impact of which had fallen very unevenly on the colonists. Correspondingly, some revolutionary citizens hoped to see their markets liberated by the new regime, whereas others naturally expected governments to promote and protect their collective American (as distinct from imperial British) prosperity. And what constituted prosperity? Should it be reckoned as the wealth of local, regional, or national communities, or merely as the sum of individual fortunes? Finally, although some Americans hoped to find a virtuous and orderly society on the far side of revolution, many others envisioned a world turned upside down. Could the same "good government" foster both? Coming out of the independence movement, republican constitutions had ensured certain means of making government policy; however, the ends of policy remained controversial and imprecise.[6]

Thus with high hopes the experiment was launched. Persons of great and small ambitions clamored after schemes to advance their fortunes and secure public improvement. But their ambitions were not harmonious, and bitter conflicts quickly distorted the practice of government in the new United States. Each proposal for government action promised its own particular results, and various internal improvers sponsored value-laden programs intended to produce economic growth, cultural change, and either local or national consolidation according to purposeful designs. Advocates of commerce and manufacturing projected different images of ideal future development than did their agricultural neighbors. Some individuals charted their visions on a local scale; others dreamed of larger systems or even empire. Very quickly—and with no little irony—people found the seeds of paralyzing conflict within the broadly popular and virtuous objectives of internal improvement. They took to supporting or opposing public works according to their private or local interests, and sometimes according to whether they believed that the revolution had empowered the nation, the states, or private individuals to impinge on the conditions of life for the larger community.

Internal improvement, then, represented some of the work that remained for Americans as a people, once they had created their self-governing republics. How to pursue internal improvement became a question that in turn sharpened certain distinctions about the nature of liberty and the role of government within the framework of American republicanism. Some people inclined toward a modern liberal or even libertarian arrangement, where the state did little more than protect property and commercial exchanges. Others craved more energetic governments, actively shaping a bountiful future or (alternatively) shielding a comfortable people from unruly winds of change. Most Americans remained unsure of any extreme and felt their way cautiously toward things they desired, working out the principles one case at a time. Like the patriotic leaders of the revolutionary era, the many advocates of postwar internal improvement worked feverishly to advance their pet projects and also the principles of design that underlay their ambitions, shaping the world to come and defining the purpose of republican self-government. As these different underlying visions gradually came into view, American politics grew more distrustful. The true nature of the republican experiment would be determined not by wars for independence or by written constitutions, but by the firstfruits of popular governments and by the meanings that prevailed in the language of republican politics.

Americans of the late twentieth century have been conditioned to see free enterprise and government noninterference as virtues so compelling and self-evident that they must have been the goals of our revolutionary forebears. During the course of the nineteenth century, the advocates of private-sector liberty and laissez-faire policy triumphed so completely in the United States that educated persons today commonly are unaware that there ever was a contest or that any but communists and ne'er-do-wells ever supported economic planning and social design. Yet, in the early decades of the republic, articulate, even elegant designs for social and economic development sprang from leading minds of the revolutionary generation, setting the agenda for politics and competing for popular approbation. How such promotions were introduced, whose interests they promised to serve, and whether they yielded the desired results all helped shape the electorate's attitudes toward energetic government. No less important, however, was the way in which the enemies of particular projects, or of internal improvement in general, exploited the rhetoric of revolutionary republicanism to discredit positive government and advance a libertarian variation as the true legacy of the American Revolution. Within a decade of the ratification of the 1787 Constitution, all kinds of schemes for internal improvement—whether for universities, libraries, roads, canals, or river and harbor improvements—were engendering bitter debates about class rule, popular sovereignty, the virtues of agriculture or commerce, regional jealousy, states' rights, national consolidation, and the return of government corruption.

The eventual triumph in American policy of what is now called classical liberal economic thinking—or laissez-faire—owed much to the story of internal improvement and the complex web of arguments that surrounded designs for promoting roads and canals during the half century between the Revolution and the rise of "Jacksonian Democracy." Early projects often failed, soaking up great sums of investment capital while yielding little or no general benefit. Wherever improvements enjoyed the patronage of government, such disappointments enhanced the credibility of political opponents, whose real purposes ranged from a zealous hatred of modernization to selfish protection of local advantages, investments in rival projects, sincere concern for the balance of power between state and federal governments, or simply expedient partisan gain. Unable to guarantee real benefits to increasingly skeptical voters and taxpayers, politicians learned to encourage improvements in general but not to commit themselves either to public investment or to the principle of activist government. By the end of Andrew Jackson's presidency (1829–36), as new technologies matured and the popular demand for public works approached its zenith, politicians at the federal level found that designs or programs for internal improvement engendered such negative fantasies of consolidation, corruption, and antidemocratic manipulation as to make them virtually insupportable. At times state governments tried to shoulder the task, only to be ruined themselves in the panics of 1819 and 1837, leaving some partisan voices to proclaim by the middle 1840s that republican governments ought never to engage in large public works of internal improvement. Only then did the private capital market, nursed into being by a generation's experiments in public investment, step forward and claim a theoretical and practical superiority over public enterprise.[7]

The triumph of laissez-faire, then, was not the natural or intended result of American revolutionary republicanism. Rather, America's eventual devotion to the Smithian tenets of political economy that reigned as orthodoxy from the Civil War until the Great Depression resulted from an abdication of government authorities that coincided with the gradual advance of innovative entrepreneurs who took the lead in internal improvement just as the new steam railroad technology revolutionized transportation again. Fearing abuse from designing politicians, midcentury Americans thought they saw in the "invisible hand" of competition an incorruptible arbitrator for desperately clashing interests. Because markets supposedly followed "natural laws" and arrived at "inevitable" results, they seemed uniquely capable of untangling the multitude of forces that were paralyzing democratic governments. Habitually distrustful of their representatives, tutored constantly on the dangers of big government and public power, and unable to perfect a system of democratic politics they truly believed in, Americans reached for the doctrines of liberal political economy to revitalize their own hopes for liberty and equality.[8]

After midcentury, railroad developers and other innovative entrepreneurs, while they never strayed far from government subsidies and protection, trumpeted with rising conviction the superiority of strictly private enterprise over public works. In the process, such new Wall Street revolutionaries shifted American ideology onto new foundations: thereafter not the consent of the governed but the freedom or rights of private property became the central pillar of American republicanism. With property rights in the ascendant, markets moved in as more legitimate arbiters of conflict than democratic governments; almost immediately railroad corporations competing in the marketplace took steps to impose designs of integration and consolidation more complete and irreversible than any contemplated by earlier internal improvers. By the 1870s, when the process of industrialization suddenly was unmasked and the confederated agrarian republic appeared to dissolve into a modern integrated nation, this transfer of power from popular democratic governments to supposedly self-regulating markets was approaching completion. The generation of Americans who had endured a Civil War to save the Union and preserve the experiment in republicanism found itself surprisingly powerless in the face of the new liberal enterprise system. The old enemies of government power, especially national government power, were joined by new advocates of strict entrepreneurial freedom to discredit government concern for the general welfare so completely that protective or regulatory actions now seemed contrary to American liberty.[9]

The result of this entrepreneurial revolution was not what Jefferson's Republicans or Jackson's Democrats ever had intended. The triumph of laissez-faire did not usher in a golden age of liberty where small proprietors flourished unmolested beneath their own vines and fig trees. On the contrary, the new economic order yielded integrated systems of commerce and industry that reduced everybody—farmers, artisans, and small businessmen alike—to a new status of dependency more comprehensive and insidious than anything threatened by earlier schemes of consolidation or internal improvement. Furthermore, when proponents of the rights of ordinary citizens attacked the new corporate "monopolies," they encountered their own libertarian rhetoric, hurled back at them by corporate executives, federal courts, and all kinds of corrupt politicians, reminding them not to interfere with the liberties of citizens (corporations being legal "persons") or their property. By a complex and unanticipated process—a process hard to sum up in a phrase but clearly illustrated by the story of internal improvement—the promise of American republicanism was captured by the agents of modern industrial capitalism. Consolidation of the Union, long feared as a consequence of national legislation, proceeded apace in the hands of unelected captains of industry whose designs were reviewed by no constituencies save the largest of corporate stockholders. It remained for a new generation, whether Populists or so-called progressive reformers, to try to revive the tradition of positive liberty and energetic government, in service to the general welfare of the people, that once had been among the clear, "self-evident," and motivating purposes of the American Revolution.

1

Designs of the Monied Gentry

THE FIRST DESIGNS for internal improvement in the new United States were articulated by such revolutionary heroes as George Washington, Thomas Jefferson, James Madison, Robert Morris, and Philip Schuyler. Members of a class George Washington called the "monied gentry," these individuals shared a common commitment to the success of the republican experiment, the security of the Union, the preservation of the national government, and the prosperity of their countrymen. Possessed of continental experience and broad vision, such gentlemen assumed a right to lead based on superior knowledge, patriotic feeling, and what they called "wisdom." Although the Revolution was eroding all hierarchies of power, these men survived for a time as America's home-grown aristocrats.

Inland navigation particularly attracted this first generation of American improvers. They saw a rising empire of settlement and commerce in the future American West. Canals and river improvements, designed to connect the interior region with the Atlantic trading communities, promised to facilitate growth and insure the loyal integration of the frontier within the Union. When local politicians and taxpayers balked at improvers' grand schemes of public investment, they formed corporations instead, which enjoyed government sanction to solicit private subscriptions. By thus farming out the work of the sovereign government, these elite promoters appeared to pursue the public good at private expense, while they reduced the need to win public approval or taxpayer support for their futuristic schemes. In other words, such postwar gentry found that their power to tax the people had been weakened by the Revolution, but their authority to set the agenda for future development had not yet disintegrated completely.

These gentleman-entrepreneurs designed on a fluid field: commercial networks, trade routes, settlement patterns, even the opinions of scientists and technical experts—all floated as on a pool of opportunity, waiting for the organizing hand of improvers to anchor the first elements. Everything was experimental. Neither engineers nor economists yet enjoyed the skill or credibility to settle competing claims made by politicians. Yet men of large vision understood that the first few steps might define the framework of development for generations to come. The future literally depended on seizing advantages now. If these gentlemen's favorite local projects could chart the course of national growth, so much the better for them and their neighbors.

Because they planned on a large scale, members of the "monied gentry" tended to favor an energetic federal government and integrated national development. They never failed to stress moral and intellectual uplift along with material well-being as the objects of their improvements, and they renounced the vulgar interests of mere adventurers in speculation. Nevertheless, their pet projects reflected local and selfish interests as much as any others. Almost nobody promoting internal improvements conceded the importance of works outside his own region. Instead, all kinds of promoters schemed to have government favor their own improvements while deflating the claims of others. As a result, the rhetoric of disinterestedness that united such gentleman-improvers rings a little false in historians' ears—and it engendered some suspicions among their contemporaries as well.

Before long, the presumed authority of the monied gentry to make designs based on their patriotic motives, superior knowledge, benevolence, or wisdom gave way to the insistent demands of more common people to make all decisions affecting the future of American liberty through the system of popular politics. Enduring suspicions toward any ruling class predisposed many ordinary voters to question the pretensions of their "betters," while the failure of elites to prove the superiority or disinterestedness of their schemes exposed early designers as perhaps no less ambitious than other "grasping" persons. Thus belief and experience conspired to unseat traditional authorities in the experimental United States. No individual better illustrates both the impulse to create designs and the decline of authority to implement them than the nation's first president, George Washington.

George Washington's Republican Vision

October 1783 found Washington in Princeton, New Jersey, biding his time, having "the enjoyment of peace, without the final declaration of it." Formalities bound him to the army but left him nothing useful to do. Inactivity depressed him, and for relief he recently had toured the waterways of upstate New York, dreaming of interior development. Poring over available maps and information, the restless general marveled that Providence had "dealt her favors to us with so profuse a hand. Would to God," he concluded, "we may have wisdom enough to improve them."[1] It is important that Washington used the term "wisdom" in this homely context. His prayer was not for money, or time, or technical expertise; it was for wisdom. Apparently he worried about the wisdom of his newly liberated countrymen, and he questioned their ability or willingness to do the right thing.

His Continental Army had suffered scandalously at the hands of the people; just then Congress sat in exile in Princeton, driven out of Philadelphia by angry unpaid soldiers. Great possibilities—or anarchy—lay ahead. Washington's phrase resonated with the urgency and apprehension that filled the atmosphere of post-war America.

Like revolutionaries everywhere, Washington cherished a vision of the rising new nation he had worked so hard to rescue from the British. His vision comprehended the existing Atlantic community, while his imagination leaped across the mountains to embrace seemingly limitless space in the continental interior. Western lands had fascinated Washington since his 1748 trip as a youthful surveyor into Lord Fairfax's western claims. In the last years before the Revolution, he had labored to pry open the western country and to interest provincial legislatures in the Potomac route to the West. "Immense advantages" awaited Virginia and Maryland, he argued in 1770, if they would make the Potomac a great "Channel of Commerce between Great Britain" and the interior.[2]

The word "channel" here originally meant less than modern readers might expect, for Washington's early vision was extremely limited, and therefore practicable. By clearing boulders and trash from the riverbeds and building portage roads between streams (or around unmovable obstructions), he hoped to facilitate the passage of canoes and flat-bottomed bateaux from the western to the eastern waterways, especially during high-water seasons. The downstream movement of bulky furs and foodstuffs concerned him more than return shipments of manufactured goods, which could better stand the cost of land transportation. Such limited expectations justified the small sums often spent by individuals and local governments toward the improvement of these rivers. At the same time European engineering offered splendid encouragement for greater ambitions. For nearly a century the famous Languedoc Canal had carried passengers and goods across the south of France, through more than one hundred locks and fifty aqueducts. More recently the duke of Bridgewater's English canal convinced American dreamers that technical solutions lay just ahead even for the Great Falls of the Potomac, an eighty-foot shelf of rock some twenty miles upstream from Washington's Mount Vernon.[3]

The Revolutionary War postponed the improvement of the Potomac, but Washington's interest in the project only increased with the winning of independence. In early 1784 he explained again to Jefferson the compelling advantages of the Potomac navigation, adding now his fear that the "Yorkers" would lose "no time" in improving their own route to the Great Lakes. Most Virginians did not see the "truly wise policy" of Potomac improvement, and they certainly resisted "drawing money from them for such a purpose." Even so, Washington hoped, as he went west in September to explore the Ohio country, that men of "discernment and liberality" could be made to see the value of the project.[4]

Firsthand knowledge only quickened Washington's convictions. He saw or

"Great Falls of the Potomac," upstream a few miles from the new federal capital city. The falls symbolized both literally and figuratively the enormous challenge facing American internal improvers. Lithograph by T. Cartwright after a painting by George Beck, 1802. Courtesy Library of Congress.

heard how a short portage between the Miami and Sandusky Rivers might link the whole Great Lakes system with the Ohio; how the Allegheny, the Monongahela, the Kanawha, and their many branches might be connected with the Susquehannah, Potomac, and James to form passages from the Ohio waters to the Atlantic coast. Geographical features came so near to meeting in a network that it seemed to Washington as if nature had designed the interior region expressly for improvement by the new United States (Map 1). As things stood in 1784, however, such improvements were not forthcoming. Western Pennsylvanians talked of opening the Susquehannah (which ran to Baltimore), but Philadelphia's merchants blocked their efforts. New York's water-level route to the lakes was well known, but British troops still occupied Niagara and other Great Lakes forts. The people of the West themselves had not the means to make improvements and—more distressing to Washington—had no "excitements to industry" because the "luxuriency of the Soil" gave too easy a living, while the impossibility of trade discouraged ambition. Open a good communication with these settlements, however, and exports to the East must be increased "astonishingly." Even more important, he presumed that the political allegiance of the pioneers would follow their commerce: so long as Spain blocked the Mississippi

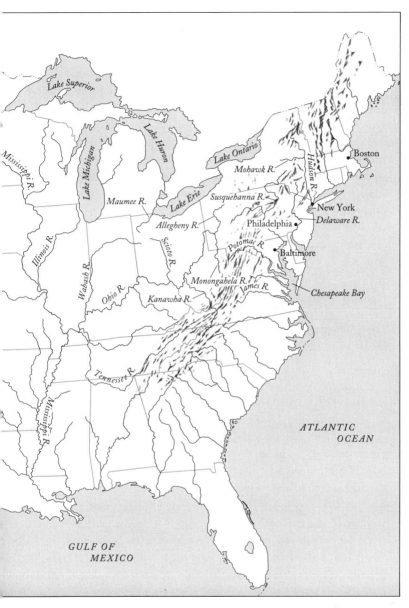

Map 1. Geographical features of the eastern United States, showing the potential routes that captured George Washington's geopolitical imagination.

and Britain the Great Lakes, the Atlantic states enjoyed a unique opportunity to "apply the cement of interest," binding all parts of the Union with "one indissolv able band."[5]

The Potomac navigation activated Washington's whole vision of the rising American empire. The West held the key to America's future greatness. The "vacant" lands back of the Atlantic states promised safety and prosperity fo generations to come. Agriculture, he assumed, would occupy the masses; bu without markets frontier farmers regressed toward a state of nature. Therefore commerce must propel the nation forward, and inland navigation would bind the wilderness communities to the Union by chains of commercial interest. Nationa character, prosperity, respect among nations, the security of the Union (and by implication the liberty that flowed from independence)—public issues at the center of Washington's concern—all depended on embracing westward emigra- tion within the American national system. Inland navigation made the Unitec States conceivable, and Washington's vision soared high above the diggings: " wish to see the sons and daughters of the world in Peace and busily employed ir the more agreeable amusement of fulfilling the first and great commandment *Increase and Multiply*: as an encouragement to which we have opened the fertile plains of the Ohio to the poor, the needy and the oppressed of the Earth." Washington's America was nothing less than "the Land of promise, with milk and honey."[6]

Private interest, Virginia pride, and concern for the welfare of the Union mingled in Washington's mind as he gazed west from the banks of his river. The value of nearly 60,000 acres of his own western lands promised to rise with the opening of tramontane commerce.[7] His sense of urgency and his insistence that the Potomac was *by nature* the ideal route reflected a keen spirit of rivalry with other states that antedated the Revolution. Yet his persistent use of the language of national interest and political security rang true despite his obvious persona interests. For years he had cultivated national credibility; now he would use it to promote his design for the river, Virginia, and the new United States.

Washington pressed his vision on everyone he knew. Henry Knox, Richard Henry Lee, Benjamin Harrison, Lafayette, Chastellux, James Madison, Thomas Jefferson, Charles Carroll, Robert Morris—all received long letters full of enthu- siasm about inland navigation and the western country. In these same letters Washington often brooded over signs of chaos and disorder that seemed to be multiplying across America, reflecting the close connection in his mind between the question of government power and the opportunity to found an American empire. Petty visions competed everywhere. Interested parties worked against his navigation schemes in order to advance their own or to protect transient advantages. In the West, squatters seized Washington's unimproved lands and dared any man to dispossess them. Speculators engrossed huge tracts, while northwest of the Ohio settlers provoked Indian reprisals. It seemed as if nothing could be done about these outrages, the general confided to his friend Henry Knox, because the people in the states were "torn by internal disputes, or supinely negligent and inattentive to every thing which is not local and selfinteresting."[8]

In a seamless tapestry Washington saw his trouble with frontier squatters, the selfish localism of his Virginia neighbors, the indifference of the states toward the federal Congress, irresponsibility in public finance, and reckless assaults on the public domain all springing from the same malaise. "The want of energy in the Federal government," he concluded, "has brought our politics and credit to the brink of a precipice; a step or two farther must plunge us into a Sea of Troubles, perhaps anarchy and confusion." Similar conflicts plagued the Potomac navigation. Such engineers as could be found assured Washington and his friends that all technical problems could be solved. The objective was compelling, and the estimates by "experts" were encouraging; only human folly seemed to stand in the way. His prescription for national health? Instill vigor in the federal government, adopt an orderly plan for settling the West, and set to work immediately on inland navigation.[9]

Because the Potomac formed the boundary between Maryland and Virginia, both states had to sanction improvements. But Baltimore merchants schemed to block the project in favor of a Susquehannah Canal chartered in Maryland in 1783, while Virginians outside the Potomac Valley showed a maddening indifference to the general's grand design. Finally in late 1784, the two legislatures authorized a joint-stock company to improve the river and collect tolls in perpetuity, according to fixed schedules. Commissioners were named to lay out and construct good roads (at public expense) from the head of navigation to the "most convenient" western waters, thereby completing communications with the frontier.[10]

The charter delighted Washington, yet his thoughts kept drifting back to the political urgency behind the project. He seemed disappointed that the two states "under their present pressure of debts" were so "incompetent" to carry on the work: would private parties really take hold? To Robert Morris, Washington explained that were he "disposed to encounter present inconvenience for a future income" he would "hazard all the money" he could raise on the Potomac navigation. But in fact he did not hazard all his money, and there lingered in his views a nagging concern that where his own purse failed others would too. Friends of the measure were "sanguine," he wrote to Lafayette, but "good wishes" were "more at command, than money." Because "extensive political consequences" depended on these projects, he felt "pained by every doubt of obtaining the means" for their completion.[11]

In Washington's mind there was much more to inland navigation than clearing boulders from a riverbed and digging canals. He was building a nation as well as a waterway, and he preferred to think that men of vision would see the wisdom of his plan, seize it with the sovereign hands of government, and pursue it to the benefit of all. But Washington knew how investors behaved. Some subscribers were "actuated" by "public spirit," and others by the hope of "salutary effects." The latter "*must* naturally incline" toward support, but those who were "unconnected with the river" would not. Why not vest such an enterprise by law with "a kind of property in the Navigation" (that is, tolls) to gain support of a third class of men, "the monied gentry, who tempted by lucrative views would advance largely on account of high interest." The corporation thus became a useful instrument for hitching self-interest to the public good.[12]

The Potomac Company charter reflected these assumptions. Because local jealousies prevented him from getting "public money," Washington proposed "a happy medium": a charter that did not "vest too much power and profit in a private company" but still held out "sufficient inducements to engage men to hazard their fortunes." To "give vigor to the undertaking," he then convinced each state to subscribe for blocks of shares. Profit served as bait to lure investors, while the legislators prescribed rates of tolls to protect their unextinguished public interest in the operations.[13] No modern liberal, Washington never imagined that government action in the economy violated any principle. Neither did he fantasize that, in their selfish pursuit of private gain, individuals would accomplish automatically what was best for all. Interest required guidance from wisdom, and now that American governments were safely republican, they might exercise power to promote the common welfare more appropriately than ever. If well-designed government policies gave shape to popular freedoms, then a free people could achieve greatness. He explained for Thomas Jefferson the example of foreign trade: "our Citizens *will not* be restrained" from commerce, so "it behooves us to place it in the most convenient channels, under proper regulations, freed *as much as possible* from those vices which luxury, the consequence of wealth and power, naturally introduce."[14] Interest guided by wisdom. Right policies alone could secure the new nation, its commerce, and its frontier domain. Otherwise the new United States would be torn apart from without or from within.

But making wise policies proved almost impossible in the Confederation era, especially on a national scale. At every step men of narrow views seemed to prove that mere liberation, without energetic governance, led to chaos and certain destruction. Throughout 1785, as the Potomac Company set to work on his river, Washington watched national harmony dissolve. "It does not appear to me," he wrote in February, "that we have wisdom, or national policy enough to avert the evils which are impending. How should we, when contracted ideas, local pursuits, and absurd jealousy are continually leading us from those great and fundamental principles which are characteristic of wise and powerful Nations?"[15]

For Washington, liberty itself depended on restoring order and forging a national community in the postrevolutionary United States. For example, on the question of western lands, which had produced so much squabbling among the states, Washington pressed for "compact and progressive seating" in order to "give strength to the Union; admit law and good government; and foederal aids at an early period." Restrict development of the interior, he argued, to one or two states at a time: too free access to western lands would only advance "private interest," perhaps at the expense of "public welfare."[16] On the equally desperate matter of commercial regulation, Washington supported national protection and promotion. When his fellow Virginians objected that navigation acts would profit New England at the expense of southern consumers, Washington rebuked them. "Every matter of general utility" would benefit some states more than others, but too jealous a regard for these particular interests undermined "national character" and made the United States look "ridiculous" in the eyes of the world. "We are either a united people under one head, and for federal purposes," thundered the general, "or we are thirteen independent sovereignties, eternally counteracting each other."[17]

By the autumn of 1785 Washington's frustration with Congress was complete. Local jealousy had rendered it a "nugatory body." The truly extraordinary thing was, "that we should confederate as a Nation, and yet be afraid to give the rulers of that nation, who are the creatures of our own making . . . sufficient powers to order and direct the affairs of the same." Disappointments mounted apace. A commercial depression undercut America's economic recovery. The 1786 Annapolis Convention on interstate commerce, born of Washington's own Mount Vernon Conference the year before, collapsed in apathy. Shays's Rebellion in Massachusetts raised the specter of domestic insurrection, while a vote in Congress to "forbear" American claims to the Mississippi River produced an explosion of separatist fever in the West.[18]

During this "critical period" Washington's despair steadily deepened and his faith in a strong but virtuous government took final form. The stubborn refusal of state leaders to empower the Congress with "ample" authority appeared to be the "very climax of popular absurdity and madness." Still the crisis would not pass. "I am mortified beyond expression," he wrote in 1786, afraid that Americans had proved mankind to be "unfit for their own Government."[19] About the only good news he received in these years was of the Potomac navigation, where by early reports difficulties seemed to "rather vanish than increase." The lack of a trained engineer left the directors uncertain at times precisely how to proceed, but by the summer of 1786 some two hundred men labored to good effect at several sites along the river. With hope perhaps intensified by the confusion rising around him, Washington reported to his foreign correspondents that the "seeds of population" were scattering "far into the wilderness," agriculture was "prosecuted with industry," and the "works of Peace, such as opening rivers, building bridges, &c.," were "carried on with spirit."[20]

During this volatile period Washington invariably juxtaposed in his correspondence gloomy accounts of the state of national affairs with reports of prog-

ress on the Potomac navigation. The one endangered, the other advanced his
cherished objective of securing the extended American republic. As winter approached in 1786, Washington entertained no doubts about the Potomac canal,
but he wondered if the Union would survive to enjoy it. "Public virtue" had
deteriorated so rapidly that he thought only some "means of coercion" could
"enforce Obedience" to the federal government. Some Virginians, led by Governor Patrick Henry, promised to bolt the Union rather than suffer any national
tyranny. Others, led by James Madison, plotted desperately to bring Virginia
into just such a "proper federal System." As the movement for constitutional
reform progressed, Washington nervously watched, his private delight shielded
by his scrupulous public neutrality. In the end, at the final hour, he agreed to
attend the Philadelphia convention, where he did not speak but presided in
symbolic silence.[21]

Gradually, during the long hot summer in Philadelphia, a more substantial
frame of government took shape. Very late in the convention Benjamin Franklin,
who shared Washington's vision of a rising empire in the West, moved to insert
"a power to provide for cutting canals where deemed necessary." Roger Sherman
of Connecticut objected to expenses that would benefit only "places where the
canals may be cut." Such local jealousy always pained the general who chaired
the proceedings. James Madison tried to substitute a broader power "to grant
charters" for promoting internal improvement, and James Wilson defended the
power "to prevent a *State* from obstructing the *general* welfare." But local feeling
and fear of monopolies prevailed. The nationalists fell back on what they had
secured so far: a government resting on the people, empowered to raise revenues
and enforce its laws, independent of state authorities, and competent to regulate
trade, finance, and foreign policy. More than that they could not win.[22]

Was Washington pleased with the Constitution? It was "the best that could be
obtained at this time," he explained to Patrick Henry. Certainly he felt it was not
too strong: "No man is a warmer advocate for proper restraints and wholesome
checks in every department of government than I am; but I have never yet been
able to discover the propriety of placing it absolutely out of the power of men to
render essential Services, because a possibility remains of their doing ill." Still,
the ratification contests were bitter, and Washington knew that the Constitution
enjoyed fragile support, especially among state politicians. Hardly endowed with
the "general *controuling* power" Washington originally desired, the new regime
would need nurturing before it could be used to accomplish greater things.[23]
Once elected by acclamation to the presidency, Washington held unprecedented
new powers; but the sensitivities of office forced him to quiet his advocacy of
national authority and western canals, in order to protect the constitutional
framework itself.

Fragments of a 1789 address, probably intended for the opening of Congress
but abandoned without explanation, reveal how much the new president *wished*

to say as he took up his novel station. Much depended on the character of Americans and their actions in the decade ahead. "If the blessings of Heaven showered thick around us," Washington wrote, "should be spilled on the ground or converted to curses, through the fault of those for whom they were intended, it would not be the first instance of folly or perverseness in short-sighted mortals."[24] With Congress his intended audience, the president poured out his larger vision of improvement and positive government:

It belongs to you [Congress] especially to take measures for promoting the general welfare. It belongs to you to make men honest in their dealings with each other, by regulating the coinage and currency of money upon equitable principles; as well as by establishing just weights and measures upon an uniform plan. Whenever an opportunity shall be furnished to you as public or as private men, I trust you will not fail to use your best endeavors to improve the education and manners of a people; to accelerate the progress of arts and Sciences; to patronize works of genius; to confer rewards for inventions of utility; and to cherish institutions favourable to humanity.

This was energetic government, the president's purposes laid down in strong, active verbs. Good things were brought about, not just allowed to emerge by themselves. Before Alexander Hamilton ever whispered in the president's ear, Washington had opened the window of "loose construction" through which enemies of the Federal Party one day would think they saw tyranny returning.

But the new president did not deliver these opinions. He said far less on 8 January 1790, when he finally addressed the federal Congress. Gone were his challenge to "short-sighted mortals" and his outline of the nation's business. This message indulged only the briefest nod toward internal improvements and education. Swirling passions and conflicting interests burdened the new regime with extravagant and jealous expectations. At the center of it all, Washington trembled for fear that "public measures" would disappoint the people and their praises would turn to "censures."[25] Possessed of sovereign power, he chose to use it delicately for fear of fracturing public confidence and unleashing once more the disintegrative forces of jealousy, greed, and a popular distrust of government.

Washington's vision of a rising empire, guided from the center by benevolent government and striving toward some splendid republican future, derived from habits of thought that he shared with most of America's politically conscious elites and many small proprietors as well. Never much of a scholar, this self-educated Tidewater planter imbibed classical and Enlightenment ideas primarily in conversations at dinner and gaming tables, at theaters or country tavern hearths. Like most of his peers, he reasoned inductively, drawing universal principles from personal experience. At the center of his vision lay American liberation, the freeing of his people from the control of distant tyrants, not to splinter into atoms but combine in the pursuit of a common, republican destiny. At the same time, many of Washington's most deeply held convictions about wisdom, power, and improvement did not square with those of his countrymen. His assumptions were more aristocratic, authoritarian, and nationalistic than many citizens, rich or poor, would freely sanction. Taken at face value, his views should have bothered the American people at least as much as their behavior worried him. Only his unique prestige as the hero of the Revolutionary War shielded him from early repudiation.[26]

Washington had yearned for a national government because he presumed that a class of men much like himself could use it to regulate the passionate masses. In practice Americans recognized no such leadership class (even if the rhetoric lingered), and they distrusted the opinions of strangers. Washington thought power, once properly derived, should be wielded freely by legitimate authorities—what other earthly purpose for government? But Americans had just escaped the grip of power, and most of them would not "glide insensibly," to use John Adams's unfortunate phrase, into submission to new authorities.[27] Washington conceived of liberty in the commonwealth tradition, a blessing enjoyed by communities of people, not atomistic individuals, and he dreamed of a rising American empire—giving pause to many good republicans who thought that "empire" was the opposite of "liberty." Finally, Washington conceived improvement in terms of benevolence—a gift enhancing the receiver according to the purpose of the benefactor—whereas many contemporaries thought more of innovation, the fruit of liberation and ambition, without moral or political design.[28]

For this reason, instead of defining the promise of the new regime, Washington's design for a rising empire (including internal improvement) marked only one end of a spectrum on which Americans would paint many shades of meaning for the terms of revolutionary republicanism. True, the new regime under Washington's guidance saved the experiment with liberty from probable disintegration; but liberty itself, even with the Constitution in place, produced an explosion of innovation and ambition that more resembled the chaos men like Washington had tried to avert. At the start of the 1790s, the glory of his reputation and widespread habits of deference to benevolent elites exempted Washington himself from most partisan attacks. Yet he could do very little to pursue a specific national agenda, and nothing at all to stop the transformation of a culture that revered his name, his deeds, his very words, even while it disregarded the meaning of his vision and perverted his designs for national integration, wise legislation, and improved inland navigation.

Rivals in the "Spirit of Improvement"

By the 1790s Americans in almost every state felt a "spirit of improvement" moving over the land. What they meant by this, however, varied greatly. Like everything else in this self-creating culture, the words "internal improvement" endured continual redefinition, shifting meanings and serving new purposes in a swiftly changing universe. Individuals such as George Washington took comfort in the apparent quickening of enthusiasm for local works of internal improvement, blithely overlooking the different foundations on which contemporaries erected their competing designs. A more critical observer, however, might have noticed that the rise of many different schemes of improvement and the competition among them for public approbation invited not the unity of vision idealized by Washington, but a bare-knuckles contest for favor and advantage that owed nothing to the commonwealth tradition. Washington's dream of harmonious interests, centered on the Potomac, shattered within a generation, partly because his friends and countrymen had independent visions of their own, partly because his class of "monied gentry" lost the political authority to impose design, and partly because his own vision (like everybody else's) was far more local and self-serving than he ever was able to admit.

Many of Washington's Virginia friends and neighbors shared his interest in the Potomac navigation without embracing the interlocking purposes of his grand developmental vision. Henry Lee, for example, laid more extravagant expectations on the canal at Great Falls than Washington ever imagined. The two men employed the same language of liberty and Union, but where Washington sought national salvation, Lee saw mostly speculative gain. Rather than invest in the company itself, Lee plunged recklessly to buy up doubtful titles to lands that would be "improved" by the Potomac navigation. As nominal owner of a townsite at the Great Falls, Lee tried to sting the company for land on its own canal. Eventually bankrupt, he went to prison at the hands of his long-suffering creditors, yet this gentleman of reputation and good family never doubted that he was victimized by cutthroats who did not recognize the service he performed. He was, he thought, a virtuous improver. To others he was simply a cheat, "the swindling Harry Lee."[29]

James Madison worked hand in glove with Washington to promote the Potomac navigation, but Madison shared only parts of the general's larger vision, and his own faith in energetic government depended on the quality of politics in practice. In 1784–85 Madison viewed the Potomac and James river projects more as benefits to Virginia than as parts of a national design. He disagreed strongly with Washington's notion that western settlement could be controlled or that Spain's closing of the Mississippi River to American trade was a blessing in disguise for the Atlantic states. Spain could no more "resist the current of such a trade" than it could "stop that [of] the river itself," Madison explained to Thomas Jefferson, characterizing the westward movement as natural and uncontrollable. To Lafayette, Madison argued that "Nature" had given the Mississippi to "those who may settle on its waters," and those nations would "shew most wisdom" and "acquire most glory, who, instead of forcing her current into artifi-cial channels," endeavored to "ascertain its tendency & anticipate its effects."[30]

A more liberal republican than Washington, more bookish and far less im-pressed with the wisdom of any ruling class, Madison nevertheless emerged by 1787 as one of the boldest advocates of nation at the Philadelphia convention. Reasoning from principles like a political scientist, Madison wished to curb injustice in state legislation with an absolute national veto. He sought a govern-ment empowered to do many things that Washington desired; but where Wash-ington was tempted to impose design, Madison preferred to induce results by tapping the inclinations of free people. The difference often was subtle, and over time Madison appeared to contradict himself as he searched for the practical balance that he saw clearly in theory. More than any of the first-generation leaders, Madison would feel the irony of quashing improvements that he ar-dently supported because the means of promoting them opened the way for constitutional mischief.[31]

Thomas Jefferson shared Washington's passion for the Potomac route, but he also favored Madison's views about a free and natural process of westward migra-tion. A thoroughgoing Virginian, Jefferson early sketched a defensive strategy of internal improvement designed to capture for the Old Dominion "as large a portion as we can of this modern source of wealth and power"—that is, com-merce. In a contest with the Hudson and the Mississippi, Jefferson argued, the return trip up the latter was too "tedious" for the import trade while the former route measured twice as long: "Nature then has declared in favour of the Pa-towmac, and through that channel offers to pour into our lap the whole com-merce of the Western world." As to expense, Jefferson wrote in 1789 that he hardly knew "what expense would be too great for the object in question"; and he further observed, "it is much better that these should be done at public than private expense."[32]

At the same time that he shared so much of Washington's vision for a naviga-tion system, Jefferson cherished a much more daring commitment to democracy than either Washington or Madison could sanction. He had authored the first drafts of the 1785 Land Ordinance that Washington thought mistaken. He placed more confidence in "men from the Western side of the mountains" and proposed to give frontiersmen much greater local autonomy than Washington desired (or than Congress later prescribed in the 1787 Northwest Ordinance). He worried far more than Madison about consolidation of power under the new Constitution, and he seemed to care less about a rising American empire than about the rights of private citizens at home. Where Washington feared lawlessness, Jefferson (viewing the problem from Paris) deferred to the will of the disorderly. Always the speculative radical, he found ideas of design appealing even while the imple-mentation or enforcement of design often repulsed him.[33]

Three famous Virginians—Lee, Madison, and Jefferson, each closely allied with Washington in the Potomac River improvement—exhibited important variations in their thinking about internal improvements, social control, private profit, and public power. Yet all employed the same words and phrases and exchanged views as if they were saying essentially comparable things. Time and experience with specific projects and policies often exposed these underlying disagreements, but in the early years of the new nation the "spirit of improvement" promiscuously covered a multitude of plans, designs, and objectives. The possibilities of harmony and Union, liberty and improvement, on which the hopes of the nation stood, seemed most secure at the level of abstractions. But where policies touched the lives of persons, where projects physically altered the ground, where the fortunes of individuals and places materially rose and fell, there consensus eluded the founders of the republic.

Few examples mocked the "spirit of improvement" more than the bitter rivalry between Baltimore and Philadelphia over the Susquehanna River. Rocky and treacherous for its first 50 miles, the Susquehanna drained much of central Pennsylvania and southern New York into Chesapeake Bay. In its natural condition the upper river provided a useful highway for country produce as far as the Conewago Falls at Middletown (just south of modern Harrisburg). From there shippers faced about 100 miles of bad roads to Philadelphia or fifty to Baltimore. Pennsylvanians disagreed whether to open their central waterway or preserve those natural barriers that kept the backcountry subservient to the seaport. Meanwhile, since the late 1730s Baltimore's merchants had sought to raid Philadelphia's commerce by building roads north into Pennsylvania. Inhabitants of the Susquehanna Valley begged for better access to their own state's metropolis, but Philadelphia's ruling elites turned deaf ears to their frontier dependents.[34]

Serious study of the Susquehanna route began before the Revolution. In 1769 a committee of the American Philosophical Society of Philadelphia reported that this river was "the natural channel through which the produce of *three-fourths of this province must* in time be conveyed to market." Thomas Gilpin and his fellow "philosophers" exhibited a broad regional perspective by encouraging improvements in the river, a canal uniting the Delaware River with Chesapeake Bay, and one or more roads between the lower Susquehanna and the port of Philadelphia. While not unmindful of Philadelphia's interests (or of generous contributions to their labors from that city's merchants), members of the committee nevertheless recommended opening the river and digging the canal as a convenience to "all the Western trade" and "the commercial interest of all the colonies adjoining" Chesapeake Bay.[35]

Such a generous regional perspective met with stern resistance from ardent home-market enthusiasts. Writing in 1770 in the *Pennsylvania Chronicle*, "Patrius" praised the civilizing influence of internal improvement, especially upon

the character of isolated frontiersmen who were becoming "uncivilized," "se
ditious," and "dangerous to the community." But this writer condemned an
Chesapeake & Delaware Canal as "chimerical," while improvements in the Sus
quehanna promised only to convey trade "to the first convenient market in
Maryland." Only an all-Pennsylvania route would do. These sentiments pre
vailed in the legislature as new statutes in 1771 and 1773 encouraged work on the
Susquehanna but prohibited improvements below Wright's Ferry, where traffi
soon would pass out of state.[36]

After the Revolution, Baltimore merchants stirred their new state assembly to
charter "Proprietors of the Susquehanna Canal," capitalized at £20,000, to open
a canal from tidewater to Love Island, just south of the Pennsylvania line. Responding to this challenge in 1789, Robert Morris, David Rittenhouse, and other
Philadelphia leaders organized "A Society for Promoting the Improvement of
Roads and Inland Navigation in the State of Pennsylvania," which took a strictly
home-market approach to internal improvement. This society whipped up a
public demand for improvements in the Susquehanna (above Wright's Ferry, of
course) and for a canal leading eastward to Philadelphia. By 1792 Pennsylvania
had appropriated £5,250 to open a passage at Conewago Falls and had chartered
corporations to build the Schuylkill & Susquehanna Navigation and to canalize
the Schuylkill itself.[37]

The Schuylkill and Susquehanna route—from Philadelphia to Reading, then
westward to Middletown—had been recommended by Rittenhouse in 1762 and
resurveyed in 1770 for the Philosophical Society. The 1792 companies enjoyed
wide public support and investors quickly oversubscribed their stocks; but practical difficulties overwhelmed both projects. Early expenses far exceeded estimates, and subscribers fell into delinquency when they saw large additional
assessments looming. Lured by a cash-paying customer, the directors agreed to
build the state-funded Conewago bypass, which further divided their energies
and embroiled them in conflict with enterprising Susquehanna boatmen, who
after 1794 employed huge flat-bottomed "arks" to shoot the falls on spring fresh-
ets and ride the wild river to Baltimore.[38]

On behalf of the failing companies in 1795, Pennsylvania authorized lotteries
to raise $400,000. Later the state subscribed to 400 shares of stock as well. Still
the works foundered. A good British engineer, William Weston, was hired, but a
French tourist reported that the directors of the Schuylkill and Susquehanna
(Robert Morris in particular) had overruled him in order that the canal should
"pass through their estates." Charges of corruption and private speculation burdened every technical failure with a hint of malfeasance that was not altogether
undeserved. By century's end canal enthusiasm had died in Pennsylvania in
favor of more modest but successful roads, such as the newly finished Lancaster
Turnpike.[39]

A kind of state-level mercantilism underlay the purposes of Pennsylvania's Improvement Society. Robert Morris's private interest was enhanced perhaps by hopes of luring the seat of the new federal government to lands in the state that he owned, but everybody's larger objective was prosperity for Pennsylvania. "To combine the interests of all parts of the State, and to cement them in a perpetual commercial and political union, by the improvement of . . . natural advantages," wrote Morris in 1791, was "one of the greatest works" that could be "submitted to Legislative wisdom." The "present moment" was "particularly auspicious," he continued; if neglected, the loss would be "hard to retrieve." Addressing directly the competition with New York and Virginia for the trade of the American West, Morris conceded certain virtues to the Potomac but claimed for Pennsylvania a natural right to the entire trade of Lake Erie.[40]

In his plea for opening the West, in his urgent recognition of a singular opportunity, and in his references to "natural" advantages requiring minimal human intervention, Morris sounded just like George Washington. Yet Morris proposed a state rather than a national program, the centerpiece of which was an expensive canal diverting traffic to Philadelphia, where nature did not intend it to go. The Susquehanna, he insisted, "we may properly call our own"; if "duly improved," it opened "such numerous sources and channels of inland trade, all leading to the port of Philadelphia, as perhaps no other nation or sea-port on the whole globe can boast of."[41] Here "duly improved" did not mean easier or safe; here improved meant wholly changed.

This manipulative use of the spirit and the language of improvement found its best expression in the contest for a Chesapeake & Delaware Canal. Philadelphia desperately wanted it for the obvious purpose of tapping Baltimore's markets and recapturing whatever commerce got away down the Susquehanna. Unfortunately for Pennsylvania, such a canal lay entirely in Maryland and Delaware. Delaware feared the loss of local carrying trade across the fourteen-mile land bridge that naturally divided these waters; Maryland bitterly opposed a canal as long as Pennsylvania law threatened fines of up to $2,000 for removing obstructions in the lower Susquehanna. Baltimore voices protested that a canal across the peninsula of Delaware would "entirely suppress every expectation of advantage from opening the Susquehanna"—which was, of course, the whole point of Philadelphia's interest in canals. In 1799 Maryland finally passed a charter authorizing the canal on the condition that Pennsylvania improve the lower Susquehanna. Two years later the Quaker state removed its "friendly" impediment to Baltimore's natural hinterland trade, but the spirit of cooperation never flourished. In this tight geographical hub, where political boundaries contradicted natural economic regions, internal improvement could not serve politically neutral objectives.[42]

New York City stood poised, like Baltimore, at the mouth of a great waterway that drained a rich and developing hinterland. Unlike the upstart Maryland city, however, New York possessed within the borders of the state the new nation's only nearly "water-level" route to the Great Lakes. New York's awareness of its "natural advantage" dated back to Surveyor General Cadwallader Colden's 1724 report, that the colony's interior waters opened "such a scene of inland navigation as can not be paralleled in any other part of the world." Little came of Colden's insights until after the Revolution, when Christopher Colles, a young Irish engineer, approached the legislature with a plan for inland navigation. At first the lawmakers found his proposals "inexpedient" to undertake "at public expense." In 1785, however, Colles won a small stipend to mount a survey, which resulted in a detailed, articulate proposal.[43]

Colles's *Proposals for the Speedy Settlement of the Waste and Unappropriated Lands on the Western Frontiers of the State of New York, and for the Improvement of the Inland Navigation between Albany and Oswego* combined familiar improvement themes with a unique land grant provision that anticipated features of later American public works policy. Incorporate a company of projectors, Colles suggested, and give them 250,000 acres of "waste land." Require them to settle 500 residents in the region within three years and open the waterway to Lake Ontario within five. He proposed that the company recruit workmen-pioneers by offering 150 acres of land to all who spent 150 days on the diggings. In the end the company would own 166,250 acres, the value of which was enhanced by the waterworks and the neighborhood of settlers.[44]

The advantage to investors appeared obvious, but why should the state of New York embrace this plan? Because, Colles answered, domestic and foreign trade might be increased, the backcountry settled, valuable naval stores brought to market, and the Great Lakes trade secured for the port of New York City. "Providence indeed seems to favor this design," argued the enterprising engineer; "the Allegheny mountains which pass thro' all the States, seem to die away as they approach the Mohawk River, and the ground between the upper parts of this river and Wood Creek is perfectly level, as if designed to permit us to pass." America—and especially New York—found its "natural prerogative" not in overseas trade but in the backlands. When "any proper, well-concerted design" for their development appeared, he concluded, the "Public should take it under their protection" or consign "to posterity the profits we so much need, and by timely attention may reap ourselves."[45]

Not yet worried about rivalry for the western trade, and perhaps put off by Colles's frankly self-interested role (he reserved 5 percent of the land for himself as engineer), New York's lawmakers passed up Colles's well-concerted design. They did, however, discuss inland navigation almost every year thereafter, urged on by Governor George Clinton, until in 1792 they finally incorporated two inland navigation companies. The chief movers behind these companies were Elkanah Watson, a self-appointed canal enthusiast who had made a private study of New York waterways, and Philip Schuyler, a Revolutionary War hero and leading Federalist politician who recommended Watson's proposals to New York's gentry. The Western and Northern Inland Lock Navigation companies each received permission to sell 1,000 shares of stock ($25 each with unlimited future assessments), build the appropriate waterworks, condemn land where necessary, collect tolls, pay dividends within statutory limits, and receive a "free gift" of $12,500 from the state once they exhausted the initial capital of $25,000.[46]

Even more carefully than the Virginians, New York's lawmakers designed their charters of incorporation to limit the accumulation of influence or windfall profits in the hands of wealthy elites. A ten-share limit blocked original subscribers, while an elaborate formula guaranteed the broadest possible ownership should the issues be oversubscribed. Voting power was stacked progressively against large shareholders. Casual users of the waterworks escaped tolls on vessels of less than one ton burden. Finally, future tolls were pegged to a 10 percent rate of return. A proposal to ensure monopoly by prohibiting canals to the Susquehanna failed, "it being conceived improper to oblige the inhabitants of the western country to make Hudson's river, or the commercial towns on it, the only markets." All these conditions Schuyler and Watson accepted, confident that economic growth and the rising value of land brought on by improved navigation guaranteed the success of their venture.[47]

New York's assemblymen apparently worried less about finding interested capitalists among the state's monied gentry than being exploited by them once they got control of public thoroughfares. If Watson and Schuyler were correct in their projections of private dividends and public benefit, these charters would protect the interests of the democracy; if they were wrong, the investors would lose their money and all powers would revert to the state. Blessed with an excellent seaport, a brisk urban economy, and easy access 150 miles up the Hudson River, New York voters responded less enthusiastically than their Pennsylvania neighbors to grand visions of inland navigation. Despite the state's superior natural potential—or perhaps because of it—only certain wealthy urban gentlemen and Hudson Valley landlords caught the internal improvement fever in Federalist New York.

Inexperience, error, and mismanagement consumed the capital of these early New York companies with disappointing results. The directors called repeatedly for more money, and delinquencies mounted, followed by petitions for state financial aid. But tolls from this unsettled wilderness would not immediately pay even the interest on money borrowed by the corporation. Without the benefit of a skilled engineer, Schuyler set crews to work in 1793, spending most of his company's funds in surveys, outfits, and poorly supervised efforts. Charges of fraud and mismanagement followed as the directors called on shareholders for eight additional payments in rapid succession, and almost immediately partisan politics intruded. DeWitt Clinton, speaking in 1793 for his Uncle George Clinton's Republican faction, condemned the canals as Federalist schemes to "enlist the passions of party on the side of hydraulic experiments." Most of the thirty-six directors of the Western Company shared elite mercantile interests, speculated largely in western lands, and supported Schuyler's Federalist Party, so Clinton's charges appeared to be credible. From that date forward New Yorkers took at least as much interest in who was promoting canals as they did in the progress of canals themselves.[48]

For Philip Schuyler and his Federalist friends, inland navigations were speculative investments in New York's future. Private benefit clearly was intended, but the larger investors expected to gain less from profits than from long-term growth. Good examples of Washington's "monied gentry," these New York improvers sought public cooperation for developmental projects, not private sinecures or simple graft. But the factional character of New York politics, the historical pretensions of the old Dutch elites, and the paucity of interior residents who might benefit immediately from improvements made it possible to see internal improvement as a game for the interested few. Thus, as the projects failed and appeals for public money grew more desperate, Clintonian Republicans could not resist the temptation to renounce them.[49]

Taken together, internal improvement programs in the early United States served many different purposes. Philadelphia distorted "improvement" to mean completely redirecting natural waterways, whereas New York pioneered the exploitation of improvements for the purpose of winning partisan elections. Where George Washington envisioned a Potomac Canal uniting the fledgling nation, Thomas Jefferson saw it opening a highway for autonomous pioneers to escape to the West. Improvement schemes emerged from common hopes and understandings at the dawn of the American experiment, yet they often served divergent objectives. Improvers encountered common problems and shared the same disappointments; but their troubles could be understood in very different ways that sparked bitter quarrels about the shape of the future and the practical uses of popular government.

As capital investments, these early efforts failed in every case, visiting "justice" (perhaps) on speculators such as Harry Lee, but ruining as well sincere and honest advocates of the public welfare. By December 1804 New York's canals at Little Falls, German Flats, and Rome had digested $367,743 in capital and paid one 3 percent dividend. Repairs and improvements consumed all other revenue. Comparable sums were spent on Pennsylvania's projects and on Virginia's Potomac Canal, where by 1808 nearly $450,000 invested returned only occasional dividends from earnings averaging $6,575 per year since 1800. Where had all this money gone? How could even wealthy and honest promoters like George Washington have calculated so badly?[50]

Elkanah Watson summed up in 1820 the underlying reason for so much mis-adventure: "We were all novices in this department." Lacking practical experi-ence, these amateur canal builders found that their "expenditures baffled all calculation." Large sums quickly disappeared as directors purchased equipment and outfitted crews for tasks nobody previously had performed, to be carried out deep in the backcountry where supervision was slight and the cost of victualing great. Recruiting workers proved almost impossible. The Potomac Company tried all combinations of black slaves, white laborers, and private contractors, but no system brought economical results. Afraid to tackle the most difficult engi-neering feats, early managers spent too much of their capital blowing up boulders in the riverbeds and effecting simple improvements, waiting until a skilled engi-neer (or some new inspiration?) might guide them through the mysteries of lock-and-dam construction. Early directors ordered survey after survey, groping to-ward scientific understanding; but too often their "surveyors" knew little more than real-estate measurement, and the "information" they produced amounted to laymen's observations of country the directors had never seen at all.[51]

Not that finding an engineer necessarily solved a canal company's problems in late eighteenth-century America. Men who claimed expertise roamed the land, armed with letters of recommendation from credible sources, demanding hand-some salaries in advance. James Rumsey, not an engineer but thought to be a competent "manager," spent a great deal of the Potomac Company's money giving orders and quarreling with his staff. Christopher Myers took thousands to construct the locks at Great Falls but produced mostly a stone house in which to live. George Washington fretted endlessly over the lack of an engineer. In 1786, when English canal builder James Brindly paid a call, Washington hurried him out to Great Falls for advice. Nine years later he talked Robert Morris into lending him William Weston, the British engineer hired in 1793 by the Schuylkill & Susquehanna Canal. Quickly recognized as about the only canal expert in the country, Weston became the oracle in New York and Virginia as well as Pennsyl-vania. A "judicious man" (wrote Washington), Weston's reports nevertheless reflected the enthusiasm of his patrons, tending to suppress doubt and multiply optimism among them.[52]

Specious calculations of benefits and costs contributed even more to the ap-peal of early navigations. Washington worked up pseudoscientific numbers; so did Jefferson, Robert Morris, Thomas Gilpin, Christopher Colles, Elkanah Watson, and Philip Schuyler. Everybody interested in inland navigation haz-arded projections of traffic on the new waterways and multiplied their esti-mates by the statutory rates of tolls to arrive at estimates of "minimum" receipts. Against this theoretical income they set the estimated costs of the improvements that would generate this traffic. The balance, theoretically, was profit, ready to divide among investors, pour into public treasuries, or reinvest in more improvements (rendered literally "free," so the argument went, by the earnings of the first successful works).

Robert Morris demonstrated this fortune-telling art in a 1790 appeal for Pennsylvania canals. Starting with the fact that 150,000 bushels of grain found a market that year at Middletown on the Susquehanna, and allowing a one-eighth increase per year for local growth, Morris generated a chart showing the future cost of exporting grain by land to Philadelphia between 1793 and 1800. Similarly he laid out return commerce and developed a total of £368,935 to be spent for eight years' transportation without the benefit of his canal. Then he derived a cost of £220,561 for the same commerce carried by boat—a savings to the community of £148,374. Furthermore, he argued, the "stock now vested in horses, wagons, &c." could be diverted to other productive use, and farmers could adopt oxen in place of horses for draft animals (oxen being more economical to feed— and edible besides). Philadelphia's population would continue to rise, and with it the demand for foodstuffs carried by canal. Reason piled high upon assumption until internal improvement looked incredibly compelling.[53]

Now Morris was a well-known speculator, and one might dismiss his words as buoyant fabrications. But Morris's arguments found reinforcement everywhere the spirit of improvement emerged. Even engineers such as Weston produced "scientific" estimates, projecting, for example, for the Schuylkill & Susquehanna Canal, an annual income of £62,862—excluding the "great emoluments" expected from leasing mill seats.[54] Elaborate calculations of the earth or water to be moved, detailed schedules of raw materials and labor costs, rich descriptions of topography and geology all contributed strength to improvement promotions.

Vision, hope, and self-interest combined to distort critical assessments of early improvement projects in a uniformly positive direction. Most promoters looked to indirect advantages for their greatest personal rewards. Robert Morris, Philip Schuyler, and George Washington, for example, each held large quantities of undeveloped land. Long-run developmental projects, sustained by large numbers of investors and secured by government favor, promised to multiply their assets regardless of immediate returns from canal stocks. On the other hand, public sector donations often generated much of the start-up capital that early improvers sank (without a trace) in excavations, and this lent credence to the charges that such schemes merely robbed the public treasury. Pressure from politicians and taxpayers in turn encouraged shortsighted mistakes, as directors looked for quick results to quiet their enemies. Engineers, even the best and most honest, wished to test the limits of hydraulic technology, and they knew that people hired experts to *build* canals, not to declare them prohibitively expensive. On the cutting edge of civil engineering, faced with real needs and opportunities, finding plausible methods of proceeding, and lacking scientific proof that their schemes could not succeed, internal improvers convinced themselves and their followers that their calculations were correct.

Even the opponents of early improvement programs inadvertently propelled the boosters onward. Special pleading by entrenched local interests invariably identified opponents of new bridges, roads, and waterways with antiprogressive thinking. Philadelphia's resistance to opening the Susquehanna River was a flagrant example of the common tendency of selfish groups to place immediate or private advantages ahead of general or future benefits. Fishermen on the Schuylkill and other rivers worked against improved navigation; millers and middlemen sought to protect those natural barriers to transportation that made their particular locations profitable in the first place; frontier farmers—the purported beneficiaries of interregional improvements—frequently resented paying tolls on splendid waterworks when the infrequent passage of flatboats on floodwaters suited their limited needs just as well. Such backward and small-minded arguments sometimes enhanced the contrasting wisdom of internal improvers' schemes.

The failed designs of the monied gentry produced negative memories in every state that inhibited public works in America for much of a generation. Writing in 1821, New York's DeWitt Clinton condemned his state's early navigation companies: "However laudable for good intentions," he declared, their operations had been "unfortunately calculated to dampen the zeal for internal navigation and to arrest its progress."[55] A political enemy of Federalist Philip Schuyler's canals, who converted to internal improvement soon after Jefferson's partisan triumph in 1800 (and whose candor never was complete), Clinton nevertheless revealed an important truth about the programs of the Federalist era. Investors sustained often brutal losses that left them shy of experimental ventures. Fraud and mismanagement diverted enough public treasure wrongfully into private hands to leave taxpayers skittish about public investments. More important than either of these, however, was the legacy of political suspicion that grew up around every proposal. In the 1790s American governments themselves were experimental projects; everybody wondered as they set them in motion whether their efforts served to perfect or corrupt the nation's experiment in self-government.

Language, Corruption, and the Public Interest

Corruption, of course, was the greatest political evil that stalked American liberty in the first years after independence. The American "Whig" science of politics identified the private abuse of public power as the root of political oppression, and most Americans believed they had seen enough of government conducted exclusively for the profit of the governors. Notwithstanding the claims of propagandists during the Revolution, that Americans possessed selfless or "disinterested" virtue, most people had doubts about their neighbors—if not themselves. Nothing triggered this fear of government corruption quite like schemes for internal improvement. Expensive, tangible, and sometimes irreversible, internal improvement projects committed the community, state, or nation to making alterations in the landscape and erecting great artificial installations. The costs bore down on everyone, while the benefits (if they materialized) remained inexorably local. Few things a new American government might do at any level impinged on the people more directly, more unevenly, or more permanently than did public works of internal improvement. Therefore, few issues more fiercely tested the rhetoric of "general welfare" and "common good" that inevitably justified these public initiatives. Injured individuals first denounced public works, because of their immediate interest in a ferry, a tavern, or some other private business; but as more projects swallowed capital without delivering the promised benefits, more and more people began to wonder if perhaps hidden motives did not govern the promotion of internal improvements.[56]

In the Federalist 1790s, hidden motives were not hard to find in the designs of the monied gentry. Philadelphia boosters such as Robert Morris did not hope to redirect the commerce of the Susquehanna because the river lacked an outlet, but because that outlet was not where they wanted it to be. New York's canalers sought public investments to hurry the progress of speculations in a wilderness that otherwise might have lain dormant for another generation. Virginia's Potomac route to the West *could* bind together the extremities of a rising empire, but it surely *would* increase the value of George Washington's Ohio lands and nourish a great city close by Mount Vernon. In this self-creating new United States, how was one to judge the claims of gentlemen whose rhetoric of service and the commonweal so clearly coincided with passionate self-interests? And because selfish interests were the root of all corruption, how could honest voters discern when politicians told the truth about internal improvement and when they simply blew smoke to cover speculations at public expense?

One clear and early example of how republican politics would meet the test of practical application came in the contest in the first federal Congress over the location of the seat of government—and the results were far from encouraging. Although the framers themselves had tried to breathe life into the new Constitution without triggering violent local or sectional jealousies, the first lawmakers in Congress could not indefinitely postpone such collisions. Before the first session closed, Congress had to come to terms with a concrete question that could not be settled to everybody's liking: where would they sit in the future? The location of the new seat of government carried material and symbolic rewards. The prize appealed to many localities as a certain cause of economic growth. Not surprisingly, the leading sites for a new seat of government lay at the centers of designs for internal improvement. At its founding in 1789 Congress sat in New York, which suited that state and New England but struck citizens of the South and West as too far east and too imbued with the spirit of modern speculative commerce. Pennsylvanians assumed that their location at the center of wealth, population, and geography rendered their claims as a natural capital irrefutable. Virginians, long accustomed to a central role in politics, and confident that frontier development would draw population steadily toward the Southwest, hoped to honor George Washington's lifelong dream by founding a great American emporium on the Potomac, "a place to which tribute is brought." Hoping to aggrandize themselves, half a dozen lesser places vied for selection, should the three major parties become hopelessly deadlocked.[57]

The issue came to life in the House of Representatives 26 August 1789, when Pennsylvania's Thomas Scott introduced a harmless-sounding resolution: fix the permanent seat of government "as near the center of wealth, population, and extent of territory, as may be consistent with the convenience to navigation of the Atlantic ocean, and having due regard to the particular situation of the Western country." Congressmen from South Carolina and Connecticut condemned the proposition as hasty and ill-considered, but Scott urged the House to act quickly while Congress still "possessed all their virtue and innocence." Massachusetts' Fisher Ames, future archdeacon of New England Federalism, rose to ridicule the claims of urgency from Pennsylvania and Virginia. "Every principle of local interest, of pride and honor, and even of patriotism" would be engaged in this debate, he predicted, and Ames doubted that the new government, "ill-cemented and feeble" as it was, "could stand the shock" such a measure would inflict. Massachusetts Congressman Benjamin Goodhue favored Pennsylvania's Susquehanna Valley as the proper location for the new federal town, continuing temporary residence in New York until new quarters could be prepared. Frightened by what looked like a prearranged bargain between Pennsylvania and New England, Virginia's Richard Bland Lee countered that centrality, "convenient communication with the Atlantic ocean," and "easy access to the Western territory" ought to be the criteria of judgment. Only the Potomac fit the bill. Thomas Hartley agreed in principle but declared that Wright's Ferry on the Susquehanna met Lee's description exactly.[58]

Speakers pursued two lines of argument at once, shifting focus for strategic advantage. First, they debated the merits of the rivers themselves. Fisher Ames described the Potomac route as long and "extremely difficult" for navigation, interrupted by fifteen miles of falls. Not at all, objected Charles Carroll: he could see the Potomac "from his own door," and he knew it to be far more accommodating. With wicked relish, Ames replied that his source was Thomas Jefferson's *Notes on the State of Virginia*. Jefferson's "account of the Potomac" did not "correspond with the praises now bestowed upon it," Ames concluded with a schoolmaster's sneer. The inference was plain: somebody was lying! Parallel arguments attacked the strategy of angling for votes before the issue had been fairly debated. On 3 September, with great righteousness, James Madison accosted Thomas Hartley with the charge that measures had been "preconcerted out of doors," without the consent or even knowledge of half the country. James Jackson, also from Virginia, named New York and New England as conspirators to fix the capital outside the South: "Why not also fix the principles of Government? Why not come forward and demand of us the power of legislation, and say, give us up your privileges and we will govern you?" Theodore Sedgwick sarcastically inquired what was wrong with gentlemen consulting together? Delaware's John Vining tried to educate his mind "to impartiality," and "chastise its prejudices," but observers might have wondered if such a thing were possible in Congress.[59]

Madison spent much of the next two days patiently defending the Potomac and piously denouncing the intrigues of a "silent majority," constructing for the record a pitiful example of how brazen interests might subvert the public good. But this was all a sham. We know from private writings that prearrangements did exist between New England and the Pennsylvanians, but Virginia also had a deal that quite possibly came first. Pennsylvania senator William Maclay (who kept an acid diary) reported on 29 August 1789 that "a contract was entered into" by Virginia and Pennsylvania, "to fix the permanent Residence on the Potowmac, right or Wrong." On 1 September, two days before Madison's attack on Thomas Hartley's outdoor conspiracy, an almost comic meeting convened in George Clymer's rooms, where upstairs Robert Morris entertained Rufus King of New York and Goodhue of Massachusetts while Clymer, Thomas Fitzsimons, and other Pennsylvanians negotiated with Madison below.[60]

To manage politics outside the chamber—one classic definition of legislative corruption—was neither new nor particularly shocking, but to vilify schemers while scheming yourself seems out of character for Madison, suggesting how strongly the Virginians felt about Washington's Potomac vision. Sincere and honest appeals to "natural facts" about the Potomac navigation fell on deaf and prejudiced ears. Fisher Ames struck rather close to the mark when he observed in debate that certain men (Washington, for one) "who were generally guided by the straight line of rectitude, had been most surprisingly warped on the present occasion." Tested in this fire of experience, the language of disinterested republican politics could not sustain ideal expectations. Fighting over valuable privileges and interests, American politicians cheated on the game they were inventing. No more innocent than most of his colleagues, William Maclay recorded disgust at the "rude manners Glaring folly, and the basest selfishness" that he thought marked "almost every public Transaction" in the first federal Congress. His disappointment underscored everyone's suspicions about government in this era of democratization. "I came here expecting every man to act the part of a God," he complained. The most "delicate Honor," "exalted Wisdom," and "refined Generosity," ought to have governed "every Act" of the assembly. Instead his fellow lawmakers plotted intrigues so complicated they collapsed of their own weight.[61]

Ironically, it was Thomas Jefferson, the pristine republican, who recorded for posterity his own agency in arranging a final deal between Madison and Treasury Secretary Alexander Hamilton, by which the Potomac supposedly was traded for Virginia's support on the Assumption Bill. Hamilton wished to enlarge the impact of his federal funding system by assuming the revolutionary debts of the states, a measure bitterly opposed by Virginians at home. But Virginians in Congress saw the chance for a deal, and the interlocking designs of Washington's rising empire and Hamilton's fiscal system moved each other toward fruition at the expense of ideal political practice. People quickly perceived the outlines of the bargain, and even Washington's immaculate reputation could not deflect all public criticism. Newspaper editors questioned the president's integrity, while the apocalyptic William Maclay howled in fury in his diary: "the President has become in the hands of Hamilton the Dishclout of every dirty Speculation, as his name Goes to Wipe away blame and Silence all Murmuring."[62] In the face of criticism that wounded him deeply, President Washington still picked a site for the new federal city that lay outside the boundaries set down in the 1790 statute. He named his hometown, Alexandria, as the southernmost tip of the ten-mile square, expecting Congress to ratify his preference at the next session. Meanwhile Treasury Secretary Hamilton proposed a British-style national bank as the centerpiece of his fiscal system. Virginians feared the bank even more than assumption, and Washington considered vetoing the bank bill, but once again political linkage blurred questions of policy. The Senate held the residence bill hostage until Washington sanctioned the bank. Republican rhetoric notwithstanding, certain interests proved simply too dear to be lost in an open, free-wheeling, public legislative debate.[63]

Throughout the 1790s, as recalcitrant rivers absorbed more and more American capital and practical politics engendered more bitterness, popular views of internal improvement became jaded. The projects of navigation, the gentlemen who promoted them, and the game of politics that united the two all lost credibility in the eyes of increasingly free and self-interested people. Recriminations flew in all directions. Delinquent investors who forfeited stocks often felt cheated by wealthy promoters. Large investors, in turn, complained that their fortunes were lost to the reckless defaulters. Not yet reconciled to the hazards of developmental markets and experimental investments, many Americans of common means thought they saw fraud whenever larger ventures failed while the gentlemen behind them survived. Often they were correct, for the "monied gentry" (who better understood how capital markets behaved) always sought and usually received a margin of safety in some form of public aid or protection. Such arrangements played into the hands of all the enemies of public works, who railed against schemers and scoundrels for reasons ranging from nostalgic conservatism to vested interest, localism, jealousy, and factional intrigue.

Two conclusions began to emerge during the Federalist decade that set the

terms of debate for later internal improvement policy. Some observers of these
early experiments concluded that the ideas were sound but inadequate funding,
faulty management, or incomplete jurisdiction (or some combination of the
three) had ruined these experimental works. Such stalwarts turned to government—both their local state assemblies and Congress—for help. Sovereign governments, they reasoned, could better invest huge sums in long-term programs
where public benefit appeared more certain than private profits. Tradition dic-
tated that governments should nurture the "common-wealth"; not even Adam
Smith's recent attack on the mercantilist tradition, *An Inquiry into the Nature and
Causes of the Wealth of Nations* (1776), denied such basic obligations of the sovereign, especially in underdeveloped (Smith wrote "barbarous") countries. From
these fragments of experience a second generation of builders and promoters
would construct foundations for a national system of internal improvements.[64]

Different people arrived at a second conclusion, ridiculing promoters of early
navigations and bitterly denouncing public investments as the games of visionary
gentlemen, thieves, and self-appointed engineers. Public works and corporate
charters restricted the field for enterprise and speculation to a privileged few,
while taxes collected to pay public debts pressed hard on ordinary taxpayers. As
short-term opportunities grew up around them, middling Americans in the
1790s lost faith in the distant benefits promised by expensive navigation projects.
Frankly partisan attacks on the national fiscal programs of Alexander Hamilton
mobilized popular feeling against the "monied class." As a result, the mass of
Americans in "the democracy" soon connected the failed designs of gentleman-
improvers with the Federalist conspiracies they thought lay behind funding,
assumption, and the United States Bank. The popular founders of an emerging
Republican Party, Thomas Jefferson and James Madison, loudly condemned
Hamilton's bank and its scheming capitalists. Under assault for corruption, the
"monied gentry" as a class found it almost impossible to defend the wisdom or
virtue of improvement schemes that yielded mostly disappointment.[65]

In George Washington's lifetime, neither the monied gentry nor the common
people rose to the standards of citizenship implied by his concept of "wisdom."
Even the president's favorite canal in the end was a local improvement. Only the
plan of the new federal city gave the Potomac route any hope of becoming a
major American highway, and Washington's brazen campaign to secure that
prize stretched his disinterested guise paper-thin. As controversy gained momentum during the Federalist era, the political culture that understood and sustained Washington's aristocratic leadership style collapsed. In its place developed
competitive partisan politics, rooted in interests rather than claims of wisdom,
and determined to transform the infant republic into something radically new.[66]

The Constitution survived, not as an instrument of grand design but as a framework for negotiating conflicts among these diverse and ambitious Americans. For that reason many founders felt unsure about the achievement of their revolutionary goals. Washington's 1796 "Farewell Address," for example, advised the people to "resist with care the spirit of innovation" in politics. This must have sounded quaint in light of the full-throated partisan clamor that had typified the preceding year. At that time, reacting to the infamous Jay Treaty of 1795, Philadelphia editor Benjamin Franklin Bache probed the limits of opposition with this unmeasured attack: "If ever a nation was debauched by a man, the American nation has been debauched by Washington." Alexander Hamilton was vilified regularly as a "bastard," the "American Walpole," while John Adams, the incoming Federalist president, could not shake the appellation "avowed MONARCHIST." "Democratization" scarcely conveys the sense of cultural disintegration that haunted these one-time revolutionaries in the twilight of the Washington administration.[67]

For all his genuine wisdom and delicate leadership, Washington had been unable to contain or suppress those fractious interests and local jealousies that had composed the "impending evils" of 1786. Instead, politics under the new Constitution domesticated these expressions of popular innovation, giving them permanent place in the life of the new republic. America's genteel revolutionary leaders had never intended such a radical outcome. Most of them had felt at least some degree of sympathy with John Adams's comparative assessment of the American and French revolutions: "Ours was resistance to innovation; theirs was innovation itself."[68] In the end, the designs of the monied gentry tried to foster but could not control the rising American empire.

This first generation of promoters, planners, and schemers correctly perceived that internal improvement held the key to America's future. They found the best routes, and they rightly suspected that the first one to open the West would win irreversible advantages. They proposed surprisingly appropriate technical systems, failing to execute their plans usually for want of experienced builders or sufficient supplies of money. If the people lacked "wisdom enough to improve" their rivers, as Washington once had worried, it was true only in the sense that wisdom implied authority and design. Reconceived in terms of *interest* more than *wisdom*, every project brought forth in the Federalist era found popular backing again in the early nineteenth century, as localities, states, and regions struggled to lead or at least keep pace with America's expansion. Some of the monied gentry watched in horror as the scramble of interests began to define American life. Others such as Jefferson and Madison tried to direct the release of energy. Yet even these Republican Party leaders hoped to perpetuate certain designs against the disintegrative forces of freedom. Liberty without design (called "license" by this generation) was an idea not yet appealing to Americans.

2

Toward a National Republican Alternative

THE RISE OF THE Republican opposition in the 1790s, both in Congress and out of doors, interfered with designs for internal improvement by steadily eroding public confidence in government authority and action. Guided by a conviction that the Federalists misunderstood or distorted the republican ideal, Thomas Jefferson, James Madison, and the party of Republicans they created set out to rescue the national experiment from what they perceived to be stockjobbers, aristocrats, and monarchists who would stop at nothing (they believed) to establish class rule. Members of the "monied gentry" themselves, these Republican leaders nevertheless denounced the schemes of "designing men" and encouraged a more democratic style of politics based on interests and the voice of the people. They articulated a more libertarian version of republicanism that stressed the dangers of power and office over the virtues of correct constitutions, and they urged the people to scrutinize their governments perpetually.[1]

Republicans in Congress in the 1790s failed to stop Treasury Secretary Alexander Hamilton's funding schemes or the chartering of a national bank, but these opponents of energetic government opened a campaign that gradually prevailed against the further extension of national authority in ways not clearly stated in the Constitution. Internal improvements quickly emerged as a class of initiatives the federal government *might* undertake for the "general welfare," but for which authority was not clearly granted. In an atmosphere of bad faith and deepening partisan suspicion, Republicans in Congress crafted a "strict construction" argument designed to limit national power almost regardless of the merits of the question. The result was a series of debates in the 1790s—often inconsistent and increasingly rancorous—over harbor improvements, lighthouses, coastal fortifications, and post roads, that served primarily as forums for debating the authority of Congress and the balance of power between the Union and the states.[2]

Finally in 1800, having first denounced government on behalf of a liberated people, the Republicans elected Thomas Jefferson to the presidency and seized control of the federal establishment. Jefferson refashioned both the rhetoric and institutions of the national government, stripping the tiny bureaucracy to its bare bones, scuttling a deepwater navy that embodied Federalist commercial ambitions, and personally destroying the pretentious decorum that was just taking root in Washington City. As head of the party in power, however, he now had to *govern* the nation while preserving its constitutional integrity, and before long Jefferson was looking for a positive agenda. High on his list of things a proper republican government should do was the promotion of internal improvements designed to foster harmony, Union, and interregional development. Soon Jefferson's supporters were dreaming of a national system of roads and canals to "bind the republic together" and guarantee a prosperous future.[3]

Ironically, public confidence in the virtue of government continued to decline as democratization proceeded, and with it fell people's willingness to accept the restricting influence of designs and institutions, even those laid down by Republican administrations. Unless they served immediate, measurable ends, all disciplinary frameworks—electoral procedures, courts, systems of money, cultural institutions, or public works of internal improvement—could be attacked as aristocratic, unrepublican, and contrary to the liberties of the people. Both in the states and in Congress, a frankly competitive, interest-based politics displaced the idealistic fervor (if not the rhetoric) of the Jeffersonian revolution. The movement fractured during the second Jefferson administration. Guided by shifting combinations of local interest and personal ambition, some Republicans embarked on a libertarian "states' rights" crusade against the power of the national government, while others tried to fashion a national agenda within the limits of the Jeffersonian vision.

Thomas Jefferson's Republican Vision

Jefferson's vision of the American republicanism rested on profoundly different principles than those of George Washington's Federalist gentry. Far less suspicious of popular government or the virtues of the common people, Jefferson cherished a more radical view of American liberation than did most revolutionary leaders. He saw the United States as a unique geographical place, a frontier nation blessed with abundant land on which experiments in human freedom might yield a natural, rational, egalitarian order and alter the course of history. Inclined to blame all that was wrong with old Europe on faulty institutions (especially established churches and aristocratic governments), Jefferson assumed that liberation required little more than stripping away these artifacts of error and guarding against their return. Unmolested by priests, lords, and placemen, honest majorities of ordinary people would be perfectly capable, he thought, of governing themselves and the nation. All that was required to release the energies that naturally motivated all people were conditions of peace, independence, individual liberties, and republican government. After 1783, the American Union seemed the most likely place on earth where such conditions might be secured for all time.[4]

Land sustained Jefferson's vision both literally and figuratively. In a preindustrial agricultural society, land promised independence and therefore liberty for the heads of freehold families. Western land, much of it ceded to Congress by his home state of Virginia, made it possible for Jefferson to conceive of general liberation without disturbing the proprietary interests of his own planter class. With "lands enough to employ an infinite number of people in their cultivation," he predicted, the new republic could anticipate a happy agrarian future. Vigorous, independent, and virtuous by nature, "tied to their country and wedded to its liberty and interests by the most lasting bands," cultivators made the finest citizens. These were supposed to be inherent qualities, and Jefferson trusted them to determine the results of liberation. Therefore, where Washington and others feared chaos in the West and proposed energetic government control, Jefferson preferred to introduce democracy, encourage the pioneers, and nurture bonds of friendly intercourse and mutual interest.[5]

This fortunate uniting of liberty and land promised benevolent results, but frontier democracy would not alone secure Americans' happiness. Jefferson knew that in a world of commercial empires, Americans must also engage Europe in mutually beneficial trade. "Our citizens have had too full a taste of the comforts furnished by the arts and manufactures," he conceded, "to be debarred the use of them." It was incumbent then upon the government to "endeavor to share as large a portion as we can of this modern source of wealth and power." Three great rivers—the Hudson, Potomac, and Mississippi—promised to carry the trade of the American interior, and Jefferson thought the Potomac must naturally dominate, pouring into Virginia's "lap the whole commerce of the Western world." Alas, the Potomac lay unimproved and useless while the inferior Hudson route was "already open" to navigation. Here Jefferson enthusiastically embraced the concept of internal improvement: the hand of enterprise must intervene to keep opportunities unfolding according to nature's implicit design. In this case, Jefferson thought the state of Virginia ought to mount the required improvements before accidental development awarded all commerce to New York. Like Washington, he sought the aid of the monied gentry; but he thought it even better if such works were done "at public than private expence [sic]."[6]

For Jefferson, then, abundant land, improved by wise government and enterprising people, framed the experiment in American liberation. By the middle of the 1780s, he had drafted for the Union what he took to be a "safe" and liberal program for the management of western lands, including a rectilinear survey system that reduced a continental empire to marketable numbered squares. He lent a hand in the Potomac River project expressly to bind the Atlantic states together with their frontier offspring. At stake was not just a valuable natural resource but the very playing field of American republicanism, "the common stock for man to labour and live on." For Jefferson, small landholders necessarily composed "the most precious part of a state," and while it was "too soon yet" to promise every man a farm, it was nevertheless desirable to retain and develop the western country, "that as few as possible shall be without a little portion of land." Therein lay the hope of American society.[7]

The second defining characteristic of Jefferson's republican vision was the practice of limited government. Only constitutional governments, established by consent of the governed and strictly limited in the exercise of power, could be expected to recognize the rights of the people or preserve their experiment in liberty from natural, aristocratic enemies. Abuse of power, class rule, local partiality, and pandering to the electors were among the evils that worried him, and he conjured up all kinds of schemes (at least three constitutions for Virginia alone) to make the exercise of power less hazardous. Short legislative terms, functional separations of power, weak executives, independent justices, little patronage, and broad suffrage—these were the building blocks of safe republican government. He did not think wealth a good predictor of integrity in office, and so he worried less about the "quality" of candidates than about their representativeness. "The decisions of the people, in a body," he professed, would be "more honest and more disinterested than those of wealthy men."[8]

Jefferson's commitment to majority rule and limited constitutional government survived some frustrating experiences in the years just after independence. New governments proved either unresponsive to the will of the people or too feeble to command respect. In Virginia, for example, the established gentry rejected virtually all of Jefferson's recommendations: for broad suffrage, reapportionment, land distribution, inheritance reform, and the abolition of slavery. In the Confederation Congress, he saw jealous localists (often large speculators) scheming for control of western lands without regard to the rights of frontiersmen or the good of the Union. Finally, sent to Paris in 1784 to negotiate economic treaties, Jefferson discovered that the Confederation government was too weak to impress the great powers of Europe who held the keys to Atlantic commerce.[9]

Each time these new governments disappointed him, Jefferson looked for ways to repair or redirect them. In Virginia, he pursued by ordinary legislation fundamental principles, such as religious toleration, that he preferred to see addressed in constitutions. In the Confederation Congress, he authored an ordinance for governing the West that empowered frontier settlers against the influence of absentee landlords and distant governors. In Paris, he set about arranging treaties designed to take commerce "out of the hands of the states, and to place it under the superintendence of Congress, so far as the imperfect provisions of our constitution will admit, and until the states shall by new compact make them more perfect." In every case, the champion of strictly limited government found it hard to accept the framework at hand and moved almost instinctively to amend it. Faced with compelling problems and faulty constitutions, Jefferson reconstrued his mission to conform to a higher purpose. Convinced that right procedures must produce correct results, he scrutinized the frameworks of power whenever the outcomes of governance annoyed him. A consummate designer of revolutions, he found it difficult to declare an end to experimentation and live constrained by anyone's organic designs, ancient or modern.[10]

Jefferson still resided in Paris in the winter of 1786-87, when the Confederation government began to unravel and the Philadelphia convention took shape. Never really understanding the dimensions of the crisis at home, he offered a solution that quickly became for him the key to American federalism: "make us one nation as to foreign concerns, and keep us distinct in Domestic ones." From a distance the formula made sense, but the distinction between foreign and domestic government proved elusive in practice and did nothing to relieve obstructions to national policy that derived from clashing state or local interests. Caught up in the whirlwind of events back home, James Madison tried to explain to his friend overseas how threats of secession, sectional distrust, foreign intrigue, commercial isolation, Indian wars, and domestic insurrections such as Shays's Rebellion all threatened to destroy the American Union. Madison wanted a drastic cure: there must be a new federal head "with a negative *in all cases whatsoever* on the local legislatures." Madison's assault upon the states startled Jefferson, but his more urgent fear of losing the Union—and the western lands without which republicanism could not succeed—sustained his interest in the work at Philadelphia.[11]

In the end, Jefferson welcomed the Constitution as a continuation of the process of self-creation. He watched the ratification progress with "great pleasure," not entirely happy with the document but "contented to travel on towards perfection, step by step." By June 1788 he was repeating what his friends so often told him: "It will be more difficult if we lose this instrument, to recover what is good in it, than to correct what is bad after we shall have adopted it." Ignoring the agonies that Madison and others had described for him by mail, Jefferson pronounced the whole ordeal a "beautiful example of a government reformed by reason alone," further proof that there was "virtue and good sense enough in our countrymen to correct abuses" whenever they appeared in government. Such an imaginary process, more than the new Constitution itself or the actual campaign to create it, impressed Jefferson that his own revolutionary vision had survived. To the English radical Richard Price he reported with great satisfaction "that wherever the people are well informed they can be trusted with their own government; that whenever things get so far wrong as to attract their notice, they may be relied on to set them to rights."[12]

Jefferson sailed from Paris at the end of 1789 fairly bursting with delight in the progress of American government. Still, doubts seasoned his most optimistic moments, and he never ceased to believe the enemies of freedom still coveted power. Thus he returned home and assumed the new office of secretary of state in Washington's administration, full of hope for the Constitution, yet expecting to learn its true virtues by its deeds. In principle Jefferson agreed with others in Washington's government, that the urgent needs of the Union included restoring public credit, resurrecting foreign trade, perfecting government in the West, and harmonizing the interests of the states. When he arrived at New York in March 1790, Congress swelled with bitter debates over Hamilton's funding and assumption bills. Jefferson did not like the plan to assume the debts of the states, but "for the sake of union" and to ward off bankruptcy he arranged a deal to break the southern opposition in return for a federal capital on the Potomac. Before long, however, dark suspicions accumulated around the treasury chief, whose purposes, methods, and style all convinced Jefferson that corruptors had resumed their calamitous advance. Ablaze again with partisan zeal, Jefferson began to see the actions of the Federalists not as alternative policies for national government but as designs to reverse the Revolution.[13]

It was this apparent abuse of federal power for counterrevolutionary purposes that drove Jefferson into opposition to the Federalist regime. Secure in his own vision of how a free people would choose to be governed, he could not imagine that Hamilton's stockjobbing program promoted anything but class rule. Everywhere he turned he found Hamilton ahead of him, meddling in diplomacy, maneuvering congressmen, bending the ear of the president, feeding lies and justifications to the press. When Hamilton proposed his national banking scheme, Jefferson denounced its "broad construction" foundations as destructive of the Constitution: "To take a single step beyond the boundaries thus specifically drawn around the powers of Congress, is to take possession of a boundless field of power, no longer susceptible of any definition." In early 1792, Hamilton's *Report on Manufactures* finally verified Jefferson's worst fears, and he unburdened himself to the president: a treasury system had been contrived, he explained, "for withdrawing our citizens" from "useful industry" into paper gambling. Bribery knit members of Congress into the scheme, who then assaulted the Constitution with "legislative constructions" designed to "keep the game in their hands." To perfect their usurpation, these enemies of popular government now proposed, with bounties for manufacturing, to take into the hands of Congress everything "which *they* should deem for the *public welfare*."[14]

Hamilton's actions supplied the evidence, but Jefferson's assumptions completed the analysis in this hysterical assessment of the Federalist program. Begging Washington to stay in office and expose the conspirators, Jefferson insisted that their goal was to "prepare the way" for "monarchy." Not content with such private pleading (in fact, well in advance of speaking to Washington), Jefferson also stirred up public opposition outdoors through the pages of Philip Freneau's *National Gazette*. The resulting newspaper war set a bitter tone for the elections of 1792 and drew a sharp scolding from Washington, who disbelieved Jefferson's fantasies and condemned "exciting" editorial pieces, "particularly in Freneau's paper," as more likely than Hamilton's programs to yield anarchy and disunion. Unwilling to argue with Washington, but unshaken in his view of what endangered the Union, Jefferson retreated into brooding opposition.[15]

Roots of a National Question

It was in this atmosphere of rising opposition that Congress in the 1790s tried to find its appropriate role in the promotion of internal improvements. The Constitution itself offered little guidance: Congress enjoyed explicit powers to coin money, provide for defense, regulate commerce, and collect taxes, and much vaguer obligations to secure the "general welfare" and take "necessary and proper" actions to fulfill its explicit duties. Historians know that the framers at Philadelphia refused to include in the Constitution powers to charter corporations or to cut canals in the states, but in the 1790s those debates were not yet publicly known. Hamilton thus built his case for a national bank on the implied powers of the "elastic clauses," ignoring the convention's vote to the contrary, and he used the same argument to promote manufacturing—triggering Jefferson's angry encounter with President Washington. As a result, the question of "broad" or "strict" construction threatened to attach itself to every initiative.[16]

Many congressmen came to the First Federal Congress filled with enthusiasm for the new central power. James Madison, for example, speaking on behalf of a national impost, effortlessly claimed that the power to "protect and cherish" manufactures, once belonging to the several states, had been "thrown" into national hands by the adoption of the Constitution. In another example, Massachusetts congressman Elbridge Gerry (once an ardent Antifederalist) moved to build at federal expense several lighthouses, beacons, buoys, and piers, which sailed through both houses without recorded debate. Congress protected such investments in the states by asking for deeds to the land on which they stood, but nobody objected to the improvements themselves.[17]

Throughout the Federalist decade Congress repeatedly embraced such patronage of coastal navigation with no apparent hesitation. In 1795, when Robert Goodloe Harper of South Carolina raised constitutional objections to a federal survey of the southern coast, it was James Madison, already the acknowledged leader of the congressional opposition, who nevertheless refused to call such aid "improper." On the closely related question of coastal fortifications, Congress freely voted expenditures, again requesting deeds to the actual ground. Although expensive forts generated nastier conflicts than did cheaper buoys and lighthouses, few members challenged the necessity for federal aid; by 1797, House Speaker Jonathan Dayton was calling for a planned national system of fortifications to replace the existing piecemeal approach. Saltwater politicians, regardless of party, seemed to understand their common national interest in traffic on the seas.[18]

On the system of post offices and post roads, congressmen found more arguments and precedents that later shaped the national struggle for internal improvements. Perhaps not as consequential as the bank, the debt, or foreign affairs, post road bills distributed tangible day-to-day benefits to particular constituents at home. Under the Articles of Confederation, the postmaster had enjoyed discretion in laying out routes and locating offices, but at the Philadelphia Convention Elbridge Gerry had insisted that this power be lodged in Congress. Even though the details of route selection, revenue, and office location quickly overwhelmed the legislative process, members hated to give up such a useful source of patronage. Massachusetts Federalist Theodore Sedgwick proposed in 1790 that the postmaster general be instructed to lay out a system of routes, it being "impossible for every particular member perfectly to understand" the bewildering choices before them. But this suggestion met with a storm of opposition. It abdicated the duties of Congress, objected Gerry and others; therefore, it was unconstitutional. The House rejected Sedgwick's amendment, then set about gleefully adding new roads to the post office system.[19]

The Senate in 1790 insisted on delegating to the president the selection of the so-called cross posts (roads intersecting the main post road), so the House reopened the question. Revenue would center "in the hands of the Executive," one member shrilled, where it "may be converted" in ways "destructive to the liberties of the United States." Only the "representatives of the people" were "competent" to know where the post roads should run. Nonsense, countered the advocates of delegated power. The current system was overburdened with routes laid on by popular demand. With the country changing rapidly, the routes would need revision constantly, causing "perpetual" legislation and "unnecessary expense." By the nature of his office, the postmaster general "must be the most competent judge" of the system based on "actual surveys" conducted by his staff. The two houses could not agree, and the postal bill was lost for that session.[20]

Nobody doubted that the federal government had to design and operate a postal system, but post road debates in the 1790s revealed ambiguities about both the purpose of postal services and also the separation of powers within the government or between central and local authorities. Especially in a republic information needed to circulate as widely and cheaply as possible. But should the post office run at a loss? Break even? Generate surpluses with which to extend the system of service? Was the subsidization of stagecoach lines an intentional or merely incidental benefit? Should the government concentrate postal service in commercial centers, where business was brisk (but where private carriers potentially abounded); or should the public mails favor distant and dispersed populations, leaving wealthy port cities to provide for themselves? Should trunk service follow fast, direct routes or meander to include the largest number of significant places? Quick, reliable mail tended to foster both prosperity and political influence. Should the post office department protect established centers of population or encourage frontier developments with early, cheap, high-quality service? Obviously, a vast pool of executive patronage fed by the postal system could threaten republican government, but did not benefits doled out by Congress promise a similar corrupt result? Finally, could the selection of post roads and offices safely be left to "experts" (who might have ulterior motives), or must these decisions remain in the political arena where frequent elections preserved accountability (and practically guaranteed a "pork barrel" approach)?[21]

Each of these questions found its way into post road debates, often blending eloquent high-toned rhetoric with the baser sort of political motivation. John Steele, a Federalist leader from "western" North Carolina, for example, first condemned delegation of power to the postmaster general as a violation of the Constitution, then embraced it when next year's bill promised a new route through his home region. Coastal spokesman Hugh Williamson, also of North Carolina, countered just as passionately that "the object of an established post was not to afford the most speedy conveyance, by the straightest line between two places, but to accommodate"—by wandering his sandy shoreline?—"as many persons" as possible." Georgia Federalist Abraham Baldwin declared it the "duty" of government to provide "at least some channel of communication" to all its parts—which meant that Congress owed him a road at least as deep into Georgia as Portland was into Maine. For Alexander White of Virginia (nominally a Federalist but unusually frightened of government power), the delegation of post road selection represented an advance "towards Monarchy" which, unchecked, "would tend to unhinge the present Government." James Madison agreed and asked, "Where is the necessity for departing from the principles of the Constitution?" Neither party nor principle determined where members stood in the postal debates. At best a shifting constellation of local interests, legislative logrolling, partisan affiliation (often local, not national), ideological conviction, and rhetorical strategy guided lawmakers as they talked through positions that would later help define the propriety of federal internal improvements.[22]

In 1794, Congress finally passed a comprehensive post office bill that perpetuated legislative oversight of roads and routes indefinitely. By then more dangerous matters of commercial policy, coastal fortification, and the threat of war with Britain or France were driving a bitter wedge of party division between Federalists and Jeffersonian Republicans. As leading spokesman for the Republicans in Congress, Madison continued to attack the Federalists' pro-British bias

and reckless disregard for the limits of constitutional power. Oddly, however, i
February 1796, in the midst of a desperate struggle over the Jay Treaty and th
president's high-handed method of securing its ratification, Madison introduce
a measure that seemed to enlarge the federal mandate on post roads. Perhaps i
connection with the new federal city to be raised on the Potomac, whose de
velopment he ardently supported, Madison called for a national survey of "th
main post road from Maine to Georgia—the expense to be defrayed out of th
surplus revenue of the Post Office." He identified two objectives: the "shortes
route" could be "determined upon," and consequently private parties, knowin
for sure where the post would run, "would not hesitate to make improvements
upon roads so selected. Not proposing to build such a road directly, Madison'
survey nevertheless intended to impose both rational design and permanence o
the existing system before something was done "on a worse principle." Georgi
Federalist Abraham Baldwin thought the states were burdened enough makin
roads to the different seaports: let the "cross roads" be left to "the government c
the whole." Postmaster General Joseph Habersham privately applauded the idea
believing like Baldwin that with a proper survey in hand, postal surpluses an
"private subscriptions" together could finance a "Turnpike Road of very consid
erable extent in the course of a few years."[23]

Madison's resolution met virtually no opposition in the House; and while i
died in a Senate committee, it did not seem to trigger constitutional objection
even in this time of white-hot partisan tempers. Jefferson, however, denounced i
as a "source of boundless patronage to the executive, jobbing to members c
Congress & their friends, and a bottomless abyss of public money." In a privat
lecture on the virtues of "country" government, Jefferson reminded his mor
nationalistic friend that even state legislatures hesitated to take over roads fror
the "magistracy of the county":

> What will it be when a member of N.H. is to mark out a road for Georgia?
> Does the power to *establish* post roads given you by congress, mean that you
> shall *make* the roads, or only *select* from those already made those on which
> there shall be a post? If the term be equivocal, (& I really do not think it so)
> which is the safest construction? That which permits a majority of Congress
> to go to cutting down mountains & bridging of rivers, or the other which if
> too restricted may refer it to the states for amendment?[24]

Here Jefferson conflated traditions of Virginia country justice with the on
true meaning of the federal Constitution. Recognizing that exceptions alread
had been made, he argued that only the most urgent necessity could legitimiz
innovations in government. With post roads there was no emergency as far a
Jefferson could see. Of course, by allowing an exception for urgent necessity (

window of expediency through which friends and even Jefferson himself at times would force their own favorite measures), Republicans only looked all the more like hypocrites. Connecticut Federalist Chauncey Goodrich, tracking Madison's behavior in the House, concluded that a "concerted system" was in place to "palsy the government" and bring about a change of "men, if not systems."[25]

Mutual suspicions, rooted in partisan and sectional differences, mounted steadily throughout the Washington administration and wracked congressional politics during the presidency of John Adams. Among public works projects, coastal fortifications first revealed the fault lines of jealousy, as representatives shamelessly condemned public spending outside their own port cities. Piers in the Delaware River—by 1796 a fairly routine request from Philadelphia merchants—excited surprising opposition from representatives of Virginia, New York, and Baltimore. But one of the more revealing displays of partisan bad faith came in response to George Washington's plea for a national university. Uniting his dreams for the national capital with his urgent concern about harmonizing all the people of the republic, Washington explained his objectives in his 1796 Annual Message to Congress:

> Amongst the motives to such an institution, the assimilation of the principles, opinions, and manners of our countrymen by the common education of a portion of our youth from every quarter well deserves attention. The more homogeneous our citizens can be made in these particulars the greater will be our prospect of permanent union; and a primary object of such a national institution should be the education of our youth in the science of *government*. In a republic what species of knowledge can be equally important and what duty more pressing on its legislature than to patronize a plan for communicating it to those who are to be the future guardians of the liberties of the country?

To encourage such a visionary project, the president offered twenty acres of public land in the District of Columbia and his own fifty shares of Potomac Company stock as an initial endowment.[26]

Once again, it was James Madison who carried into the House the president's nationalistic designs. Reporting for a select committee on the subject, Madison asked his colleagues to charter a corporation to receive these donations. John Nicholas of Virginia objected, afraid that once created the institution would demand financial support while benefiting only a small neighborhood. William Lyman of Massachusetts agreed. People from "remote parts of the United States" would never send their children to such a distant "Seminary" (that would probably corrupt their morals), and it would be a "natural source of discontent" to "pay their money merely for others to obtain the advantage." Friends of the measure insisted that nothing more was asked than a receptacle for private donations, but New York's Edward Livingston disagreed: "Something further seemed to be intended," warned Livingston; "I believe it will operate . . . as an 'entering wedge.'" Madison denied having hidden designs upon the national treasury, denied even that this was a "National University" but only "An University in the District of Columbia," and he pointed out that after 1800 the district would have no state government to which it could turn. Still, the enemies of national action held their ground. It might just as well be said, argued a frustrated supporter, that by "allowing a bridge to be built or a road to be cut," Congress promised to pay for the work. Precisely, retorted Nicholas. "If you adopt the plan, if you begin the building and it is left unfinished, it will remain a monument of reproach." Were this project requested by "the people," he would offer "all possible aid"; but this scheme came from promoters of the District, from "men who are sent there to manage business"—and "they are not the people."[27]

Here in miniature were critical arguments that would frustrate a generation of lawmakers interested in national internal improvements: fear of empowering the government; fear of burdening the taxpayer; fear of benefiting one locale with revenues from another; fear of plans or designs that, once adopted, tended to force their own continuation; fear of large or distant institutions that undermined authorities at home; fear of being lured by promoters into schemes that made men rich at public expense; fear of steps that fostered changes the results of which could not be foretold accurately. These were the same reasons Jefferson opposed the Maine-to-Georgia post road despite its promise of overall benefit. Worked up into an opposition creed, these principles matched the pure republicanism of "country" ideology. They became the central tenets of Jefferson's oppositional "Spirit of '98" (and they energized the schismatic "Old Republicans" who later deserted his party); yet here was Madison laboring in vain against them on behalf of a university project he and Jefferson cherished.

By the end of Washington's second administration, party differences had grown irreconcilable. Nearly everything about the Federalist regime reinforced Jefferson's belief in an organized monarchist conspiracy. George Washington himself had attacked what Madison called "the most sacred principle of our Constitution" by condemning the "self-created" Democratic Societies. Jefferson concluded that American liberty stood in mortal danger from "an Anglican monarchical, & aristocratical" party, "sprung up" to restore the substance and the form of British government. "The main body" of citizens remained "true to their republican principles" (the "whole landed interest" and the "great mass of talents"); against these stood the executive, judiciary, all officers and would-be officers of government, all "timid men who prefer the calm of despotism to the boisterous sea of liberty," British merchants and their American debtors, and "speculators" in public funds. The greatest men of the Revolution had "gone over" to the British model. The "irresistible influence" of Washington "played off by the cunning of Hamilton" accounted for the first transformation of "republicans chosen by the people into anti-republicans." After 1796 John Adams labored "with great artifice" to perpetuate the notion that his government represented the people, but for Jefferson this was not the case.[28]

Amid these developments, Jefferson and Madison organized an opposition. Electioneering, legislative "management," and outdoor agitation belonged among the evils of factional politics according to the wisdom of their day; nevertheless, both in and out of office these two Virginians orchestrated a movement against the Federalists in power. Jefferson excused his factional intrigues as nothing more than honest responses to dishonest politicians. "Were parties here divided merely by a greediness for office," he explained by 1798, participation would be "unworthy of a reasonable" person; but where "the principle of difference" was as pronounced as "between the parties of Honest men & Rogues," he felt obliged to play a "firm & decided part." An acknowledged opposition leader during the Adams administration, Vice President Jefferson tried to shape popular reactions to the Alien and Sedition Acts, the XYZ affair, the Quasi-War with France. Simultaneously he stimulated discontent while seeking to curb its disintegrative tendencies. To John Taylor in 1798 he praised the state governments yet discouraged all talk of dividing the Union into new confederations. In the 1798 Kentucky Resolutions, he proposed nullification as a local check on the pretensions of federal authority while still pledging to sacrifice "everything but the rights of self-government" to the cause of Union. By 1800, Jefferson's objective was to win the presidential election and reestablish the Constitution in the "true sense in which it was adopted by the States."[29]

Jefferson defined true republicanism in reaction to his vision of the Federalists' crimes. On the question of national power, the Federalists had tried to "seize all doubtful ground," and so he embraced a more Antifederal view of the Constitution than he had held twelve years before. He transformed Madison's reluctant Tenth Amendment, reserving to the states "the powers not yielded by them to the Union," into the centerpiece of his own interpretation. Within the federal sphere, he wished to see Congress reclaim whatever power had been usurped by the executive branch, but more importantly he nursed a jealous hatred of that government outside the most limited fields of defense and foreign affairs. He promised "rigorously frugal & simple" government, saving public revenue to pay off debts and suppress taxes, minimizing public offices, trusting the militia and minor naval forces to defend the homeland without grandeur. Convinced by the Federalists that powerful institutions served only to rob, cheat, manipulate, and oppress the people, candidate Jefferson proposed a truly Spartan federal establishment: let the "general government be reduced to foreign concerns only," with "simple" and "unexpensive" duties performed "by a few servants."[30]

Horrified by the Federalists' exercise of power, Jefferson attacked power itself.

Forgetting how narrowness of interest among the states had wrecked the postwa Confederation government (and lacking firsthand experience of the disorder o the later 1780s), Jefferson saw the Federalist responses to disintegrative tenden cies as retrograde assaults on liberty. Because Federalist programs fostered course of progress more urban, commercial, and elitist than he favored, Jeffersor assumed that their purpose was sinister and counterrevolutionary. Even while Madison continued to discriminate between what he considered good program and bad, Jefferson embraced the darkest view of every Federalist measure. He cultivated sympathy among the antigovernment radicals in Virginia and around the country, however libertarian, localistic, or backward-looking they might be and he set out to rescue the national government. In the process he left disabling marks on the American practice of government, tending—intentionally or not— to perpetuate (perhaps forever) a contingent and ambivalent relationship be tween the people and their federal government.[31]

Governing Republicans

Jefferson's election in 1800—he liked to call it a "revolution"—placed the reins o federal power in the hands of the Republicans. The creed of opposition laic down by Jefferson since 1792 had called for little government, strict construction states rights, and above all majority rule. Now the triumphant Jeffersonians se about remodeling the institutions of government according to their radical doc trines, while the Federalists steadily retreated. Confronted with the burden o government, however, Jefferson and his party soon discovered faults and contra dictions in their radical political principles.

The first task of Jefferson's government was to consolidate the support of the people and secure their fidelity to his definition of popular rule. "We are al republicans, we are all federalists," the president told his inauguration audience The same generous sentiments filled his correspondence with liturgical repeti tion, until he had constructed for himself an explanation of how the America republic had been saved. The people once were "hood-winked," he told John Dickinson, but the "band is removed, and they see for themselves." He assure James Monroe that the people once called federalists ("I always exclude thei leaders") now looked with "affection and confidence to the administration." T Joseph Priestley he penned an extravagant report that his countrymen had "re covered from the alarm into which art & industry had thrown them." The "orde & good sense displayed in this recovery from delusion" left Jefferson "bette satisfied" than ever of the promise of popular government. Once "decoyed int the net of monarchists," the people now were "coming back" to their sense rapidly.[32]

This denial of deep or lasting party differences excused Jefferson at first from defending his partisan agenda or developing a program of accommodation. H thought that reconciliation required only the restoration of good government. Accordingly, in his First Annual Message to Congress he called for an end of internal taxes, reductions in public expenditures, revision of naturalization laws, reform of the bloated judiciary, and a general scaling down of the old Federalist establishment. To Treasury Secretary Albert Gallatin he outlined a plan for retiring the public debt from the proceeds of import taxes freely paid by "the rich chiefly." Such good fortune accompanied Jefferson's arrival in office that by the end of 1802 there was "nothing scarcely to propose" for action by Congress. Wags protested that Hamilton's taxes and fiscal system made Jefferson's frugality possible, but Jefferson took the credit in the name of wise policies and sound liberal principles: "If we can prevent the government from wasting the labors of the people, under the pretense of taking care of them, they must become happy."[33]

Unfortunately, the twin pillars of Jefferson's creed—majority rule and strict construction—never yielded the simple clarity of right and wrong that Jeffersonians in opposition had described. When competitive tensions inevitably broke out among his own partisans, Jefferson blamed it on the influence of priests, lawyers, and unreconstructed Federalists. He met with anger all "malicious inquiries" from Congress, asking for explanations of his presidential actions. Astonishingly, he attacked as illegitimate the very type of self-created political societies (in this case, a Philadelphia ward committee) he once defended against Washington and Hamilton. As his own brand of popular politics took root in fractious state and local organizations, Jefferson retreated toward a very undemocratic principle of guidance: "under difficulties of this kind I have ever found one, & only one rule, *to do what is right*, & generally we shall disentangle ourselves without almost seeing how it happens."[34]

Doing "what was right" once meant doing only that which was spelled out in the Constitution, but after 1801 Jefferson found strict construction as difficult to live with as absolute majority rule. The purchase of Louisiana in 1803, for example, exceeded the limits of federal authority by Jefferson's own admission; but the measure complemented his vision and gratified the majority of voters outside of New England. Consequently, it was hurried by a Republican Congress through the elastic fabric of the Constitution, with Jefferson's uneasy acquiescence.[35] Exercising similar discretion, especially where the powers of government seemed unclear, he aggressively pursued the acquisition of Spanish Florida, pushed commercial policies that favored agriculture, manipulated Indian tribes for whom he was the ultimate legal guardian, encouraged frontier expansion, sent Lewis and Clark to explore the Far West, and finally turned the coercive power of government on his own people in an 1807 embargo of questionable wisdom or justice. At the same time, Republicans in Congress discovered many jobs that the government might do, and also how to use their orthodox principles to advance (or obstruct) special interests.[36]

Internal improvements reappeared on the Republicans' agenda because the need of the country for roads and canals simply was not being met. Politicians might condemn Federalist "schemes" or invite the attention of local county magistrates to the condition of the roads, but nothing much was accomplished by this posturing, and demands for improved transportation continued to mount. Petitions poured in to congressmen from their constituents, begging in traditional language for lighthouses, piers, and post roads, but increasingly asking as well for aid to turnpike and canal companies. If surviving documents are any guide, the volume and flow of this constituent pleading, while not extraordinary, increased nearly every year right through the Jeffersonian "revolution" in government. Neither did the form nor language change between the Federalist and Republican eras. All petitions promised a general as well as local benefit, and each particular work drew negative attention from combinations of endangered interests, niggardly taxpayers, and "conservative" characters hostile to all forms of "progress." Not surprisingly, therefore, some Republicans rediscovered the merits of internal improvements by the (now popular) national government while others dug in behind the ramparts of strict construction to prevent innovations, no matter how popular, in transportation—or in government.[37]

The Ohio Enabling Act of 1802, a perfectly Jeffersonian measure creating the first new state in the Northwest Territory, placed the question of road building before the first Republican Congress. Eager to displace the Federalist territorial establishment in Ohio and bring a new Republican state into the Union, William Branch Giles of Virginia brought forward a bill encouraging the people east of the Miami River to call a convention and prepare for statehood. Fearing that a new sovereign state might seize for taxes lands sold on credit by the federal government, Treasury Secretary Gallatin proposed three inducements to forestall such taxation, including one-tenth part of the proceeds of public land sales within the state to build "a turnpike or other roads, leading from the navigable waters emptying into the Atlantic to the Ohio, and continued afterwards through the new State." If built with the permission of the states through which it ran, such a road would not endanger local sovereignty but would benefit coastal states and the nation as much as the Northwest Territory by "cementing the bonds of union between those parts of the United States, whose local interests have been considered as most dissimilar." After a lively debate in which Federalists (reversing their original convictions) first condemned as unconstitutional all inducements put forth by Congress, Connecticut's Roger Griswold zeroed in on the road fund as a scheme merely to make roads in Virginia and Pennsylvania at national expense. Giles responded that federal lighthouses in New England bore a similarly local aspect, but if a "general benefit" accompanied expenditures, he "had no objection to them." Any policy "connecting the different parts of the Union by every tie as well of liberal policy as of facility of communication" he thought "highly desirable." Thus did the Jeffersonians in the Seventh Con-

ress move toward national aid to internal improvements (voting 47 to 29) with
scarcely a word about strict construction.[38]

Renewed interest in public works worried Jefferson, but pressure from his
supporters in the states and regular encouragement from Madison and Gallatin
helped him discover a legitimate role for the federal government to play. At first
he quarreled with Gallatin, opposing piers in the Delaware River and denouncing lighthouse construction as an "infraction" of the commerce clause likely to
expand the Constitution to "comprehend every power of government." Gallatin,
more of a nationalist by temperament and a savvy political strategist, urged the
president not to attack the Delaware piers and not to slam the door on useful
works because of occasional human failings. Meanwhile western Republicans,
anxious to throw off territorial (read "Federalist") paternalism on the frontier,
lobbied hard for the patronage of Congress to open their region and facilitate
local development. In this case, energetic government served not elite or established interests but the process of liberation and westward expansion that marked
Jefferson's original vision.[39]

Controversy attended the Ohio road project from the beginning, but for reasons of interest, not ideology. First, in the original 1802 bill the Senate reduced
Gallatin's one-tenth contribution to one-twentieth (5 percent), of which Ohio's
constitutional convention asked to have three-fifths (3 percent) turned over to
the Ohio government for roads inside the new state. The next year Ohio claimed
this "3 percent fund" as an addition to the original 5, a disingenuous move that
failed but set a new low standard of "interestedness" in legislative arguments. As
the fund accumulated, the question of routes to Ohio ignited fierce competition
among three primary contenders: from Philadelphia via Pittsburgh; from Baltimore to the upper Potomac; and from Richmond up the James and down the
Kanawha Rivers. Finally in December 1805, a Senate committee headed by
Connecticut Federalist Uriah Tracy reported a bill favoring the middle route
through Cumberland, Maryland. Their reasoning seemed compelling enough.
A Pennsylvania turnpike was being built already without federal aid, while the
James-Kanawha route served a howling wilderness where even Virginia had not
stirred to build roads. The Maryland route conveniently served Washington
City, but it could not reach Ohio without crossing two state lines—a perfect
example of the need for federal intervention. Because the fund would support at
best one road, the Senate adopted the report and sent Tracy's bill to the House.[40]

Opposition in the House of Representatives centered in Pennsylvania and
Virginia, where members clung to rival projects. Pennsylvania's Michael Leib
denounced the measure as "premature," while his colleague William Findley
called for "disinterested Commissioners" to recommend a "better" (that is, an
all-Pennsylvania) route. Virginia's Christopher Clark wished to lay out three
roads, spreading the money equally among them. John G. Jackson, also of Vir-

Thomas Coke Ruckle's "Fairview Inn or Three Mile House on Old Frederick Road"
(c. 1829). This depiction shows something of the character and volume of traffic on the
National Road. Courtesy Library of Congress.

ginia, argued absurdly that the plural noun "roads" in the Ohio Enabling Act
made it illegal to select just one. Such verbal sparring seems not to have moved
many congressmen: the bill carried 66 to 50. Federalists and westerners overwhelmingly supported the Cumberland Road bill; Republicans divided equally,
but nearly all the 38 Republicans voting nay came from Virginia or Pennsylvania
and stood against the *route*, not the road itself. Of the four Pennsylvania Republicans supporting the bill, two represented Albert Gallatin's present and former
congressional districts; of the two Virginians voting yea, one was Jefferson's son-
in-law, Thomas Mann Randolph, and the other James Madison's replacement in
Congress, John Dawson. Madison later would remember this first example of
national road building as the ill-conceived product of the session's final hours,
but members at the time must have seen it as an administration measure.[41]

Two conclusions had become inescapable by the time the Jefferson administration launched the Cumberland Road experiment. First, many Republicans
in Congress and outdoors desired a more energetic national government than
Jefferson had promised at his inauguration. Second, as the threat of "monarchical
Federalists" diminished, Republicans turned their taste and talent for factional
politics against each other in shameless displays of special pleading and local
legislation. These developments placed Jefferson's two most cherished ideological convictions—majority rule and strict construction—on a collision course.
When the "monied gentry" of the Federalist era tried to sponsor large works of

public improvement, majorities of common people had risen against them. But what if the majority of common people, represented by the members of Congress, truly wanted a more active federal hand? Increasingly, members pressed the demands of their constituents, justified often by the simple claim that commerce developed the country and cemented the bonds of Union. Could the government deny the people what they wanted because the framers had failed to see the need? Should the progress of a free and self-governing people be obstructed by artificial handicaps created in a former generation?[42]

In March 1805 Jefferson addressed this dilemma in his Second Inaugural Address. Despite having cut taxes on everything except imported "luxuries" ("what farmer, what mechanic, what laborer ever sees a tax gatherer of the United States?"), Jefferson still began his second term with the prospect of a treasury surplus. Once the national debt was retired, Jefferson proposed "by a just repartition among the states, and a corresponding amendment of the constitution," to apply the liberated revenue to "rivers, canals, roads, arts, manufactures, education, and other great objects within each state." His hope was to preserve the impost, partly to protect American manufactures and partly to keep the federal treasury supplied for the sudden demands of war. Actual hostilities, then, would require no new debts or taxes but only "a suspension of useful works, and a return to peace, a return to the progress of improvement." Missing the significance of the president's wording, Secretary of State Madison wondered, "What is the amendment alluded to as necessary to a repartition of liberated revenue amg. the states in time of peace?" But national improvements on the scale now envisioned by Jefferson and Gallatin unquestionably required, in Jefferson's view, an enlargement of federal power.[43]

Each new forecast from Gallatin's treasury increased the president's enthusiasm for national internal improvements: "it hastens the moment of liberating our revenue, and of permitting us to begin upon canals, roads, colleges, &c." By November 1806, as Jefferson worked on his Sixth Annual Message to Congress, Gallatin was promising between two and five millions per year beginning in 1809—sums "sufficient for any possible improvement." It would take, thought Gallatin, "at least the two intervening years to obtain an amendment, pass the laws designating improvements, and make the arrangements preparatory to any large expense." Confident that his program was popular, Jefferson insisted on an amendment "because the objects now recommended" were not among the government's "enumerated" powers, but also because he had no doubt that the amendment would pass and the program proceed "apace."[44]

Jefferson's desire for an amendment, logical and pristine, an artifact of theory and of bitter wars against the "broad construction" Federalists, would be the tragic undoing of Republican internal improvements. His fear of corruption, once trained on the arrogant executive, now focused on the "eternal scramble among members" of Congress "who can get the most money wasted in their State." Without constitutional limits, Jefferson believed, those would "get most who are meanest." Proportional spending in each state according to the "federal ratio" he thought might minimize the danger of logrolling. Gallatin suppressed this idea as unworkable: "neither improvements nor education can ever in practice be exactly partitioned in that manner." Consequently, Jefferson fixed his hopes on an amendment expressly covering roads, canals, and universities, so that *this* enlargement of federal power would be no precedent for other "elastic" experimentation.[45]

Jefferson's amendment, however, was not forthcoming. Die-hard Federalists who would gleefully oppose such a gift to Jefferson's government abounded, while "Old Republicans," clinging to the original Spirit of '98, opposed any step toward "consolidation." Always prone to exaggerate his own control over national affairs (Gallatin sometimes warned him to remember the importance of "the people themselves, both as electors of Congress and as influencing measures by the weight of public opinion"), Jefferson failed to notice that by 1806 he had lost control of the Republican Party. State organizations in New York and Pennsylvania were breeding grounds of faction, intrigue, and ambition, estranged either by Gallatin's abrasive personality or Jefferson's peremptory handling of patronage and the details of administration. John Randolph was leading a schismatic movement at home in Virginia that cost Jefferson the confidence of James Monroe, North Carolina's Nathaniel Macon, and many other stalwart southern partisans. With no whip to crack over Congress as he tried to steer an aggressive new course of national purpose, the president could only watch his amendment, his university, and his program of roads and canals languish unattended while conditions around him disintegrated. Utterly insensible as to how the people had become once more ungovernable, Jefferson blamed the extraordinary novelty of his program. "There is a snail-paced gait for the advance of new ideas on the general mind," he wrote to Joel Barlow, to explaining why improvements were not issuing from Congress. "A 40. years' experience of popular assemblies has taught me, that you must give them time for every step you take. If too hard pushed, they baulk, & the machine retrogrades."[46]

It was not the people who lagged behind Jefferson, but Jefferson who had lingered, tilting at monarchists, while his people and their local politicians lunged ahead toward a brave new era of prosperity, expansion, and rapid change. Divergent, competitive ambitions invaded congressional debates and fostered bare-knuckles interest-group contests where informed deliberation was supposed to prevail. The immediate result of Jefferson's effort to launch his own program of internal improvements was an explosion of special pleading that appalled even friends of the administration's design. Whether promoting a bridge at Washington City, the rival Mason's Island Causeway, the Chesapeake & Delaware

Canal, Susquehanna River improvements, the Potomac Canal, Massachusetts' Salem Turnpike or Merrimack Canal, the Cumberland or New Orleans roads, or a canal around the Ohio Falls at Louisville, members of both houses invoked high principle, sacred revolutionary rhetoric, pious recitations on integrity in politics, and simple unvarnished lies to advance their favorite projects or obstruct the progress of their enemies. In the House, Jefferson's amendment died in committee, while in the Senate Federalist James A. Bayard made a deal with Republican Henry Clay to grant land to a Louisville waterway in exchange for aid to the Chesapeake & Delaware Canal. Neither bill alone commanded a majority, but linked together by some kind of arrangement (the very definition of "corruption") they were likely to pass.[47]

In 1807 John Quincy Adams, Massachusetts Federalist by birth but recent convert to nationalistic Republicanism, objected in the Senate to this back-scratching style of legislation. With a fervor that shocked even his friends, Adams pointed out that nine states controlling a majority in Congress could, by this technique, combine "to divide the public lands, and public treasures among them." Fear not, cried supporters of the deal: "The virtue, and the honor of the Representatives of the nation should forever preclude, even the idea of such a possibility." But Adams's patience for such rhetoric was gone, and he wanted to postpone the bill until Treasury Secretary Gallatin could prepare "a plan for the application of such means as are constitutionally within the power of Congress" to assist those "objects of public improvement" as "may require and deserve the aid of Government." The Senate rejected Adams's motion and postponed aid to the Delaware canal, but a week later senators adopted a substitute motion, introduced by Thomas Worthington, ordering Gallatin to draw up a plan. There is no evidence that Gallatin engineered the resolution, and Adams's opposition to the Bayard-Clay arrangement may have sprung from hidden interests as well as a desire to formulate good policies; but the opportunity that resulted from this Senate confrontation perfectly suited the administration's need to impose leadership and order on a program of internal improvements.[48]

Gallatin seized that opportunity and produced a classic work of public planning, the 1808 *Report of the Secretary of the Treasury on the Subject of Public Roads and Canals*. First gathering and arranging into a giant appendix all evidence of projects being planned and executed throughout the United States (with engineer's reports, charters, petitions, and other supporting documents), Gallatin assembled, with the help of Benjamin Henry Latrobe (probably the best engineer in America) a comprehensive framework that elegantly blended engineering technicalities, commercial probabilities, and political sensitivities. Skillfully ignoring recent pettiness in Congress, Gallatin blamed inaction on confusion, not disharmony. Guided only by the "great geographical features of the country," he selected "those lines of communication" that appeared to "embrace all the great

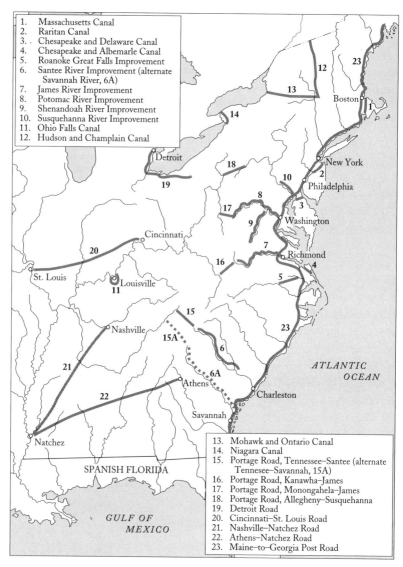

1. Massachusetts Canal
2. Raritan Canal
3. . Chesapeake and Delaware Canal
4. Chesapeake and Albemarle Canal
5. Roanoke Great Falls Improvement
6. Santee River Improvement (alternate Savannah River, 6A)
7. James River Improvement
8. Potomac River Improvement
9. Shenandoah River Improvement
10. Susquehanna River Improvement
11. Ohio Falls Canal
12. Hudson and Champlain Canal

13. Mohawk and Ontario Canal
14. Niagara Canal
15. Portage Road, Tennessee–Santee (alternate Tennesee–Savannah, 15A)
16. Portage Road, Kanawha–James
17. Portage Road, Monongahela–James
18. Portage Road, Allegheny–Susquehanna
19. Detroit Road
20. Cincinnati–St. Louis Road
21. Nashville–Natchez Road
22. Athens–Natchez Road
23. Maine–to–Georgia Post Road

Map 2. The Gallatin Plan of 1808, showing the main works selected by Gallatin for inclusion in a national program of internal improvement.

interests of the union." These included a grand Atlantic coastal waterway (with canals at Cape Cod, across New Jersey and Delaware, and through Virginia's Dismal Swamp into North Carolina), a Maine-to-Georgia post road, five inter-regional routes to the western and northern frontiers (New York, Pennsylvania, Maryland, Virginia, and Georgia), four new far-western post roads, and such critical local works as canals at Niagara and the Louisville Falls (Map 2). Of course, the realities of geography and engineering did not distribute benefits across the country with "arithmetical precision," even though taxes were collected from everyone; consequently, Gallatin proposed to "do substantial justice" and cultivate "general satisfaction" with compensatory grants to "a number of local improvements" in New England and the South.[49]

Neither private nor local public capital was competent to proceed on these major projects: the sums were too large, the fruits of investment depended on the coordination of simultaneous and distant operations, and the greatest benefits often fell outside the jurisdiction where the work was to be done. In many cases general improvements would cause immediate injury to local merchants, ferry-men, and tavern keepers—whose protests state and county governments scarcely could ignore. Only the "general government," Gallatin believed, could remove such "obstacles" to progress by defining a national plan "best calculated to suppress every bias of partiality." An amendment would be needed to empower the government for these specific purposes because Gallatin thought it was essential to override local interests with a grand design: "The national legislature alone, embracing every local interest, and superior to every local consideration, is competent to the selection of such national objects."[50]

Gallatin's appeal here was for congressmen to rise above parochial interests and demonstrate the kind of statesmanship the framers had imagined when the Congress was designed. But theories of disinterestedness in office never accurately described reality, and Republican attacks on Federalist pretensions (led by Jefferson and Madison and often carried into execution by Gallatin himself) had done more than a little to advance the style of politics that made this image sadly obsolete. Armed with an amendment clearly mandating national action, the administration might have gained authority to impose that degree of order and discrimination Gallatin recognized as central to any successful plan. But by April 1808, when Gallatin presented his report, Congress was rising, New England writhed in howling opposition to the embargo, John Randolph's "Quids" lay in wait for any threat to "states' rights," and the treasury surplus on which the program depended was disappearing before the threat of war. The next winter in the House, the internal improvement amendment was delivered by a hostile speaker to a committee chaired by Randolph, where it died. Meanwhile, everyone took advantage of Gallatin's invitation to aid existing projects where the "assent of the states" removed constitutional objections. Petitions begging aid to works named in Gallatin's report sharply increased after 1808, but the Tenth Congress, badly divided over foreign and commercial policy, showed little interest in internal improvement.[51]

The first real test of the Gallatin Plan came in the Eleventh Congress, second session, when New York congressman Peter B. Porter and Kentucky senator John Pope introduced into their respective houses a proposal for a system of funding for a network of roads and canals. This Pope-Porter bill, written by Latrobe and enthusiastically endorsed by Gallatin, committed the federal government to buying one-third of the stock of private companies chartered in the states to build every major project named in Gallatin's report—*except* the Potomac Canal. Proceeds from the sale of public lands would accumulate in a fund (like the Ohio road funds) to pay for the government's investments. The program appeared to be fully constitutional (although Virginia's John Wayles Eppes insisted it was not) because it operated only when private parties in the states initiated corporations. The omission of the Potomac Canal (not a work Latrobe found promising) doubtless bothered friends of Washington and Jefferson, and Pennsylvanians continued to subvert each other in vicious competition between Philadelphia and western factions; but the deadliest blow came from New England Federalists, who in retaliation for the embargo swore that "no measure of the [Republican] party ought to be suffered to succeed, until commerce is restored & so forth." Pope's Senate committee lost faith and stripped from the bill every project except the Delaware and Louisville canals, whose chief sponsors dominated the committee. After that, Virginia's William Branch Giles, an early supporter, moved indefinite postponement. In the House, Porter spoke to the importance of market development and of ties uniting East and West, but the bill died there as well. New York's Gouverneur Morris and DeWitt Clinton made a pilgrimage to Washington in December 1811, where President Madison received them coolly and Congress turned a deaf ear. Paralyzed by intramural rivalries and distracted by worsening conditions overseas, the national legislature did nothing more about the Pope-Porter bill before the outbreak of the War of 1812.[52]

After 1809, with Jefferson in ignominious retirement, leadership in national politics fell to many grasping individuals, few of whom enjoyed truly national support, fewer still showed much integrity as disinterested public servants, and none at all commanded the respect of their opponents. Certainly the deteriorating world condition played a central part in the disintegration of the Jeffersonian republic during Madison's administration, but internal dissension and the collapse of any shared national vision contributed as much as it derived from the swirling dangers of war. The legislative death of the Pope-Porter bill confirmed, all the rhetoric of national purpose and harmonizing interests notwithstanding, that congressmen might jockey for competitive advantage but felt no compelling obligation to devise a comprehensive system of internal improvements. Accumulated hatred for Albert Gallatin, dark suspicions of engineers like Benjamin Latrobe (who was financially invested in several of these projects and notorious for running over budget), genuine or strategic concern for preserving limits on federal power, bitter rivalries among the Atlantic seaports, calculated partisan ambitions—any or all were reason enough to do nothing for roads and canals. The Jeffersonian design for internal improvement faltered for want of discipline and authority in the national arena—the very objects of Madison's constitutional reforms in 1787, and the primary casualties of Jefferson's revolution in government after 1801.[53]

Nationalism Redux: The Bonus Bill

Deteriorating politics and war gradually destroyed executive authority in the Madison administration, while politicians seized influence wherever they could in Congress and outdoors. New England ceased cooperating altogether in national councils over Madison's stubborn policy of commercial restriction. DeWitt Clinton's New York Republicans "fused" with local Federalists to promote the Erie Canal and challenge Virginia's hold on the national party. Pennsylvania continued to nurse partisan factions, some regionally based and some driven only by a blind hatred for Albert Gallatin. Westerners demanded war and protection from Indians, but they proved unwilling to take orders from Washington. Reinstalled at Monticello, Jefferson moved once again toward the back bench of opposition. Young men in the capital city, such as Henry Clay of Kentucky and John C. Calhoun of South Carolina, watched the Virginia gentry lose control of national politics, and they trimmed their sails accordingly. By 1814 Madison's secretary of war, John Armstrong of New York, refused even to defend the national capital, and when the British burned Washington in August federal prestige collapsed. Behind it all lay the results of a generation of Jeffersonian campaigning, a new style of politics, more "actual" in representation, more local in orientation, and more participatory than ever before.[54]

If the war shook Madison's faith in popular politics, the restoration of peace in 1815 brought him new hope. Determined to put the best face on his wartime leadership, Madison dismissed his own disgrace as proof that republican government could survive a world war without abusing power. He rebuilt his cabinet and tried once more to assert that nonpartisan leadership he thought defined the American presidency. Without the distractions of war and commercial restriction, perhaps Congress would rediscover the practice of "disinterested" government. In an almost buoyant message to Congress in December 1815, he praised the conditions of peace and confidently asked for a new national bank, protective tariffs, a reformed and efficient military establishment, coastal defense works, a national university, and the construction of roads and canals for the purpose of "systematically completing" the "inestimable" work begun recently in the states. When the first session of the Fourteenth Congress failed to complete this impressive agenda, Madison reiterated his desires:

> I particularly invite again their attention to the expediency of exercising their existing powers, and, where necessary, of resorting to the prescribed mode of enlarging them, in order to effectuate a comprehensive system of roads and canals, such as will have the effect of drawing more closely together every part of our country by promoting intercourse and improvements and by increasing the share of every part in the common stock of national prosperity.[55]

Madison got his bank and tariff protection (which even Jefferson now supported), but his larger hopes remained unfulfilled. Few high-minded statesmen stalked the halls of Congress, and no effort of the president's was likely to restore public virtue or transcendent vision. Men such as House Speaker Henry Clay spoke for a new generation of politicians who knew the words but not the substance of the old genteel tradition. South Carolina's Calhoun, seeking his own niche in the new order, proved his disregard for Madison's leadership by spearheading a movement *against* the new bank that the president wanted and *for* one he felt compelled to veto. If Madison hoped to rule as Jefferson once had ruled—deferring to Congress, which, in turn, deferred to him—it never would be so. The Fourteenth Congress knew nothing of deference, and only when the voters themselves forcibly retired its members in punishment for the tactless Compensation Act did anyone realize the extent to which power had exploded out of doors.[56]

The Bonus Bill of 1817, which resurrected the Gallatin Plan, grew out of a conscious effort on the part of new nationalists in the Republican Party to reverse the effects of this political disintegration. National pride ran high in the immediate postwar years, and the lessons of the late war temporarily impressed many congressmen with the frailty of the Union. Standing squarely (he believed) on the president's platform, Calhoun announced in the House his desire to "bind the Republic together with a perfect system of roads and canals." His rhetoric conjured up earlier nationalists' dreams of orderly design; but unlike the Gallatin Plan or the 1811 Pope-Porter bill, Calhoun's measure did not attempt to select routes or appropriate money. This time the idea was to pledge the $1.5 million bonus due the government from the new federal bank, as well as the U.S. share of the bank's future dividends, to a permanent fund for "constructing roads and canals." Having set aside the money (and presumably the constitutional question), subsequent Congresses could promote different projects with "specific appropriations."[57]

On 4 February 1817, Calhoun finally rose to present his case. Party and sectional feeling, he began, were "imerged in a liberal and enlightened regard to the general concerns of the nation." Peace prevailed and revenues abounded; the time was right to embark on internal improvements. Nothing promised so great advantage to the "wealth, the strength, and the political prosperity" of the country as good roads and canals. State and private efforts were important, but certain crucial projects either cost too much or stimulated too much "rival jealousy of the States" to be completed without national direction. "Let it not be said," therefore, "that internal improvements may be wholly left to the enterprise of the States and individuals."[58]

According to Calhoun, commercial advantage was not the most compelling reason for establishing the system. The *political* health of the republic was at stake. "No country enjoying freedom, ever occupied anything like as great an extent of country as this Republic," he argued. Distance fostered the threat of disunion, and Calhoun felt a "most imperious obligation to counteract" every such tendency. Whatever impeded "the intercourse of the extremes with this, the centre of the Republic"—whatever compromised the effectiveness of the federal government at a distance—weakened the Union. "Let us conquer space," he pleaded in a famous peroration. "Belted around" as was the Union "by lakes and oceans, intersected in every direction by bays and rivers, the hand of industry and art" was everywhere "tempted to improvement." Blessed "with a form of Government" that combined "liberty and strength," Americans might anticipate "a most splendid future" if only they would "act in a manner worthy of" their advantages. Neglect these advantages, however, permitting "a low, sordid, selfish, and sectional spirit to take possession of this House," and this "happy scene" would vanish. "We will divide," Calhoun warned darkly, "and in its consequences will follow misery and despotism."[59]

What objections to a system could be raised? Had Congress the power to build roads and canals in the states? Technically irrelevant, ruled Calhoun. His bill appropriated money only: no real work was contemplated anywhere. But what if it were? The Constitution "was not intended as a thesis for the logician to exercise his ingenuity on. It ought to be construed with plain good sense." True, roads and canals were not among the enumerated powers of Congress, but "our laws are full of instances of money appropriated without reference to the enumerated powers." Congresses since the very first had appropriated money for objects not enumerated but contributing to defense or the general welfare, and those precedents furnished "better evidence of the true interpretation of the Constitution than the most refined and subtle arguments." Some objected that ours was a government of principles, not precedents. Fair enough, admitted Calhoun; yet he had introduced examples of flexible construction (including the popular Louisiana Purchase) to "prove the uniform sense of Congress, and the country (for they had not been objected to), as to our powers." Others complained that without a list of projects members could not know what they were buying. Maybe so, Calhoun agreed, but it was proper, or at least practicable, to set apart money first because a detailed bill could not be passed: "The enemies to any possible system in detail and those who are opposed in principle, would unite and defeat it."[60]

Two novel points emerged in Calhoun's arguments. First, the young South Carolinian could not imagine constitutional restrictions that endangered the Union itself. Many postwar nationalists in Congress agreed. Second, what was politically expedient was indistinguishable in his mind from what was natural and proper. If the fund must precede the system because rival interests would lay waste detailed designs, then such was the correct approach. Having made his case, Calhoun urged the Fourteenth Congress to seize the initiative and get the credit for establishing the system. "No body of men," he thought, "ever better merited the confidence of the country." They had been slandered by the public over the Compensation Act, and Calhoun wished to restore their reputation by adding internal improvements to "the many useful measures already adopted." In much the same way Madison had tried to rescue leadership by setting out a positive agenda, Calhoun was trying to bind the people to their federal government before state and local politics completely mastered their allegiances.[61]

Responses to Calhoun's arguments occupied the House all week. Friends of the bill identified different sources of congressional authority: the general welfare clause, the commerce clause, or the several defense provisions. Some opponents claimed they would support the bill if it specified a system, but most speakers attacked the question of constitutional power. Thomas Bolling Robertson of Louisiana blasted Calhoun's entire premise, pointing out that equal benefits had been offered by history's greatest tyrants. Expediency did not make the system safe or republican. Give the money to the states, Robertson concluded, and avoid the "disgraceful scene" that surely would follow, "when we shall be called upon to designate the position and course of the contemplated roads and canals, when all our local feelings will be up in arms, and, under a pretense of a general welfare, we shall have in view exclusively the interests of the State or district which we represent." Having thus pulled down the mask of disinterestedness, Robertson touched upon what for many states' righters was the heart of the matter: this bill promised to create "one grand, magnificent, consolidated empire."[62]

To prevent these scheming nationalists from using roads and canals to consolidate their national empire, Robertson moved to distribute funds directly to the states according to population—terms once proposed by Jefferson but rejected by Gallatin as incompetent to guide a national system. Henry Clay descended from the speaker's chair to oppose the change. Proportional spending destroyed the potential for a system because funds could not be concentrated for national objectives. Timothy Pickering of Massachusetts inserted "with the consent of the State" into a substitute motion, which Calhoun denounced as ruining the bill. State consent, like proportional spending, stripped away federal power to design or direct improvements. Both amendments prevailed; yet even so disarmed, the Bonus Bill passed by only two votes over the combined resistance of radical Virginia Republicans and unreconstructed New England Federalists.[63]

In these debates, new Republican nationalists clashed with states' rights anti-consolidationists, each side drawing proudly from the political legacy of Jeffersonian and Madisonian Republicanism. Frustrated in their pursuit of great national objectives by vindictive party spirits and petty local interests, Clay and Calhoun labored (as had Madison himself in 1786 on behalf of a new frame of government) to gain power to do what they thought was the right thing by whatever means seemed to be available. "Old Republicans" like Randolph and Robertson took their cues from Jefferson's bitter opposition to Hamilton's banking system, condemning legislative construction and the schemes of national improvers as if they were latter-day monarchists. Remnant Federalists watched with glee, voting against what they probably supported just to stir up the ranks of their enemies. Thinking they had snatched the hope of the Union from this irresponsible melee in Congress, Clay and Calhoun proudly delivered the Bonus Bill to President Madison three days before his term expired. Perhaps the nationalist agenda was secure after all.

On 2 March 1817, at a farewell reception at the White House, Madison stunned Calhoun with news that he would veto the Bonus Bill. The next day Clay sent a confidential letter to Madison begging a reprieve: "Knowing that we cannot differ on the question of the *object* of the Internal Improvement bill, however we may on the Constitutional point, will you excuse me for respectfully suggesting whether you could not leave the bill to your successor?" But Madison could support neither the effect of the bill they presented nor the reasoning by which they had obtained it. In their desperation to get authority into national hands, Clay and Calhoun had accepted a bill with no power to control local spoilsmen except by packaging their greed in pork barrels. Further, they had reinterpreted the Constitution to suit the wishes of majorities outdoors—a revolutionary practice virtually invented by Jefferson and Madison in the early years of the republic, but one the aging framer could not sanction in the hands of the coming generation. Much as he wanted progress toward internal improvements, Madison could not authorize such corruption in both the practice and structure of the American federal government.[64]

Madison's veto surprised the entire Washington community. The president's nationalism had risen steadily since the 1800 election. His last several messages had begged for energetic government, while his most recent veto (of an imperfect bank) raised only the most tentative objections, which he invited Congress to override. But this time he flatly denied that Congress possessed satisfactory powers or an adequate precedent to proceed with roads and canals. Such a power could not be "deduced," he argued, without an "inadmissible latitude of construction." Such latitude threatened the "definite partition" between the "General and State Governments" on which the "permanent success of the Constitution" depended. This time Madison did not invite Congress to override his scruples; instead he directed it to the "safe and practicable mode" of a constitutional amendment.[65]

Such rigid strict construction did not harmonize with Madison's confident and flexible outlook over the past sixteen years. Just two years before he had dismissed objections to the national bank on the simple ground that the legislators approved it, presidents and judges (all Federalist) upheld it, investors found it useful, and the "general will of the nation" seemed to concur. Now suddenly, in his final days in office, he renounced his own post road arguments of twenty years past, Jefferson's Cumberland Road, and all the accumulated improvements in rivers, harbors, and fortifications as inadequate precedents to sustain a similar reading of the Constitution. The positive spirit of nationalism that had brought him to embrace protective tariffs and the second bank abruptly disappeared behind a firm conviction that this bill gave to Congress a "general power of legislation" that no state, no court, no executive could restrain.[66]

What had triggered Madison's reaction? Part of the answer lay in the provisions of the bill itself. Specifying no plan or projects to be funded, and guaranteeing proportional spending according to federal ratio in the states, the bill could not discriminate among improvements or unify a network. It was a bad bill, which could accomplish almost none of the coherence or control that earlier designs attempted. Gallatin later denounced it. Jefferson condemned it as threatening to "loosen all the bands of the constitution." Madison himself had shared with Jefferson a private note of alarm, one of very few direct clues to the president's motivation: the House was trying "to compass by law only an authority over roads and Canals." Legislative construction was the offense that caught the president's eye. Strict construction as a doctrine had been forged to stop designs of overweening executives, but the same dangers could arise if the people themselves, greedy for the patronage of Congress, mounted an assault on the balanced Constitution. More than ever, outdoor partisan behavior looked to Madison like factious combination, and special-interest issues like internal improvements inexorably corrupted the legislative process.[67]

Behind his fear of legislative corruption and the chaos of popular politics, Madison harbored a growing concern for the meaning of the Constitution itself. Of all the surviving framers, Madison probably knew best what the Constitution was supposed to have meant: after all he had drafted the Virginia Plan, kept notes of the convention debates, orchestrated ratification (especially in Virginia), written much of *The Federalist*, and designed the Bill of Rights. In the 1790s he had raised an opposition with Jefferson confident that he knew where the Federalists had strayed from the path of virtue, and after 1800 he had relaxed believing that the enemies were driven from the field. Adhering like a gentleman to the Philadelphia pledge not to exploit the convention debates, Madison tried to let the public ratification in the states set the standard for "original intent." But surely he could see how even he and Jefferson had twisted their own memories, reason, and words to meet the ever-changing needs of politics. As the framers' generation passed away, Madison watched young men with no roots in the founding take up the game of constitutional construction. Because he knew how men of the highest reputation and virtue had struggled to secure a system that was rational, balanced, and stable—one supposed to yield proper outcomes as well as right procedures—he knew the peril that would follow if the frame became too loose or the limits too dependent on the passing fancies of the people. In a way, his Bonus Bill veto represented an attempt to keep the Constitution anchored in the history of the founding. With Calhoun's utilitarian principles echoing in his ears, Madison hoped to bind the rising generation with the authority of the Union's creators.[68]

Madison's veto of the Bonus Bill effectively spread the burden of internal improvements, at least for the moment, on the backs of the states or private enterprises. Thirty years of frustration with local jealousies, rival jurisdictions, vested interests, straitened purses, and the preferences of local capital for less extravagant (and more immediately rewarding) projects all had failed to establish the legitimacy of a national system or design. Jefferson and Madison still believed (wrongly) that, if asked for an amendment, the states would "certainly concede the power." Therefore, out of no hostility to national improvements, but to defend the Constitution against additional future encroachments, the leading architects of a Republican alternative to the designs of the Federalist gentry finally denied themselves—or at least their successors—the exercise of power for the general good.[69]

In rejoining the battle against consolidation, broad construction, and the enlargement of federal authority, Madison and Jefferson underestimated the danger that was building from resurgent antifederal sentiments in the states. National purpose drifted dangerously while the kind of minimal caretaker governments promised by the Spirit of '98 struggled to meet the demands of a changing world. Gallatin's *Report* had perfectly described the need to integrate and arbitrate any differences among the states before they fostered more desperate rivalries; but "states' rights" and "strict construction"—polemical tools from another context—now were being used by the strong to immobilize the weak (and, perversely, by the weak to immobilize themselves), blocking any effort to cultivate fairness in a general system.

3

The Problems with State Initiatives

EXASPERATED WITH the gamesmanship in Congress that frustrated the Pope-Porter bill and finally resulted in Madison's veto of the Bonus Bill, New York canal promoters seized the initiative in 1817 to build with their own resources America's most famous internal improvement, the Erie Canal. New Yorkers enjoyed two advantages that made their actions compelling if no less bold: first, nature offered them a route through the mountains that rose little more than 600 feet; and second, New York possessed undivided political sovereignty over this "water-level route" and the territory it would enrich. New York's initiative urgently challenged other states to help themselves to the blessings of progress, and it seemed to validate Madison's desire that the states carry out a national program without federal funding or control. Unfortunately, no other single state could raise the money, control the work, or monopolize the rewards of a project of comparable importance. New York's example stimulated not cooperation and mutual benefit but a competitive scramble for local advantages. This experience recalled the wisdom of Albert Gallatin's original analysis, that only the national legislature—"embracing every local interest, and superior to every local consideration"—could promote an integrated national system.[1]

Several factors conspired to frustrate improvers who labored at the state and local level. First, nature's gifts had been distributed unequally. Whereas some places naturally were better suited to improvement with roads and canals, others, even places with "natural advantages" in the unimproved environment, were not susceptible to the same degree of enhancement. Second, political geography seldom worked in concert with nature to encourage public works. Major rivers often ran out of state, feeding cities outside the jurisdiction of the improving government. Third, local resources seldom could support expensive, experimental works. Private investors found greater immediate return in commerce, agriculture, and manufacturing, while taxpayers resisted public expenditures for roads and canals (or spread them far too broadly, trying to satisfy clamorous, democratic interests). Fourth, transportation technology evolved so dramatically

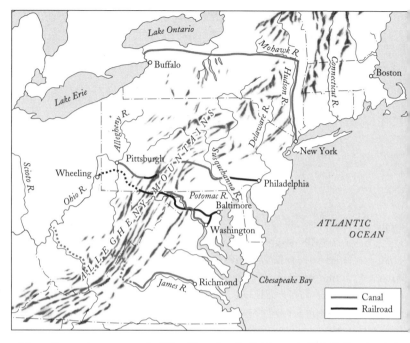

Map 3. Competing routes to the West. Note that the Baltimore & Ohio Railroad and the Chesapeake & Ohio Canal fought for exactly the same passes through the mountains of western Virginia and southwestern Pennsylvania.

in the first four decades after 1800 that even clear-sighted public or private investors could not tell what was the right thing to do. Fifth, some Americans opposed improvement itself, denouncing all development as inherently exploitative, corrupt, and unrepublican. Few Americans truly lived outside the market or intended never to exploit their opportunities for profit, but some people saw their economic options embedded in structures of power and social relations that might be threatened by the rise of more starkly capitalistic institutions. Finally, shrewd politicians often found it tempting to exaggerate any of these factors for transient partisan advantage, introducing a tactical (sometimes dishonest) dimension to the discourse that further muddied the waters.

Different combinations of these factors influenced the internal improvement story of each state in the American Union (Map 3). In every case the details of local geography, economic potential, and political history gave the experience a character sufficiently unique that historians have been discouraged from drawing them together in a single view. For most states, a rich historical literature details the course of individual projects, initiatives, and programs, but the idiosyncrasies of local experience and the complexity of interacting variables have rendered historical generalization unsatisfying and sometimes misleading.[2] The five brief cases that follow serve to illustrate these problems with state initiatives. New York, of course, showed the benefits of natural advantages. Pennsylvania confronted a discouraging, mountainous interior with an alarming sense of urgency caused by the sudden rise of New York. Maryland, lacking jurisdiction altogether over major routes and torn between railroads and waterways, struggled to support various projects and avoid comparative disadvantage despite its relatively small resource base. Virginians talked theoretically about developing their vast western hinterland; but few planters saw any urgent need, so they spread too little capital across worthy projects at far too leisurely a pace. And North Carolina, endowed with a daunting landscape and an equally contrary political inheritance, sank backward into a libertarian malaise that seemed to be ineradicable. Hardly comprehensive or original, these sketches strive only to reveal the contexts in which politicians and internal improvers in the states responded to the Bonus Bill veto. In every case except New York the results were disappointing. Each of those disappointments derived to some extent from problems of scale, clashing local interests, and the lack of an overall national design. Almost inevitably, sooner or later, frustration led improvers back to Washington to inquire once more after federal aid to internal improvements.

New York: The Magnificent Erie Canal

The extraordinary opportunity afforded by natural geography, to open an artificial waterway 350 miles across New York from Lake Erie to the Hudson River, long had teased the imaginations of New York's canal enthusiasts. Earlier efforts to open navigations to Lake Ontario and the St. Lawrence River (the Western and Northern Inland Lock Navigation companies respectively) had come to naught, but so much the better for the present generation. As the wilderness slowly developed, New Yorkers came to realize that Great Lakes traffic, once it reached Lake Ontario, probably would flow toward Montreal and the St. Lawrence rather than follow a complicated route to the Hudson. Therefore opening canals to Canadian waters only threatened to drain away commerce into the hands of foreign competitors. Abandoning the wisdom of an earlier day, which sought to make short connections between natural waterways, new visionaries—especially Canandaigua merchant Jesse Hawley and the irrepressible nationalist Gouvernor Morris—seized boldly on a plan for a man-made canal across the interior reaches of the state. There gentle grades and abundant supplies of water convinced a local surveyor, James Geddes, who examined the landscape in 1808, that an Erie route was practicable. With the Gallatin *Report* stirring talk of federal investments in roads and canals, New Yorkers' enthusiasm mounted. Writing in March 1811 for a new state board of canal commissioners, Morris laid the merits of a man-made Erie Canal before the state and the nation: "there is no part of the civilized world," he proclaimed, "in which an object of such great magnitude can be encompassed at so small an expense."[3]

Posting their best (admittedly wild) estimate at $5 million, New York's commissioners insisted that such a significant undertaking must be a public work. "Too great a national interest" was at stake. This rare advantage ought not to be the "subject of a job, or a fund for speculation," and anyway, "such large expenditures" could be "more economically made under public authority, than by the care and vigilance of any company." The legislature agreed, authorizing Morris, DeWitt Clinton, and their fellow commissioners to apply once more to Congress for aid, to approach landowners for rights-of-way, and to employ engineers for preparatory work. It was with this legislation in hand that Morris and Clinton visited Washington in December 1811, trying to reanimate a variation of the dying Pope-Porter land grant scheme. They were sent home empty-handed by a Congress too riven by jealousies and distracted by thoughts of war to think about the progress of the "civilized world." In March 1812 Morris reported back to the New York Assembly that no immediate aid was forthcoming from Congress and that whatever help might someday appear would be in the form of a grant of land to offset local expenditures. Either way, he concluded, "the canal is to be made by the state."[4]

Having offered New York's geographical advantage to the Union, and having been spurned, Morris now urged the state to make the canal "for her own account." It showed a "want of wisdom, and almost of piety," he believed, "not to employ for public advantage those means which Divine Providence has placed so completely within our power." New calculations of cost and benefits suggested earnings as high as a million dollars "net revenue" per year that might be used to lower state taxes for every voter. Merchants in New York City surely understood that their future control of interior trade was at stake. And if public revenues and private profits did not tempt New Yorkers, consider the glory this canal promised to fix upon its makers "when the records of history shall have been obliterated, and the tongue of tradition have converted (as in China) the shadowy remembrance of ancient events into childish tales of miracle, this national work shall remain. It shall bear testimony to the genius, the learning, the industry and intelligence of the present age." All this for $6 million which the state might borrow in Europe on favorable terms at 6 percent. Rather than delay or suffer the indignity of repeated supplications before jealous enemies in Congress, Morris recommended a "manly and dignified appeal" to New Yorkers' "own power." The legislature responded with authorization to borrow $5 million and further prepare for building the grand canal.[5]

The War of 1812 killed all progress on the Erie Canal, and a combination of discouraging forces nearly prevented its postwar resurrection. Doubts flourished as experts ridiculed the 1811 "inclined plane" design, which promised to carry

Lake Erie water all the way to Albany on a continuous slope of six inches per mile. Equal uncertainty surrounded the prospect of the state borrowing $5 or $6 million in unstable postwar European markets. Local interests not served by the proposed canal—Long Island farmers, settlers in the southern tier of counties bordering Pennsylvania, and villagers along the Lake Ontario's eastern shore— begged for more equitable distributions of the state's investment resources. And taxpayers everywhere, eager to avoid the risk of burdensome future levies, re-kindled interest in the simpler Ontario route, in cheaper turnpike roads, and in wrangling financial assistance out of the national government. Confronted up close with the hazards of grand experimentation, New Yorkers balked in the face of what everyone later would see as their destiny.[6]

DeWitt Clinton breathed new life into the Erie Canal during its darkest hour. Nephew of former New York governor and Antifederalist political boss George Clinton, onetime United States senator, Republican challenger for the presi-dency, and longtime mayor of New York City, Clinton had been turned out of City Hall in 1815 by Tammany Hall Republicans and was casting about for a niche in the vicious game of New York state politics. Never zealous about inter-nal improvements before 1815, Clinton now took up the cause with a vengeance and built a new popular movement around the vision of the grand canal. He wrote a powerful "Memorial" promoting the canal and took it to public meetings all along the route, where over 100,000 citizens signed petitions to the assembly. Clinton painted marvelous, even biblical images of "boats loaded with flour, pork, beef, pot and pearl ashes, flaxseed, wheat, barley, corn, hemp, wool, flax, iron, lead, copper, salt, gypsum, coal, tar, fur, peltry, ginseng, bees-wax, cheese, butter, lard, staves, lumber," and of "merchandise from all parts of the world." Manufacturing establishments would spring up; agriculture and commerce flourish; villages, towns, and cities "line the banks" of the canal and the Hudson River. "The wilderness and the solitary place will become glad, and the desert will rejoice and blossom as the rose."[7]

Technical difficulties collapsed before Clinton's detailed explanations, while the cultural imperative for action gained momentum. "Delays" were the "refuge of weak minds," Clinton scoffed. Expenses would increase over time; contrary interests would become more entrenched; and the national Union itself might be threatened by the divergence of Atlantic and western interests. New York alone among the states was "both Atlantic and western"; New York alone could strengthen the Union with the "great centripetal power" of mutual interest. Finally, reaching for perspectives far above the sordid realm of local interest and factional intrigue, Clinton touched the challenge of American republicanism: "It remains for a free state to create a new era in history, and to erect a work more stupendous, more magnificent, and more beneficial, than has hitherto been achieved by the human race."[8]

Enemies abounded to Clinton's ambition. Tammany's urban artisans and Martin Van Buren's so-called Albany Regency labored together to defeat him. But with the "Memorial" Clinton had seized the high ground, and opponents were left to take selfish, parochial stands against courage, progress, republicanism, and the Union. Such "harpies" put off the improvers with another year's technical study, but the tide was beginning to turn. The next winter Clinton's commissioners delivered one more report heavy-laden with engineering details and estimates supporting a conventional lock canal along the Erie route. While the assembly debated, James Madison vetoed the national Bonus Bill, killing all hope for immediate aid from the deeper pockets of the general government. In the New York Senate, where lower-house bills twice had failed before, Clinton's nemesis, Van Buren, came about in the popular wind and abruptly ended his opposition. A canal bill passed in 1817, authorizing the Erie (and also a Champlain) canal. Ironically, the grand improvement that would fix forever New York's national commercial hegemony prevailed against the opposition of every single delegate from New York City.

New Yorkers had not spontaneously accepted their historic role, but Clinton's deft combination of engineering science and political rhetoric had brought this vision to the moment of realization. Now it remained to be seen if they could find the financial wherewithal or the technical expertise to execute the ditch itself. This was a public work of unprecedented dimensions, and money was not the greatest problem facing its advocates. Men of vision could sell loans well enough, but could they master hydraulic engineering? Could they raise, equip, and command the requisite army of workers? And could they quiet the demands of a democratic people who were quick to see in every local or temporary injury the outlines of designs to subvert their liberties? Supplied at last with permission to begin, New York's internal improvers turned to details of implementation.

The 1817 legislation created a "canal fund" comprising revenues from the salt tax, a portion of New York City's auction duties, new taxes on lands along the route of the canal (never levied), revenues collected on the finished canal, and loans against the credit of the state, the whole sum not to exceed $400,000 per year. Special "canal fund commissioners" managed this pool of money, freeing the regular "canal commissioners" to focus on the daunting task of spending what the fund brought in. The special tax on frontier canal land had quieted opponents in the city and along the Hudson River who feared being taxed to death for a wilderness experiment they thought would surely fail. The canal builders themselves hoped that public debt would build the waterways, designated revenues pay current interest, and future profits from tolls retire the debt eventually.[9]

In June 1817, when the canal fund commissioners opened subscription books for the first loan of $200,000, New Yorkers had seen very little of debt or taxes. Just two years before, to meet wartime expenses, New York had resorted to its first general tax on property and had floated (with apprehension) its first $1.3 million state loan. By contrast, the Erie Canal now was expected to cost $7 million. With little hope of European borrowing (because of the war), and facing stiff competition from shares of the reborn Bank of the United States, Clinton wondered if the capitalists of New York City would back his vision with cash. In fact, New York's "monied gentry" avoided canal subscriptions for several years; still the money poured in from middling investors—and even working people, through the local Bank for Savings. The early success of state subscriptions, backed up by progress on the diggings, stimulated public interest, so that despite the panic of 1819 New York loans attracted ever-stronger buyers in the city as well as in England. By starting small, spending wisely on parts of the canal most easily completed, and crowing loudly about their progress, New York's canal commissioners raised their own stock in the money markets of the world.[10]

Common sense assisted by good fortune contributed to the success of the grand canal. Failing to attract a European engineer, the commissioners selected four local amateurs who trained themselves to serve as the Erie's principal technicians. Armed with the spirit level, a few books, a tour of Boston's Middlesex Canal, and whatever expertise one assistant could pick up on a quick trip to England, James Geddes, Benjamin Wright, Charles Broadhead, and N. S. Roberts set to work on the "experimental" middle section connecting Utica with the Seneca River. Here the engineers perfected the use of the level, worked out techniques for excavating different kinds of soil and rock, and developed bidding procedures that turned hundreds of farmers into construction contractors, who then transformed common laborers into American "navvies." By trial and error they discovered the inadequacies of wooden locks, the mysteries of hydraulic cement, the relative merits of deep cuts and long embankments. They invented simple machines to pull stumps, cut roots, and handle soil. They learned (oh so slowly) how to "puddle" the ditch with clay slurries until it stopped "weeping." By early 1820 94 miles of the middle section had been completed, relatively close to budget, and eager users were contributing tolls to the fund intended for servicing debt. Over 200 miles were open by the end of 1822 and technical feats such as the long stone aqueduct over the Genesee River at Rochester bore witness to the talent of the men in charge. Ahead lay the most difficult parts: the narrow channel east of Little Falls where the Mohawk cut through rock to reach the Hudson, and a seventy-foot escarpment at Lockport separating the broad interior from the Erie shore. But the cumulative impact of successful experimentation, steady financing, and a rising tide of traffic on the finished canal guaranteed victory over these final barriers.[11]

General success did not entirely quiet contrary voices around the state. Petty rivalries and speculations—in land along the route, in materials and supplies, in construction contracts—generated dissatisfactions. Long Island and Hudson

"Process of Excavation," Lockport. Innovative—often jerry-rigged—techniques for moving earth and rock marked the process of constructing the Erie Canal. From Cadwallader D. Colden, *Memoir* (1825). Courtesy Library of Congress.

River farmers continued to grouse about "subsidized" commodities flooding their once-protected markets. In 1820, after the middle section reached Utica, local partisans tried to stop all further digging on the western section until the route to the Hudson River was complete; but Clinton insisted on working in both directions at once, and the legislature agreed. A stiff rivalry developed for the terminus of the canal between Black Rock, home of the politically influential Peter B. Porter, and Buffalo, where the engineers hoped to take water at a higher elevation. In 1822, as the grand canal was progressing, Clinton suffered an unexpected political defeat at the hands of Martin Van Buren's "Bucktail" faction and was dismissed in 1824 from the Canal Commission as well. In the treacherous game of New York politics no good deed went long unpunished.[12]

By October 1825 the Erie Canal was finished. Swelling with pride, New Yorkers began a ten-day celebration. They had made, claimed Jesse Hawley, the "longest Canal—in the least time—with the least experience—for the least money—and of the greatest public utility of any other in the world." As the ceremonial flotilla sailed slowly eastward from Buffalo toward New York City, headed by the *Seneca Chief* bearing Governor Clinton (newly returned to office by the voters in 1824) together with a host of dignitaries and two kegs of Lake Erie water soon to be poured into New York Harbor, crowds thronged to share the ritual excitement of this wonderful achievement. Speakers everywhere praised the "wisdom, public spirit, and energy of the people of the state of New York." Congratulatory letters poured in from outside the state, as people everywhere recognized the

"Entrance to the Harbour," Lockport. Here a staircase of locks lifted canal boats over the final ridge separating the Atlantic waters from those draining into the Great Lakes. From Cadwallader D. Colden, *Memoir* (1825). Courtesy Library of Congress.

magnitude of the achievement. President John Quincy Adams declared the moment an "Event" in the "progress of human Affairs." Former President James Monroe acknowledged that it would give "new and powerful support, to our free and most excellent system of government." James Madison, whose Bonus Bill veto had forced New York to act alone, called it a "precious contribution" to the happiness of the country, "worthy of emulating" in other states. Thomas Jefferson—the man whose 1805 enthusiasm for internal improvement had reinspired New York canallers even while his libertarian political pronouncements gave comfort to anti-improvers nationwide—noticed (as he had predicted for Washington's benefit in 1784) that the Erie Canal would bless New York's "descendants with wealth and prosperity" while proving to "mankind the superior wisdom of employing the resources of industry in works of improvement."[13]

Jefferson, of course, was correct. The Erie Canal poured into New York City a "river of gold" far exceeding that which its early friends had predicted.[14] Lured by the canal itself and the prospects of immediate access to markets, ambitious pioneers flocked into upstate New York. Lumber, grain, and flour poured down into the city and out into the markets of the Atlantic world. Immigrants and trade goods found a better route to the Old Northwest, and farm exports from the Great Lakes basin added to New York's groaning trade. In the city, merchants, bankers, warehousemen, shippers—entrepreneurs of all sorts—seized the opportunity to perfect and specialize their services, fostering round after round of business innovations that within a decade of the opening of the Erie Canal had made New York by far the best place in America to engage in commerce. So successful was the grand canal that everybody then—and most persons since—forgot it had ever been opposed. And so complete was the commercial transformation of New York that when the railroads of the next generation made it possible to divert trade virtually anywhere, the city captured the railroads instead. No one could know for sure at this early date, but with the opening of the Erie Canal, New York had redrawn the economic map of the United States forever in its own favor.[15]

Pennsylvania: A Desperate Imitation

Forceful leadership, clear vision, and unique geographical gifts combined in New York to produce spectacularly successful results. As the Erie Canal approached completion, even before its economic benefits were realized fully, rival seaports with hopes of tapping interior trade began to imagine dreadful prospects of permanent eclipse. Whatever spirit of mutual good feeling and national welfare once greeted the Gallatin Plan now disappeared behind desperate efforts in cities such as Philadelphia to create for themselves a westward connection and thereby secure a prosperous future. But no other state enjoyed the natural invitation to canal construction that made New York's initiative so compelling. In Pennsylvania, physical geography tended to fracture the body politic and orient the interests of the citizens toward out-of-state markets. Such a divisive landscape exacerbated the sectional jealousies that naturally plagued local politics. Finally, a mountain barrier 3,000 feet high shielded Philadelphia from the so-called western waters. Everything about the Pennsylvania situation cried out for a different solution. But the race was on, New York was winning, and canals were the instruments of choice for this generation of internal improvers. Therefore, whipped to a frenzy of desire by a small, ardent band of Philadelphia promoters, Pennsylvania boosters plunged their state into one of the most controversial projects of the American internal improvement movement, the Pennsylvania "Main Line" Canal.[16]

The state of Pennsylvania is raked through the middle diagonally by a series of mountains rising to a summit on the Allegheny range near the center of the state. The Susquehanna River further subdivides eastern Pennsylvania, creating a north-south path through the mountains but also directing the commerce of its users—and many settlers southwest of Harrisburg—to the port of Baltimore, Maryland. West of the mountains, downstream traffic gathers at the three-rivers confluence at Pittsburgh and proceeds down the Ohio to the West. Northwestern Pennsylvania faces Lake Erie, and elsewhere in the northern counties water flows northward into New York's Finger Lakes, where in 1825 the Erie Canal and its branches promised up-to-date communion with New York City. For Philadelphia, once the proudest colonial metropolis in British North America and the thriving center of a hinterland reaching well over fifty miles inland nothing in this landscape suggested growth in the next generation.[17]

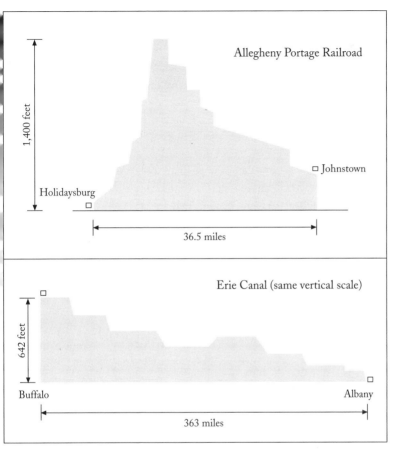

Profiles of the Allegheny Portage Railroad and the Erie Canal. Pennsylvania improvers confronted over twice the total rise of the Erie Canal in this one section one-tenth as long as the New York project. Engineers finally mastered the summit with a railroad using stationary engines and inclined planes.

Philadelphians were no less aware of the limits of their hinterland than other American seaports. Since before the Revolution, leading figures had dreamed of cutting canals across the Delaware peninsula to recapture the Susquehanna trade and also of linking by canal the waters of the Schulykill and Susquehanna Rivers. During the improvement movement of the 1790s, chartered companies pursued various river and canal improvements, but geography and immediate commercial demand had made turnpike development far more rewarding in Pennsylvania. In 1794 the sixty-two mile Lancaster Turnpike brought reliable (for that day) land transportation to the banks of the Susquehanna. Additional pikes laced the Philadelphia hinterland, bearing a steadily rising traffic and paying handsome dividends to the shareholders who built them; two additional companies worked on turnpikes to Pittsburgh. By 1808, Albert Gallatin reported that "artificial roads of the most substantial kind" had been completed or were "progressing, from Philadelphia, in sundry directions." In 1811 the state bestowed $825,000 in public aid to turnpike companies that soon reached Pittsburgh and various points on the New York state border. Thus favored by turnpike developers, Philadelphians contented themselves with trying to block improvements in the lower Susquehanna and trying to open a ditch through the state of Delaware— that is, until New York built the Erie Canal.[18]

Mathew Carey, a Philadelphia publisher and political economist, sounded the new alarm. In 1821 he launched a campaign to revive the moribund Chesapeake & Delaware Canal. On this question, as in the cause of protective tariffs and industrial development generally, Carey found his shortsighted friends and neighbors to be woefully indifferent to the urgent dangers confronting them. Energized by their apathy, he threw himself into agitations of every description, including a Society for the Promotion of Internal Improvement, which met with surprising favor among Philadelphia's merchant elites. By December 1824 forty-eight individuals had paid $100 each to join the society, whose mission was to gather and disseminate information on roads, canals, and railroads. Carey set to work immediately, and by March 1825 he had flooded the state with eight "unbiased" technical pamphlets. At the same time, thinly veiled by the pseudonym "Fulton," Carey issued his own manifesto for the Mainline Canal.[19]

Citing "exhilarating views" of New York's "magnificent and liberal canal policy," Carey proclaimed in his "Fulton" essays that a canal between the Susquehanna and Allegheny Rivers would be "as beneficial to the State of Pennsylvania as the Erie canal to New York." Such a canal, he continued (echoing Clinton), could not be "undertaken or completed by private subscription. It must be executed by the state, as the Erie and Champlain canals have been." After treating his readers to a long column of statistics documenting New York's burgeoning trade, Carey reminded them that since 1817 Pennsylvania exports had dropped 40 percent. The open question, he averred, was not whether to build the canal, but when? "Which of our legislatures will have the honour of so magnificent a benefaction to the present and future generations?" Carey proposed a town meeting to draw up a petition to the legislature, and by 10 February the text of that memorial appeared in the daily *United States Gazette*.[20]

Carey's memorial neatly summarized the case for immediate state action. Thanks to the pioneering work of New York, skill and experience now were available as never before. An "abundance of capital" sought employment in Pennsylvania and the state's excellent credit rendered it "almost certain that the requisite funds" could be borrowed on "moderate terms." Such a great western waterway had once seemed too risky, but with "canals in active and profitable operation" all around, the technology no longer seemed in doubt:

Henceforward the intercourse between the East and the West is to be carried on by means of inland navigation. This is decided by what is already done. No State, therefore, can expect to participate largely or beneficially in this interesting intercourse, unless she offer such a channel of communication. . . . This single fact your Memorialists believe to be of sufficient weight to render all argument superfluous, unless we are disposed to give up the well-earned reputation of Pennsylvania, and to suffer her to fall back from her established character and standing.

In conclusion the petitioners begged for the suppression of local interests. Admittedly, the first benefits of any canal would fall on its immediate locale, but "every part of the State" would "in some degree feel its happy influence," and eventually "other works" would be "contrived" to satisfy "every quarter."[21]

In Carey's mind, urgency was everything. Virginia and Maryland had chartered a new Chesapeake & Ohio Canal Company that someday would satisfy the commerce of southwestern Pennsylvania, thereby killing support in that region for state public works. New York's future branch canals promised to do the same for northern counties already accustomed to out-of-state connections. Past experience had satisfied Carey that private investors always wrecked chartered companies, such as the Schuylkill & Susquehanna Canal Company, by subscribing to their shares in hopes of speculative gain and then refusing to pay their installments. Only the state could be expected to mount and finish such monumental works of improvement. Yet the progress of democratization (at least according to the "better class" of Philadelphia merchants) was filling the Pennsylvania legislature with narrow, selfish office seekers, ill-disposed to take risks or impose taxes no matter what the prospects of the object in question. In short, Carey feared that the people of Pennsylvania all too readily would settle for cheap and easy access through foreign markets, leaving their metropolis to fend for itself. That was the real reason behind the Society for the Promotion of Internal Improvement, and it was the reason in 1825 for whipping up a frenzied public support for grand Pennsylvania canal.[22]

Driven by this terrible sense of urgency, the Society for the Promotion of Internal Improvement pushed in early 1825 for immediate passage of a navigation program even as they sent an engineer, William Strickland, to England to investigate canal and railway technology. Experimental railroads were just beginning to attract attention in America: for example, Nicholas Biddle, a member of Carey's society and president of the Bank of the United States, thought railway experiments promising enough to hazard the opinion that "whoever will establish a rail way & Steam waggon between Philadelphia and Pittsburgh, will do more honor to himself & more service to the State than by any other measure which I can imagine." But Carey viewed this discussion of a rival technology

Detail of stone aqueduct section, from Strickland's report prepared for the Pennsylvania Society for the Promotion of Internal Improvement, 1826. While railway technology remained strictly experimental, Strickland found canal engineering in England to have reached a mature state by the 1820s. Nevertheless, Strickland himself found railroads more promising than his patrons chose to believe. From a copy in the Goss Collection, Purdue University Libraries.

with alarm. Any "differences of opinion" as to route or mode served only t divide the ranks of improvers, producing delay and confusion and inviting th enemies of progress to unite against the program. Pretending to review th evidence about the new mode of transport, Carey marshaled available facts an figures to show that railroads probably cost more, performed less well, an carried far greater uncertainties than their advocates dared to admit. By 16 Jun when Strickland's first report reached Philadelphia, recommending railroads i mountainous country for reasons of "*safety, speed*, and *economy*," Carey and hi society already were committed irretrievably to canals.[23]

The promotional campaign of Carey and the Philadelphia improvers lit fire under legislators who had been moving more slowly in a similar directior The previous legislative assembly had created a Board of Canal Commissioner whose February 1825 report was marred by one commissioner's preference fo railways over canals. As signed copies of Carey's petitions piled up in Harrisburg Philadelphia representative William Lehman, chairman of the Inland Naviga tion Committee, reported a bill repealing the 1824 law (dismissing its indecisiv commissioners) and compelling the state to build precisely the canal described i Carey's memorial—from the Susquehanna to the Allegheny River with a cor nection north to Lake Erie. Lehman's committee bill became law in April 182 and a new board of canal commissioners was charged with finalizing the rout drawing up the plans, and securing appropriate financing. Railroad advocate launched a full-scale propaganda campaign to convert the people (and the commissioners) to the merits of alternative technology; Carey's society pressed relentlessly for canals and began organizing a huge statewide convention to be held in Harrisburg in August. Pamphlets and newspaper editorials circulated freely during the spring and summer, spreading all kinds of estimates, rumors, and testimonials in behalf of either tried-and-true canals or hypothetical railroads.[24]

The August convention labored to smother the railroad party and document instead a public consensus for an all-water route to the West. Fearing years of delay that necessarily would follow a switch to experimental railroads, and suspecting (or perhaps knowing what cannot readily be proved in retrospect) that the advocates of railways truly were the enemies of state public works, Philadelphia improvers forcefully managed the affair so as to ratify a set of prepared resolutions embodying the canallers' "party line." The "character and standing," permanent prosperity and happiness" of the state depended on connecting "the eastern and the western waters." The application of resources to that end "ought not to be regarded as an expenditure, but as a most beneficial investment." The magnitude of that investment was set at $8 million. Private capital was said to be incapable of such an undertaking—nor should private interests command the source of such enormous future benefits and revenues. Railroads were assigned a "subsidiary" place, useful to feed traffic to the canals or to surmount abrupt elevations. Finally, "local objects" were denounced as tending to diffuse public resources and endanger the accomplishment of the central undertaking, without which local fragments must remain relatively useless. Published and circulated as the settled will of the whole people of Pennsylvania, the report of the canal convention apparently set the agenda for the Pennsylvania legislature that convened in December. By January 1826 Lehman's committee reported a bill for the "Pennsylvania Canal"; before the end of February it was signed into law.[25]

The Main Line story ends less happily than the story of the Erie Canal. Panic in the face of stagnation moved its advocates to close the door too quickly on technological investigations, especially research into railroads. Haste also encouraged improvers to cut deals in the legislative process, trading local branch-line construction for votes—especially in the anthracite coal-producing regions—thereby spreading efforts too thinly before the main canal could be finished. Work began at once on those sections of the canal and its branches that did not pass through the mountains, while engineers continued to study how best to conquer the summit. A portage railway gradually emerged as the technically appropriate solution, but die-hard canallers called for survey after survey, looking for an all-water route. In 1831 they finally accepted defeat, but by then hundreds of miles of canal were completed, and the state was committing to an awkward, amphibious network despite impressive railway advances at the summit and on a new Philadelphia-to-Columbia railroad line.[26]

Through-service to the western waters—the grand objective of the Pennsylva-

nia Main Line and its primary source of anticipated revenue—did not begin unt
1834, long after interest on debt had overwhelmed revenues from fragmentar
branch operations. The system truly was an engineering marvel in its day-
running 395 miles from Philadelphia to Pittsburgh (including 36 miles of Alle
gheny Portage Railway and 82 miles of railroad from Philadelphia to the Sus
quehanna), climbing 2,322 feet above sea level (compared to Erie's 650) with 17
locks, an 800-foot tunnel, and ten inclined planes, five on each side of th
mountains, equipped with stationary winding engines to haul up or lower th
barges. Unfortunately, the Main Line never facilitated the interregional trad
never serviced its own debt, and never poured revenues into the coffers of th
state quite the way the Erie did in New York. Perhaps most cruelly, the necessar
substitution of railways for canals in parts of the Pennsylvania system helpe
demonstrate the merits of the railroads themselves; and once perfected by experi
ence, railroads displaced the canals, whose own perfection had been proclaime
so recently. Before it had much chance to repay its long-suffering promoters, th
Pennsylvania Main Line confronted competition from a new Baltimore & Ohi
Railroad and, after 1846, from a private Pennsylvania Railroad Company a
well.[27]

What went wrong in Pennsylvania's internal improvement movement? His
torical economist Julius Rubin, laboring meticulously with reason and hindsigh
has shown that Pennsylvania enjoyed "a real choice of methods" and that clearl
"a mistake was made." Carey and his Main Line enthusiasts ignored commo
logic, suppressed evidence, and otherwise manipulated events to prevent th
adoption of a railway system—or, more accurately, to avoid the delay any rail
road design necessarily entailed. Their behavior rested neither on science no
venal selfish interests but on a matrix of assumptions about government, societ
human nature, and economic development that clearly justified (in their ow
minds) the most stubborn perseverance. New York, as a state, was growing ricl
off the Erie Canal. Only states, they reasoned, could mount such expensive pub
lic works, and those that did so would reap irreversible rewards. Common voter
naturally would shrink from bold initiatives and public debt, while private buyer
and sellers just as naturally would drift into subservience to out-of-state market
unless the state of Pennsylvania gave them better ones. Once diverted by th
designs of ambitious neighbors, local taxpayers in much of Pennsylvania neve
would support public works of their own. The commonwealth itself, in this di
sastrous scenario, would be recolonized by New York, Virginia, even Maryland.[2]

In 1825 Philadelphia's merchant elites perceived a last fleeting chance to bin
their restless neighbors in an all-Pennsylvania market network. They dared no
wait, or all would be lost. They could not back the visionary railroads: how coulc
any responsible government overlook the stunning example of New York's cana
initiative and plunge instead into an untried railway scheme? Technical measure

ments alone could not address the subtle links between political and economic culture that marked the trauma of internal improvement in Pennsylvania. Questions of pride, sovereignty, and public honor played as great a part as calculations of expense, elevation, and tolls.

Carey himself penned an explanation in 1831 for the disappointments of the state public works. These "magnificent projects," worthy of the "influential citizens" who planned them and the "powerful state" that undertook them, had been hobbled by two "radical" mistakes. First, fearing loss of support from disappointed voters, legislators committed to "too many objects simultaneously," driving up immediate expenses while fatally postponing the start of profitable through traffic. The second "egregious error" lay in not providing for initial interest from an independent source of revenue (such as New York's salt tax and auction duties). This too Carey blamed on the politicians' "paltry dread of unpopularity." Yet despite crippling failures of statesmanship, Carey still believed the Mainline system would achieve its original objective—ensuring the survival of Pennsylvania as an independent state by engendering prosperity among its citizens. The Keystone State possessed better resources than New York, more valuable exports (salt, iron, and coal), and a shorter winter; there was no reason to doubt that its canal would have a similar effect. Besides, considering the $15 million pumped into the state economy, plus untold millions in ancillary economic development, rising land values, and the immeasurable elevation of the "character" of the citizens, Pennsylvania already enjoyed a fair value for the investment—and still had reason to believe that "in fifteen or twenty years, the surplus revenues" would pay off the debt and "afford a fund for the support of government, and ample provisions for public schools." Against this cornucopia of present and future blessings was charged a mere $775,000 in annual interest, most of which would be covered by canal tolls as early as next year.[29]

Self-justifying as it seems in retrospect, Carey's explanation perfectly reflected the character and purpose of internal improvement as it was understood in his generation. Pennsylvania's plunge into internal improvements was guided by a remnant of the old commercial gentry hoping to preserve their sovereign state and fend off the chaos of unguided competition in either the political or economic marketplace. Reasoning as statesmen rather than entrepreneurs, they thought they did the "prudent" thing in copying the tested New York model; reacting as gentlemen whose prerogative was under siege, they dismissed the advocates of railroads as obfuscators in disguise. About the railroads they could not have been more wrong; about the danger of intercity rivalry, however, they were essentially correct. Confronted with fierce competition, Pennsylvania leaders concluded that they simply had to promote development. What they failed to understand was that states could not entirely control the market revolution no matter where and how they built their improvements.

Maryland: A Multitude of Frustrations

Philadelphia's worries pale when compared with the challenge as seen fror Maryland. None of the great objects of internal improvement lay entirely i Maryland's political control. The famed Potomac route to the West belonge« equally to Virginia while it served the developmental interests of Ohio or west ern Pennsylvania. The Chesapeake & Delaware Canal—Philadelphia's instru ment for capturing Susquehanna traffic bound for Baltimore—enjoyed fair sup port as a "national" project, but Baltimore's corresponding demands to open th« lower Susquehanna met with flat rejection in Pennsylvania and no sympathy i» Congress. Finally, the showdown between canal and railroad technologies tha» Mathew Carey suppressed in Pennsylvania found full expression in the contes» between Washington-based friends of the Potomac Canal and Baltimore pro moters of a pioneer railroad. Considering its limited capital, compromised juris- diction, and technological uncertainty, along with the usual sectional conflicts» petty local interests, and games of political ambition, it is a wonder Marylan« accomplished anything at all during the era of state initiatives.[30]

According to Gallatin's *Report*, by 1808 Maryland already was "extending" incorporated turnpike roads from Baltimore "in various directions." The mos» ambitious of these, the Frederick Town Pike, capitalized at $500,000, in 180« began opening a road to Boonsboro, just beyond the Blue Ridge near Haggers- town. In 1812 another corporation was chartered to build a road through th« howling wilderness west of Big Conococheague Creek to meet the nationa] "Cumberland Road" that since 1806 had been building westward toward Wheel- ing. Two additional corporations filled in the gaps through punishing country between the Frederick Town Pike and the Cumberland Road, creating the fines» through route to the West by the early 1820s—just in time to be displaced by New York's brand-new water-level service. The state had lured private capitalists into road building by attaching it to profitable banking privileges, but that resource» lay close to exhaustion precisely at the moment when renewed interstate compe- tition demanded canal or railroad development.[31]

Agricultural exports, especially flour for the West Indies, had fueled Bal- timore's rise to commercial prosperity after the Revolution, and while much of the wheat handled in Baltimore came down turnpikes from the Maryland pied- mont, another large portion arrived on Pennsylvania "arks" via the Susquehanna River. Philadelphia knew it and prohibited improvements in the river south of the falls at Conawego. Baltimore retaliated by building a canal, opened in 1802, from the state line south to tidewater, but Pennsylvania declined to extend the "improvement" upstream. Gallatin noticed this frustrating rivalry in his *Report*, and for years Baltimore merchants tried to get concessions without success. Despite a gift of lottery privileges in 1804, Baltimore's Susquehanna Canal was old by the sheriff in 1817, and the two states did not cooperate to improve the route until the middle 1830s.[32]

Baltimore's frustration with Philadelphia only increased in the case of the Chesapeake & Delaware Canal. If Pennsylvania could forcibly engross its own Susquehanna hinterland trade, then surely Delaware and Maryland could justify blocking a canal through their own sovereign soil that would give Philadelphia access to upper Chesapeake Bay. But the Delaware peninsula was one of those barriers to navigation, like the hook of Cape Cod or the Great Dismal Swamp, that seemed designed "by nature" for immediate improvement. Gallatin had named it as part of a protected coastal navigation of unparalleled national importance. In 1799 Maryland first passed a charter of incorporation for Philadelphia's pet project, contingent on the free and unobstructed navigation of the Susquehanna. Delaware balked until 1802, and the company finally was organized in May 1803 with $103,000 capital paid in. All of this and more it exhausted by 1806, when work was suspended for want of funds and friends of the project approached Congress for assistance, triggering the call for Gallatin's *Report* and the first debate over an integrated national system. Then, like everything else, the project stalled until after the War of 1812, coming forward again as a national project made more compelling in the early 1820s by the progress of the Erie Canal.[33]

The challenge of the Erie Canal rekindled another improvement project of great interest to Baltimore, one that had lain nearly dormant since the 1790s—George Washington's Potomac Canal. The original Potomac Company intended to dig canals around several rapids, including Great and Little Falls. By 1799 their capital had been exhausted with the locks at Great Falls only partially carved through a wall of solid rock. Thanks to a timely investment of £13,000 by the state of Maryland, the work at Great Falls was completed in 1802; from then until the end of the War of 1812, the company employed itself in relatively futile efforts to improve the bed of the river and its branches. In 1816 a new Virginia Board of Public Works began exploring more ambitious improvements along the Potomac route. Its efforts culminated in 1823 in chartering a new corporation empowered, with the assent of Maryland and the aid of Congress, to build a $1.5 million canal to meet the National Road at Cumberland.[34]

The state of Maryland refused its assent to this new Potomac corporation because Baltimore merchants hated the enhancement of Georgetown and Washington almost as much as they feared invasion from Philadelphia. Immediately promoters expanded their vision, pushing their canal past Cumberland to the Ohio River and courting Baltimore with promises of a branch connection, hopefully near Point of Rocks (due west of Baltimore). From there, the argument ran, traffic could choose a Potomac or Chesapeake terminal without backtracking any distance. Preliminary surveys condemned the Point of Rocks junction as impracticable, but Baltimore's interest in the project continued to rise, especially since the greatest share of the estimated costs (now closer to $3 million) would be paid by Congress, Virginia, and the cities in the District of Columbia. Virginia chartered a third corporation in 1824, and Baltimore merchants, convinced that the Chesapeake & Ohio Canal would be built with or without them, exchanged their power to obstruct for a much larger hope that the new canal would bring them a piece of the western trade. Maryland and Congress affirmed the charter in 1825 and Pennsylvania in 1826. The U.S. Corps of Engineers estimates later that year placed a stunning $22 million price on this fabled national objective, but with four states, three cities, and the federal government backing the project improvers pressed ahead.[35]

The Chesapeake & Ohio Canal might have rescued Baltimore's future, but the Maryland city stood virtually powerless to control a work directed by so many governments and funded by outside resources. Furthermore, the proposed canal could not help but foster the commercial pretensions of Georgetown, Washington, and Alexandria, Virginia, eventually eclipsing Baltimore. Therefore, in the fall of 1826, when Quaker merchant Evan Thomas brought home striking accounts of England's Stockton & Darlington Railroad, even canallers in Baltimore paused to hear him out. By February 1827 public meetings had concluded that a railroad to Ohio would be one-third shorter and half as expensive as any Potomac Canal. Newspaper commentators seized upon the railroad as the last best hope of Baltimore: *"Depend upon it,"* wrote one, *"you will never see a canal between this city and the Ohio River."* Others pointed out that a canal to Georgetown, even if completed, would be frozen in winter, dried up in summer, and "of no use to *us*" in Baltimore. The *"construction of a double railroad on the most improved plan,"* however, promised to "bring the great bend of the Ohio almost to our very doors." In less than two weeks railroad mania swept the city. Promoters secured a $3 million charter with shares reserved for state and municipal subscriptions. Private shares sold quickly, the company organized itself in April 1827, and the following May, from preliminary surveys supplied by the federal Corps of Engineers, the directors adopted a route to Point of Rocks and thence up the Potomac Valley to the summit—right beside the projected canal.[36]

On 4 July 1828, just two years after the coincidental deaths of Thomas Jefferson and John Adams had reminded even cynics of the hovering hand of Providence, another coincidence marked the dawn of a new age as surely as the deaths of the patriarchs had drawn an older one to a close. On that day at Little Falls on the Potomac, John Quincy Adams, son of the founder and now president in his own right, turned a spadeful of earth to launch the Chesapeake & Ohio Canal, one of the great national public works to come out of the internal improvements movement. Forty miles away, ninety-year-old Charles Carroll of Carrollton, sole surviving signer of the Declaration of Independence, performed a similar service on behalf of the Baltimore & Ohio Railroad. Unknown to both parties—and still unknowable—the aging Carroll broke ground that day on the model for American transportation, industry, and enterprise that would dominate the century to come. The vigorous president by contrast, had begun one of the last of the great canals, celebrating an approach to public enterprise that he thought marked the progress of civilization—an approach that had stirred the founders but would stand repudiated altogether within the younger Adams's lifetime.[37]

Why had Baltimore taken the radical "step in the dark" to build a railroad through the mountains to Ohio? Conventional wisdom everywhere supported canals and public works of inland navigation—in New York where it was working fabulously, in Pennsylvania, in Virginia, in Congress, and even elsewhere in Maryland. But conventional wisdom threatened to isolate a city such as Baltimore that neither could command the resources of a sizable state nor direct the flow of waterborne commerce through its hands. Driven by the same desperation found in all the seaport cities as a result of the Erie Canal, thrown back on local resources by the Bonus Bill veto and the lack of a national program of internal improvements, and unwilling to trust entirely to the uncertain patronage of Congress or the voluntary contributions of rival taxpayers in Virginia, Georgetown, and Washington, D.C., Baltimore merchants took the only risk they could be certain served their local interests alone. Like the Philadelphia gentry, Baltimore's leaders feared for their collective, not just their private, fortunes; but unlike their neighbors to the north, they could not build a consensus in politics and tried instead to cultivate a common interest with a broad-based stock subscription to a business corporation. Twenty-thousand of their townsmen purchased shares in the railroad venture, a stunning pledge of popular support, and in the very long run we know that their gamble was warranted. For much of the next twenty years, however, as the B&O struggled up the valley, consuming more time and money than anyone expected, Baltimore's solution must have seemed about as hopeless as the Mainline system or the Chesapeake & Ohio Canal.[38]

Virginia: The Virtue of Theory

The Commonwealth of Virginia approached the transportation revolution with more philosophical detachment than New York, Pennsylvania, or Maryland. Dominated by plantation oligarchs who nursed theories of political perfection while governing unchallenged at home, Virginia in 1816 adopted an approach to public works that seemed to combine the virtues of private enterprise and the benefits of public support—while supposedly avoiding the perils of both. Known as the system of "mixed enterprise," Virginia's approach left initiative in the hands of interested parties, assuming that persons would risk their own capital only when worthy and promising ventures appeared. Projects thus brought for-

Lake Drummond Hotel, on the Dismal Swamp Canal, c. 1830. Never capable of handling much of the coastal trade, the canal served more tourists and small shippers. This out-of-the-way hostelry, situated exactly astride the North Carolina–Virginia border, catered to a shady clientele of lovers and duelists. In this print, sailboats bracket a brand-new steam launch, *Lady of the Lake*. Courtesy The Mariners' Museum, Newport News, Virginia.

ward by local investors were assumed to be deserving of state support. The motive behind this approach was to avoid the enlargements of government that encouraged corruption in office, fostered unfair advantage, or imposed unequal burdens on voting and tax-paying citizens. At the same time, Virginians professed to understand the unique public character of internal improvements, and they wished to subsidize efforts to undertake works that would not command private capital.[39]

Internal improvements had been on the minds of some of Virginia's leaders long before the challenge of the Erie Canal. Plans for improving piedmont rivers, the Potomac and James river routes to the West, and a ship canal through the Dismal Swamp connecting Norfolk to Albemarle Sound, all had late colonial roots. The postrevolutionary era had seen the chartering of three major companies—the Potomac (1785) and James River (1785), both headed at least nominally by George Washington, and the Dismal Swamp (1790), all private joint-stock corporations with sizable public subscriptions. Having thus placed the most compelling projects into the hands of the prominent "monied gentry," and confident that works of similar merit would be brought forward the same way, political leaders relaxed.

The work itself proceeded slowly. Technical problems and a shortage of skilled laborers stymied inexperienced, sometimes amateur engineers, while delinquent subscribers defaulted on their assessments. The Potomac Company ran out of money for building the locks at Great Falls, and even after being rescued by the state of Maryland, it failed to open the kind of navigation envisioned in its charter. By 1799 the undertakers of the Dismal Swamp project had opened a road along the length of the canal; but, carelessly assuming that their great bog was "perfectly level," they neglected even to measure elevations and so did not know until sometime after 1800 that locks rising twenty feet would be required. Only the James River Company had been successful, clearing the natural bed of the river upstream over 200 miles, through the Blue Ridge to Crow's Ferry, and opening canals to circumvent the falls at Richmond. But this success only cultivated rising expectations; and the collection of tolls during the early years of construction, while it kept the company solvent, engendered popular complaints resulting by 1805 in an investigation into the company's affairs.[40]

By the time of Gallatin's 1808 *Report*, evidence was mounting that Virginia's internal improvement efforts were inadequate. The Dismal Swamp Canal served only local "shingle flats," having been dug at first too shallow and too narrow for sloop navigation. Neither the James nor the Potomac navigation met the present needs of their communities, let alone future interregional traffic. Gallatin could find but one twelve-mile turnpike in Virginia. Something of the "urgency" with which Virginians tended to these questions can be seen in the example of a legislative commission named in 1805 to see if the James River Company had fulfilled its charter: it never examined the stream. A second commission, named in 1811 and headed by John Marshall, concluded the following year that the company had not satisfied the terms of its incorporation. More important, Marshall's commissioners encouraged the perfection of a water route up the James, across the Allegheny Mountains by road to the Greenbriar River, and thence downstream via the New and Kanawha Rivers to the Ohio. For immediate local service no such grand expenditures were required, these explorers conceded, but to secure a piece of the western trade the improvement ought to be "complete and effectual." Considering the "exertions which other States" were making to secure such a commerce, the commissioners hoped to "awaken the attention of Virginia to that part of it which should naturally belong to them." Thus the stage was set for Virginia's postwar bid for the commerce of the interior.[41]

Considering the role Virginia politicians played—and would continue to play—in the frustration of the national internal improvement movement, it seems surprising to find in the 1816 report of the Committee on Roads and Internal Navigation of the Virginia House of Delegates a positively ringing testimonial to the virtue of public works, especially in the hands of republican governments. "Next to the enjoyment of civil liberty itself," the lawmakers could find "no greater blessing than an open, free and easy intercourse" among the citizens of the "nation." Transportation improvements enriched the planter, farmer, and manufacturer, opened lands "too remote from market to tempt cultivation," developed mineral resources, fossil fuels, and commerce, and facilitated defense. Especially in a republic,

> where public opinion exerts a controuling influence, and public virtue should be the spring of all public action, they may be considered an important auxiliary, if not a necessary ingredient of political liberty. They tend to diffuse more equally the knowledge which experience acquires, and the leisure which wealth alone can purchase; they strengthen the cords of social union, and quicken that generous feeling of patriotism, which is ever ready to exclaim at the contemplation of an extended scene of public improvement, "I love my country, because she is worthy of my affection."[42]

By nature, the committee continued, Virginia simultaneously was gifted and challenged: no other state was "intersected by so many navigable rivers, nor divided by so many chains of lofty mountains," none abounded "with such happy varieties of climate and soil, and so many resources for internal commerce." Yet, while other states advanced with a rapidity that "astonished themselves," Virginia, "the ancient dominion and elder sister of the Union," had "remained stationary." Quickly reviewing familiar scenes of poverty and decline in the tidewater region—"of wasted and deserted fields! of dwellings abandoned by their proprietors! of Churches in ruins!"—the committee warned of a "revolution" in the West, where the sons of Virginia were bound, that threatened to alienate frontiersmen from the Atlantic states. Through a "connection between the Roanoke, the James, or the Potomac rivers, with the waters of the Kanawha or Ohio," Virginia could arrest the "progress of this revolution," securing its own welfare and that of "the Union at large."[43]

No loftier or more compelling arguments could be heard anywhere on the eve of the Bonus Bill veto. Therefore, it must have been questions of method, jurisdiction, and competitive advantage—not doubts about improvements themselves—that darkened the minds of President Madison and other Virginians who stubbornly resisted a national program. To these questions the Virginia committee turned its earnest consideration. Private capitalists, argued these oft-called "agrarian" statesmen, ought to furnish any roads and canals that could generate adequate tolls. That way expenses would be born "equitably" in sums "proportioned to the benefit" of those who used them. But for some works essential to the Commonwealth, local capitalists lacked the money or could not bear the long delay between expenditure and eventual repayment. These deserved the patronage of government, but because both theory and experience warned against programs that wasted the taxpayers' money and encouraged jobbing in the legislature, it was important to improve as well "the mode . . . of extending . . . that patronage."[44]

The first problem associated with public works in the states had been the lack of skilled engineers. Let the state employ such an expert, reasoned the committee, and relieve individual companies of this expensive burden. The second plague upon improvement schemes had been the jealousy encountered when selecting the projects and making appropriations. Therefore, create a permanent common fund and then appropriate monies to each enterprise according to priority and merit as guided by the state engineer. Finally, these lawmakers flatly rejected the model of direct public enterprise then prevailing in New York and Pennsylvania: "Experience testifies" that public works "will be more economically made, and better repaired, if their management be left to the individuals who subscribe to their stock with a view to private gain, than if confided to public officers or agents." Because none of the James, Potomac, or Dismal Swamp companies had fulfilled their charters or satisfied the expectations of their customers, it seems unclear just where this experience was gathered; but the committee's convictions were unequivocal.[45]

The recommendations that concluded the report of this delegates' committee established Virginia's mixed enterprise approach. From an initial pool of banking, canal, and turnpike shares already owned by the state, totaling $1.25 million, a new Board of Public Works would support a state engineer, order appropriate surveys, and subscribe up to two-fifths of the stock of any corporations "the General Assembly may, from time to time, agree to patronize." As an added incentive to the private sector, the state waived its dividends, effectively subsidizing profits for the early investors until the rate of return reached 6 percent. Equally sensitive to profiteering with a state-granted franchise, the Board of Public Works set tolls at such rates as to guarantee 10 but not more than 15 percent net profits. Revenues from completed works supposedly would refresh the fund, creating a revolving source for continuous improvement. Reflecting a preoccupation in Virginia with pristine republicanism, and lodging surprising faith in the capitalist incentive (even while carefully restraining the greed of the capitalists), the mixed enterprise formula appeared to help investor-owned projects without wagering the credit of the state or the political capital of legislators who might otherwise be forced to select a route or rank the merits of different local pet projects. However, the Virginia Board of Public Works never was empowered to design a coherent system or to authorize particular appropriations. Initiative remained in private hands, and all appropriations (and even engineering specifications) passed through a popular assembly accustomed to guarding its own power.[46]

Virginia's theoretical approach to internal improvement worked rather poorly in practice. The routes begging for improvement sprawled across the western wilderness, while most of the private capital—and a disproportionate majority of legislative seats—remained entrenched in the tidewater East. Neither investors nor customers resided where the real work needed to be done. What Old Dominion required (even more than in New York or Pennsylvania) was a transfer of wealth from the East to the West in behalf of future development, and Virginia's approach effectively prevented exactly that result. Beginning in 1817, from the annual income of the Internal Improvements Fund (derived mostly from state-owned bank stock), the Board of Public Works doled out $40,000, $50,000, sometimes $60,000 per year in subscriptions, mostly for turnpike shares—a full order of magnitude below the investments in comparable works elsewhere.[47]

By far the most important and ambitious project undertaken by the Virginia Board was the James River route to Ohio. Guided by reports of their new state engineer, and noticing more urgent competition for the commerce of the West, the Board of Public Works pressed the old James River Company to replace its existing sluice navigation with a lock-and-dam canal through Blue Ridge Mountains, build a $100,000 turnpike from the head of James navigation to the Great Falls of the Kanawha, and improve the Kanawha down to the Ohio to a minimum depth of three feet. Satisfied with their earlier achievements (and the handsome dividends they were collecting), the James River shareholders balked at risking their capital further; therefore, in 1820 the legislature reduced the corporation to an agency of the state. Continuing frustration with high expenses, faulty estimates, and engineering difficulties necessitated loans against the credit of the state and led to another reorganization in 1823. By 1826 Virginia had borrowed and spent over $1.2 million on the James River–Kanawha route. Interest alone consumed well over half the income in the public works fund, leaving little to invest in other worthy improvement projects. Engineers promised that another $4.75 million would complete the work, but the legislature refused to borrow more. A grand convention in Charlottesville in 1828 (with the aging James Madison in the chair) tried to rekindle government support; but nothing could be done without borrowing huge sums and pledging tax revenues to pay interest, something the "slave-rich, cash-poor" tidewater planters stubbornly resisted. In 1832 the stalled enterprise was sold to yet another new corporation, the state retaining three-fifths of the stock.[48]

The Virginia system not only failed to support internal improvements, it failed as well to prevent either government corruption or sectional jealousy. Charges of "speculation and avarice" echoed in Virginia as much as anywhere when costs ballooned and results proved disappointing. The very creation of the Fund for Internal Improvements attracted schemes for its diversion. In 1818, with the program barely organized, Charles Yancey (reporting for the Committee of Roads and Internal Navigation, no less) proposed opening a bank with the money. His reasoning was plausible: because banking was immediately profitable, and because no great works could be built without taxes "too burthensome to the people," then let the bank loan the money to the capitalists and use the interest they pay to buy the state's two-fifths shares. But Yancey's hedge threw the risk back on the very private investors the fund was intended to relieve, and it might have encouraged borrowing for purposes other than internal improvement. Meanwhile, a select committee in 1818 churned out thousands of words condemning the previous assembly for placing wide discretionary powers to distribute privileges and incur obligations—powers clearly "*legislative*" in nature— in the hands of executive and judicial officers (the governor and attorney general) as well as nonelected regional members of the Board of Public Works, all in flagrant violation of the Virginia Constitution and the "inherent rights" of men. Although the system survived these early skirmishes, the board found its program competing with the legitimate claims of Potomac River enthusiasts and sabotaged at every turn by planter-lawmakers who insisted on sharing the wealth with minor, local improvements—and who enjoyed the power to ignore the appeals of the underrepresented West as well as the unrepresented future.[49]

Where could the problems with state initiative better be seen than in President Madison's own Virginia? Awake to the opportunities for grand developmental projects, capable of articulating beautifully the political and economic blessings associated with internal improvements, and recently prodded by the brash competition taking shape in New York, Pennsylvania, and Maryland, Virginia's landed elites nevertheless refused to commit themselves to anything but local and partial endeavors. For one thing, tidewater planters simply did not need internal improvements to facilitate their own economic transactions, so the case for state initiatives seemed abstract at best. Furthermore, since the long decline of the tobacco economy many small and middling planters struggled to turn a profit on exhausted soils with too many expensive slaves (for which they were just now finding a market in the cotton South). Taking refuge in claims that private companies worked more efficiently, and that users ought to pay for local internal improvements, such planters seemed more frightened of taxes (that would fall, of course, most heavily on them) than of government corruption or ineptitude. At the same time, the fixation of anti-improvers on the threat of government doling out privileges and favors unfairly seems ironically revealing: since colonial times, Virginia's narrow governing class had done little else with power, notwithstanding their conversion to republicanism and doctrines of disinterested service. Virginia's improvers also were planters, men of wealth and extraordinary influence. But while they pressed their neighbors to invest in Virginia's future, they did not press them very hard. Too fixed in their conviction that Old Dominion controlled the Union as long as they controlled national politics, Virginia's gentry did not see, even as it happened in front of them, that New York's commercial rise would undermine their power in the Union that was to come.

North Carolina: The Cult of True Republicanism

In early North Carolina, state internal improvements fared even worse than in Virginia. Much of the story south of William Byrd's famous "dividing line" paralleled Virginia's experience: insufficient capital, difficult geography, faulty engineering, sectional jealousy, and the unfair distribution of local political power. But in North Carolina, improvers confronted a more stubborn, rigid resistance, not just from selfish tidewater planters with little to gain but also from backcountry farmers who needed roads and canals but so distrusted government that they sometimes joined with their enemies to oppose internal improvements. Overrepresented in the North Carolina General Assembly by the original state constitution, eastern landowning gentry exercised power without shame to deny the needs of the rapidly growing interior, and the rising majority of inland voters seemed powerless to help themselves. Local jealousies undercut appeals to the "general welfare," while county politicians, firmly entrenched in "court house rings," exploited republican rhetoric to protect their unreconstructed right to rule. A grim inheritance, rooted in bitter colonial political experience and reinforced by daunting landscapes, seemed to foster in North Carolina a libertarian cult of "true" republicanism that virtually prohibited government initiative.[50]

The land itself in North Carolina seemed created to frustrate human ambition. In the northeastern region, an intricate maze of inlets and estuaries touching Albemarle and Pamlico Sounds scattered settlers in isolated pockets. The sandy Outer Banks, broken only by treacherous, shifting inlets, diverted large oceangoing vessels to the friendlier waters of Chesapeake Bay. Sandbars restricted the entrance to every major river, preventing easy movement in or out of the fertile piedmont, while tidewater swamps and sandy pinelands supported more turpentine stills than large, staple-crop plantations. Such natural conditions insulated North Carolina from the British Atlantic community, frustrated colonists hoping to establish grand estates, and favored subsistence farmers who hiked into the backcountry and rafted their meager surplus down the shallow rivers to market. As a result, the region filled up with what colonial Governor Gabriel Johnston once called "a wild Barbarous people," over whom the resident gentry wielded power with a selfish misanthropy nourished by despair. By the time of the Revolution, "Poor Carolina" was notorious for its corrupt and ruthless magistrates; at the same time it was, in the view of one inhabitant, "the Best poor mans Cuntry I Ever heard of."[51]

Everyone in revolutionary North Carolina cherished political independence, but in practice local autonomy meant different things. For common farmers, independence meant freedom to scramble and make a living unmolested, if possible, by governments of any description. For members of the tidewater gentry who had struggled to assert themselves against imperial authorities, independence meant the chance to govern their own state like a private club. Resenting coercion from outside as much as pressure from below, members of North Carolina's country gentry perfected a doctrine of liberation that led them to oppose the federal Constitution of 1787 and to join the Jeffersonian attack on strong central government during the Washington administration. Applying the same principles at home (augmented by a dreadful fear of paying taxes on their estates), slaveholding legislators set about limiting the role of government to the minimal functions of raising a militia, naming local magistrates, distributing privileges and patronage among themselves, and preserving the autonomous power of the General Assembly.[52]

In 1800, after a decade of frustrating efforts by local Federalist elites to cultivate a spirit of improvement, Jeffersonian Republicans were swept into power and backwardness became the hallmark of North Carolina. Newly elected Republicans revoked the funding for the fledgling state university—a Federalist novelty and the first such institution in the United States. In fact, they seemed determined to reverse all evidence of progress in the government. William Polk reported bitterly that "never was so much ignorance collected in a Legislative capacity since the days when Laws were enacted prohibiting the frying of Pancakes on Sundays." William Richardson Davie observed in 1803 that North Carolina was so "debased as to think herself honored with the permission 'to wallow in the mire of Virginia politics.'" One young attorney (a fraternity not known to be fastidious) observed in 1807 that his fair prospects among this "contentious people" were "blasted by the illness, the poverty, and I may add the villainy of the people."[53]

We might dismiss such spirited language as partisan screed, but Republicans themselves relished the picture of a cheap, inactive government that their enemies painted. In 1809 North Carolina budgeted expenditures of only fourteen cents per person while Virginia, frugal enough by ordinary standards, lavished upon its citizens thirty-six cents apiece. North Carolina's favorite son in national politics, Congressman Nathaniel Macon, an ascetic political rustic from Buck Spring, rose to national prominence beside John Randolph of Roanoke as a leader in the Old Republican movement and an enemy of extravagant, spendthrift politicians such as Jefferson and Madison. It was Macon who toasted his home state's political culture: "The State of North Carolina. Truly Republican without ostentation."[54]

Public works found little support in such a libertarian climate. North Carolina governors, beginning with Alexander Martin in 1784, repeatedly begged for legislative "interposition and patronage" to improve the state's trade and navigation. In 1791 Martin pointed to neighboring states that were "opening their rivers and cutting canals" while North Carolina "but feebly aided" such improvements. Still, the assembly refused to appropriate public funds. As North Carolina grew increasingly "dependent" on its "sister States for markets and for merchandise," governors reiterated their concern, focusing more each passing year on the danger to security and independence that wanton backwardness implied. Listen to Governor Nathanial Alexander's delicately worded overture to an 1806 pitch for better roads and inland navigation:

> In a government constituted as ours, where the people are every thing, where they are the fountain of all power, it becomes infinitely important that they be sufficiently enlightened to realize their interests, and to comprehend the best means of advancing them. . . . If this be true . . . how deeply interesting becomes the enquiry, whether the citizens of this State are sufficiently enlightened to know the value of their own rights, to discern and to provide against invasion of them, to distinguish between oppression and the necessary exercise of lawful authority, to discriminate the spirit of liberty from that of licentiousness, to cherish the one and to avoid the other.[55]

Alexander went so far as to suggest that "nothing" was "more congenial to the spirit of republican government, than the application of resources derived from all to the benefit of all." Tarheel lawmakers disagreed. If capitalists wanted progress, let them pay for it themselves. Occasional private bills authorized individuals or corporations to build toll roads or collect donations to effect improvements in navigation, but no public works (and precious little else) found the favor of public patronage. Of the thirty-some private acts aimed at road or river improvements between 1784 and 1815, only a few ever raised subscriptions. The Dismal Swamp Canal, the Neuse River Navigation Company, the Cape Fear Navigation Company, and the Clubfoot & Harlowe's Creek Canal accomplished some parts of their objectives, but none fulfilled the expectations of its promoters or the transporting public.[56]

Well aware of the forces against them, a state Senate committee on inland navigation first reported a comprehensive plan in December 1815. Committee chairman Archibald D. Murphey, self-taught lawyer from Orange County, self-appointed expert in school reform, circuit judge, and indefatigable booster of internal improvements, opened with a blast at prevailing conditions. Local agriculture was "at a stand" and thousands fled to Tennessee each year, while the remaining citizens abandoned all hope of "getting rich by the cultivation of the soil" and turned instead to the game of speculation. What cause could be assigned to these conditions? "We have as good a soil," Murphey argued, "as any" on the southern seaboard and better rivers than "our neighboring states," but "we have suffered year after year to pass by without seizing opportunities to improve our condition."[57]

According to the modern "science of political economy," Murphey argued, North Carolinians were wrong to hamstring their government. France, England,

and several American states all had learned that public spending on internal improvements brought the "blessings of the government" to "every man's door." Public labor thus was encouraged and "the wealth of the state" kept pace with "the wealth of its citizens." It was time for North Carolina, he concluded, "to take effectual steps to develop her territorial resources." Canals improving the principle rivers—Neuse, Tar, Cape Fear, Yadkin, and Catawba—claimed first priority, followed by a network of turnpike roads, all designed to build up home-market towns and "break the spell" that bound people in dependency to Virginia and South Carolina. To that end, Murphey sketched out a plan of state aid to those patriotic investors who undertook internal improvement. Existing navigation charters would be amended and two new ones created, bringing all canal companies into a common form. A new state board of commissioners would oversee these private companies, subscribe for the state up to one-third of their stock, and provide "scientific topographical engineers" for technical support. Calculating the public revenue surplus from state-owned bank stock and existing taxes at nearly $60,000, Murphey proposed spending $40,000 per year to fund the internal improvement program.[58]

Murphey's design failed in the Commons, 59 percent opposed, although limited aid was extended to the Roanoke and Cape Fear companies, commissioners were named to survey four other principal rivers, and a petition was sent to Congress begging national help in opening an outlet from Albemarle Sound. For a time Murphey was everywhere: accompanying surveyors down the Yadkin River, lobbying assemblymen in Raleigh, whipping up support in Fayetteville and down the Cape Fear Valley. As he encountered opposition he formulated rejoinders for next year's committee report. "No considerations of local policy," he reminded the 1816 Senate, "should divert our views," nor should "paltry considerations of expense." Members of the Commons disagreed. "Isolated measures, without plan and without system" Murphey insisted, baffled the "efforts of honest industry," often "giving wrong direction" and disappointing "expectations" by their "frequent abortion." Yet the legislators balked at a long-term program or system. Addressing particular local interests, Murphey arranged his projects in sections, directing the "whole trade of North-Carolina into three channels, each having an outlet in the state." Finally, the guiding hands of commissioners and a state engineer were "essential to the success of any general plan." Again, the Commons did less than Murphey requested: four new charters were granted and the commissioners appointed in 1815 were authorized to hire a "Principal Engineer," the search for whom consumed the next two years. Meanwhile local talent conducted various surveys, all of which were printed by the North Carolina General Assembly in 1818 and placed the following year in the hands of an English professional, Hamilton Fulton, who accepted the position of state engineer for the startling salary of £1,200 (about $5,300) per year.[59]

By the time engineer Fulton arrived on the scene in July 1819, a financial panic had struck hard in the South and West, exploding paper fortunes, collapsing land and commodities prices, closing banks, and generally depressing trade. While Fulton set to work acquainting himself with the sandy outlets, rivers, and swamps he was hired to improve, Archibald Murphey set pen to paper once more, producing an imposing ninety-page *Memoir of Internal Improvements* (1819) that blamed hard times not on banks and swindlers but on the failure of the state to concentrate its commerce in a "home market." Recycling familiar arguments, Murphey claimed that nothing but "supineness and want of public spirit" stood in the way of recovery and growth. He carefully reviewed what could be done, and with elaborate statistical tables he demonstrated how the state, albeit reeling from the panic, could easily afford to pledge $150,000 annually to support internal improvements. His objective, again, was a permanent fund, a standing board, and a comprehensive statewide system.[60]

Sensing a turning point in local history, Murphey closed his *Memoir* with a scathing attack on North Carolina's political culture. Ideologues such as Macon might see great virtue in the people's commitment to "*stern Republicanism*," but Murphey thought this was the cause of their neglect and steady decay. On the national level the state was ignored except for the "Farce" of presidential elections, after which Tarheels were "laughed at for a few weeks, and no more remembered." At home, North Carolina cultivated neither "respect for herself" nor "character in the Union," allowing her citizens to chase their own fortunes without regard for the state of their homeland. Quoting New York's DeWitt Clinton, that the "glory of the State is the common property of its citizens," Murphey saw around him only humiliation: "would it not be better," he quipped, "to surrender our Charter as an Independent state and incorporate ourselves with Virginia and South Carolina?" The favorite explanation in the General Assembly, "that we are too poor to get out of this condition," was but an "*off-hand* excuse" for politicians "not doing their duty." States with "inferior resources" had "rendered themselves . . . ornaments of this Republic." Invoking the hopes of the coming generation, Murphey called for the long view: "A good name is a richer inheritance than property; and posterity will venerate much more, those who transmit to them renown and manly virtues, than those who transmit only lands and negro slaves."[61]

Murphey's frustration ran deep. Eleven years after the Gallatin *Report*, and four years into the wave of postwar local initiatives, North Carolina still had done almost nothing in its own behalf. Opportunities abounded, and now an engineer was hard at work setting priorities; still the General Assembly refused to commit more than paltry resources and private capital disappeared into fragmentary amateur projects or ancillary speculations. Bitter rivalries split voters and promoters into local factions. Accustomed to taxing local exports like mythical trolls, river-town merchants refused to believe that public works or better market services would redirect business that "rightfully" was theirs. Even among those who supported internal improvements, a "perverse and contrary Spirit" (Murphey's words) drove men to "ridicule every plan of Operations that can be devised." Outside the commercial towns, backwardness reigned supreme: "I had no Idea," Murphey reported after riding the frontier circuit, "that we had such a poor, ignorant, and squalid Population." Even as he drafted his famous *Memoir*, Murphey grew "disgusted with North Carolina." Another generation, he concluded, might eventually see the benefits, but the "Spirit of the present" was "radically mean and groveling."[62]

Murphey despaired of improving North Carolina. His private fortune gone by 1820—swept away in the very speculations he so often deplored—he sheltered what property he could in the hands of a trustee and fled to Tennessee, where he scrambled to rescue something from his ill-fated frontier investments.[63] Meanwhile, the North Carolina legislature adopted in December 1819 the shell of his proposals—a permanent fund and a board of commissioners—but the program got no cash appropriations, depending instead on proceeds from Cherokee lands that were not yet ready for market. Over the next decade the cumulative fund for internal improvement barely reached the $150,000 Murphey now wanted to spend every year, and as these meager appropriations disappeared without significant results, original doubts about improvements hardened into a fixed determination not to encumber either the taxpayers or the public credit.[64]

Almost annually after 1820 the House of Commons moved to abolish the Board of Internal Improvements and reabsorb its pathetic resources, attacks that were deflected by the Senate. Almost annually the board reported that all the companies were "deficient in funds to complete their works" and begged for additional appropriations and stock subscriptions, appeals that fell on deaf or disaffected ears. Engineer Fulton had been ordered to introduce science and control into all public projects at once, a charge guaranteed to produce friction with existing contractors while exhausting the expert himself in making hasty, superficial studies. Enthusiasm for opening coastal inlets, made urgent by the possibility of federal patronage to such national objectives, consumed much of Fulton's overtaxed energies. Demands for new roads into frontier Buncombe and Haywood counties and the Cherokee treaty lands further stretched scarce resources into the extremities of the state. Nothing was "more injurious" to the system than the "jealousy" of existing towns, yet the board encountered such intramural contests everywhere. Enemies condemned the slow, expensive gathering of information by a foreign engineer whose reports always called for more money.[65]

In 1824, a presidential election year that introduced powerful distractions of rhetoric and ambition to an already superheated controversy, the board and the state engineer barely survived an all-out attack in the North Carolina House of Commons. Upward of $200,000 (about one-fortieth of New York's investment, one-sixth of what Virginia spent on the James River Canal) had disappeared since 1815, much of it utterly unaccounted for, yet the board could show for it only a few primitive roads, failed experiments at dredging and scouring tidal inlets and rivers, some sections of imperfect canals, and $50,000 worth of inconclusive engineer's reports—most of which called for ever-higher public investments. In his own defense, Fulton attributed these disappointments to unforeseen technical difficulties substantially aggravated by inadequate funding, local jealousies, incompetent contractors, and the casual inattention of navigation company directors with whom he was obliged to work.[66]

Where fabulous success rewarded New York's bold canallers, relentless failure stalked North Carolina's partial, tentative initiatives and verified the claims of detractors, that internal improvement was a game for wasting money. By 1824 popular enthusiasm for internal improvements (never great) gave way to the habitual suspicion of public officials and government programs that marked North Carolina's libertarian political culture. Friends of the Murphey program, especially State Senate Speaker Bartlett Yancey, labored to keep up public support; but defenders of the status quo (both political and economic) scoffed at the engineers and warned the tax-paying public against the promises of wild-eyed dreamers. Overwhelmed by technical problems and unable to focus on a single dramatic operation, the advocates of North Carolina's state public works never posted the kind of success that saved DeWitt Clinton from disaster. However one wonders what might have been done with thirty or forty times as much money, the order of magnitude of investments in New York? In one year (1811) Pennsylvania gave to private turnpikes alone four times as much money as North Carolina spent in a decade of "feverish" improvement.

From Washington, the venerable Macon scolded Yancey for his exuberant support of internal improvements and especially federal aid. "Be not deceived, I speak soberly in the fear of God, and the love of the constitution," thundered the voice of Old Republicanism. "Let not the love of improvement, or a thirst for glory blind that sober discretion and sound sense with which the Lord has blest you." Remember, Macon continued, that "you belong to a meek State" and a "just people" who want nothing more than "to enjoy the fruits of their labor honestly" and to "lay out their profits in their own way." Macon spoke not from sober calculations of the merits of roads and canals but from a priori convictions that development itself was a fraud. There was no need for government programs, plans, or designs because private parties would invest where the necessity was real (and for Macon it seldom was): "In all countries, those who have sense enough to get and keep money, may be safely trusted as to the manner of disbursing it." It was not just the high costs or technical uncertainties of public works that worried Macon, or even their harmful impact on government, but concern for the seamless integrity of the old order that was threatened by activist government, modern technology, and progressive commercial development.[67]

Macon's constitutional purity was aimed primarily at federal authority, to be sure, and he delivered to Yancey in 1818 a warning that would echo through internal improvement debates for a generation: "If Congress can make canals they can with more propriety emancipate." But resistance to federal power was only one tenet of Old Republicanism, and slavery was but a piece of a complex prerogative that sustained the rule of established planters, minimized government, stayed the hands of merchants and bankers, and celebrated a radical individualism that could never challenge the existing inequalities of social class. In North Carolina, as long as interior counties remained landlocked, underdeveloped, and underrepresented in the assembly, tidewater planters had nothing to fear. Such were the virtues of independence under the cult of true republicanism that gentlemen in power defined as vice anything likely to change their ways. Internal improvements promised to enrich the people, and as Congressman Willis Alston, Macon acolyte (and nephew) and Halifax County planter reminded a 4 July crowd of patriots in 1824, riches fostered luxury, luxury corrupted morals, and immorality threatened republicanism: "*The tables of Sinai could not control the Jews—so* must the provisions of our constitution lose their influence over *us* when we reject our simplicity of manners and our regard for virtue."[68]

It was nobody's fault, really, that North Carolina was a very hard place to improve, but local history and culture did foster negativity among the people that transformed resignation into a virtue. Widespread torpor in the face of such daunting obstacles—what Archibald Murphey called "supineness" and "want of spirit"—served the interests of gentlemen in power, who stood to lose more than gain from commercial and material development. Furthermore, it was in very conscious defense of those interests that North Carolina's politicians polished the libertarian rhetoric of true republicanism, hauling back from temptation poor souls (like Yancey) who were dazzled by visions of a better future, and reaffirming at home and in the counsels of the national government that the interests of ordinary people were served, not by the patronage of Congress (once it paid the fiddler, might it not call the tune?) or even state-level programs (spending every man's taxes to benefit somebody else), but by vigilant attention to the blessings of simplicity, the sacred charge of liberty, the joys of independence, and the virtues of the natural order of things as they were—and always should be. Bested by conditions and opponents at home, North Carolina improvers turned their hopes once more toward Congress for a national program of internal improvement that would bring progress to the Old North State in spite of its prevailing temperament.

In every case except New York, state-level initiatives in the wake of the Bonus Bill veto of 1817 brought disappointment to even the most practical internal improvers. Shortage of capital and imperfect technical expertise—the two causes most often cited by historians for the failure of early public works—surely frustrated anyone who turned his hand to the business; but money and engineers were no more readily available in New York than in other states in the Union, and the Erie Canal prospered famously. In some ways the time was "right" for the Erie route to the West while other programs seemed "premature" or "ill-conceived." But the time had been *made* right for Erie by the role of improvement promoters in generating public support, marshaling the power of the state, finding technical experts, and recruiting armies of laborers for a concentrated effort so large that in 1817 no private firm or business corporation could imagine undertaking it. As the Erie project approached completion, showering money and economic growth on the taxpayers of New York, it was hard to resist the conclusion throughout the rest of the country that wealth and power flowed to those who seized that kind of initiative. Yet boldness alone was not rewarded in any other case, and determined promoters who modeled themselves on the heroic DeWitt Clinton sometimes found themselves covered with shame.

While the Erie Canal was being built—a period of time that coincided almost exactly with the presidential administrations of James Monroe—internal improvers in every state found themselves awash in grand designs, extravagant claims, false starts, failed experiments, stubborn opponents, political adventurers, local protectionists, and endless expenditures for digging, designing, and surveying. They quickly discovered that private investors did not always—in fact did not often—lead the way in public works, even when the future of whole communities seemed to hang in the balance. They learned that technological innovation did not proceed in straight lines but offered uncertain choices, some of which led to expensive mistakes. They found that interstate and interurban rivalries always subverted cooperative ventures despite the most elevated promises of mutuality or harmony of interests. They discovered that engineers chronically "low-balled" projected costs in order to maximize public enthusiasm (and they learned to encourage this treacherous practice by hiring the man whose figures most closely matched the public purse). They found that the instant roads and canals became fixed to the ground, voters and taxpayers quickly divided into those who felt well served and those who felt neglected by the exact location of the route. In short, internal improvements often suffered as much from cultural as from economic or technological shortcomings.

Taken all together, experience showed that successful large public works of internal improvement required an authority sufficient to command resources, make discriminating judgments, suffer the trials and errors of experimentation, and retain the faith and confidence of the people in whose behalf improvements were pursued. Even then major programs might fail. At the time James Monroe assumed the presidency in 1817, government alone held the power to sponsor and coordinate projects of this magnitude; but everywhere Americans questioned the wisdom of encouraging their governments to act. Even when voters authorized their states to pursue internal improvements, problems of scale and jurisdiction easily distorted their objectives and undermined their freedom to make the best decisions. Consequently, even while the states took up the initiative in the wake of the Bonus Bill veto, demands for federal aid, guidance, and integration bombarded Congress and the executive throughout the Monroe era. Unfortunately, in the national arena, the complex merits of internal improvements frequently disappeared beneath ever more strident debates about the legitimate use of power, the consolidation of the federal Union, and the rights of the sovereign states under the Constitution.

4

The "Progress" of Consolidation

DURING THE presidency of James Monroe (1817–24), politicians and internal improvers staged some of the most thorough debates yet on national public works—their widespread popularity, their economic and cultural impact, the power of Congress to support them, and the right (or duty) of the states to resist them under the federal Constitution. Shocked by Madison's veto of the 1817 Bonus Bill, reiterated by Monroe in his First Annual Message to Congress, the advocates of federal improvements redoubled their efforts in the Fifteenth Congress to salvage the platform of custom and precedent that Madison's veto sought to deny them. Private advocates for roads and canals and the representatives of various states in need of help directed a widening stream of remonstrances to Congress, begging for aid to pet projects of "compelling" national interest. Each new gambit called out voices of opposition, sometimes bitter and narrowly selfish, but always mouthing high principles and gradually coming to focus their opposition on what they called "consolidation."

Consolidation called to mind unfinished business reaching back to the ratification of the Constitution. Was the Union a mere confederation of states or was it a national government? Unable to build a solid consensus in 1788 on this essential structural issue, the champions of ratification originally embraced a studied ambiguity, hoping that the blessings of peace and prosperity under the new frame of government would quiet their Antifederalist enemies. Bitter policy struggles followed—over funding the national debt, the first Bank of the United States, the Quasi-War with France, the Alien and Sedition Acts, Jefferson's reforms, Louisiana, the embargo, and finally the War of 1812—repeatedly opening the wound and nourishing competing interpretations of American federalism. But with the Treaty of Ghent in hand (and the providential victory of Andrew Jackson at New Orleans fresh in memory), postwar nationalists took hope once more. Congress reestablished the national bank, adopted a modest protective tariff, and tried to begin, with the Bonus Bill, a system of national public works. By the time James Monroe addressed his first Congress in December 1817, it seemed to him that "local jealousies"—those natural enemies of al confederations—were "rapidly yielding to more generous, enlarged, and enlightened views of national policy." The United States was poised at the threshold o greatness, and for these advantages "so numerous and highly important" Monroe offered thanks to the "Omnipotent Being," praying for "virtue and strength tc maintain and hand them down in their utmost purity to our latest posterity."[1]

What looked to Monroe in 1817 like "generous" and "enlightened" views may have been nothing more than a euphoric sense that there was plenty enough fo all in the face of postwar expansion. But harmony and hope more than jealousy and fear had marked at least very recent public discourse—especially in Congress, especially compared with any other moment save the opening years of George Washington's first administration—and so Monroe chose to believe. Alert to the dangers of regional jealousy, he began his administration with a tour of New England the summer after his inauguration. Witnessing the president's amazingly warm reception in Boston, someone called it an "era of good feelings," and people everywhere, including the new president, began to see barriers to progress melting away. But these "good feelings" proved evanescent. In pursuit of progress, and confident that the Constitution allowed the general government sufficient authority to promote Americans' collective prosperity, Republican nationalists—Henry Clay, John C. Calhoun, and John Quincy Adams chief among them—advocated policies designed to promote economic development. Clay pressed the question tirelessly in the House, and it was there he first spoke of the "American System" that would guide his politics for thirty years. Calhoun, now heading Monroe's War Department, tried to implement public works under the cover of national defense (a latitudinarian strategy he would repudiate completely within the decade). Such Republican nationalists cast the federal government in an energetic role as a patron of ambition, a handmaiden of entrepreneurs, and an advocate of the general welfare. It was, they believed, the necessary path to modernization and greatness.[2]

States' rights radicals, however, reacted in horror to such activist policies. Frightened by rapid change, high mobility, the proliferation of new western states, and the emergence of a less local, more national identity among young Americans (whose roots tapped the founding era but not the colonial stories that the old states cherished), determined localists and ideologues (sometimes known as "Old Republicans") launched a drive to restore the original limited vision of a mere confederation of states. Placing states' rights ahead of the Union, these particularists reached back past the Jeffersonian Revolution of 1800 (from which they pretended to draw their authority) to demand the restoration of Antifederalist claims for undiminished state sovereignty, before the progress of consolidation awarded legitimate force and permanency to a supreme national state.[3]

Beginning in the winter of 1817–18 and working with fervor and premedi-

ation, led by congressmen Philip Pendleton Barbour, James Johnson, Hugh
Nelson, and others, but drawing critical support and verbal ammunition from
Virginia appellate judge Spencer Roane, Richmond *Enquirer* editor Thomas
Ritchie, John Taylor of Caroline (the cultural heir of conservative jurist Edmund
Pendleton), and of course John Randolph of Roanoke, Virginia particularists
seized every opportunity to obstruct the progress of national programs and redefine the terms of the Union's original founding. The result was the start of a
new constitutional struggle that wrecked the fragile Jeffersonian consensus, polarizing Republicans in Congress fully a year before fierce debates about slavery
in Missouri and painful losses from the panic of 1819 fortuitously clothed these
"neo-Antifederalists" with a mantle of prophetic legitimacy. The great "danger"
against which they labored was the consolidation of a national state. The practical target of their initial opposition was support for internal improvements. The
immediate occasion for the start of this crisis was Henry Clay's attempt in the
House in early 1818 to reverse the effect of Madison's Bonus Bill veto.

Bonus Bill Redux

The Bonus Bill veto of 1817 had been crafted by Madison to make it clear that he
did not fear internal improvements or an active federal program. As tangible
projects fixed to the ground, roads and canals triggered ancient jealousies and
fears of unequal government favor—indeed, that was the point of Gallatin's
argument for national planning—and Madison recognized the value of a *system*
of public works. But the Constitution's principle author feared the effects of too
loose a construction of law, and he worried that embracing a congressional
program by implication might engender too free a game of logrolling legislation.
Standing squarely on the same ground, incoming President Monroe tried to fix
the attention of the Fifteenth Congress on securing the requisite amendment by
issuing his opinion in advance "that Congress do not possess the right." Enter-
taining a "high sense of the advantage" to the nation from "good roads and
canals," and hoping to clarify the issue once for all, Monroe urged Congress to
amend the Constitution to embrace internal improvements and national "semi-
naries of learning" as well. He was "happy to observe" that the "benign spirit of
conciliation and harmony" that prevailed "throughout our Union" surely would
bring to such an effort a "prompt and favorable result."[4]

So advised, Congress set quickly to work. In the Senate, James Barbour introduced a constitutional amendment granting Congress explicit power "to pass
laws appropriating money for constructing roads and canals, and improving the
navigation of water-courses." Barbour himself believed Congress already possessed the authority requested, but since Monroe had pronounced a contrary
opinion, the "impracticality" of passing it through Congress seemed "palpable."

Good Virginian that he was, Barbour harbored no sinister wish to "enlarge th
powers" in Washington; but military roads across "this extensive empire, or a
internal navigation on the same scale, clearly required the resources and th
superintending power of the General Government." Barbour's language, al
though demanding an amendment, seemed perfectly in sympathy with Gallatin'
original *Report*.[5]

It was exactly what Monroe had asked for, but the Barbour amendment die
without fanfare in the Senate. Meanwhile, members of the House of Represen
tatives staged a more raucous debate on the limits of congressional power. Barel
two weeks into the session, Henry St. George Tucker—a Virginian but also a
internal improver—delivered a long committee report denying that either Madi
son's veto or Monroe's preemptive opinion should influence "the disposition o
Congress to legislate on this interesting subject."[6] Congress already enjoye
authority to "establish post offices and post roads" and with it a "correspondin
obligation of transporting the mails," which surely justified bridging rivers, re
moving obstructions, and leveling mountains that stood in the way. Nationa
defense justified the opening of roads during actual hostilities: why not in time
of peace as well? The power to cut canals was no less incidental to the regulatio
of internal commerce than were the navy, lighthouses, breakwaters, piers, an
harbors essential to the regulation of foreign trade. Precedents abounded fo
appropriating money to purposes not specified in the Constitution: how els
could the government have purchased Louisiana, or Jefferson's library, or paint
ings for the Capitol? How could it aid manufacturing, encourage fisheries, re
lieve the victims of misfortune? If the Congress could not appropriate money, i
could not legislate at all, and surely this was not the framers' intention. Take
altogether, Congress had the right to make roads and canals; therefore, th
committee resolved, "it is expedient" to set aside the bonus from the nationa
bank as a "fund for internal improvement."[7]

Tucker's report contained what by now were standard claims of internal im
provers for adequate national power. On 6 March 1818, in Committee of th
Whole, Tucker spelled out his arguments in detail, reaching back to Jefferson'
day and the original Gallatin *Report* for the roots of what he insisted on calling
"Republican party" objective. Until recently nothing but war and penury ha
frustrated national improvements, but now interstate rivalries and "the inefficac
of State efforts" threatened to stop progress altogether.[8] To advocates of a
amendment Tucker explained the hidden hazard in that seemingly innocen
precaution: seeking amendments to ratify powers already lodged by the framer
in Congress invited states to encroach upon the power of the nation. Six sma
states might deny to the federal government powers it already possessed; further
more, an amendment might fail, not because the people disapproved, but be
cause a few genuine opponents were joined by friends of internal improvement
who thought that *asking* for power endangered the government. Members wor

ried about states' rights, but Tucker could not understand why. Disintegration, not consolidation, posed the greater threat to the United States, and it was "to the preservation of this Union" that "national improvements" would contribute.[9]

States' rights Virginians answered with a blistering attack on the exercise of power in Washington. First Alexander Smyth laid down the general rule that wherever the powers of the states and the Union overlapped, the latter must withdraw. The power to build roads and canals rightly was exercised by every state government, and while precedents existed for federal encroachments (the Cumberland Road, for example), these precedents were wrong and no excuse for encroaching again. Echoing the rhetoric of recent legislation in Virginia, Smyth reported (without foundation) that "experience has proved" that internal improvements were "most economically made, and best managed" by private corporations: "So soon as the wants of society shall render such works profitable, individuals will associate, unite their stock, and construct the works."[10] Philip Pendleton Barbour continued the constitutional exegesis. Whatever Congress or the executive may have done in the past had been done without legitimate authority. Pretending that the meaning of the Constitution was transparent and incontestable, Barbour disallowed all inferential precedents as tending to perpetuate the struggles for power that constitutions intended to settle. However desirable the object in question, it was best, he concluded, not to disturb "that political balance which our ancestors had settled between the several governments of this country."[11]

Such appeals to original intention usually covered an interested position, and this renewed fundamentalism after seventeen years of Virginia control of the national executive seemed especially self-serving. Could it be Old Dominion was afraid to play a declining role in a rapidly growing Union? Such, at least, was the inference when Speaker Clay finally rose to rebut the particularists with an alternative version of Jefferson's Republican legacy. Claiming to draw "from the same source" as Barbour and Smyth—that is, the campaign of 1798 against the crimes of the Federalists—Clay disagreed with the "water-gruel regimen" the Virginians now would feed the Constitution. Common sense discovered that the United States comprised "twenty local sovereignties having charge of their interior concerns" and "one great sovereignty, for the purpose of general defense, for the preservation of the general peace, and for the regulation of commerce both internal and external." For Clay, all governments existed "for the benefit of the people," and all powers given them were "so many duties" to be "exercised by the governors for the benefit of the governed." What was the power that excited such "alarm" among the friends of states' rights? To "promote social intercourse; to facilitate commerce between the States; to strengthen the bonds of our Union; to make us really and truly one family—one community in interest and in feeling." Where was the danger in that?[12]

Seizing boldly on the language of his enemies, Clay allowed that his program

would bring consolidation; but compared to disintegration, nothing could be
more virtuous. Quoting George Washington's original endorsement at the close
of the Philadelphia Convention, Clay recalled that there was no higher purpose
in the founding than "*the consolidation of our* Union [Clay's emphasis], in which
is involved our prosperity, felicity, safety, perhaps our national existence.'" Especially with the rise of the West, where a scarcity of capital and enormous developmental needs crippled the efforts of pioneer societies, clinging tightly to government inaction and principles of strict construction actually perpetuated unequal
treatment among the states. The preservation of the Union was the first objective
of the federal government; internal improvements promised greatly to promote
that objective; and in exercising such benevolent powers Congress did no harm.
Ridiculing Philip Barbour's paralyzing, negative principles, Clay contrasted their
concepts of federalism: "he considers everything gained to the States from the
General Government as something snatched from a foreign Power. I consider it
as a Government co-ordinate with them, and the true construction, I think, is to
give it all that vigor and vitality which rightfully belong to it."[13]

Over the Sabbath congressmen rested, but on Monday debates raged anew.
John Paine Cushman of New York, an unashamed advocate of national improvements, chastised Virginians for pushing Confederation era principles. Virginians
could not now reclaim for the states more power than they had demanded at
ratification, nor was recourse to prior sovereignty appropriate in a Union where
nearly half the states, born of this Constitution, had existed under no other.[14] If
Barbour's theory were correct, Cushman reasoned, the whole "history of our
legislation" was "a record of continued usurpations upon the rights of the States."
The flexible authority that currently legitimated policies governing commerce,
the post office, Indian trade, the purchase of Louisiana, the territorial system,
and the prohibition of the African slave trade sustained the ambition of internal
improvers to make roads and canals in behalf of interior intercourse. (Barbour
himself had approved such actions as recently as last year.) Finally, Cushman
warned, a frequent recurrence to the people by the process of amendment, as
requested by President Monroe, threatened to bestow "extraordinary powers" on
a tiny "doubting minority."[15]

The internal improvers' dilemma, articulated here by Cushman, was the same
one that had dogged friends of the central government since Madison's brooding
treatise on "Vices of the Political System of the U. States" back in 1787: the power
required to effect what nationalists called good government never would be
surrendered by states whose leaders took advantage of their freedom. Perfectly
cognizant of this dilemma, Madison had squeezed from the Philadelphia Convention the potential framework of a central government and secured its ratification by artful exposition and timely concession, hoping its benevolent impact,
once established, would quiet fears and reservations. The dishonesty latent in the

rategies of desperate advocates of ratification infected constitutional politics
vith a strain of disingenuousness that now came back to haunt some of the archi-
ects of the nation—especially Madison, who labored now to stop or even reverse
1e flow of energy to the center. Having first invented a national majority, the
We the people" of the Constitution's Preamble, in order to skirt the obstruction-
st states, Madison himself had come to fear a popular majority in Congress.[16]

Leaving Monroe in awkward possession of the middle ground, Virginia's
ounger generation—with Jefferson's blessing and Madison's acquiescence, and
ided enthusiastically by notorious particularists like Roane and Randolph (men
ho never had embraced the nationalists' principles)—sought now to place strict
mits on the elastic powers of the instrument that had served them well so far.
he reasons for this reversal lay buried beneath the strident insistence that the
Constitution always had been so. Utterly rejecting Clay's artful gloss on the term
consolidation," for example, Archibald Austin claimed for the states complete,
istinct, uncompromised sovereignty exactly as if they were independent coun-
ries "only bound to each other" by a "league or confederation between them."[17]
Convinced of the alien nature of federal power, Austin imagined that if Congress
ould build roads and canals, Congress could take jurisdiction over taverns and
ost office buildings, seize and destroy a man's house or farm, or "level the State
overnments." Why it should do so required no explanation: such was the nature
f power. National improvements, he concluded perceptively, necessarily implied
"large national plan" that must sometimes contradict "the interest of the State,
1e people, and the commercial town." Wanting no part of a rising, consolidated
ation, Austin opposed every new "accumulation of power."[18]

Such local men, who perhaps had never truly accepted abridgments of state
overeignty within the Union (and who frequently envisioned no society more
omplex than the tidewater plantations on which they were called "master")
eadily dismissed the demands of merchants, capitalists, and western pioneers as
eedless designs against liberty. Eventually this would become a southern re-
ional perspective, but in 1818 not all southerners or planters agreed. Eldred
imkins, a freshman congressman from South Carolina, jumped to praise the
realth and prosperity that flowed from the "spirit of industry and commerce."
No country on earth," he explained in an oft-repeated observation, "was capable
f greater improvements" than "our own"; and no greater "evil" could "assail a
eople, spread over such a vast surface" than "local jealousies—as unfounded in
1eir nature as dangerous in their consequences." Was it not precisely the fail-
re of the Confederation Congress to discipline the sovereign states that had
rought about the Constitution? Could it be the framers of 1787 had failed in
1eir principal objective?[19]

Virginian James Johnson rose to direct members' attention away from the
enefits of present initiatives toward potential dangers in the future when "some

bold, adventurous, and daring spirit" might gain control of unrestrained govern
ment and "drive with desolating fury over the rights and liberties of the people
Johnson zeroed in on Clay's intentional design or "system of political economy
"commerce is to be diverted from its wonted channel; agriculture to assume
new character; human skill and industry to be placed under the tutelage of th
Government; the condition of the people, in the different sections of the countr
to be rendered precisely equal, by an artificial system of legislation." Dangerou
monopolies and hothouse development resulted whenever government intro
duced arbitrary favors. Blending Bolingbroke's critique of administrative corru
tion with Adam Smith's more modern proscription against any policy of eco
nomic management, Johnson pledged his liberal faith that "that system was th
most perfect, which left the citizen the most freedom, and permitted him und
the influence of interest, to pursue his own fortune and prosperity."[20]

Johnson's theory privileged the status quo as an artifact of "nature," tending
see all change in the world as the consequence of fraud and manipulation, and
did not square completely with progressive talk about a rising American empi
so popular beyond the Appalachians and long cherished by nationalistic Virgin
ians such as Jefferson, Madison, and Monroe. Further, the dismissal by Virgin
ians of all precedent, custom, and experience resurrected Antifederalist position
that had not prevailed in the founding era. South Carolina's William Lowndes i
fact accused the particularists of proposing limitations no less "constructive" ar
novel than anybody's brief for implied powers. North Carolina's Lemuel Sawy
rejoined luridly that federal invaders who entered his state with "axes, spade
and shovels, to tear the virgin bosom of our country," should be prepared fo
violence: he, for one, would fight "till the flesh were hacked from my bones
Virginia's Hugh Nelson, clinging to Madison's "Virginia Resolutions" of 179
declared this the "last battle" in the House for "the preservation of State rights
and summoned his colleagues who cherished the Spirit of '98 to return to th
same "field of triumph—a triumph of the States over the Federal Constitution."

Nelson's diatribe elicited from Charles Fenton Mercer, a Virginian but n
party to this states' rights campaign, another historical lecture on the nature
the founding event, replete with quotations from original "Publius" letters rejec
ing exactly Nelson's position. Quoting Madison's *Federalist 45*: "in all the exam
ples of ancient and modern confederacies, the strongest tendency continual
displaying itself in the members, [is] to despoil the General Government of i
authorities; with a very ineffectual capacity in the latter to defend itself again
their encroachments." Instead of mounting this threatening campaign, Merc
wondered why Virginia didn't welcome the chance to stand as the "key of th
expanded arch, which stretching from North to South, binds the whole East
union . . . [with] our Western Empire."[22] Henry St. George Tucker then took
parting shot at the pious claims of his fellow Virginians: if precedent and a

quiescence had no force in a republican regime, how did they account for their own state constitution, which was formed "by the ordinary Legislature," never ratified, and now revered because of long acceptance by the people? None of the Virginians opposing internal improvements agreed with each other on the limit of congressional power, yet all insisted on the strictest principles of construction. "With these things before your eyes," Tucker wondered, "who shall pretend to say what is orthodoxy—what is heterodoxy?"[23]

Speaker Clay tried to bring closure to the debate. The present arguments of the Virginians threatened a "relapse" into that "debility which existed in the old Confederation." Crisply restating Adam Smith's contention in *Wealth of Nations*, that "in a new country" conditions may be "ripe for public works long before" private capital was able "to effect them," Clay concluded that nothing a government could do was more "permanently beneficial" than "durable" internal improvements, "part of the land itself, diffusing comfort and activity, and animation on all sides." Therefore on behalf of a wholly benevolent objective as well as the rightful powers of government, he begged his fellow lawmakers to "assert, uphold, and maintain, the authority of Congress, notwithstanding all that has been, or may be, said against it."[24]

When the debates finally expired a series of roll calls measured the sentiments of the House on four propositions (Table 1). Might Congress appropriate money for national roads and canals? (Answer: yes, by vote of 89 to 75.) Did national defense or the needs of the postal system justify building national roads? Or canals? (No, 84 to 81 and 83 to 81.) Under the elastic clauses could Congress build roads and canals to promote commercial development? (No, 93 to 70.) Virginians and North Carolinians overwhelmingly rejected all of these propositions; New England did the same. South Carolina and Georgia divided evenly on each, as did Maryland in the Middle Atlantic region. Strong support for federal improvements came from the largest Middle Atlantic states (three-to-one for New York, even higher for Pennsylvania) and the new states of the West, although Kentucky and Tennessee posted significant ambivalence to federal action.[25]

What did the voting mean? Hugh Nelson had thought the improvers would win by "an overwhelming constitutional majority," and he must have been surprised and encouraged. Clay, of course, was chastened and desperately seized upon his single victory as proof of congressional authority. But did the failure of the other propositions truly legitimate the strictest claims of the states' rights radicals? Virginia particularists had labored to make these polls referenda on their neo-Antifederalist doctrines (not necessarily shared by Jeffersonians everywhere), but the meaning of the result was ambivalent. For example, New England members, including at least eleven die-hard Federalists whose sense of the framers' intent could not have coincided with the radical Virginians', nevertheless opposed internal improvements across the board. Were the Yankees voting

TABLE I. Internal Improvement Votes, 15th Congress, 1st Session,
House of Representatives, March 1818

	Resolution 1		Resolution 2		Resolution 3		Resolution 4	
	Yea	Nay	Yea	Nay	Yea	Nay	Yea	Nay
New England	10	27	8	31	7	31	8	29
Vermont	1	5	2	5	2	5	2	4
New Hampshire	3	2	3	2	2	2	3	2
Massachusetts	6	12	3	15	3	15	3	15
Connecticut	0	7	0	7	0	7	0	6
Rhode Island	0	1	0	2	0	2	0	2
Middle Atlantic	49	13	46	15	42	15	46	15
New York	20	7	19	6	19	5	20	6
Pennsylvania	17	2	16	4	14	5	16	4
New Jersey	5	1	5	1	3	1	5	1
Delaware	2	0	2	0	2	0	2	0
Maryland	5	3	4	4	4	4	3	4
South Atlantic	14	29	11	31	9	35	12	30
Virginia	4	12	3	14	2	16	3	15
North Carolina	2	11	2	11	1	12	2	10
South Carolina	4	4	3	3	3	4	3	3
Georgia	4	2	3	3	3	3	4	2
West, Free	7	0	7	0	5	2	6	1
Ohio	6	0	6	0	5	1	5	1
Indiana	1	0	1	0	0	1	1	0
West, Slave	9	6	9	7	7	10	9	8
Kentucky	5	3	6	2	5	4	6	3
Tennessee	2	3	2	4	1	5	2	4
Mississippi	1	0	0	1	0	1	0	1
Louisiana	1	0	1	0	1	0	1	0
Totals	89	75	81	84	70	93	81	83

Source: *Annals*, 15th Cong., 1st sess., 1384–89.
Note: Resolution 1 = power to appropriate money; 2 = build postal or military roads
3 = build postal or military canals; 4 = build roads and canals for commerce.

regional interests this time instead of abstract principles? Or were they merely
toying with their enemies, giving comfort to renegades among the southern
party? What about South Carolina and Georgia? These later wellsprings of
southern sectionalism seemed not yet awake to the dangers of consolidation: they
found as much to gain as fear in the promise of national internal improvements
Although the propositions distinguished with care between justifications based

on the post office mandate, national defense, and the infamous elastic clauses, all but a handful of members voted straight across, yea or nay. Were these stalwarts set against Clay? Against consolidation? Or against roads and canals in any form with all their modernizing consequences? The Fifteenth Congress contained an extraordinary number of new members (thanks to the backlash against the 1816 Compensation Act, 59 percent of those voting in the House were novices), but inexperienced freshmen divided almost exactly as their veteran colleagues on the internal improvement questions.

In the end these debates, long on passion and rhetorical art, had failed to settle a quarrel that began with the Bonus Bill veto. Instead, they fueled a new campaign to redefine the American Union and tilt the balance of power in federalism, a campaign that would spread and last into Andrew Jackson's presidency—and beyond. By the spring of 1818 the problem of internal improvements embodied the question of liberty and power for a new generation of American republicans.[26]

What Did the Principals Want?

What makes these internal improvement debates at once opaque and profoundly suggestive is the fact that all parties responded to designs (or apparitions) that were thought to lie beneath the surface propositions. Hurt feelings and deep suspicions abounded in Congress and among the people outdoors, some freshly rooted in the bitter treason of the Hartford Convention, others reaching back to the embargo, Jefferson's election, or the crises of the Federalist decade. At the same time enormous creative energies and economic ambitions strained to find expression as the postwar boom multiplied opportunities for truly explosive growth. Even as they celebrated peace and prosperity, Americans worried reflexively that some other class, party, or region was gaining advantage behind the smiling mask of public amity. Still guided by a Manichaean notion of politics that comprehended opposition as subversion or intrigue, American voters and their representatives readily peered behind the curtain, searching for the agents of corruption that their ideology led them expect. Often they found what they were seeking, and the ubiquitous evidence of narrow selfish interest that tainted nearly every appeal to principle seemed to validate the cynical view.[27] As a result, public works seldom were seen as simply roads or river improvements, and policy initiatives easily stood condemned as stalking horses for interested factions and their sinister designs.

What, for example, did Henry Clay want when he pushed so fervently in 1818 for public works by existing congressional authority? Young, brash, driving leader of that party of "War Hawks" who forced the Madison administration into battle, now flush with the "victory" he liked to think he had helped to engineer as a peace commissioner at Ghent, Clay was seen by his colleagues as dangerously ambitious. Impatient and plain-spoken (some thought blunt and, frankly, ar rogant), he cared little for the poses of disinterestedness that marked the firs generation's leadership (of which Monroe survived as an antique example). Lik a boy released from a suffocating apprenticeship, young Clay had seized the rein of the speakership to which he was elected in 1811, determined to defend nationa honor and to *use* the general government to accomplish its fullest purposes Instinct rather than breeding made him an impressive political leader, a genius a legislative management.[28]

Since his return to the speaker's chair in December 1815, Clay had led th campaign to restore the credibility of the federal government in the wake of difficult war. Under his gavel the House had authorized a new central bank an adopted protective tariffs—two of the objectives that together with internal im provements would later constitute his trademark American System. He mad few speeches in the Fourteenth Congress, but he spoke without shame about th usefulness of power. He looked with pride upon the exercise of power to "distrib ute benefits" widely to the people, and he urged as a reason for passing the Bonu Bill in 1817 the "claim to the public gratitude" it would establish in the Fourteent Congress. Clay was frank to admit that conflicts of interest and local feeling inevitably threatened to fracture the body politic; he disbelieved Monroe's tal about a "spirit of conciliation," and he consequently labored always to strengther the Union with bonds of interest.[29]

Whenever he was thwarted by claims of strict constructionists, that he wa bending the Constitution, Clay turned their attention to the "great aim anc object of its framers"—the preservation of the Union. What endangered tha Union now, he believed, was not an abuse of central power but the return o irresponsible localism such as prevailed in the critical period before the Phila delphia Convention. National policies facilitating commerce, the transportatior of "military force and means," even the "circulation of intelligence necessary to the existence of our government" all served the original purpose of the architects of Union. Despite the probable impact of Fulton's steamboats on the western river trade, Clay still predicted that if Congress sponsored turnpikes to connect the Atlantic with the western waters they could retain "in the old channel" two-thirds of the commerce with Ohio Valley states. "Could there be a better basis for the union, a stronger tie to connect the various parts of the country together?" The vision was Washington's verbatim, and Clay never saw the least contradic-tion between strengthening the bonds of Union by promoting internal improve-ments and the survival of the sovereign states: "to them is still left every munici-pal power, and every power essential to their sovereign character as federated states."[30]

Steeped in the fire-tempered nationalism of Madison's wartime government and naturally inclined as a gambler, frontier planter, attorney, and entrepreneur welcome the rush of commercial development, Clay saw his path to the future clearly. So confident was he of the error in the Bonus Bill veto (and Monroe's reiteration of the same) that he had shunned the Barbour amendment and pressed instead for a declaratory bill, apparently hoping that a clear majority (perhaps even two-thirds) would affirm what to him and his friends seemed perfectly obvious: Congress possessed all the power it needed to build roads and canals in the states. That Clay hoped to ride a wave of nationalist feeling into the hearts of all posterity—and into the newly painted "White House" on the way—cannot be doubted; but he seemed to have no more sinister object in view. Hardly a monarchist, as plausible a "common man" as Andrew Jackson, never an abolitionist, not known to be a party to ancient Federalist cabals or aristocratic designs against the rights of the people, Clay wanted to be president of a rising, prosperous nation made up of sovereign states but firmly united by interest and purpose on a grand scale. When he narrowly lost his claim for congressional authority to what sounded like resurgent Antifederalism laid down by hysterical Virginians whose sovereignty, principles, and interests seemed in no way seriously endangered, Clay must have wondered what it was these Virginians really feared?

They said they feared consolidation—at least that was the word emanating from the editorial offices of Thomas Ritchie's Richmond *Enquirer*. Reputed by his enemies (and subsequent historians) to be the leader of a fiercely states' rights 'Richmond Junto" that was said to pull all the strings of Virginia politics, at first Ritchie seemed about as smitten as anyone by postwar optimism. An ardent supporter of the War of 1812, Ritchie had celebrated Clay's congressional belligerence and, in the face of New England's treason, he wrote intemperately of 'Holy Union" as the "pillar of Peace, our Safety, our Prosperity." At the end of the war he eschewed any hint of relaxation: had Americans "no *water-courses* to clear? No *Canals* to construct? No *Roads* to form? No *Bridges* to erect?" Let them not remain the "laughing-stock of strangers" but "seize this precious leisure and devote it to *Internal Improvements*."[31]

Beating the drum for Virginia's own links to the frontier region, Ritchie urged the *Enquirer*'s readers in August 1817 to develop the "Western Trade." State works in Pennsylvania and New York, plus the "National Cumberland Road" that directed traffic toward Baltimore, already reached for the wealth of the backcountry. Steamboats on the Mississippi further threatened to "divest the Atlantic States" of their share of western commerce. But money alone was not the reason to link the James and Kanawha Rivers: commercial ties would "rivet still more strongly" the bonds of Union. "The East and West bound together by the ordinary intercourse of business, and a sense of mutual benefits, will eye with still more jealousy and abhorrence, the wretch who would propose to dissolve or enfeeble the political bands which bind us together."[32]

In his fervor for internal improvements Ritchie sounded much like Clay or

Calhoun—or even Washington before them—but there was an important diffe:
ence: Ritchie feared any loose construction of power to achieve even wortr
goals. In 1816, for example, fearing the creation of a weak, imperfect bank as
result of questionable national authority, Ritchie called for an amendment to th
Constitution to legitimize such a bank and disable its state-chartered rivals. I
his attention to procedural delicacy, Ritchie anticipated by a year Madison
insistence in the Bonus Bill veto, that federal power be enlarged by intention:
action and not by artful construction. (Madison himself embraced the bank wit
no such scruples but later adopted Ritchie's position in the case of roads an
canals.) When the Bonus Bill debates reached the pages of the *Enquirer*, Ritchi
printed a sterner warning against excessively loose construction. Denying that h
resented national power (Virginia's patriotism, he said, was intact but he "depre
cated the conduct of Massachusetts" during the War of 1812), Ritchie neverthe
less called for a "pause in the career we are running." Quoting extensively th
arguments in Madison's 1799 "Virginia Report," he concluded that if one coul
establish "a system of Roads and Canals, on the grounds which have been statec
what power may not the U. States assume?" The popularity of public work
caused him special alarm: "We dread these institutions, the more on account o
the benefits which they promise—because these benefits are calculated to concea
the encroachment on which they are founded."[33]

Three shadings distinguished Ritchie's postwar position from that of Henr
Clay. First, he seemed less eager to forget the recent war and the traitorou
behavior of New England (on which he blamed the failure of the Canada campaign as well as the sack of Washington). Northern states, he thought, harbore
jealousies against Virginia, its culture (a "slave state," wrote one Philadelphian
"no commerce, no manufactures"), and its influence in the government of th
Union. Where was safety for Virginia if a strengthened federal establishment fel
into the hands of bitter partisans in Pennsylvania, New York, or unrepentan
Massachusetts? Second, he wished to see Virginia prosper and develop but he
did not see federal public works as the only (or even the most likely) way to
realize that objective. In Clay's mind, federal public works benefited Kentuck
almost regardless of where they were built: if they did not touch Kentucky's interests then they stood as precedents for others that did. Ritchie saw that federa
aid potentially benefited powerful rivals (New York and Pennsylvania) at the
expense of Virginia, whose influence in the Congress already was diminishing.
Third, he refused to see as innocent any constructive increase of power, and he
tended to conflate ends with means in the internal improvement debates. "Calculated to conceal the encroachment," he charged, Clay's program of distributive
benefits had been *designed* to consolidate power whether or not it built any useful
roads and canals. Maybe Clay believed that Jefferson's Revolution of 1800 had
purged the republic of its Federalist disease, but Ritchie worried (in the words of

Edmund Pendleton's cautionary pamphlet celebrating Jefferson's election) that "THE DANGER WAS NOT OVER." Pendleton had written his dark warning in 1801 to remind a celebrating people of the "melancholy truth" that men in power could never be expected to preserve liberty from destruction. Steeped in a traditional outlook far more negative than that which guided Jefferson, Ritchie feared instinctively the creeping hand of power that fed on "necessary and proper" extensions in pursuit of the "general welfare." He could not look at Clay's objectives without seeing corrupt designs.[34]

One example of corrupt designs that struck Ritchie as too flagrant to deny was the campaign for national supremacy conducted by John Marshall at the Supreme Court. From the beginning Antifederalists had worried that the federal courts might offer safe haven for well-connected malefactors seeking to escape the people's justice, and just such a story was unfolding in the case of John Marshall and the Fairfax claims on Virginia's Northern Neck. Hoping to avoid the loss through revolutionary confiscation of 160,000 acres, the heir of Thomas Lord Fairfax in 1793 sold his inheritance to James and John Marshall, who in turn traded part of the wilderness tract to the state for clear title to the remainder. Armed with this private bill dated 1796 (which said nothing at all about special fees), the Marshalls tried to collect quitrents from their tenants. Northern Neck citizens refused and took the Marshalls to court. In 1805 the Court of Appeals supported the Marshalls' claim, but Justice Spencer Roane filed a blistering dissent. John Marshall, Roane reminded the people, once had promised the Ratifying Convention that Virginians would never again pay feudal dues—and here he was trying to collect them. Encouraged by Roane's scolding (and Marshall's unpopularity in Jefferson's Virginia) people refused to pay, forcing the matter back into the courts. In 1809 Roane found against the proprietors, denouncing the legislative bargain of 1796 and suggesting that the state would own the whole free and clear if not for the Marshalls' greedy maneuvering. Desperate for revenue, Marshall sued to remove the case to the federal Supreme Court under section 25 of the 1789 Judiciary Act. There in 1813 Associate Justice Joseph Story (Marshall recusing himself) ignored the existence of the legislative settlement and affirmed the Marshalls' rents and fees on the whole—including waste lands deeded away in 1796.[35]

Cloaking high political objectives with innocent judicial rhetoric, both of these courts were gambling for power. Whether Story overreached in 1813 out of deference to Marshall's interests or his own fierce commitment to federal judicial supremacy hardly matters. Here was Chief Justice Marshall, surviving Federalist strongman in a Jeffersonian government, author of the hated *Marbury* v. *Madison* ruling, architect of judicial nationalism, and stubborn enemy of the states' rights "Spirit of '98," flouting state sovereignty with tortured constructions apparently for naked private interest. Appalled by Story's "errors," by the high court's breathtaking reach, and by what he took to be a grasping intention by the Marshalls to escape "country" justice, Roane moved in December 1815 to stop such usurpation by claiming final jurisdiction in his own Virginia Court of Appeals. Whereas Story and Marshall repaired for authority to Hamilton's "Publius" essays, Roane chose as his key to the Constitution Madison's 1799 "Virginia Report." Containing, he wrote, "the *renewed* sense, of the people of Virginia" about the nature of the Union, this catechism served a "new Era, in the American republic." Consolidationists might look to the Preamble's "We the People" for roots of a truly national government, but Virginia already had dismissed that expansive language as contradicting the "plain meaning" of the "body of the instrument" and so irrelevant to it. In the end Roane simply rejected Story's decision, declaring section 25 of the federal Judiciary Act—on which rested Story's jurisdiction—"unconstitutional, and void."[36]

Roane's decision amounted to judicial state nullification. In haste Marshall drafted a petition for a writ of error and thrust the case once more on the high court's docket for a term just weeks away. Roane refused even to forward the files. Marshall's attorneys cobbled together the documents, the court heard oral arguments, and in April 1816 Story released *Martin* v. *Hunter's Lessee*, a nationalistic pronouncement even more sweeping than his last. The Constitution, Story stated as a fact on which no disagreement "ought to be indulged," was established by the people, not the states, which people could (and did) "make the powers of the state governments, in given cases, subordinate to those of the nation." Moreover, the charter was intended to "endure through a long lapse of ages":

> It could not be foreseen what new changes and modifications of power might be indispensable to effectuate the general objects of the charter; and restrictions and specifications which, at present, might seem salutary, might, in the end, prove the overthrow of the system itself. Hence its powers are expressed in general terms, leaving to the legislature, from time to time . . . to mold and model the exercise of its powers, as its own wisdom and the public interests should require.

Having thus swept away all ground for strict construction as well as the Confederation model of the Union, Story then claimed as incontestable (even mandated by the Constitution) the right of Congress to assign the Supreme Court appellate jurisdiction over state causes. Stubbornly ignoring Roane's assertions that the case turned not on treaties but on state legislation, Story kept his focus tightly on the fact that Roane was trying to nullify a statute of the United States.[37]

For Spencer Roane, *Martin* v. *Hunter's Lessee* marked the beginning of a death struggle to preserve states' rights from the limitless claims of the Marshall court and other pretenders to consolidated national power. Principals on neither side seemed interested in finding an accommodation. Roane had used the case not to settle the Fairfax claims but to dramatize the dangers of consolidation and advance his neo-Antifederalist principles. Story sought the opposite extreme, taking advantage of Roane's indiscretion to claim greater power than ever before. Associate Supreme Court Justice William Johnson begged for parties to accommodate each other. Roane had assumed "an alarming latitude of judicial power" in striking down an act of Congress. On the other hand, the Supreme Court might have chosen to execute its own judgment rather than insult Virginia's judges with a mandate. Language was "essentially defective in precision," Johnson sighed, and he had found no "good result from hypercritical severity, in examining the distinct force of words." But with Story and Marshall seizing every fragmentary stone in their effort to erect a great national edifice of power, men like Roane took up a brooding vigilance.[38]

Thomas Ritchie shared the views of his cousin, Spencer Roane, about the Marshall court, consolidation, and the Antifederal nature of the Union. Sitting comfortably in 1817 atop the Virginia establishment, together with Bank of Virginia president John Brockenbrough (another cousin), the erratic John Randolph of Roanoke, John Taylor of Caroline, John Floyd, and the young John Tyler, Ritchie saw more to lose than gain by the consolidation of power in the general government. Therefore he took up the cause of opposition to federal power from which he never again would waver (except for the annexation of Texas). The members of Congress from Virginia who staged the 1818 attack on Clay's internal improvement proposals—especially Philip Pendleton Barbour and Hugh Nelson—drew their arguments directly from Ritchie's and Roane's assaults on "constructive" powers. Thomas Jefferson joined their cabal from his retirement at Monticello, guided by his hatred of John Marshall and his persistent belief that a phalanx of Yankee monarchists might yet spring from the bushes of the federal judiciary. By vetoing the Bonus Bill, Madison seemed to repudiate his own and Jefferson's nationalism; and while the so-called father of the Constitution gave no aid and comfort in 1818 to the neo-Antifederalist forces, neither was he sure that men like Clay understood the delicate balance that sustained his beloved Union.[39]

Not everybody in 1818 embraced the kind of polarizing attitudes that motivated strident nationalists like Marshall or particularists like Ritchie and Roane, and nothing yet defined these arguments in regional or sectional terms. Some states' rights radicals could be found throughout the country, while other southern voices vigorously defended a national program of internal improvement. South Carolina congressmen William Lowndes and Eldred Simkins, for example, thought the benefits of national improvements far outweighed any fanciful dangers that Congress or the Court might pose for their constituents. Philip Barbour's brother James, whose amendment stood as the solution Ritchie called for (but did not promote), clung to Jeffersonian nationalism throughout the Monroe era. North Carolina's Bartlett Yancey, another young southern friend of internal improvement, could not understand what was wrong with national roads and canals. At the height of the 1818 debates Nathaniel Macon, the North State's original "Old Republican," spelled it out for Yancey in a private letter using the most frightening terms he knew. Sometimes "great events" took time to unfold, but already he observed there were "colonizing bible and peace societies" forming in the United States: "their intentions cannot be known; but [if] the character and spirit of one may without injustice be considered that of all it is a character and spirit of perseverance, bordering on enthusiasm; and if the general government shall continue to stretch their powers, these societies will undoubtedly push them to try the question of emancipation." Time would be unkind, Macon feared, to southern slaveholding republicans, and the "states having no slaves may not feel as strongly . . . about stretching the constitution." Who would have thought "when Mr. Jefferson went out of office" that his principles "would so soon" become "unfashionable"? Who would have predicted that Madison, "the champion against banks, should have signed an act to establish one"? Who would have believed "that Mr. Monroe" could return from his northern tour as "apparently the favorite of the federalists"? No, warned the dark old voice of worry (not yet prophesy), the "camp that is not always guarded may be surprised; and the people which do not always watch their rulers may be enslaved, too much confidence is the ruin of both."[40]

Birth of a Counterideology

Why lavish our attention on this revolt of the Virginia particularists? They spoke for no party or movement (Old Republicans never really coalesced as a faction, and even the fabled Richmond Junto probably was more of a fiction than a force), their claim to speak for the founders was suspect if not specious, and their "disinterestedness" was seen as a pose by all of their opponents. Proponents of internal improvements mounted logical and forceful arguments supporting their national program, and the interests of Americans everywhere stood to benefit from some well-distributed form of federal aid. Yet the attack on the general government begun by Virginians in 1818 grew into an anticonsolidationist ideology that, during the Monroe administration increasingly nourished a campaign to restore the confederation to what radicals called the framers "original" intentions.[41]

Nobody knew when Congress returned to Washington at the end of 1818 (what we can barely bring ourselves to ignore) that they were nearing a special precipice. If anything, they confidently thought they could foresee the shape of the future. Rhetorical excesses and legislative grandstanding—even threats of disunion—had been the stock-in-trade of politicians at the federal level since the founding, and they continued to be employed freely. It may even be that the sense of well-being that followed the War of 1812 actually encouraged a more daring style of political fencing. But a series of misadventures soon bathed this ritual quarreling in bitterness, leaving an ugly feeling of foreboding in its wake. While crisis after crisis broke over the second session of the Fifteenth Congress, three members of the cabinet—Adams at State, Calhoun at War, and William H. Crawford at the Treasury—along with Speaker Clay and General Andrew Jackson (commander of the southern army) all found themselves distracted by dreams of succeeding Monroe in the presidency. In such an atmosphere, objectives that were merely local, personal, or strategic easily could strike a spark in the Congress that members, had they *known* they stood in a powderhouse, might have labored to avoid. More by accident than design, national politics and the balance of power within the constitutional Union were approaching a turning point in 1819 faster than anybody could have predicted.

The first of these misadventures grew out of John C. Calhoun's attempt to recover through his cabinet position some of the internal improvement ground lost in the Bonus Bill veto. Entering Monroe's administration as secretary of war in late 1817, young Calhoun quickly moved to give shape and direction to the largest federal department with a comparatively huge budget—and a yet-unchallenged tradition of building national public works. Knowing that a peace-time Congress would press to reduce the size of the army, Calhoun rushed to complete a line of coastal fortifications, expand West Point and the engineering program, press an aggressive program of frontier exploration, and organize a permanent command that could be filled up quickly with local militia and raw recruits. Asked if he expected to clash with Monroe on internal improvements, Calhoun replied that his sentiments were "so well known in relation to the constitution" that the president expected him to act "in conformity with my established opinion." With the president's apparent support, Calhoun set to work on some of the most nationalistic undertakings of Monroe's administration.[42]

Henry Clay was naturally sympathetic to Calhoun's designs but wary of the young South Carolinian's ambition and especially the chance that Calhoun might get by executive order results that Clay hoped to claim as his own legislative achievements. Having failed in 1818 to overthrow the Bonus Bill veto, the House Committee on Roads and Canals requested from secretaries Crawford and Calhoun detailed plans "for the application of such means as are within the power of Congress" to make national roads and canals. The question could only be a trap, in light of Monroe's repeated insistence that Congress had no such power. Crawford ignored the request, but Calhoun took the bait. Deftly stepping around Clay's constitutional snare, he acknowledged the "intimate connexion" between the defense of the nation and its "improvement and prosperity"; indeed, he thought a "judicious system of roads and canals" serving civilian purposes would constitute the "most efficient means" of a complete national defense. But he had been asked to confine himself to narrower concerns of strictly military necessity. His first objective (in addition to the coastal fortifications already under contract) was a great inland coastal waterway from Boston to Savannah with which to frustrate a blockading naval power. The transappalachian links so central to Gallatin's plan now seemed likely to be built by states or rival cities, but roads and canals on the northern and southern frontiers must fall to the federal arm. As the "*basis* of a system" and the beginning of a "plan" Calhoun urged Congress to direct a survey of the various routes he described.[43]

Calhoun's report, dated 7 January 1819, was an olive branch of sorts. "Should Congress approve" of a "military survey" of roads and canals, he offered the army as a source of engineers and labor, and he volunteered to have "disbursements" made by the War Department. Where chartered companies or states already were at work, subscriptions in aid might be appropriate; elsewhere work might be done on contract, with officers of the engineer corps supervising operations. He closed by listing those frontier roads on which troops already labored on so-called fatigue duty. In a cabinet meeting called to discuss this report, Monroe fretted that Clay's appeal to department heads (bypassing the president) constituted an "irregularity." Adams did not think so. The real problem lay in the fact that Calhoun, like so many members of Congress, disagreed with the need for a constitutional amendment. Still, he had avoided taking sides against the president, and his recommendations were in line with actions Monroe already supported. The report was approved to go forward.[44]

Oddly, Clay did not wait to receive Calhoun's report before launching his attack on the War Department's road-building program. Out of the blue on 6 January (one day before the date of Calhoun's document), House Ways and Means chairman Samuel Smith suddenly moved to take up military funding. Probably with Clay's connivance, Henry St. George Tucker rose to ask where in the military appropriations bill he could find money for the roads that Calhoun was building. Having been forced, Tucker argued, to fight the administration (and his Virginia colleagues) for "every inch of ground" pertaining to internal improvements and the Cumberland Road, he thought it was "proper" to ask by what authority the executive undertook similar projects? Clay jumped in, begging to know the same thing—not for himself, he said (bowing with sarcasm) but for congressmen Barbour and Nelson, conservative Virginians in danger of voting for things in disguise that they ardently opposed in the open. Barbour thanked the speaker not to worry: he opposed internal improvements but not appropriations to maintain the army. Gleefully Clay asked, would not Barbour's principles prevent him from "voting to pay men who are thus to be unconstitutionally employed"?[45]

Uncertain where this debate was headed, members fired off all kinds of missiles until late in the afternoon, when Smith read a note from Calhoun explaining that $10,000 of the quartermaster's budget was intended to go toward extra road-building pay. The following morning Kentucky's David Trimble moved to deduct from the quartermaster's line the amount of $10,000 and insert instead an appropriation for "extra pay" for soldiers "employed in constructing and repairing military roads." Clay then uncloaked his intention: he wished to present Monroe with a practical bill appropriating money for national roads and say to him "here it is—sign it or not sign it." If he refused, Clay threatened to "withhold every appropriation until he conceded the point." It was a surly gesture, but Clay believed the people were with him. Conventional wisdom in Washington already marked Monroe as a powerless man. "The House of Representatives," wrote Joseph Story, "has absorbed all the popular feeling and all the effective power of the country." Treasury Secretary Crawford privately admitted what he would not say in public, that a majority in Congress would indeed support internal improvements without a constitutional amendment. And in the end Clay got his Trimble amendment and Calhoun got his money; but nobody believed internal improvements had been legitimated.[46]

A second major problem, the panic of 1819, resulted from erratic world market fluctuations following the end of the Napoleonic Wars and fueled cruelly in the United States by the land-and-cotton boom that was making so many Americans rich. The panic of 1819 as it was *experienced* by contemporaries, however, was a "paper bubble" (Jefferson's term), a speculative disaster stemming from the reckless expansion of the currency, made worse by the sordid operations of the Second Bank of the United States. That the bank received blame for more than it deserved cannot be doubted; but for understanding the impact of the crisis on federal policies and political ideology, it is enough to expose the bank's record of incompetence, fraud, and embezzlement, juxtaposed with Chief Justice Marshall's pronouncement of its final constitutionality, all played out against the backdrop of crashing land and cotton prices, failing state and local banks, declining government revenues, and private bankruptcies—especially in the West, where state relief laws often seemed a man's only defense against well-to-do out-of-state crooks.[47]

The trouble with the national bank began immediately in 1817. Taking advantage of the private authority within this mixed corporation (private stockholders elected four-fifths of the directors), President William Jones and a band of intensely self-interested directors virtually hijacked the new central bank, subverting all requirements (most notoriously the requirement to stock the vault with specie), expanding loans (often to themselves) far in excess of authorized limits, and covering their misappropriations by freely issuing notes to all who desired them. Eighteen branches floated drafts on each other, never bothering to transfer funds, until the summer of 1818, when total system obligations exceeded

reserves ten times over! Retrenchment—specifically requiring state banks to re
deem in specie and ordering branches not to pay notes issued by other branches—
started the downward spiral. By October a government call for $2 million in
specie to pay off the Louisiana Purchase (virtually all the cash in the bank) could
not be met.[48]

As state banks collapsed and the currency crisis deepened, alarmed members
of Congress launched an investigation that verified the ugliest rumors. The
bank's directors blithely had accepted each others' notes in lieu of specie for
capital stock installments, paid themselves dividends on stock they did not own
and kept control by rigging elections with fake registrations and powers of attorney. Hardly misinterpretations of law, these were flagrant crimes, purposefully
indulged by men who claimed it was their right, as private investors, to manipulate their bank for maximum gain. Virginia's James Johnson, an old-school hater
of banks, moved to repeal of the firm's charter, but the House showed a curious
disinclination to punish the institution. On 25 February, by a large majority (121
to 30) it rejected repeal. Langden Cheves replaced William Jones as president
and he was handed a writ from Congress requiring the bank to justify itself; but
armed with unusually clear evidence of official malfeasance, even self-appointed
guardians of public morality such as Virginia's Hugh Nelson chose not to redress
this wrongdoing.[49]

It may have been the intimate involvement of certain members that blunted
the congressional temper, or perhaps it was the darkening skies of the panic itself
that dissuaded lawmakers from taking precipitate action. By February 1819, cotton prices in Liverpool had turned (American prices soon would drop from
thirty-two to fourteen cents) and over the next several months the force of the
international stringency ruined banks, commercial firms, and private fortunes
Ways and Means chairman Samuel Smith's company, Smith and Buchanan,
came down "in a crash that staggered" the city of Baltimore and helped expose
the dishonorable dealings of the Baltimore branch of the Second Bank of the
United States. Henry Clay accumulated tens of thousands of dollars in debts as
friends failed whose notes he had endorsed. Men argued in Congress that closing
the national bank at a time like this, whatever its crimes or culpability, was
unwise, perhaps unlawful. Such arguments fed paranoid fears that no corporation, once created, could be made to pay for the hardships it engendered, and this
hardened irrational antibank feeling out of doors. David Walker of Kentucky
wondered if the all-powerful national bank, if backed up by the Marshall Court,
did not endanger states' rights more than efforts to restrict slavery in Missouri.[50]

Barely more than a week later, the Marshall Court pronounced exactly such a
blessing on the bank as Walker predicted. Political friends of state-chartered
banks had been searching for ways to protect their creations from the return of a
federal competitor, and Maryland's solution was to tax the notes of banks not

chartered by the state. The Baltimore branch objected, giving rise to the suit of *McCulloch* v. *Maryland*. Hearing the case in late February 1819, exactly when Congress was debating whether to repeal the bank's charter, the court kept its attention tightly focused on constitutional questions. Taking no notice of the scandals, the unfolding panic, or the merits of this particular (deeply flawed) bank, Marshall affirmed in the boldest terms yet his sweeping understanding of the extent of implied powers under the Constitution. Contrary to Maryland's claim (made to bolster its views of state sovereignty), the Constitution did not emanate from the states but established "emphatically, and truly, a government of the people." Wherever the ends were legitimate and the means not specifically prohibited, and Congress acted within its limits. The bank itself thus sustained, Marshall denied any right of Maryland to tax it: a tax could effectively destroy the bank, absurdly contradicting the will of Congress.[51]

Marshall's ruling in *McCulloch* v. *Maryland* considerably narrowed the Tenth Amendment's reservation of power to the states, a tenet that was central to the Spirit of '98 and the Virginia doctrines of neo-Antifederalism. Here Marshall reserved almost nothing to the states except what was local and self-contained, and he gathered under the umbrella of federal supremacy all things not prohibited by the Constitution—as construed by his court and no other authority. Much of this was old ground for nationalists and states' rights radicals alike, and nothing but the persistent force of Marshall's claim that the court should decide—and the fact that *he* got to speak for the court—gave his arguments force. What was new were the conditions into which Marshall's arguments fell. Until now consolidationist language had promised much and cost very little. But as scandalous crooks like the Baltimore bankers suffered exposure but not conviction, and as the hated bank itself recovered its losses through contraction and foreclosures, popular sympathy for Marshall's economic nationalism momentarily receded. A hard-money critic of the 1830s put it succinctly: "The Bank was saved, and the people were ruined." Even Nicholas Biddle, newly appointed director of the bank and soon to be its most famous president, complained to his friend James Monroe about the unfairness of the law: if a postal employee "embezzles or secretes the smallest amount of property confided to him he may be publicly whipped and imprisoned for ten years," whereas an officer of the Bank of the United States "may defraud the institution of millions & escape the criminal law of the United States." In the depths of the panic of 1819, Marshall's nationalistic vision seemed to shelter not the people but their oppressors.[52]

In Ohio, a state much abused by the national bank, authorities greeted the *McCulloch* decision by exacting a tax of their own and seizing by force some $50,000 from the vault of the Chillicothe branch (for which the agents of Ohio promptly were arrested by a federal marshal). In states across the West—Tennessee, Kentucky, Illinois, Indiana, and Missouri—democratic lawmakers adopted schemes aimed at stopping local collections (measures almost as obnoxious to Marshall as state nullification). By 1820 even Congress was moved to pass debt relief legislation. In Richmond, Virginia, the Junto sprang into action once more. Cheered by the fact that Marshall's nationalistic claims now shielded the vastly unpopular bank, Thomas Ritchie, Spencer Roane, and John Taylor launched a propaganda offensive that furthered the process by which Virginia's neo-Antifederalist rhetoric would acquire status as a legitimate understanding of American federalism.[53]

Ritchie's campaign began 30 March 1819 with the publication in the *Enquirer* of an essay by "Amphictyon" (now believed to be Judge William Brockenbrough, another member of the clan that included cousins Ritchie, Roane, and Bank of Virginia president John Brockenbrough). Amphictyon refuted Marshall's theory of the founding in favor of Virginia's claim that the states, not the people, had forged the compact of the Union. Such revisionist history gained plausibility wherever people wished to remember a founding that primarily supported states' rights. More damaging was a second effort 2 April to discredit the effects of Marshall's ruling: accept Marshall's doctrine, Amphictyon argued, and Congress may spend money on roads and canals or "create boards for internal improvement," build universities or even churches, and incorporate companies for all kinds of purposes.[54]

Northern nationalists such as Joseph Story thought nobody believed the antiquarian diatribes that filled the pages of Ritchie's *Enquirer*, but Marshall himself took serious alarm and wrote two essays as "A Friend to the Union" trying to contain the virus before it gained new credibility. Spencer Roane weighed in next with four ponderous essays signed "Hampden," each topped with the headline "Rights of 'The States,' and of 'The People'" and carrying a footnote containing the text of the Tenth Amendment. Roane sounded the alarm against a dangerous "judicial *coup de main*" that would extend by simple assertion, through the words of *McCulloch* v. *Maryland*, a "*general* power of attorney" to Congress to legislate on all matters. People "sodden in the *luxuries* of banking" might be careless of their liberties, but Roane intended to speak "with the spirit of a freeman" against this creeping tyranny. Deftly touching the "hot buttons" of republican propaganda, Roane proceeded to ridicule Marshall's tortured dilations on the nature of "necessary" powers (*McCulloch's* most vulnerable passages) and he likened the "latitude of construction now favored by the supreme court" with that "which brought the memorable sedition act into our code." Posing as a fair-minded patriot, Roane pretended to object not to the enlargement of federal power but to the dishonest means of the consolidationist court: "Let us extend their powers, but let this be the act of the *people*, and not that of subordinate agents." It was a masterful political argument. Whatever the merits of his legal opinions, Roane brilliantly deployed the rhetoric of natural rights and republican self-government while fixing on Marshall the hated objective of "consolidation." Marshall answered with nine more pieces in the *Alexandria Gazette*, but nothing he wrote could recapture the ground Roane had seized.[55]

Of course, the most dramatic confrontation of 1819—the one that seeded abstract principles of states' rights radicalism with urgent, tangible interests—touched on the status of slavery in Missouri. On 13 February 1819, after weeks of rancorous debates about military appropriations, Andrew Jackson's conduct in the Seminole War, and misbehavior at the national bank, James Tallmadge Jr. of New York proposed amendments to an act that would enable Missouri to prepare for statehood. First, he moved to prohibit the further introduction of slaves into Missouri, and then he proposed freeing the children born of slaves already there when they reached age twenty-five. One of the architects in 1817 of New York's similar emancipation program, Tallmadge appeared to be continuing his antislavery work on the southwestern frontier (although contemporary charges and his own record of party changeability suggest less elevated motives of personal ambition may have been at work here as well). Whatever his true purpose, Tallmadge's motions caught a wave of northern sympathy. Slaves constituted only 16 percent of Missouri's population in 1819—not much higher than in New York when it began emancipation a generation before. What a perfect time and place to take the next step in what most Americans (including southerners) had *said* they desired since the founding of the Union: the end of African slavery.[56]

Tallmadge's amendments sparked an "interesting and pretty wide debate," most of which unfortunately was not transcribed by Gales and Seaton's reporters. Speaker Clay opposed the restrictions, partly on the grounds that Congress had no right to attach conditions to an incoming state; but he also introduced the South's increasingly popular "diffusion" theory, that the cause of abolition was best served by *extending* slavery into the West. Other southerners lined up behind Virginia's now-familiar views about the limits of federal authority and the sanctity of states' rights: Philip Barbour likened conditional admissions to "shearing one beam more of sovereignty" from new states. Friends of the Tallmadge amendments made bold to argue that slavery flatly contradicted republican government, and while it had been tolerated in the old states this was no reason to extend it to the new. Heaping scorn upon the peculiar institution and its apologists, Arthur Livermore dared his colleagues either to redeem "national character" or "declare that our Constitution was made to impose slavery," not "establish liberty."[57]

Tempers rose steadily as slaveholders felt the sting of northern critics who laughed at their paternalistic guises and taunted them to tell no "idle tales" about "the gradual abolition of slavery." By the third day Tallmadge himself took the floor to decry the "violence" and "intemperance" of debates in which disunion had been threatened freely, along with civil war! But far from calming the assembly, Tallmadge delivered a blistering sermon on the evils of slavery, which he said his constituents hated "in every shape." Referring to yesterday's arguments he asked, were members who spoke against slavery now to be accused of treason and threatened with execution (like Arbuthnot and Ambrister)? And still people sought to encourage and extend to Missouri this "monstrous scourge of the human race?" If civil war, "which gentlemen so much threaten, must come, I can only say, let it come!" With such a defect as slavery spreading in the Union, he thundered, "your Government must crumble to pieces, and your people become the scoff of the world."[58]

The decorum of the House in shambles, a solid block of northern members proceeded to pass the Tallmadge amendments over even more solid southern opposition. Bitter partisans on either side had unmasked new sectional agenda: some northerners apparently stood ready to contain (perhaps to terminate?) slavery, while some planters in the South drifted toward an unashamed insistence that the right to exploit human chattel was essential to American freedom. Raw numbers told the frightening truth, that the free states of the North, once animated by a sectional passion, soon could dictate national policy. Only the Senate's refusal of the Tallmadge amendments saved Missouri from "outside" abolitionists, setting the stage for a year-long propaganda war before the Sixteenth Congress finally crafted a compromise package. Even then, New York senator Rufus King's bitter denunciation of the three-fifths clause (by which the South up to now had held its grip on national power) gave notice of a sectional intention to beat the slaveholding states out of their predominance in Washington and turn the federal government into a servant of northern regional objectives. In this way, the Missouri debates served up dark proof for the enemies of consolidation of what jealous northerners would do with centralized power if ever freed from constitutional restraints.[59]

The importance of Tallmadge's amendments came into focus slowly through the balance of 1819. "Congress are about to assemble and the clouds look black and thick," wrote old John Adams in November, pointing to the Spanish treaty, Missouri, the clamor for protective tariffs, bankruptcies, banks, "perhaps even the monument for Washington" as items that were likely to raise great controversy.[60] Since the spring, noisy public meetings in the North had seemed to verify a willingness to sacrifice the South upon an alter of emancipation. Jefferson and Madison as well as others saw it always as a plot by unrepentant Federalists to split the Republican Party and climb to power again. President Monroe agreed and downplayed the crisis in his 1819 message to Congress; but soon enough Missouri talk overwhelmed the Washington community, "awakening sectional feelings," according to Clay, and "exasperating them to the highest degree." The words "civil war, and disunion" were "uttered almost without emotion," and one senator was heard to say he "would rather have both" than lose the Missouri restrictions. Slaveholders could not hear the speeches of Rufus King (reported Adams) "without being seized with cramps." Monroe's cabinet could not agree about the power to bar slavery from a state. Crawford thought it could not be done, but Adams felt that it could—if not by the Constitution, then by the Declaration of Independence. Slavery, he argued (indiscreetly for a man in conference primarily with slaveholders), was not a "sovereign power" but a "wrongful and despotic power" that could not be instituted by any legitimate republican government. Walking home with Adams that evening, Calhoun suggested that Adams's principles were true but applied only to "white men," which brought another outburst against a "vicious" Constitution that pledged "the faith of freedom" to perpetuate the "tyranny of the master." If "the Union must be dissolved," Adams concluded in his diary entry (but did he actually say as much to Calhoun?), "slavery is precisely the question upon which it ought to break."[61]

Slowly waking to the magnitude of danger, Henry Clay finally engineered acceptance of a compromise suggested by the Senate, linking the admission of Maine and Missouri (balancing the Senate, where slavery was safe from sectional majorities in the House) and adding (as a sop to the eighteen northern "doughfaces" who abandoned the Tallmadge amendments) the exclusion of slavery throughout the balance of the Louisiana Purchase north of the 36°30′ line. Monroe signed the bill 6 March, and the Washington community breathed a collective sigh of relief; but men like Adams grieved the loss of a moral opportunity, while Thomas Ritchie gave words to the darkest fears the southern master class: "If we yield now, beware.—they will ride us forever." Perhaps to quiet this extremism into which both sides had fallen, Jefferson broke a self-imposed vow of public silence and sent a letter to John Holmes of Massachusetts designed to highlight the importance of the compromise, not the confrontation: "This momentous question, like a fire bell in the night, awakened and filled me with terror," wrote the Republican patriarch. "I considered it at once as the knell of the Union." The states' rights radicals had done their work, and now Virginia's neo-Antifederalist theories circulated widely in opposition circles as the pure milk of original republican intentions. But the point was to restore the Confederation model of the Union, not to break up the Union altogether.[62]

Press On Regardless

Two convictions, each of them centering on consolidation, emerged in people's minds as they reflected on the calamities of 1819. Some Americans thought they saw the sinister designs of old Federalism returning, supported as usual by stock-jobbing bankers but made more dangerous now by the addition of fanatical abolitionists. Concentrated in the South and scattering into the West (but never only there) such people began to view the world through Ritchie's states' rights lens, and they drew their understanding of liberty and justice from new revisionist political treatises such as John Taylor's *Construction Construed and Constitutions Vindicated* (1820) and *Tyranny Unmasked* (1822). In these learned and forceful works, Taylor found the "original" sources of the American Union not in the propaganda of Publius's *Federalist* or in the rulings of John Marshall's court but in natural law, the universal law of nations, the state ratification conventions, and such anticonsolidationist documents as Madison's 1799 "Virginia Report." An agrarian, a liberal, and a slaveholder, Taylor conceived of the people as the community of landowners and of governments as necessary evils, prone to corruption, and far more likely to threaten property than promote the general welfare. His contribution lay in crafting a history of the founding that would sustain the principles of states' rights radicalism through the critical 1820s (until the interests of the next generation could be knit together into a genuine southern sectionalism). Old Virginians such as Taylor, Jefferson, and Roane, all living links to the founding generation, labored to control and redirect their usable past because they feared and resented what they saw in their country's future. In the process they reenergized a negative rhetoric of watchfulness that did not require real harmony of interests to sustain a community of opposition.[63]

The second conviction growing out of 1819 ran in just the opposite direction. Some frightened observers detected what looked like a movement by narrow-minded planters to disempower the federal government, default on promises implicit in the Constitution, block commercial and industrial development, and sacrifice every national interest to their singular fixation on protecting their peculiar institution. Viewed from this perspective, the possible spread of Virginia's states' rights doctrines signaled an urgent need to shore up authority in government and strengthen the bonds of Union before those local jealousies that Monroe and every president before him had denounced destroyed forever the hard-won gains of the Constitution. In response to the panic of 1819, Pennsylvania's Mathew Carey, long an advocate for systems of improvement, sketched out a program of domestic development through tariff protection and public works investment aimed specifically at forging a national market where different interests and sections would find mutual prosperity instead of competition. Carey's works offered consolidationists a theoretical foundation (as John Taylor's works did for states' rights), and Henry Clay drew on them freely as he began to press in Congress and outdoors for what he called the American System.[64]

Clay previewed his rapidly maturing thoughts on a systematic program of national development during an 1820 speech supporting protective tariffs. Reliance on foreign markets for staple crop exports, Clay argued, undermined American independence. In fact, we had become "a sort of independent colonies of England—politically free, commercially slaves." Domestic manufactures, on the other hand, promised to developed home markets and foster economic independence, contributing in the bargain to "the preservation & strength of our confederacy." Gentlemen might agree about the need for home markets, Clay admitted, and still doubt the government's role: "let things alone," they argued, "and all will come right in the end." So it would, but only after "a long period of disorder and distress, terminating in the impoverishment, and perhaps ruin of the country." "Free trade" and the popular liberal "maxim" of "let things alone" in fact were not practiced by European states with ancient, mature economies. Why impose them here in America, where "every thing is new and unfixed," and therefore in greater need of protection? Our table "is now loaded" with petitions, he concluded, playing the popular card. "Let us not turn a deaf ear" to the people.[65]

Ever since the Bonus Bill veto Clay had kept an ear turned toward the people, and he believed that popular demand for policies adequately justified their passage. Such was the simplest meaning of democratic self-determination. Now Congress neared the end of another contentious session that was long on obfuscation and short on action dealing with the currency, banking, declining federal revenue, or a national bankruptcy act: Clay asked with palpable frustration, What shall we tell our constituents? The House responded in April 1820 by passing his tariff bill, but the Senate refused it by one vote, causing Baltimore journalist Hezekiah Niles to call for disciplinary action by the voters.[66] Impatience was mounting among the friends of developmental government, and the idea spread that things could not *truly* be unconstitutional if most of the people desired them. Strident prophets of negativity would always remain, howling about rights and warning against consolidation; but it fell to genuine statesmen (by this line of thinking) to press on and govern regardless.

While consolidationists and their enemies quarreled bitterly over power and principles, advocates of particular roads and canals pressed their objectives as if the larger general issue were not related. At the War Department, Secretary Calhoun answered calls for engineering help in behalf of canals in Illinois, Ohio, and (of all places) Virginia, as well as road-building projects in Iowa, Louisiana, Mississippi, Tennessee, Georgia, New York, and Maine. In Congress, friends of the Cumberland Road fought annually to preserve appropriations to complete (and increasingly repair) that rapidly deteriorating turnpike and extend it to the Mississippi River. Sponsors of the Chesapeake & Delaware Canal still sought a stock subscription from Congress (widely thought to be constitutional without an empowering amendment). Refusing to be hobbled by consistency, westerners who used states' rights language to thrash the national bank nevertheless demanded territorial highways and "3 percent" set-aside schemes to funnel money from the sale of federal land into roads and canals for new states. Rival corporations begged for aid to canals around the falls of the Ohio at Louisville—one in Kentucky, one in Indiana. Visionaries already talked of canals linking Lake Erie with the Ohio, Lake Michigan with the Mississippi, and the Tombigbee and Tennessee Rivers. The states and their mixed corporations were "busily employed in planning and executing systems of internal improvements," observed Kentucky senator Richard M. Johnson; "shall Congress invigorate the spirit of enterprise, which characterizes the States and the people of the States, by timely and reasonable appropriations, or shall we refuse our aid, and thus indirectly condemn, and positively protract, that system which will give to this nation so much wealth, so much power, and so much union?"[67]

The extension of the Cumberland Road squeezed through the Sixteenth Congress in the waning days of an exhausting first session, but bankruptcies, Missouri, and declining federal revenues depleted the lawmakers' energies. Other than a brief Senate discussion of an Ohio and Erie waterway and a stillborn House proposal for granting land to state-made canals, the second session did almost nothing more about aid to internal improvements. After 1821, however, economic recovery brought a return of confidence and new pressure on Congress to act. At the end of the Sixteenth Congress, Henry Clay retired from the House to repair his ruined fortune (and also to assess the political winds and prepare his campaign for the presidency). In his absence, like-minded members of the Seventeenth Congress entertained appeals from states and their citizens for aid to various roads and canals, military highways, river and harbor improvements, the Chesapeake & Delaware Canal, and the Potomac navigation. Old Nathaniel Macon from North Carolina continued his prophetic warnings: "Commence these roads, and there is no telling where it will end; for legislation might be compared to shingling a house—the first row is useless unless you go on, lapping one row over another to the top." Still, improvers once more grew optimistic.[68]

Buoyed by evidence of popular demand, the House Committee on Roads and Canals in 1822 ventured to report another forceful proposal for a national system. Reiterating Gallatin's claim, that certain projects could not be done by state or private enterprise, committee members listed five examples of urgent national projects: the Atlantic coastal waterway; a Washington-to-New Orleans road; canals around the falls of the Ohio and connecting that stream with Lake Erie and the Potomac; a waterway linking the Susquehannah with New York's Finger Lakes drainage; and canals linking the Tennessee with the Savannah, Alabama, and Tombigbee Rivers. The report culminated in a bill for a program of surveys to "lay the foundation of a well-digested and regular system," that would enable Congress "the better to decide on the propriety of engaging in these undertakings." New York State's bold and ambitious example was held up to prove that governments could mount public works "with dispatch and economy" and that public credit could pay for the work. West Point cadets, argued Joseph Hemphill of Pennsylvania (still a Federalist but destined to abandon Clay and Adams for the Jackson movement) could perform these surveys cheaply, gaining valuable experience for the army while gathering expert information perfectly free from local partiality. The time was right to commence a system; the greatest burden of expense would be deferred until such time when the improvements themselves helped pay the debt; and the power of Congress to do so had been settled by precedent (if not by presidential blessing). Nothing came of it in 1822, but two years hence this General Survey Bill would replace the Bonus Bill as the central piece of legislation in the national campaign for a system of internal improvements.[69]

Meanwhile, repairs to the Cumberland Road focused the next big confrontation. This first great national road had been neglected by the states through which it passed and quickly fell into a state of disrepair. Having barely finished the work to Wheeling (and having just authorized its extension to the Mississippi River), Congress now faced the difficult question of how to maintain—at whose expense and by whose authority?—a road that many states' rights radicals believed never should have been built. Supporters in the Senate introduced a bill to erect toll gates for the "preservation" of the road, hoping to burden its users rather than taxpayers at large and eliminate the fights for appropriations that invariably sparked constitutional debates. In the House, John W. Taylor moved to cede the road to the states through which it ran, dismantling forever this hated example of national public works. Taylor's motion lost two-to-one even though the toll gate bill itself received a narrower approval of 87 to 68 on its third reading.[70]

Apparently pushed too far by this resurgent latitudinarianism, Monroe finally struck back. With "deep regret," he wrote, "approving as I do the policy," the president vetoed the bill erecting toll gates on the Cumberland Road. He felt "compelled to object" because the "power to establish" these gates implied "a power to adopt and execute a complete system of internal improvement," and the latter he could not support. He then attached a 25,000-word treatise that he said was the fruit of ruminations on the subject since the beginning of his presidency. Starting with the overthrow of royal authority, Monroe traced the evolution of government from the Articles of Confederation through the Constitution. Always a Virginian, he distorted the story just enough to praise state governments for promoting "the diminution of their own powers" in order to enlarge those of the general government. But still an honest Madisonian, he also acknowledged that the people, not the states, had formed the Union. As the "highest authority known to our system," the people had the power (if they chose to use it) to create for themselves a great nation, "one community, under one government. They wisely stopped, however, at a certain point . . . making the National Government thus far a consolidated Government, and preserving the State governments without that limit perfectly sovereign and independent of the National Government." Two "complete sovereignties" thus existed, each circumscribed within limits, each a "representative" sovereignty, for "real sovereignty" remained "in the people alone." Because the people had drawn the federal boundary, only the people by amendment could alter it. Therefore, an amendment was required before Congress could proceed with a system of internal improvement.[71]

Having checked (he hoped) the worst neo-Antifederalist heresies, Monroe turned to the much more elusive question of where the line had been drawn between the states and the federal government. With excruciating patience, learning, and historical sense, the president waded through all the arguments that ever had been offered in behalf of the power to build roads and canals, and he rejected every one. If he did not share the conclusions of the neo-Antifederalists, that the Union was a mere confederation, Monroe nonetheless affirmed their every argument for why the Congress did not posses the power to send out "men of science" running surveys, "take land at a valuation," "construct the works," regulate their use, "raise a revenue from them," or "keep them in repair." At the same time he insisted that "such a power vested in Congress and wisely executed would have the happiest effect on all the great interests of our Union." Ask for an amendment, then, to enlarge the power of the Union: it can be done by no other means.[72]

Monroe's pronouncement only heightened the stalemate. The improvers' majority in the House disappeared as the vote to override failed 68 to 72. Congress stood prohibited from doing what the people (and the president) wanted because the guardians of constitutional balance feared the prospect of further encroachment. By demanding an amendment that could not be secured, Monroe empowered the neo-Antifederalists he clearly intended to disarm, yet by approving of a system of roads and canals he also encouraged the improvers to cling to their agenda. An amendment would clear away objections, but improvers dared not press for it now because the neo-Antifederalists had staked the limits of a redefined Union far less powerful than the one that was ratified originally. If they killed an internal improvement amendment, this could affirm their new interpretation and undermine powers long acknowledged, opening the Constitution to eventual recision, clause by clause. As long as states' rights proponents insisted on restoring the confederation model, nationalistic improvers pressed ahead wherever they found votes to act—thereby proving themselves "guilty" of aggressively loose construction.[73]

Renewed talk about a system of surveys, together with the controversy stirred by Monroe's veto of the Cumberland Road toll gate bill, produced another flurry of popular demands from the states and private corporations for federal aid to roads and canals. Most appeals were transparently self-interested, but some were more generous than others. Anticipating aid to the Potomac navigation, for example, the legislature of Maryland promised to "highly approbate, and zealously co-operate" with any program of public works "best calculated for the interests of the Union at large, and especially of this State." Frontier states begged for land grants and aid to build roads into nearby territories, mixing freely as justifications military defense, postal service, the government's duty to facilitate settlement, and the increasing value of lands in the public domain once internal improvements were made. Opponents still warned that any gift was "but a beginning" that would run into endless commitments; but often (as in the case of a Tennessee congressman speaking against a road in Michigan) these principled objections "fell" from members whose states begged preferment themselves. In 1823 the House revisited the General Survey Bill. Philip Pendleton Barbour, now speaker of the House, moved to kill it, trying to "determine at once" if a majority "would or would not commence" a "system" he believed was unconstitutional. Pennsylvania's Hemphill, author of the bill, agreed that its purpose was to foster the design of a "general system," and then he spoke for hours reviewing all the proofs for internal improvement. Barbour's motion failed in a thinly attended House, after which the bill itself was tabled. The next day Silas Wood of New York (revealing that state's conversion to strict construction now that the Erie Canal was successful) delivered the contrary argument, decrying the "fashionable" habit, "the cant of the day," of calling every subject of "general utility" a "national subject." Once again the bill was tabled by a close vote, and then a large majority (including many friends of the bill) refused to consider it further.[74]

The demand for internal improvements clearly was mounting, and if the "cant of the day," changed the minds of no states' rights members of Congress, it seemed increasingly to represent the popular desires of the people. Traveling widely through Kentucky and Ohio during his brief retirement from Congress (collecting debts for the national bank and support for his presidential campaign), Henry Clay decided that the people were ready to support his developmental vision, and he prepared to return to Washington. Secretary of War Calhoun (another candidate) arrived at the same conclusion: "The people are for internal improvement, domestick manufacturers, &c., &c." Addressing the incoming lawmakers in December 1823, President Monroe opened a hole in his own constitutional levee by suggesting that Congress might "authorize by an adequate appropriation" (no amendment required) the assignment of army engineers to surveying roads and canals—an invitation congressmen eagerly accepted. It looked as if the Eighteenth Congress finally would measure the mood of the country and test the progress of consolidation.[75]

A Legislative Victory

Filled with hope, Congressman Hemphill reintroduced his bill for a system of surveys by army engineers, this time shrewdly leaving all route selection to presidential discretion and stressing that no constitutional objection could be raised to such a routine executive task as ordering out the troops. Heralding a new era, in which "the spirit of the nation" justified national action, Hemphill opened debate 12 January. Philip Barbour entered a brief defense of originalis states' rights dogma, adding one new argument that probably revealed Virginia's greatest fear: federal disbursements necessarily would fall disproportionately outside Virginia. But spending was always redistributive, scoffed Clay: otherwise "we should restore to each man's pocket precisely what was taken from it." Hopelessly distracted at the moment by underground presidential politics, Clay delivered an uninspired speech too freely toying with Monroe's arguments in his 1822 treatise and placing incautious weight on his own "philological" conviction that the power to "establish" post roads obviously meant power to build them. Silas Wood rose again to denounce consolidation, and Vermont's Rollin Mallary expanded on Wood's fears, warning that the government would soon seize control of state roads, perhaps even the new Erie Canal. With New York on the verge of claiming through innovation the commerce of the interior, he wondered if Congress could resist demands from disappointed rivals to redistribute trade in the name of interstate "fairness." Both sides agreed that, while the bill before them called only for surveys, the real intention of this measure was to launch a general system of national internal improvements.[76]

For three solid weeks of mind-numbing argument the advocates of public works rang familiar changes on the sources of road-building power—the post office mandate, national defense, commercial regulation, the right of appropriations, and the "necessary and proper" and "general welfare" clauses. Opposing speakers (once again almost exclusively from Virginia) met them thrust-for-parry with dire warnings about the progress of consolidation and the "prostration of the States." Pennsylvania's Andrew Stewart gave a stirring review of the record of past public works (lighthouses, beacons, piers, post roads, and fortifications), the relative neglect by Congress of the West, the danger to the Union of centrifugal forces, and the urgent need for consolidation. "Defeat this bill," he concluded, "and you give the death-blow to the best hopes and best interests of the nation." Pass it (along with the tariff) and the Eighteenth Congress would "be hailed by future generations as having laid the foundation of a system of policy which would soon raise this nation to the high and brilliant destiny that awaits it."[77]

Of course, nothing frightened states' rights radicals quite like these visions of national grandeur resulting from intentional policy, and the Virginians flocked to denounce them. William Segar Archer reminded the House that the point of the Constitution was to limit their power, not enlarge it: the "importance of the work" simply could not make it constitutional. Articulating Virginia's trademark agrarian liberalism, Alexander Stevenson added that roads and canals *always* were local, *never* national, and were executed better by the states, best by private enterprise. Unequal spending, he continued (in a new tack offered by several

Virginians to soften their apparent particularism), must inflame desperate jealousies among the states—placing the Union in far greater danger than the naturally uneven process of local development. Dark conspiracies filled the radicals' scenarios, of men in office grasping for power, relentlessly pursuing the destruction of the state governments. If Congress can act to improve interstate commerce, argued Randolph of Roanoke, can it not just as surely "*prohibit*, altogether the commerce between the States"? And take notice, "every man who has the misfortune . . . to be born a slaveholder," that "if Congress possesses the power to do what is proposed in this bill . . . they may emancipate every slave in the United States—and with stronger color of reason than they can exercise the power now contended for." Here, on the public record, was the warning that Macon had circulated privately for years, linking neo-Antifederalist principles to the defense of the peculiar institution.[78]

Doubtless this fear of emancipation helped feed the development of southern sectionalism that flourished in the years just ahead; but Randolph and Macon were famous cranks, and in 1824 prominent slaveholders such as Clay and Calhoun still led the campaign for national internal improvements.[79] Constitutional fundamentalism and neo-Antifederalism (younger members such as William Cabel Rives invariably referred to "this Confederacy" rather than "the Union") continued to dominate Virginians' rhetoric, as if principle alone guided their political obstructionism. This time, however, Old Dominion's spokesmen opposed not just the improvers' loose construction of power (Monroe's position, and Madison's) but also their developmental vision itself. Never one to mince words, Randolph sneered at the "pathetic ejaculations" he had heard about the suffering of the West. In his mind too much had been done for the West already—lands purchased, Indian treaties signed, frontier states admitted with skeletal populations. Too profligate to develop themselves, westerners now begged the Congress to stimulate their growth so they might prosper and drive original states such as Virginia into relative insignificance. At the founding, calculated George Tucker, Virginia wielded one-sixth of the power in the national government; now her share was one-tenth and rapidly declining. New York currently enjoyed Virginia's former rank (thanks to its Grand Canal) but in ten or twenty years the "fertile valley of the Mississippi" would overwhelm it too. The bill "comes too late," argued Alexander Smyth, revealing perhaps more candidly than he intended both the self-satisfaction and the limited vision of Virginia's ruling class. Links from the East to the West were "made already"; the New York canal was complete, and Virginia had done all it needed. The present "scheme" was "deceptive," appearing to "confer benefits on the States" while primarily consolidating power in the national government.[80]

As they had since the first Bonus Bill, improvers found important support among Calhoun's friends in South Carolina. George McDuffie (soon to remake himself, like Calhoun, into a fire-eating states' rights radical) delivered a spirited rejoinder as soon as the parading Virginians resumed their seats. They had "conjured up a phantom which they denominate consolidation," and McDuffie endeavored now to "exorcise" that demon. All powers could be abused, and liberty depended not on paper structures but the accountability of officials to the people. "Destroy this tie, and any portion of power" could generate despotism; preserve it and the "ordinary powers of Government"—state or federal—became "both safe and salutary." Virginia was no "barometer of the national feeling on this question"—McDuffie doubted if the people of Virginia even comprehended the "metaphysical" productions of their politicians. Let us have, he said, the "*splendid* government" Virginians so feared: let it promote "the happiness, the wealth, and the security" of the people; let it provide "substantial ties of commercial interest" to bind the Union; let us "substitute moral for military glory" and "create, by our common toil and common treasure, some great monuments of the enterprise of the nation, which the people of this Union will contemplate with a common pride and regard as their common property."[81]

Looking back on these debates, it seems that Americans in 1824 inescapably faced a public choice. The world the framers had cherished—organic, predictable, cyclical—always had been tainted with nostalgia and now stood visibly crumbling before the onslaught of what we know as the "century of progress." The revolutionary generation had hoped that by creating good governments they could exempt themselves from cycles of decay they believed resulted from corruption; but the market revolution just ahead was caused by liberty, not tyranny, and it seemed to wield unprecedented force. American republicanism had promised that right structures would yield correct policies, tempting statesmen (who now increasingly were mere politicians) to avoid deliberation and conscious choice by resorting to constitutional exegesis: we cannot choose what the framers did not choose! In the face of the new era, such a practice faltered. Thanks to the profound ambiguities embedded in the framers' handiwork, the Constitution could be stretched to embrace a modernizing vision—or it could with equal plausibility prohibit innovations not foreseen a generation earlier. Both sides portrayed themselves as innocents. Improvers posed as midwives to a destiny beyond their control. This was true; but staggering expenditures and irreversible changes surely would follow from their program, resulting in injuries that private individuals and local communities understandably sought to avoid. Virginians prided themselves on their love of liberty and the Constitution, in defense of which they saw only themselves (and maybe North Carolina) arrayed against the heedless juggernaut of change. But their obsession with their own fading preeminence never slipped entirely from view.[82] Everybody came to these debates guided by fear, desire, or ambition, and they had to make a choice where the outcome could not be controlled (the very definition of statesmanship). What

Virginians feared—and what almost surely would befall them either way—was that public choice in an expanding national community would not accommodate their particular desires.

A call of the roll on 10 February brought the exercise to a close. A solid majority (113 to 86) voted to engross the General Survey Bill for a third reading in the House. The next day by an unrecorded vote the bill was passed and sent to the Senate. Virginia was joined in its opposition by New York and the New England states, where much had been done already and little benefit was expected, and by ideological North Carolina; slave-dependent South Carolina and Georgia split their votes despite Randolph's lurid talk about emancipation, while the West, free and slave, cast not a vote against internal improvements (Table 2). Granting Virginians their claim, that they only loved the Constitution, states' rights convictions accounted for probably less than half the negative votes, or less than a quarter of the whole. More telling, thirteen out of twenty-four state delegations embraced without a dissenting vote the promise of internal improvement—and presumably the vision of consolidation. Considering the exhaustive debates spread across the pages of the newspapers and the strength of the vote in the House, it would be hard (but, we shall see, not impossible) to argue that the people in 1824 did not understand and apparently approve the public choice being made in their behalf.

In the Senate, Thomas Hart Benton of Missouri tried to introduce a measure of control and political ownership over the final design of the system by offering a substitute bill that specified exactly which projects merited national attention. John Holmes of Maine voiced the standard "Virginia" opposition. Richard M. Johnson of Kentucky dismissed Holmes's worries: this bill *made* no roads but authorized surveys only—to which John Taylor of Carolina responded with appropriate reference to the "foolish Trojans" and their wooden horse. Benton's amendment failed on a tie, and eventually the Senate passed the House bill 25 to 21. Again, with virtually no states' rights tradition to stand on, New York and New England lent their solid, interest-based support to the "principled" objections of Virginia and North Carolina. The Middle Atlantic states (except Delaware) favored the bill, as did the West (two senators dissenting, but *not* Andrew Jackson, who voted silently for it). As in the House, South Carolina split. So by April 1824, seven years after the Bonus Bill veto, internal improvers stood possessed once again the possible shell of a system of national public works.[83]

Did the General Survey Act finally mark the beginning of a program fondly imagined by every president since Washington yet postponed for so long by combinations of theoretical and "interested" opponents? Perhaps—but maybe not. Monroe signed it 30 April, apparently content that the Constitution was

TABLE 2. General Survey Bill Votes, 18th Congress, 1st Session,
House of Representatives, February 1824

	Yea	Nay
New England	11	26
Maine	1	5
Vermont	0	4
New Hampshire	0	6
Massachusetts	8	5
Connecticut	0	6
Rhode Island	2	0
Middle Atlantic	45	26
New York	7	24
Pennsylvania	23	2
New Jersey	6	0
Delaware	1	0
Maryland	8	0
South Atlantic	15	34
Virginia	6	15
North Carolina	1	12
South Carolina	5	4
Georgia	3	3
West, Free	17	0
Ohio	13	0
Indiana	3	0
Illinois	1	0
West, Slave	25	0
Kentucky	10	0
Tennessee	7	0
Mississippi	1	0
Louisiana	3	0
Alabama	3	0
Missouri	1	0
Totals	113	86

Source: *Annals*, 18th Cong., 1st sess., 1468–69.

Note: The vote is to engross for a third reading in Committee of the Whole. The roll call on final passage in the House was not recorded.

reserved (or at least grateful for the face-saving modesty of this preliminary step). The bill itself was but an authorization, charging the president to "cause the necessary surveys, plans and estimates to be made of the routes of such roads and Canals as he may deem of national importance in a commercial or military point of view, or necessary to the transportation of the publick mail." To that end, secretary of War Calhoun organized a Board of Engineers and ordered it to sift among proposals and petitions (the tide of which swelled again because of the passage of the bill), select the truly national routes, and send forth teams of engineers. If we take the December 1824 report of that board as a guide, Calhoun construed the bill broadly as an order to design a national system. Already on his preliminary agenda stood a Potomac canal to the Ohio and another from the Ohio to Lake Erie; various improvements in the Ohio, Mississippi, and Tennessee Rivers; the extension of the Cumberland Road; the Atlantic coastal waterway, comprising canals linking Barnstable, Buzzard's, and Narragansett Bays, the Delaware & Raritan and Chesapeake & Delaware Canals; and a "durable road" from Washington southwest to New Orleans. Several other routes, after full investigation, might be added to round out the system. Calhoun seemed to treat the matter as a fait accompli.[84]

Henry Clay probably was cheered by the passage of the General Survey Act, but it did not divert his preoccupied mind from the crucial tariff debates that immediately followed (or the presidential scheming that overshadowed everything). Convinced that he could win back the votes of New York and New England (dissenters on roads and canals) by protecting home manufactures, Clay laid down in March another forceful brief for home market development. Thinking the Virginians in retreat, Clay mocked their insistence that the Constitution forbid both public works and the protection of domestic manufactures: if so, it must be a "most singular instrument" made "for any other people than our own." Invoking the "saving spirit of mutual concession" under which the Constitution had been drafted, Clay asked his colleagues in the House to "imitate" the framers' courageous "example" and adopt a "genuine AMERICAN SYSTEM." The bill before them was less of a system than a grab bag of favors given out industry by industry; but enough of Clay's colleagues concurred that a program of protection by special legislation was begun.[85]

Taken together, the Tariff of 1824 and the General Survey Act could have been—and could have been seen to be—foundation stones for a new federal policy. Such was the intention of the rhetoric, and also what the states' rights radicals feared when they thought of consolidation. At the same time, both bills, and the American System idea behind them, could be seen just as well as invitations to various interests to look for plunder in the national treasury. This second outcome was equally despised by states' rights radicals, yet their opposition would contribute to its realization. Only the element of design implicit in consolidation could rescue these programs from the rush of plunderers, yet the rad‌ cals hated design and control as much as they hated corruption.[86] Curiously, ou‌ side of Congress, the people paid relatively little attention to these landmark ac‌ For all the present year (and several months of the past), except for the routi‌ reprinting of congressional debates, the papers—even Ritchie's *Enquirer*—h‌ devoted their columns almost exclusively to the men and maneuvers that ma‌ up the game of presidential politics. Americans lost themselves in 1824 in the fi‌ real presidential contest since the revolution of 1800. But lacking nearly all t‌ required apparatus for a meaningful national campaign (and inclined to think‌ presidents in largely emotional terms), they conducted less a policy referendu‌ than a national game of comparative personal celebrity. The results would ‌ disastrous and would alter profoundly the national political culture and t‌ future of internal improvements.

5

Spoiling Internal Improvements

A S THE PRESIDENTIAL election of 1824 drew near, it might have seemed as if a national system of internal improvements lay just over the horizon. Most of the leading candidates were either strongly in favor of federal action or had not come out openly against it. The General Survey Act authorized the gathering of detailed information with which the administration or the Congress could assemble a system of national projects. Alas, developments prevented the realization of this potential and set the stage for the destruction of the nationalist ideal represented by the Gallatin Plan. One was an unseemly scramble for preferment that followed the passage of the survey bill itself, drawing into the legislative process such a swarm of special interests that neither Congress nor the White House could (or would) impose design. The other was a campaign of political revenge conducted by the friends of Andrew Jackson for what they thought was theft of the presidency in 1824 by John Quincy Adams, Henry Clay, and their supporters. Claiming that "the people" had been cheated of their choice, the Jacksonians coupled their opposition with Virginia's neo-Antifederalist movement to fix upon the younger Adams the taint of illegitimacy long associated with Alexander Hamilton, old John Adams, the hated Alien and Sedition Acts, corruption, monarchy, and class rule. In this campaign Jackson's friends redeployed the Spirit of '98 and those revolutionary-era fables that always portrayed a virtuous people struggling against corrupt and wily governors. That a corrupt and wily people might disable virtuous government was not a possibility anybody could yet imagine.

The spoiling of internal improvements that took place during the Adams administration included both senses of the term "spoiling." In the hands of Congress armed with the General Survey Act, roads and canals became mere spoils of victory as surveys were ordered for ever more obscure creeks and byways. Lacking the political or moral authority to impose order and design (in part because of the campaign against his own legitimacy), Adams further spoiled the national system by accepting pork-barrel methods in place of a coherent design, because he (rightly) feared he could proceed no other way. Although he tried in his infamous First Annual Message to Congress to raise the sights of the legisla tive body, nothing could prevent a democratic Congress from indulging in the patronage and benefits implied by federal aid to local roads and canals.

The forces that buoyed the Jackson movement, wrecked the Adams admin istration, and spoiled the national system of internal improvements reflected two great fears that had stalked the American experiment from the first days of the Revolution. One was the enduring fear of monarchy and class rule, and while seems implausible to us, men and women in a world still governed by royalty saw real danger from an evil they had escaped not so long ago. The second fear was of the oft-denounced tendency of men in office to abuse their power, building u networks of support for their continuance by handing out favors, benefits, an offices to unscrupulous armies of placemen. As democratization proceeded it was the people themselves who plagued the government for favors, yet they con tinued to respond to the rhetoric of old that decried the tendency of "ministries to subvert the people's virtue.

Feeding off this process of democratization was the capitalist market revolu tion. Schooled by experience to fear navigation acts, bounties, monopolies, tar iffs, and restrictions—all designed in former times to benefit favorites or enrich the government—most Americans gravitated unconsciously toward laissez-faire the liberal "free trade" promise that the end of interference in the marketplace guaranteed equality for all. Having no experience yet with consolidated power in the hands of private firms and corporations, most Americans believed that libera markets favored business on a human scale. Lingering amid their assumption was the hope they could enjoy the fruits of economic development withou sacrificing local control or the easy access to opportunities they believed wer essential to the legacy of freedom. Thus when Adams announced that he though liberty *was* power and promised to stimulate and shape economic developments doubters took alarm on both the liberal and conservative ends of the politica spectrum.

Striking an intentionally ambivalent pose in the face of this market revolution Andrew Jackson won the hearts of Old Republicans and new market liberal alike by attacking Adams and Clay and their blueprint for planning and develop ment. Shrewdly sensing that the people wanted rhetoric *and* benefits, Jackson never promised to stop the flow of aid to local projects of internal improvement Once in office he struggled to deliver patronage and virtue simultaneously, finall trusting more-or-less unregulated markets to generate prosperity while the whip of party regularity bound his factious constituents to the fold. Turning on inter nal improvements in May 1830, in an effort to stop Clay's American System Jackson brought on the final destruction of the concept of "system" and ordered retreat from interlocking policies on a national scale.

An Electoral Fiasco

It might have fallen to the presidential election of 1824 to try to resolve the constitutional dilemma that had plagued internal improvers and states' rights radicals during the Monroe administration. Return to the people was the mantra of republican purists, and a presidential election was the closest thing going to a general canvass of the voters. But presidential politics in 1824 were frightfully imperfect. Americans never had been happy with the method for electing their "Chief Magistrate." Obsessed with the fear of demagoguery, the framers had adopted byzantine procedures that failed to anticipate party nominations or even distinguish between candidates for president and vice president. States named electors who nominally were free to choose anyone for president. In the first contested election of 1796 these procedures yoked together (absurdly) the campaign rivals, John Adams and Thomas Jefferson, in one administration. In 1800 the same flawed procedures produced a tie between Jefferson and Aaron Burr, tempting Burr and some angry Federalists to attempt to displace the obvious victor. The Twelfth Amendment (1804) closed this loophole, giving parties effective control over the top of the ticket. An informal caucus of Republican congressmen then guaranteed their success against the Federalists by fixing nationwide attention on a single pair of nominees. Electors themselves were named by the state legislatures, by voters who elected them in districts, or on statewide "general tickets"—and local pols changed these procedures often to manipulate the outcome of elections. Virginia, birthplace of the Republican movement, home of the party's most talented leaders, and proud caster of the largest bloc of electoral votes, tightly controlled the caucus—and the presidency—through the next five elections.[1]

Dissatisfaction with this "Virginia Game" grew steadily as other states and regions resented Virginia's presumptive claim on the executive, its prestige, and its patronage; but factional divisions among Republicans in New York and Pennsylvania and the survival of Federalism in Massachusetts disabled potential rivals. By 1817 everybody knew that James Monroe must be the last of the present dynasty, but after Monroe who should stand—or run—for office? How should he be nominated? On what basis should the voters choose? There were no rules and hardly any underlying principles to guide political innovators. Most states by 1824 had given the vote to virtually all adult white males, but the impact of this new democracy could not yet be predicted. With their Federalist enemies destroyed, Republicans in the congressional caucus now seemed interested less in saving the Revolution than in preempting the people's choice, and friends of all the candidates but William H. Crawford turned against the caucus as a fraud. Republican tradition proscribed active campaigning. The role of the president as a party leader or a champion of programs had not yet found legitimate expres-

sion, so no one knew what to say about his favorite—except that he did not see
the office and would never use the power to favor his friends, his interests, or hi
geographical locale. But, of course, no other reasons existed for preferring on
candidate to another, so a "popular" election would turn on exactly those issue
that etiquette barred from discussion.[2]

Monroe had taken office fully aware that the scramble for succession mus
accompany his whole administration, and he brought into his cabinet in 181
several likely candidates representing each of the sectional interests kept at bay s
long by Virginia's control. Georgia's William H. Crawford at Treasury had beer
Monroe's fiercest rival in 1816 and was the choice of the decaying caucus for 1824
Secretary of State John Quincy Adams, a New Englander with Republica
credentials reaching back to 1807, held the place reserved for the heir since the
beginning of the "Virginia Game." By his appointment Monroe seems to have
intended to signal it was time for a northern succession. Young John C. Calhour
(he was only thirty-six when he joined the administration) developed his ambitions while transforming the War Department into an engine of national development. Henry Clay, the "Harry of the West," refused appointment to the
cabinet, preferring to manage his campaign from the speaker's platform in the
House of Representatives, where he led a systematic opposition to Monroe and
the Virginia party.[3]

As Monroe's second term gradually expired, these contenders and their friends
adopted different strategies for securing election. Crawford sabotaged his president wherever possible and clung to the favor of the Republican caucus (Adams
styled him "a worm preying upon the vitals of the Administration within its own
body"). For his part, Adams performed his diplomatic functions with frosty
brilliance and hoped that the rights of the northern states to have a president,
together with his intellect, integrity, and long years of public service would bring
the desired result. Sensing narrowly sectional foundations beneath each of these
contenders, Calhoun launched an intentionally nationalistic bid, hoping his
sponsorship of roads and canals, fortifications, Indian negotiations, and western
exploration would bring recognition and gratitude from electors across the country. Clay pursued a similar strategy, openly proclaiming in Congress and at occasional campaign dinners the "prominent measures" that constituted his American System, in the process linking his candidacy closely to a legislative program.[4]

Newspapers polished the image of their favorites and vilified the others, often
printing forgeries and fictional attacks, the refutation of which occupied rival
prints for weeks and kept the public entertained if not enlightened. Misinforma-
tion filled the papers, mostly touching character (rarely issues or candidate positions), and "truth" often floated on a sea of mere plausibility. Crawford was
attacked for corrupting the Treasury (in charges that were not exactly true), yet
the press never mentioned that paralytic strokes had left him truly incapacitated a

ear before the election! Taking unfair advantage of the comic misadventures of
he War Department's Yellowstone Expedition, Crawford attacked Calhoun for
wasting money extravagantly, while his Old Republican allies accused all rivals of
plotting "consolidation." Adams was denounced as a Federalist ("his father's
on") and as an enemy of internal improvements (a mistake built on the fact that
New England Federalists typically voted against a national system). Adams tried
o correct this last impression in a letter explaining his position going back to
Gallatin's famous report; but nobody in the West would believe him, while
Virginians who inclined his way (as a substitute for Crawford should he die)
recoiled and lurched absurdly toward Henry Clay instead. Clay was portrayed in
Indiana as a slavery expansionist (because of his role on Missouri), in the Deep
South as a restrictionist (because of his role on Missouri), in Ohio as a heartless
bill collector (for the Bank of the United States), and as a reckless gambler
everywhere. Nobody quite knew the protocol: how or how much to address the
electorate, and whether to promote their man or deflect the lies and deceptions of
others.[5]

   Behind all the posturing, local pols seeking patronage and influence brokered
commitments in whatever forum would pick the electors—state assemblies or
caucuses, innovative nominating conventions, or old-fashioned "junto" offices—
while the candidates worked their private networks of correspondents. Who
could win? By what combination of supporters? What would be the practical
result of throwing in with this or that man? These were the issues that dominated
private letters. As early as 1822 Henry Clay seemed completely obsessed with
electoral strategy, and his hundreds of surviving letters for 1823 and 1824 deal with
little else. Were Virginians so committed to Crawford, Clay asked Francis T.
Brooke, that they would "hazard all consequences"? It seemed of no importance
that leading Virginians hated his American System: what was that compared to
backing the winner? Calhoun likewise schemed among his friends, seeking nominations and endorsements that might fall, like dominoes, to spell out victory.
Convince the "leading men" of Maryland, he counseled Virgil Maxcy, "that Clay
and myself are the only two, who are openly in favour of a system of internal
improvement." Because the West approved already there was nothing to be
gained electing Clay; but as a southern man, Calhoun could hold that section *and*
"do most to effect this great object of national policy."[6]

   None of this elaborate scheming anticipated the most dramatic innovation of
1824 that would transform a simple donneybrook into a system-altering event.
General Andrew Jackson occasionally was mentioned by friends in Tennessee as
a possible candidate, but (to quote Thomas Ritchie's *Enquirer*) "we never supposed by anyone, seriously." The popular hero of New Orleans lately had been
smeared by reports of arbitrary tirades and by acrimonious debates in Congress
over his murderous conduct in Florida during the Seminole War. Having retired

to his plantation since the Army Reduction Act, Jackson the "military chieftain, a hot-tempered man without breeding, education, or experience in office, struc almost no one as a plausible candidate. "Incomprehensible" wrote Albert Gal latin. "Violence is in his blood," shouted Clay. "He is one of the most unfit men I know of for such a place," pronounced the aging Jefferson. Precisely because h was dismissed universally by leading politicians across the country, Jackson' manager, John Henry Eaton, decided to invent and then expose a great conspir acy against the people's right to elect their own president—a conspiracy from which General Jackson alone could rescue the American people. Through the artful pages of *The Letters of Wyoming*, appearing first in 1823 in the *Columbian Observer*, then in pamphlet form in 1824, Eaton crafted America's first revolt o the outsiders against the Washington establishment.[7]

There was a time, Eaton began, baiting his trap with venerable images o General Washington, when "no controversy existed as to who should" be presi dent. Nobody asked if Washington could "write a paragraph with classical pu rity" or practiced perfectly the "finished" arts of "intrigue." There was "virtue" i America then; but now the "leading men . . . like Alexander's generals" maneu vered "after power," ready to "stake the happiness of their country on the succes of some favourite." The "original design of the Constitution" intended for "th freemen of the nation" to call some "meritorious citizen to this high and dis tinguished post," but now "intrigue" passed for "talent" and "corruption" had "usurped the place of virtue." The ancestors had feared that "an elective govern ment could not endure," that some day the people would surrender their virtue for interest. Had such a period arrived?

> Look to the city of Washington, and let the virtuous patriots of the country weep at the spectacle. There corruption is springing into existence, and fast flourishing, Gentlemen, candidates for the first office in the gift of a free people, are found electioneering and intriguing, to worm themselves into the confidence of the members of congress, who in support of their particu lar favourites, are bye and bye to go forth and dictate to the people what is right.[8]

Here was a paranoid tract worthy of the 1760s, warning of Walpolean corrup tion and calling the "yeomanry" back to revolution: "If you are freemen act fearlessly as such; or at once surrender and be slaves." The rhetoric invoked the strictest construction of the Constitution, whose meaning to the "man of ordi nary intelligence" was as "plain and obvious," as "the Holy Bible." "Usurpation" was condemned, as was the "ARISTOCRACY . . . rising in our land." But to what great dangers did *The Letters of Wyoming* refer? Considering the recent cam paigns of the Virginia radicals, one might have expected Eaton's tirade to con demn public works and consolidation. Yet according to *Wyoming*, grave danger lurked not in the policies or programs of the government but in the caucus (Virginia's instrument), in campaigning for office, and in the claims of the politicians that experience, learning, or superior achievement ought to qualify men for advancement. Particular scorn fell on "THE LEADING MEN of the COUNTRY," especially those with access to federal patronage, which they were said to manipulate for personal advantage. Crawford (the man least associated with Clay's American System) took the greatest drubbing by name, and the program of retrenchment recently demanded by Virginia radicals—especially army reduction and the drastic cuts in fortifications and defensive public works—was the only recent policy initiative singled out for critical notice. Practically every one of Eaton's hundred pages focused on faulty electoral procedures, the alleged conspiracy in Washington, and the virtues of Andrew Jackson.[9]

Despite references to original intention and strict construction of the Constitution, Eaton's *Letters of Wyoming* owed nothing to the opposition movement Virginia radicals had been building since the War of 1812. Eaton was constructing for Jackson out of older republican cloth a coat of virtue and simplicity that made other candidates appear to be draped in ancient, British-style corruption. The argument was cut to order perfectly: every fault in Jackson became a virtue. Not a dangerous chieftain but a patriotic warrior, only Jackson had "bled" for his country on fields of glory. He alone "rested" on his farm while others schemed and scattered favors, angling for votes. He alone *lacked* polish, education, and experience—all proofs of a taste for courtly intrigue. He did not desire election; "none certainly" had "courted it less." Other presidential hopefuls paraded their accomplishments in college, on diplomatic missions, or in different branches of the federal service, but what were these to the honest yeoman of the country? Jackson too had been in Congress (sent there by the people against his own desires), but he had never been "in Europe" and never the "HEAD OF A DEPARTMENT." What he had been was "head of an army contending for independence, and for his country, and repelling the invaders of her rights."[10]

To anyone familiar with the presidential game in the 1820s, Eaton's interest in a Jackson presidency was perfectly transparent. (Indeed, Eaton found his just reward, not in Heaven but as the head of Jackson's War Department.) The hysterical rhetoric with which he condemned both the candidates and procedures of 1824 rivaled Jefferson's worst fulminations against the "Monocrats" of 1800. By erecting a phantom conspiracy and making an emotional appeal directly to the people, Eaton tapped once again the deep roots of revolutionary fervor that had nourished the Spirit of '98 and then had found an enduring place in the rhetoric of the Jeffersonian "persuasion." Anti-institutional, anti-intellectual, and essentially libertarian, these popular sentiments deflected all attention from programs, policies, or candidates' qualifications, and flattered the instincts of a people who in fact were not inclined to study national affairs or take the large, "disinterested" view. It fostered the belief that virtue alone prepared a man for public service, that there was nothing to the science of statecraft except character.

Whatever might have been wrong with the presidential game in 1824—and clearly nobody found it satisfactory—statesman of experience could hardly welcome or applaud Eaton's strategy on Jackson's behalf. Yet here it was, spread across the Pennsylvania papers, and having the desired effect. In a rush of enthusiasm in March 1824, the delegates to Pennsylvania's new nominating convention overthrew the arrangements of the pols (who favored Calhoun) and voted Jackson 124 to 1! The bandwagon swept into Maryland, New Jersey, and North Carolina, then on through the South and West. Letters to the newspapers repeated the warnings of *Wyoming*, adding almost nothing new and frequently repeating Eaton's phrases word for word. By November 1824, when all the ballots were counted, Jackson held the largest number of electoral votes and an even larger share of what was called (prematurely) the popular vote. Had it not been for the Constitution (that required an absolute majority of electoral votes), Jackson would have won the 1824 election. As it was (and Eaton had invited such an outcome in *The Letters of Wyoming*), the election was thrown to the House of Representatives.[11]

Nobody honestly believed that the presidential canvass of 1824 reflected the opinions of the people on programs or policies—nor, in six states with appointed electors, did it even yield a sense of popularity among the candidates. Barely 25 percent of the voters took part in the election, and their choices supported no clear pattern of interpretation. Responding to what he took to be the mood of the West, Henry Clay had come the closest to campaigning on the promise of a program. He won only 37 electoral votes; but most objections to Clay turned on personality, and men *seeming* to promise similar programs (Adams and Jackson) together claimed another 183 electors. Adams could not shake his enemies no matter what he said, yet he collected 84 votes; Crawford could not lose his friends despite his hopeless physical infirmities, and he polled 41. Jackson won 99 electoral votes vaguely promising "judicious" tariffs and "National" internal improvements while he tilted at phantom hordes of placemen to reclaim the government for virtuous republicans. Where the people voted for Jackson, they voted to be saved from corrupt politicians who they thought planned to rob them of their liberties. But the people had been shammed: there was no conspiracy, nor was there evidence that Jackson's friends desired less ardently to seize the honors and offices of government. Skeptical observers could not fail to wonder if such "popular" elections cultivated anything more than the demagoguery that so frightened the framers a generation before.[12]

The failure of the 1824 election placed John Quincy Adams in a difficult personal position. Adams knew himself to be far from popular. "Cold, austere, and forbidding" were his own judgments on his personality, and he had done nothing in his long career to endear himself to a mass electorate. Adams first had entered the public fray in 1791 with an anti-Jacobin attack on Tom Paine (and therefore his American enthusiast, Thomas Jefferson) for dazzling the people with the "party-colored garments of democracy." In the early 1800s, as Jeffersonians in power showed a willingness to govern (and New England Federalists drifted toward the treasonous Hartford Convention), Adams joined the Republican Party; but he never abandoned his faith in the elevating powers of reason and discipline in politics. The point of liberation, he believed, was to cultivate human improvement. Since 1815 Republicans everywhere (except for the states' rights radicals) seemed to be moving in that general direction, and in 1824 it looked as if the breakthrough might be at hand. Now Adams stood upon the threshold of power, the one candidate (other than Clay) who was certain to proceed with national development, yet bested in a four-way race by the worst display of demagoguery since Jefferson's campaigns against Adams's father. Two possibilities loomed: enlist the support of any one of the contestants and rescue the power of the presidency; retreat before the claims of the so-called popular vote, and watch the experiment in rational government be torn apart by an inflamed democracy. How could Adams distinguish temptation from duty?[13]

The outcome of the drama is well known. After weeks of intrigue in Washington, congressmen from the three Clay states threw their votes to Adams, raising him to the presidency on 9 February 1825. Shortly after, Clay accepted an appointment as secretary of state. Jacksonians howled that through "bargain and corruption" Clay and Adams had stolen their election. "The *Judas* of the West," roared Jackson, "has closed the contract and will receive the thirty pieces of silver. his end will be the same. Was there ever witnessed such a bare faced corruption in any country before?" The lawful procedures established by the framers, and reiterated by Jefferson's people in the wording of the Twelfth Amendment, had produced the Adams election. To this day there is no proof of a deal beyond the fact of the appointment itself. Everyone in Washington was angling for something that winter. For notorious brokers such as Martin Van Buren to object, as he did, that "the people" had been cheated, strains credibility then and now. Legitimate considerations could just as well have moved Clay supporters toward Adams without any reference to the makeup of the cabinet, and Clay was a logical choice for the State Department job. At the same time, no proof of innocence could ever contradict the "evidence," when viewed through the lens of *The Letters of Wyoming*, that leading men at Washington, with arrogance and forethought, had overthrown the people's choice.[14]

The Grandest of Visions

With a tragedian's sense of foreboding, Adams took up the yoke of the presidency determined to do what was "right"—and convinced he would likely be despised for it. Adams's historical appreciation for the Constitution, with all the perils attendant to freedom and self-government, received brief exposure in the Inaugural Address, but in his First Annual Message to Congress in December 1825 the tremendous force of his anxiety and hope found expression in a stunning political composition. "I might not be destined to send another," he told his worried cabinet; however flawed his election, he felt an "indispensable duty" to suggest "these views." At stake was the American experiment.[15]

The president reviewed with satisfaction the state of the Union in 1825. The treasury at home was flourishing. The Board of Engineers for Internal Improvement, created the previous year under the General Survey Act, was actively exploring routes for roads and canals all across the land. Moral, political, and intellectual improvement were "duties assigned by the Author of Our Existence," for which governments were "invested with power." To "the attainment of that end—the progressive improvement of the condition of the governed—the exercise of delegated powers" was as "sacred" as the "usurpation of powers not granted" would be "criminal and odious." Employing both the style and vocabulary of seventeenth- and eighteenth-century moral philosophers—John Locke, David Hume, Adam Smith, Thomas Reid (all of whom he studied as a youth)—Adams offered a short course on the nature of the republic and its mission on earth. Steeped in Protestant religion or faculty psychology (or both), revolutionary leaders had hoped that liberty would foster improvement, that citizens would cultivate their "higher faculties" once they enjoyed the freedom and encouragement to do so. So convinced of this had been President Washington that he often recommended to Congress the creation of a national university, where improvement could be gained through knowledge. Shamefully, no university had been started: the "spot of earth" that Washington "bequeathed" for that purpose remained to this day "still bare and barren."[16]

Shielded for the moment by the name of Washington, Adams proceeded with a stinging critique of present-day Americans as a people who drew freely from the stock of human knowledge but did not labor to contribute their share. For the fifteenth-century voyages of discovery that gave birth to America, he thought, we still owed "a sacred debt" to the world. Even now Great Britain and France spared no expense in patronizing research into weights and measures, earth science, and astronomy. It was "with no feeling of pride as an American" that Adams counted in Europe 130 observatories but "not one" of these "light-houses of the skies" in the American hemisphere. If knowledge provided the footings for moral, political, and economic progress, then Americans were not tending their foundations. The Old World, supposedly corrupt and decaying, surged ahead; but "upon our half of the globe," and the earth revolved "in perpetual darkness to our unsearching eyes."[17]

Astronomy, of course, was not the point but just an example of what worried the new president. His countrymen's lack of scientific interest reflected a preoccupation with selfish gain, private ambition, and jealous individualism that their fathers had associated with degeneracy and dissipation. People might object that patronizing science and exploration was unconstitutional, but Adams could not believe that a constitution adopted by men of the framers' intelligence intended to prohibit the exercise of sovereignty where local and private agents failed. (Could the framers have been, he once asked in print, "so ineffably stupid, as to deny themselves the means of bettering their own condition"?) In fact he felt required by the nature of the Constitution to act in cases where improvement *might* result: to "refrain" from doing so constituted "treachery to the most sacred of trusts."[18]

Having established that Americans' exceptional freedoms laid on them a duty to humankind (if not to God), Adams closed with a soaring peroration that pressed his argument to a splendid consummation:

> The spirit of improvement is abroad upon the earth. It stimulates the hearts and sharpens the faculties not of our fellow-citizens alone, but of the nations of Europe and of their rulers. While dwelling with pleasing satisfaction upon the superior excellence of our political institutions, let us not be unmindful that liberty is power; that the nation blessed with the largest portion of liberty must in proportion to its numbers be the most powerful nation upon the earth, and that the tenure of power by man is, in the moral purposes of his Creator, upon the condition that it shall be exercised to ends of beneficence, to improve the condition of himself and his fellow-men. While foreign nations less blessed with that freedom which is power . . . are advancing with gigantic strides in the career of public improvement, were we to slumber in indolence or fold up our arms and proclaim to the world that we are palsied by the will of our constituents, would it not be to cast away the bounties of Providence and doom ourselves to perpetual inferiority?[19]

Here was a picture of liberty rich with the cautions of the revolutionary gentry. All freedoms were contingent, and all people were required in the end to account for their use of such a gift. The close connection in Adams's mind between human improvement and economic development emerged in his final illustrations of the "spirit of improvement": the opening of Thomas Jefferson's new University of Virginia, and the completion of New York's Erie Canal. Each represented the accomplishment by a single state of objectives first placed by George Washington on the original national agenda. States' rights advocates often cited these examples as proof that the federal government should not sponsor developmental projects, but Adams drew just the opposite conclusion. If such things could be achieved "by the authority of single members of our Confederation," should the "representative authorities of the whole Union" be allowed to "fall behind"? Consciously referring to the separate spheres that made dual sovereignty comprehensible at all, Adams challenged his listeners in the Nineteenth Congress to perform the sovereign functions for the *whole* people that these two model states had performed each for their own particular inhabitants.[20]

For Adams, the United States faced an important juncture. Positive action would be needed if the country were to meet its destiny in the century ahead. Earlier presidents had been willing (and able) to pacify the localists and limit their reach to matters of national defense, the public credit, and foreign affairs. But the progress of other nations now required an activist government, eager to design and build roads and canals, establish national standards of weights and measures, encourage inventors through patent protection, support universities and scientific institutions, and explore the vast interior of the national domain. The constitutional issue was a needless distraction: the "great majority" of people "now think with me," Adams argued, "that Congress do possess the power" to make roads and canals without an amendment (which could not be secured). "Why should they beat about the bush for a bird which they have in hand?"[21] Continued assaults on federal authority, whether cynical or sincere, served to undermine the legitimacy of power itself, endangering the very concept of government while inflaming selfish individualism. Nothing could be farther, Adams thought, from the original intentions of the founders of the American republic.[22]

It was partly to recover the intentions of the founders that Adams now pronounced his views on power and the national government. Thirty years of Jeffersonian rhetoric had privileged one aspect of the Revolution's legacy—the assault on government power—while ignoring the problems of anarchy and license that had equally concerned the revolutionaries themselves. It was true that power might corrupt those who wield it; but power itself was not corrupt, and it only became so when turned to dishonorable ends, such as the disunionist plots that drove him from the old Federalist Party. By the same token, liberty alone did not guarantee virtue. If liberation yielded nothing more than the widespread gratification of animal passions it was surely as corrupt as the indulgences of voluptuous aristocrats. Liberty *is* power! The phrase was an equation. If Adams placed greater emphasis on the duties of republican citizens, he differed in degree, not in kind, from Jefferson's position. Governments instituted merely to protect private greed or to frustrate the exercise of human ingenuity failed to serve their greatest purpose. Adams's word "improvement" implied an upward moral trajectory; so did Jefferson's term "happiness." Nobody wanted liberty that did not promise betterment. For Adams, the founders' gift of freedom belonged not to selfish individuals who sharpened their wits in trade and competition, but to those who pushed the architecture of human achievement ever higher.[23]

None of this made Adams a Federalist or neomercantilist (as his enemies tried to label him). Impressed by the energy released in a liberal market economy, Adams also grasped what Adam Smith called the "third and last duty of the sovereign," which was to provide "those public institutions and those public works" that were too costly to "repay the expense" to private investors. Especially in a new country (Smith's term was "barbarous"), government had to intervene to encourage capital formation and provide essential facilities. Following Smith's formulation exactly, Adams stressed the need for education and internal improvements, coupling in his closing illustration for Congress the dramatic feat of opening the Erie Canal with the supporting promise of the University of Virginia. Finally, Adams claimed that his vision differed little from the dreams and programs of Monroe, Madison, Gallatin, and Jefferson—all reflecting at bottom their common commitment to the "federalism of Washington, Union, and Internal Improvement." These had been the "three hinges" on which Adams's own political life had turned, and they provided, he thought, a common thread in the American experiment that survived the corruption of political intrigue. In his claim to represent the original republicanism of Washington *and* Jefferson, Adams tried to cut away the damage of partisan mythology and reestablish continuity in American history between the worlds of the Adamses, father and son. Given his keen sense of the workings of an active God, John Quincy Adams probably saw his extraordinary election as a prophetic opportunity.[24]

Because we know too well how it all came out, historians typically have treated Adams's vision as hopelessly at odds with American traditions and the popular spirit of the times. In fact, it was the last great articulation of a strain of revolutionary republicanism that soon would fade away amid the boisterous demands of mass popular democracy and the market revolution. In that sense it marked, like its mirror image, *The Letters of Wyoming*, a rhetorical turning point in American politics. At the time Adams's message was surprisingly well received by editors and members of Congress, although many of his audience probably noticed only the green light for popular programs and not the civics lesson in which it was embedded. Only in Virginia were the protests unequivocal. Ritchie recognized at once that the president's pretensions contradicted the neo-Antifederalist dogma of the states' rights radicals, and he condemned them as the "wildest construction" of the Constitution. Apocalyptic to the end, Jefferson could only see in Adams the return of "aristocracy, founded on banking institutions, and moneyed incorporations" cloaked in promises to trade and manufacturing, "riding and ruling over the plundered ploughman and beggared yeomanry." Jefferson was right: an aristocracy was rising to displace the landed gentry that had spoken for the yeomanry of Jefferson's day; but would it feed on privilege and corruption in government? Or on democratic politics and "natural" market forces? The spoiling of internal improvements owed something to both possibilities, and the outcome would not be clear for another generation.[25]

The Scramble for Preferment

What most Americans desired in 1825 was something far less grand than Adams's vision and yet more generous than the strict construction and rigid economy of orthodox Virginia-style radicals. And what most of them heard in Adams's message was encouragement to press for federal aid to public works that could be dressed up as having "national importance." Even before the fateful election, a boom of promotions greeted the General Survey Act and the attendant expectation that the bar to national assistance had come down. Teams of army engineers ordered out by Secretary of War Calhoun gathered the details for three monumental objectives: a Potomac Valley canal to the Ohio River, thence to Lake Erie, together with improvements in the Ohio and Mississippi Rivers, all of which would constitute a complete interregional waterway; a turnpike extending the Cumberland Road from its terminus at Wheeling to St. Louis; and a grand Atlantic thoroughfare comprising canals across Cape Cod, Rhode Island, New Jersey, Delaware, and Maryland together with a great southern national road terminating at New Orleans. Secondary goals for Calhoun included the Dismal Swamp Canal, a cut through the Florida peninsula, and links between coastal and interior waters such as the James and Kanawha Rivers, the Alabama and Tennessee, the Savannah and Tennessee, the Susquehannah and Allegheny, and the St. Lawrence and Hudson via Lake Champlain. Many projects lay entirely within individual states, but Calhoun insisted that improvements in the Susquehannah River, for example, served "not only Pennsylvania" but a "large portion of the community." His correspondence for 1824 teemed with assurances to interested parties that their favorite road or canal would be studied just as soon as the Board of Engineers found the time.[26]

Unwilling to wait for the results of the engineers' surveys, members of the lame duck Eighteenth Congress had explored a number of legislative routes to the goal of internal improvement. The House charged its Committee on Roads and Canals to work up a bill pledging the surplus revenue from land sales and national bank stock dividends "as a permanent fund for the purpose of internal improvement." Daniel Pope Cook of Illinois brought in a plea in behalf of the Illinois & Michigan Canal (to which Congress last year had given a right-of-way but no real money): if Congress would not put up the capital, could Illinois cash in its school lands and use the canal tolls to fund education? The Chesapeake & Delaware Canal Company was back asking Congress to subscribe for $300,000 of its stock, while Ohio pushed hard for an extension of the Cumberland Road eighty miles from Wheeling to Zanesville, on its way to the Mississippi River. Late in the session friends of the Chesapeake & Ohio Canal Company, already chartered in Virginia and Maryland, sought congressional affirmation (but not yet cash) for their resuscitation of the old Potomac Canal. Content at last (so they repeatedly assured each other) with the "settled" state of their constitutional power, most lawmakers turned enthusiastically to the challenge of implementation, where they quickly exposed fissures within the improvement community that would tend to fracture the system approach and transform any program into a barrel of pork.[27]

First, genuine support for a national system required that everyone take a generous view of the advantages (and costs) of any specific road or canal. In practice neither advocates nor their opponents could resist the temptation to snipe at each other. In defending the extension of the Cumberland Road from those who wanted to wait for a system design, Ohio's Philemon Beecher asked why men approached each other with such "mutual suspicion": did they think that members of Congress were tied so narrowly to local interest that they would "abandon the system as soon as each district . . . had secured its own object?" An answer of sorts came quickly from Beecher's rear. Both Illinois and Indiana declared opposition to the present bill because it applied the national "2 percent fund"—money set aside from the sale of public lands to build roads to the new western states—to a road in eastern Ohio. Members asked in astonishment how they should manage to build roads *to* Indiana without going *through* Ohio; but the westerners would not recede from a reductionist demand that 2 percent funds raised in their states be spent only on roads touching their borders. Never mind that Congress already had spent seven times the amount in the 2 percent fund on the national road to Wheeling, or that the road to St. Louis would cost more than the fund ever could raise.[28]

Questions of fair treatment within the Union permeated discussions of this national road. One New Yorker snarled that the people of the West did not "lift a shovel to preserve" the Cumberland Road, ignoring the fact that the road actually lay in *eastern* states and was lawfully a burden on Congress, not the people of the states. The western states complained that they had been stripped of their public lands by Congress, so they could not help themselves the way Pennsylvania, New York, and Virginia so smugly recommended. Furthermore, the West had received not a tenth of the money lavished on ships and forts and everything else in the East since the adoption of the Constitution. Preferring not to be tied to this new system of internal improvements, western spokesmen insisted that their national road derived from earlier commitments and had nothing to do with the program begun by the General Survey Act. Both Henry Clay and Daniel Webster begged their colleagues to eschew such bickering and take the large view, but jealousy could not be stifled. South Carolina's George McDuffie observed (correctly) that the urgent case for this western road rested entirely on "sectional" arguments: "The whole nation does not call for the present undertaking of the work, but two or three, or four of the Western States." Despite its long history and impeccable Jeffersonian roots, this original national internal improvement—the extension of which was implied in the laws admitting each new western state—struggled to command a national base of support.[29]

The case of the Chesapeake & Delaware Canal exposed equally difficult questions about a private-sector approach. This project had failed once before, and in 1824 it was stalled again for want of regional investor support. Obviously a central link in the much discussed "chain of internal communication" along the

"Atlantic frontier," the Chesapeake & Delaware Canal brought little benefit to the land where it lay and actually contradicted the interests of Baltimore, the city near its western outlet. Philadelphia stood to gain most, but Pennsylvania was deeply in debt for its own internal improvements, and Philadelphia capitalists, explained Congressman Hemphill, could not "undertake every public work" no matter how "profitable" it promised to be. Opinions varied widely and in new constellations. Members of Congress who tended to oppose national public works nevertheless liked this proposal for a federal stock subscription because it did not transgress the rights of the states or enlarge federal authority. Some congressmen worried on the other side that through such investments agents of the states gained undue access to the federal treasury. Others wondered if they should invest in eastern works that were sure to be profitable, or if it would be better to save federal money for riskier ventures in the capital-starved West. A few (especially from South Carolina, where the tariff was becoming a political hobby) groused that all federal revenue should pay off the debt and then reduce the hated import duties. Flush with pride in their own self-sufficiency, New Yorkers questioned the wisdom of federal aid, thanking Congress sarcastically for rejecting their earlier pleas and forcing them to develop their own resources. Dudley Marvin of New York (whose motives were likely corrupt but whose prophesy still rang true) warned the House not to buy stocks based on the claims of the corporations without independent engineering advice: to do so would "lay the foundation for innumerable applications from all associations of persons, who show, or think they can show, that they are engaged in an undertaking of public utility."[30]

In the Senate, Littleton Tazewell of Virginia moved to encumber the Chesapeake & Delaware Canal bill with a grant to the Dismal Swamp Canal. If Congress insisted on making unconstitutional gifts to local interests (which he intended to vote against), Tazewell wanted Virginia to get its share. Thomas Hart Benton preferred public works over aid to private or mixed corporations, and he decried the hasty piecemeal approach reflected in the House bill before him. Georgia's Thomas W. Cobb resurrected the Virginia and Kentucky Resolutions in an effort to rekindle the fundamentalist issue, and old Macon of North Carolina bemoaned all the schemes for "tying the people together"—banking, tariffs, and internal improvements: "The end of them all would be, in the vulgar tongue, taxation." If Macon's fear underlay many practical objections to appropriations, the one more chilling to politicians was that expressed in the House by Samuel Clesson Allen of Massachusetts, who opposed all appropriations for "local objects." It would produce, he feared, "a scrambling on this floor for the benefits which were to be dispensed, and, instead of strengthening Union," its "practical tendency would be to weaken, if not destroy it."[31]

Bills for the Cumberland Road and the Chesapeake & Delaware Canal both prevailed in the Eighteenth Congress, but several flags had been raised in the course of debates that would mark the future course of internal improvements. First, local interests in every quarter stood ready to scrambled for federal aid, and few politicians could resist the temptation to color them all with "national importance." Second, it became clear that spending much money in any one place engendered such quick and forceful objections from places not served as to endanger the consensus on which all appropriations depended. This posed a significant problem because the alternatives—scattering limited resources too thinly over many projects, or proportional distributions to the states—crippled expensive works and destroyed the potential for coherent integration. Outgoing war secretary Calhoun and incoming president Adams ardently hoped that scientific experts from the corps of engineers could point out selections, removing politics from the process of design; but few members of Congress really were prepared to surrender the fate of their constituents to the bloodless calculations of surveyors employed by the army. Furthermore, friends of the large-scale system approach, such as Henry Clay and Charles Fenton Mercer, discovered that the call for systematic surveys quickly replaced the demand for amendments in the mouths of those who intended to frustrate the progress of all improvements. In a community defined by goodwill and mutual objectives, engineers might direct the selection of projects for a comprehensive plan; but in a hotly contested political universe, no surveyor's prospectus could match the force of determined local spoilsmen or the enemies of federal aid who could block every action with calls for better technical data. Louis McLane of Delaware, gave voice to a new lament: "The friends of the cause create impediments, of which its opponents take advantage. . . . We are forbidden to exert our new power in one part of the country, unless we employ it in every other."[32]

With this inheritance from the Monroe administration, the Nineteenth Congress hardly needed John Quincy Adams's oratorical inspiration to strike off on an ambitious course—or to find ground for continuing controversy. By the time of Adams's famous message to Congress in December 1825, army engineers had completed their surveys of the Chesapeake & Ohio Canal route, two of three routes for the Washington–New Orleans turnpike, and a Connecticut River project. Over a dozen detailed reports on these and other projects were delivered to Congress before the end of the first session, touching canals in New England, Tennessee, Alabama, Mississippi, Louisiana, New York, Virginia, and Ohio, roads in Pennsylvania, Michigan, and upstate New York, and improvements in the Ohio and Mississippi Rivers. Not yet a coherent system or even a comprehensive plan, this flow of information created the potential for a fundamentally different approach to making appropriations and selecting worthy objects for the attention of the national legislature. Unfortunately, members of Congress—pressed by the desires of their constituents—took this opportunity in the other direction, advancing pet projects with increasingly dubious claims of national significance and indulging in ever more bitter attacks on each other.[33]

Four separate ideas floated through the Nineteenth Congress for regularizing a program—a variant of the old Bonus Bill fund; an amendment to the Constitution authorizing appropriations to the states for internal improvements, education, and colonization; a plan for granting public lands; and another distributing to states some portion of the surplus in the federal treasury—but no systematic approach commanded the attention of lawmakers filled with either desire or righteous indignation.[34] Instead, major debates raged over the Cumberland Road (a perennial sink for rhetoric and money that forever rekindled bitter disputes: Michael Hoffman of New York said "it haunted him like a ghost"); surveys for a canal across Florida and possibly on through the cotton South to New Orleans; grants of land for canals to link the Great Lakes with the Wabash and Illinois Rivers; stock subscriptions to the Dismal Swamp and the Louisville & Portland Canals and the Columbus & Sandusky Turnpike; and an outright appropriation for a new breakwater at Philadelphia (in addition to the dozens of harbor improvements routinely funded for saltwater commerce). The success of these promotions brought in further demands in the Twentieth Congress for grants of land to Michigan for a cross-state canal, Alabama for various river improvements, and Ohio for two canals the state already was building with borrowed money on the New York "do-it-yourself" plan. The fledgling Baltimore & Ohio Railroad sought a drawback of duties on imported iron, and the state-federal-private Chesapeake & Ohio Canal Company still wanted a million-dollar subscription. All the while specific appeals poured in from petitioners everywhere begging a survey of this or that creek, bog, trail, or portage, the improvement of which might result in some "great national advantage."[35]

Each of these gambits could be perceived as a legitimate part of a comprehensive system, but almost nobody brought to the table a spirit of accommodation. All talk of the Cumberland Road produced bitter attacks on the western states as if they were bastard offspring angling for an inheritance. John Randolph claimed now to be so "stupid" ("he would not say 'ineffably' so") as to doubt the power of Congress even in territories like Florida. When someone suggested that a Florida canal might someday complement one through Panama, Randolph asked nastily if Congress planned to cut that one next? John Branch of North Carolina broke ranks to support the Dismal Swamp Canal, on the grounds that his own constitutional "squeamishness" ought not "deny his People" a place at the "feast which had been prepared out of their money." Knowing improvers dared not discriminate openly against Virginia and North Carolina, Randolph, Macon, and Littleton Tazewell chose instead to flaunt their own righteousness by voting against public works for their constituents, while John Chandler of Maine (another unrelenting enemy of federal aid) twitted Branch for biting "the first bait held out to him." After Indiana's Hendricks defended the Wabash & Erie Canal as a "great national work," William Findlay of Pennsylvania answered derisively that the same could be said for the Pittsburgh Canal, "but the Nation certainly never thought of giving a quantity of land for its completion." Infuriated by such rebuffs, westerners pressed in their counter assertion that the new states deserved to hold title to their own public lands—just like original states—which raised an objection from John Holmes of Maine (a frontier state whose lands never passed to Congress) against this "new doctrine" on public lands. In opposing an Ohio turnpike subscription, William Smith of South Carolina denounced these new mixed corporations as "pernicious co-partnerships." Congress, he feared, was "fast becoming a finished stock-jobber." Macon had said as much before, point-ing out (tautologically) that solvent companies thrived on private investments and only the bankrupt ones came to Congress. How, Macon asked at Ohio's expense, had Kentucky, Tennessee, and Pennsylvania been settled? "Why, they had to work their own way, and do as well as they could." All this aid to the western states, he thought, was a "step too far, and anticipating prosperity."[36]

None of these insults stopped the progress of public works, and friends of the national program reiterated time and again (*too* often perhaps) that the question of power finally was settled. A few new voices in the Senate, such as New York's Martin Van Buren and South Carolina's Smith, joined the unconverted radicals in rejecting all constitutional authority; but most arguments now turned on the expediency of granting aid, the likelihood of success, the potential national importance, and the fair distribution of federal largesse. Virtually all federal expenditures for tangible installations—forts, piers, lighthouses, naval yards, ar-mories, customshouses—generated local advantages: all could be sustained or condemned as appropriate "national" works. How else was "the general welfare" to be "promoted," pleaded House Roads and Canals chairman Mercer, in frus-tration, "but by promoting a part at a time?" Virginia's resentment of all spending on the West, argued Joseph Vance, was more selfish and local than all the West's demands together, and their precious "States' rights" doctrines threatened to "shake this Union to its centre." If it ever fell, the Ohioan predicted, it would be "from State jealousies, State factions; and the want of equal distributions of the national disbursements." Such scoldings had no visible effect on the sons of the Old Dominion, and the relentless attack of the states' rights minority, together with shifting coalitions opposed to particular projects or methods, kept local jealousies inflamed and hope alive for the enemies of general systems.[37]

The most relentless opposition centered in New York (protective of Erie), Virginia (obsessed, they said, with principle), and the Carolinas (now fixated on public economy and the tariff); the West alone voted "yes" to almost any appro-priation (see Table 3). In the Senate, Maine and Tennessee split their votes oddly, with Jacksonians Holmes and Eaton solidly supporting internal improvements

TABLE 3. Senate Roll Calls, 19th Congress, 1826–1827

State	Senator	Cumberland Road	L&P Canal	Dismal Swamp	Wabash-Erie	Cumberland Road
ME	Chandler	N	N	N	N	N
ME	Holmes	Y	Y	Y	Y	Y
NH	Bell		N	N	Y	
NH	Woodbury	N	N	N	N	N
VT	Chase	Y	Y	Y	Y	Y
VT	Seymour	Y		Y	Y	Y
MA	Lloyd/Silsbee			Y	Y	Y
MA	Mills	Y	Y			Y
RI	Knight	Y	N	N	Y	Y
RI	Robbins	Y	Y	Y	Y	Y
CT	Edwards	Y	Y	Y	N	Y
CT	Willey	N	N		Y	
NY	Van Buren	N	N	N		N
NY	Sanford	N	N	N	N	N
NJ	Dickerson	N	N	N	N	
NJ	McIlvaine/Bateman				Y	Y
PA	Findlay	N	Y	Y	N	N
PA	Marks	Y	Y	Y	Y	Y
DE	Clayton	N	N		N	N
DE	Van Dyke/Ridgely				Y	Y
MD	Lloyd/Chambers				Y	Y
MD	Smith	Y		Y	Y	Y
VA	Tazewell		N	N	N	N
VA	Randolph	N			N	N
NC	Branch		N	Y	N	
NC	Macon	N	N	N	N	N
SC	Gaillard/Harper/Smith			N	N	N
SC	Hayne	N	N	N	N	N
GA	Berrien	N		N		N
GA	Cobb	N	N		N	N
KY	Johnson	Y			Y	Y
KY	Rowan		Y	N		
TN	Eaton	Y		Y	Y	Y
TN	White	N	N	N		N
OH	Harrison	Y	Y	Y	Y	Y
OH	Ruggles	Y	Y		Y	
IN	Hendricks	Y	Y	Y	Y	Y
IN	Noble	Y	Y	Y	Y	Y
IL	Kane	Y	Y	N	Y	Y
IL	Thomas	Y	Y	Y	Y	Y

TABLE 3. *continued*

State	Senator	Cumberland Road	L&P Canal	Dismal Swamp	Wabash-Erie	Cumberland Road
AL	Chambers/McKinley		Y	Y	Y	Y
AL	King	N	Y	Y	Y	N
MS	Ellis/Reed	Y	Y	N	Y	Y
MS	Williams					
LA	Bouligney		Y	Y	Y	Y
LA	Johnston	Y		Y	Y	Y
MO	Barton	Y	Y	Y	Y	Y
MO	Benton	Y	Y		Y	Y

Source: *Register of Debates*, 19th Cong., 1st. sess., 364, 620, 720; 19th Cong., 2nd sess., 338, 490.

Note: Both Cumberland Road votes came on motions to strike appropriations: I reversed the yeas and nays so that yea always means support for the proposed internal improvement. Louisville & Portland Canal and Dismal Swamp Canal bills involved stock subscriptions. The Wabash & Erie was a land grant.

while Chandler and Hugh Lawson White (the latter a *Whig* presidential candidate in 1836) stood immovably opposed. In the House, New York's Hoffman said he wanted a "general plan, having equal relation to all the States," but apparently he meant that when other states had burdened themselves much as New York they could talk about federal aid. As was the case so frequently, John Randolph expressed the opposition perspective in its extreme: "No Government can be safe for Virginia, that is not a Government of persons having a common feeling—a common interest—a common right with Virginia." Gentlemen came to Congress, he shrilled, for no other reason than "to be faithful Representatives of the States" that sent them.[38]

Partisan politics broke through the surface of internal improvement debates in December 1826, when Virginia's William Cabel Rives asked the House Ways and Means Committee to discontinue appropriations under the General Survey Act of 1824. Too much discretion had been handed the president, and now it was too easy, added Charles A. Wickliffe of Kentucky, to order up a survey and inflame the hopes of every local population. Take back control, urged Rives, and limit the work of the engineers to projects authorized specifically by Congress. Silas Wood of New York protested that such a move would stop the flow of scientific information and throw the House back on the "*opinions* of gentlemen given on this floor, or the interested representations made by others to us." Daniel Pope Cook saw its purpose more bluntly: "to cut up by the roots the entire system of Internal Improvements." More likely, Rives's intention was to neutralize the popularity of national improvements and lay the foundation for campaign charges by friends of Andrew Jackson against the administration of Adams and Clay.[39]

The Ways and Means Committee buried Rives's resolution, but on 20 February he insisted on the privilege of being heard. Given annually $30,000 with no oversight on how it must be spent, the administration, Rives explained, was enlarging its "immense patronage" and influence. Unlimited discretion allowed the president to stir up people's hopes in return for electoral support. Whenever the federal government rescued a failing project, Rives saw only an "occasion for impressing the important lesson of the inefficiency of the State authorities, and that the General Government only was to be relied upon for aid to these useful enterprises." Of all the War Department's efforts since 1824, Rives claimed that only six of thirty-five surveys (the ones ordered by Calhoun and Monroe) truly qualified as national objects. The rest examined local creeks in the wilds of New England, Pennsylvania, and Indiana—all centers of Jacksonian support in the 1824 election. The whole reason, he claimed, for lavishing efforts on the Chesapeake & Ohio Canal was to bring around Jacksonian Maryland; the same could be said for Adams's efforts to revive Virginia projects deemed impossible or insignificant by that state's Board of Engineers. With all this activity, what had *not* been accomplished by Adams's busy engineers? Nothing for Muscle Shoals, the Florida Canal, the Tennessee, Savannah, or Alabama Rivers—all "too near the Military Chieftain both in feeling and position to admit any hope of alluring them from their unfortunate attachment." Supplying sinister motives for verifiable actions, Rives artfully tightened a vise on Adams, Clay, and Secretary of War James Barbour, who stood condemned for what they did *and* for what they did not. It was a brilliant political speech that fell with striking effect on a House not yet accustomed to such flagrant presidential campaigning.[40]

Charles Fenton Mercer leveled a blistering rebuke at Rives for turning the "Legislative Hall into an arena for the tilts of the champions for Presidential Candidates." He explained away each of Rives's circumstantial proofs and sketched out ideal procedures by which the House might use engineering results instead of politics and local desires to guide their selections and appropriations. (Unfortunately even Mercer could not resist what Hoffman called "Congressional engineering": when army engineers calculated $23 million for the Chesapeake & Ohio Canal, Mercer called in James Geddes from the Erie Canal to cut those estimates in half.) Other members rose in turn to defend Adams and Barbour or to deny that their constituents could be "melted down" so easily in "the sordid crucible of self-interest." Bartlett of New Hampshire reminded Rives that if he thought the streams of New England seemed a long way north of Virginia, that Virginia to him was "quite as far" to the South. Many members seemed offended by Rives's insinuations, regardless of their stance on public

works; still, the party card had been played, and presidential aspirations increasingly would color debates on internal improvement until the 1828 election
was decided.[41]

The effect of Rives's resolution was to show friends of Andrew Jackson how
they could oppose the Adams administration on internal improvement without
embracing the cause of old radicals such as Macon and Randolph. Voters in the
West naturally were drawn by sentiment to Jackson—his violence, heroism, character, primitive rhetoric, and humble origins; but westerners equally were drawn
by interest to internal improvements, and they would not join a party built on
states' rights and hostility to federal developmental programs. Taking their cues
from Rives, members of the Twentieth Congress began presenting themselves as
friends of a "system" of improvement yet enemies of executive influence, patronage, corruption, and the rise of a monied "Aristocracy." John Eaton (of all
people)—author of *The Letters of Wyoming* and a recognized voice of the Jackson
camp—gave a speech worthy of the early Calhoun, praising the "stronger bond of
Union" that resulted from improvements and urging the adoption of "such measures" as would "make the citizens of this extended continent one People." At the
same time friends and enemies of internal improvement rushed to document
their opposition to this administration's alleged excesses. "No great system . . .
had been reported to Congress," complained Louis McLane: "The Secretary of
War had departed entirely from the object of the law of '24." By now sixty-nine
separate surveys had been commenced and over thirty more were pending. Robert Y. Hayne, who had once asked Calhoun why the Charleston harbor found no
place in his national system, now said that he had learned a great lesson from
supporting the General Survey Act: "the most important question, in passing a
law, was not 'what' its benefit would be, but to what extent its provisions might be
abused."[42]

South Carolinians in both houses led such effective new attacks on the annual
appropriation for the Board of Engineers that both the wisdom and constitutionality of the present system began to slip from view. The proliferation of
petitions for aid, and the reluctance of anyone to find his own project too local to
deserve assistance, left the cause of *national* improvements wide open to attack.
Congressman William Dickinson Martin moved to strike out the whole appropriation, disavowing any sectional feeling yet noticing that no federal engineers
had been to South Carolina. Philip Barbour worried that the day was coming
when the $10 million now annually servicing debt would be freed up for internal
improvement: such a boon would "destroy" the "equilibrium between the General and State Governments." Afraid that work enough had been identified to
last fifty or a hundred years, Charles Wickliffe of Kentucky called for a "bird's
eye view of the probable expense of those already surveyed." South Carolina
senator William Smith delivered a huge speech ridiculing Adams for favoring

every local petition with a visit from the engineers. (What might they have said if he had not?) The wisdom of the framers in depriving Congress of the right to make roads and canals now stood verified in Smith's mind: tens of millions of dollars were about to be spent, scattering unequal benefits across the states—too much going to the West and little coming to the cotton South, which generated most of the country's export wealth. How could even "national" projects be constitutional? The word "national" was "unknown to the origin and theory of our Government." At Philadelphia the framers themselves had bothered to "expunge" it from the draft of the Constitution by "unanimous vote." Who "pushed this doctrine" transforming a republic into a nation? "Those who were looking to empire":

> Sir, the tariff of 1816, for a system of protecting duties to manufactures; the bonus bill of 1817, for a system of Internal Improvements; the report of the Secretary of War of 1819, recommending an extensive system of military road [sic] and canals; and the law of 1824, for procuring plans, estimates, and surveys for national roads and canals, were the priests that bound your Constitution fast in cords, and laid it at the foot of the alter of caprice, avarice, interest, and ambition, and we, their surrogates, are about to immolate the victim.[43]

Vice President John C. Calhoun—onetime sponsor with Henry Clay of the Bonus Bill and author of that 1819 War Department blueprint for an "extensive system"—now slipped out of the priestly vestments Smith had given him, casting a tie-breaking vote in the Senate, to *restrict* appropriations for the Board of Engineers. This was the second such move (he had two years before killed an Illinois canal), yet he angrily denied that he espoused any new opinions. With critics murmuring in their seats, Calhoun explained from the chair that he always had feared that congressional authority would be "diverted from national objects or made subservient to political combinations." James Noble accused him of treachery and speaking out of order but was gaveled down himself in a heated exchange. Tempers flared in the House as well during the frantic closing days of a very long session, as members washed their hands of particular surveys they once had demanded. Feuding Ohioans tried to pass a land grant for the Miami canal while scuttling a second through Cleveland. And in Kentucky, local Jacksonians turned against a turnpike through Maysville that would become the tree on which to hoist Henry Clay. Charles Wickliffe hoped that by restricting the system to "national" projects selected only by Congress they could rescue internal improvements from the "little army of civil agents, blood-suckers, hangers-on and dependents" who fed "from the public crib" and together with the officer corps made up a "formidable phalanx in the field" of men beholden to executive power. It boiled down, as always, said George Gilmer of Georgia, to "the strife between Democracy and Aristocracy."[44]

Albert Gallatin had written back in 1808 that only Congress, "embracing every local interest, and superior to every local consideration" was "competent to the election of such national objects" as belonged in a system of internal improvements. That claim rested on a model of the legislative process, belonging to an earlier republicanism, in which Congress gathered not to broker the interests of constituents but to discern their common welfare as a people. Adams's message of 1825 sought in vain to resurrect that conception of Congress; but democratization and atomization had progressed too far. Driven by ambition, greed, and opportunity, and fostered (or at least justified) by the rhetoric of disbelief and citizen vigilance that rested at the center of Jefferson's creed, private interests and public officials had drifted toward an image of Congress as a market where members traded as little as they could of their constituents' rights and interests for the greatest share of national benefits they could command. Such a Congress proved utterly incapable of "embracing every interest" or transcending "local considerations." If they delegated power to the president, someone conjured up fantasies of patronage, privilege, corruption. Surrendering to the experts proved even less acceptable: how could the people's representatives dare to let a hireling belonging to the War Department set aside forever as "local" or "impractical" the projects dearest to the hearts of their constituents? Historians note with alarm the rise of "sectional feelings" in this period, but sectional resentments sprang as much from intentional and distorted propaganda complaining of alleged "unequal treatment" as from real injuries or conflicts of interests. This propaganda, in turn, grew out of the habits of politicians who inflamed local jealousies in order to advance particular interests or enhance their power in Congress. As long as plausible statesmen—Randolph, Macon, Philip Barbour, Tazewell, and now Calhoun, William Smith, and Martin Van Buren—denied the existence of a national interest independent of immediate benefits for people at home in their states, it would be impossible to sell the short-term inequities that must result from federal spending on a genuinely national system. And so the program launched with the General Survey Act was spoiled by its major beneficiaries, overwhelmed by limitless desires, torn apart by jealousies, and corrupted by the willingness of candidates for office to torture both the principles and language of republican politics in order to secure themselves a place at the trough.[45]

Acts of Political Revenge

Given the "progress" of internal improvement through the Nineteenth and Twentieth Congresses, the election of 1828 might have been expected to turn on a general revulsion against the American System, consolidation, and the vision of integrated national development that Adams so clearly (one might say foolishly) articulated. A casual reading of national histories would not much disturb the impression that Adams's vision and programs were rejected flatly by voters in the

Jackson landslide, but such was not precisely the case. Too much of Adams' vision satisfied too many people for Jackson (or any candidate) to prevail by promising a simple return to Virginia-style strict construction or the limited reach of a neo-Antifederalist Union. Instead, the Jacksonians crafted their campaign in 1828 as a drama of the worthy against the licentious, and to some extent everything that happened during the Adams years—even the spoiling of internal improvements that took place in congressional debates—found its impetus in part in the determination of wounded Jacksonians to place in the White House in 1828 the one they considered the rightful winner in 1824.

At the center of this opposition movement stood Vice President John C. Calhoun, whose political metamorphosis after February 1825 was nothing short of spectacular. Calhoun had campaigned through 1824 as a champion of internal improvement and protective tariffs and an implacable foe of the caucus and Virginia radicalism. Sensing the immanent triumph of a new Republican synthesis, Calhoun prophesied destruction for "intriguing statesmen" such as Martin Van Buren, whose Crawfordite "Albany Junto" he styled "the most dangerous faction, which has ever appeared in our country." Calhoun's objectives seemed perfectly clear in the months preceding the election: continue Monroe's nationalistic policies, destroy the congressional caucus, and liberate the electorate from the domination of Virginia "Radicalism" (which threatened the first and nourished the second). He loved (he said) the balance of power within the Constitution as much as any Virginian; but he disagreed that the rules of construction should be "invariably rigid against the power of the general government," he believed that Congress should protect manufactures and build roads and canals, and he felt some exasperation toward critics who resisted the whole evolution of Republican policies. When his own candidacy sank in Pennsylvania beneath the surging Jackson movement, Calhoun sought endorsements for vice president from Adams and Jackson both. In late November 1824, when Jackson and Adams emerged as leaders over Crawford and Clay, he proclaimed his satisfaction gleefully: "Let either succeed[,] the victory will be equally decisive." Already elected to the vice presidency, Calhoun pretended complete indifference through December and January as to whom he thought the House should make president, and he gave no hint of displeasure with the constitutional procedure for completing the election. Through it all, as secretary of war, he continued eagerly to pursue the internal improvement mandate resulting from the General Survey Act, juggling the impatient demands of local promoters for visits from the Board of Engineers.[46]

Behind the scenes, however, Calhoun's friends had been threatening Adams with the direst of consequences if he secured his election or built his administration around an alliance with Henry Clay. George McDuffie warned Adams darkly that "a tremendous storm" would drive him from the White House "at the end of four years," and Samuel Ingham promised an opposition, uniting the South and West against Adams, "so powerful that it must break him down." But according to Adams's informants, this opposition was assured either way, and so he opened his hand to Clay. The election took place 9 February, and two days later Adams offered Clay the State Department post. Leading players still hoped Clay would be ashamed to accept; as a test Calhoun pressed instead the name of Joel R. Poinsett. But on 18 February Clay accepted his appointment, and the promised storm began. That day, Calhoun wrote to an intimate friend, things in Washington had "taken a strange turn." In early March, after taking his oath of office, he startled the Senate by claiming his right to preside over that chamber's sessions and appoint its committees—a function no vice president ever had performed before. In a "strictly confidential" letter 10 March he again reported many "strange events during the last winter, which are but little known to the country." The result, he explained, was "that we have triumphed in part and been defeated in part":

> In the final stages of the election, the voice and the power of the people has [*sic*] been set at naught; & the result has been a President elected not by them, but by a few ambitious men with a view to their own interest, I fear. There is a solid feeling of duty, that it must be corrected at the next election, or the liberty of the country will be in danger. It is my opinion, that the country will never be quiet till the example is corrected, and the Constitution so amended as to prevent the recurrence of the danger.[47]

Here was the declaration of opposition that would guide Calhoun's behavior throughout Adams's four years as president. What exactly were the crimes that rendered illegitimate a president, not yet a week in office, who Calhoun had intimated six weeks before he would be happy to see elected? The faulty procedures for contingent elections could not truly explain his reaction; for Calhoun (like everybody else) had long expected an election by the House, and he had schemed no less than any man to influence the outcome. But while Calhoun had won the second highest office in the land, he had played a losing hand. After eight years at the head of a large and influential federal department, he now stood isolated in the executive, without patronage or positive influence, parked in the line of succession behind Clay, whose presumptions might postpone Calhoun's hope for the presidency by as much as sixteen years. His only recovery lay with the friends of Andrew Jackson, whose complaint about the theft of an election at least could be aired before the public without shame.[48]

Throwing the cloak of righteousness over one shoulder, Calhoun now made it his cause to restore political integrity and the people's right to elect their president. He promised to amend the constitution to "prostrate political juglers [*sic*]," and he embraced as a sacred mission the task of keeping the people inflamed

until this egregious wrong could be righted. Eloquent letters poured forth, extol
ling the virtues of popular election, denying any personal ambition, and de
nouncing every form of "management" that might be practiced in political cam
paigns. He went back home to South Carolina for the first extended stay in
several years, where he apparently took stock in the mood of his constituents and
began to trim his ardent nationalism. As he gradually transformed himself into a
leading states' rights radical, he bristled at every suggestion that his course had
been anything but "uniform": "in every public act of my life," he told an audience
at Pendleton in April 1825, "I have at least been governed by a disinterested and
ardent attachment to our admirable system of government."[49]

By the fall of 1825 Calhoun believed himself *driven* into opposition by what he
imagined to be Adams's systematic policy of favoring Federalists and Clay's
southern friends to the exclusion of his own and Jackson's partisans. Why those
in the Adams administration should oppose Calhoun was obvious: he alone
stood firm on principle, whereas they had come to power by "the hope of patronage," with which they now endeavored to support themselves. Satisfied that
Adams and Clay craved monarchy and ministerial rule, he concluded that "the
struggle" was engaged "between liberty and power; and as I have taken my side
fearlessly, I must expect the natural consequences, bitter and deep denuncia
tions." Calhoun's apostasy culminated in June 1826 in an extraordinary letter to
Jackson pledging the vice president's allegiance to "this great struggle" in which
Jackson's name was found, "as it always has been, on the side of liberty, and your
country."[50]

It was a breathtaking reinvention. In barely a year Calhoun had reconfigured
all his rhetoric as well as his alliances around the Jacksonian cause. Power must
flow from "the gift of the people," but the people were easily deceived and might
be persuaded by its works that this administration served them well. It was up to
men like Calhoun to correct any "partial indications of publick sentiments" and
keep people focused on "truth and principles." To Martin Van Buren (managing
wizard of that "most dangerous faction" in New York—on which Jacksonians
now pinned their hopes) he wrote, "I rejoice that your prospect in the State is so
good." To Levi Woodbury he likened the administration to a coalition of the "old
Federal party of '98 and the bargin [*sic*] and sale party of the West." By January
1827 he claimed it was his "pride" to be "the object of unceasing attack by the
corrupt occupants of power," while this opposition role kept moving him steadily
into new company and away from the programs he pretended to hold dear. To
Virginia (over whose radicalism he had celebrated "complete victory") he now
looked for "zeal and union": "every resolution in favor of liberty in our system,
must be effected by the South . . . headed by Virginia." He began to treat the
national tariff as an intentional fraud upon the South, a "system of monopoly and
extortion against the consuming States" for which he saw but one "effectual"

emedy: a "veto . . . on the part of the State." He turned against the "American System," the effect of which he said had distressed him for "the last 5 years." In the wake of the 1828 "Tariff of Abominations," Calhoun's protests grew so strident that Duff Green tried to warn him away. As winter came on, instead of celebrating Jackson's victory Calhoun took up his pen to justify nullification in the "South Carolina Exposition," a manifesto that took him straight past Jackson's democratic nationalism into a neo-Antifederalist position more extreme than that of Virginia against which he had battled his whole public life.[51]

In Congress, the Adams administration was treated to extremely rough handling from the beginning. Senate committees stacked by Calhoun pounced on various parts of the president's December 1825 message. Martin Van Buren introduced a resolution declaring that Congress possessed no power to build roads and canals in the states. Thomas Hart Benton called for an amendment to the Constitution requiring the election of presidents in popular districts, and Robert Y. Hayne added a provision explicitly barring interference by the House of Representatives. But nothing exploded quite so dramatically as Adams's appointment of delegates to the international Panama Congress. Day after day senators leveled the most scurrilous charges of conspiracy and usurpation at Adams and Clay, always reaching back to touch their "corrupt" accession to power. On March 30, at the end of a rambling diatribe, John Randolph became so personally abusive that Henry Clay called him out and tried to shoot him in a duel. House debates showed more balance if not more respect for the administration, but angry confrontations persistently refocused everyone's attention to the "bargain" of February 1825. When the session finally expired Calhoun told Jackson he was "neither surprised nor displeased at the depth of feeling displayed by the members on several occasions." The agony had been by design.[52]

This chronic opposition plagued policy initiatives throughout the life of the Adams administration. National bankruptcy legislation, the national university, a scientific expedition to the South Seas, the Atlantic coastal survey, even Treasury Secretary Richard Rush's well-intentioned efforts to save interest charges by refunding the national debt—all drew predictable opposition that found amplification in the efforts of Calhoun and the Jacksonians to embarrass the administration. In 1828 eastern Jacksonians helped kill Thomas Hart Benton's pet bill for gradually reducing the price of public lands, yet campaigning friends of Jackson managed to focus the blame on the federal government. Efforts to stay Georgia's criminal assault on the rights of Creeks and Cherokees only verified Adams's putative indifference to the rights of the states. Plans to increase the tariff to protect home markets yielded the "Giles Resolutions" reiterating Virginia's unbending conviction that protective tariffs *and* internal improvements were simply unconstitutional. Around this antitariff standard the South quickly rallied in a solid block, while some Jacksonians hijacked tariff reform and cyn-

ically "larded" the 1828 Tariff of Abominations to favor critical states such a
Pennsylvania, New York, Ohio, and Kentucky. Unable to escape the taint o
illegitimacy, Adams found goodwill on which to balance his desired programs o
national improvement, scientific discovery, and economic integration.[53]

So afraid of charges of corruption was Adams that he refused to remove his op
ponents from offices of power and influence. As a result, many true friends of the
administration remained empty-handed while active enemies labored to destroy
him from the comfort and protection of their government positions. The betray-
als of Postmaster General John McLean were positively scandalous, but ever
when the president acknowledged McLean's "deep and treacherous duplicity," he
would not have him sacked for fear of being charged with electioneering. (I:
Adams intended to be venal he was singularly stupid about it, and his temperament inclined him to self-defeating perseverance when trimming would be better.) Grueling workloads coupled with the stress of constant opposition took their
toll on the whole administration. Believing he was dying in April 1828, Henry
Clay tendered his resignation but recovered to serve out his term. James Barbour
left a few weeks later—to "save himself from the wreck," Adams noted with
characteristic gloom. The Jackson "tempest" now raged and Adams thought the
administration's chances were "desperate." Ever the optimist, Clay spent his
campaign summer in Kentucky absorbed in political strategy; Adams stayed in
Washington, tending to business as usual, swimming almost daily against the tide
in the Potomac, and counting walnut seedlings in the White House nursery as
they sprouted—then withered and died.[54]

On 4 July 1828, dignitaries gathered to break ground for the Chesapeake &
Ohio Canal, the long-awaited continuation under federal, state, and private
auspices of George Washington's fabled Potomac route to the West. This project
was the crown jewel of national public works resulting from the General Survey
Act of 1824, and President Adams was proud to be present for the ceremony. In a
brief speech he declared the arrival of a third stage in the development of America's vision. The first was embodied in the Declaration of Independence, and the
second in the Constitution; now, with the application of the powers "of the
whole Union" to national improvement, the country finally was addressing God's
commandment to "replenish the Earth, *and subdue it.*" The sentiment offered a
closing bracket to the chronicle of his administration, begun in such grandeur
back in 1825, but he was wrong about the new era dawning. Just ahead lay not the
age of national improvement but the heyday of popular democracy, of rule by the
people in a marketplace of politics unrestrained by pretensions of breeding,
public spirit, or self-sacrificing virtue. Adams's vision marked the end of the
second era, not the beginning of the third, and as he reached for a shovelful of
earth to inaugurate the project before him, Adams inadvertently performed his
first truly popular presidential act. The spade struck a root, and in exasperation

e president peeled off his coat and hacked furiously at the ground to loosen the
quisite soil. In this homely display of frustration and labor, the press and the
eople glimpsed for once what they craved but had never seen behind the elegant
rose and frosty manners of John Quincy Adams—evidence of a human connec-
on with the common man.[55]

By the time Adams wrestled with his shovel, Jackson and his friends had per-
cted a formidable campaign machine, the construction of which began imme-
lately after the Adams election. On 20 February 1825, Jackson himself had au-
norized "the papers" back home to "speak out" with "disapprobation" on the
cent election. In Washington Calhoun became the first recognized focus of
le new Jackson movement, reportedly hosting a strategy dinner a week *before*
dams's inauguration. In October 1825 the Tennessee legislature nominated
ckson for president in 1828, at which point Old Hickory resigned from the
enate and retired once more to the Hermitage. Before long the Nashville cadre
f John Henry Eaton and others was joined by Calhoun (whose formal pledge
ame in June 1826), Benton of Missouri (riding the hobby of cheap frontier land),
nd Van Buren (master magician of the old New York–Virginia coalition of
rawfordite "radicals," who struck a deal with Calhoun in December).[56] Strat-
ςy flowed from a Nashville Central Committee, to whom Old Hickory himself
ave orders. Grass-roots "Hickory Clubs" mobilized support among the people,
ho were fed a steady stream of partisan doctrine via committees of correspon-
ence and local editors, who in turn relied on Duff Green's Washington *United
tates Telegraph* or Amos Kendall's *Argus of Western America*. Outside the Old
outh (where the tariff had been made intensely unpopular by the arguments of
alhoun), Jacksonians chose not to criticize—and even pretended at times to
ipport—internal improvements and tariff protection. Instead they marched
eneath the banner of "Jackson and Reform." Liberty and democracy hung in the
alance; aristocracy crouched by the gates of Washington. Near the end of the
ampaign William Cabel Rives predicted certain victory and opined that the next
our years would determine "whether we are to remain an united & happy
eople."[57]

Everything about the opposition to Adams found its impetus in the claim that
le people—and the general—had been cheated in the previous election. Having
un as an outsider in 1824, promising to clean the "Augean stables" of Wash-
igton corruption, Jackson claimed to have been robbed by arrogant pretenders,
pitomized by Clay, aristocrats who scorned the people's wishes and hungered
or power and wealth. The idea of popular election was novel and unfounded in
onstitutional traditions, but it resonated perfectly with the changes that had
iken place already within the political culture. Once their new Jacksonian narra-
ve took hold of the people out of doors, opposition factions climbed aboard. In
lis way Virginia's neo-Antifederalist dogma and the selfish briefs of New York

and South Carolina found new life as tenets of original "republicanism." In this way the gambits of politicians, *against* whom Monroe, Calhoun, Clay, and Adams had struggled for a decade to promote policies the people seemed to favor, were rehabilitated as *popular* reforms against the politicians. Jackson himself defined "demagogues" as men who pursued "a course of self-aggrandizement regardless of public good" and "attempted to prostrate the character of those who pursued an "independent course."[58] The irony is paralyzing; but with the eye of a zealot Jackson saw himself entirely outside the system of corruption he so eloquently hated, and he invited the voters to join him for an assault on the wicked men in power. Such a perspective blinded him to the "management" and bargains that greased the wheels of his own new party. It blinded the voters to their own complicity in spoiling federal programs by begging for themselves benefits they would not extend to others. In deference (they said) to the unmanaged voice of the people, the Jacksonians formed a coalition with their worst caucus enemies (the original "Leading Men of Washington") and organized party to manage the people's voice more effectively than ever had been done before. These acts of political revenge redefined the nature of presidential politics and profoundly disabled the potential implicit in the Constitution for the kind of national Union Adams tried to rescue from what looked to him like demagoguery and disintegration.

Retreat from Systems of Policy

The 1828 election delivered to Jackson the first real landslide victory in an American presidential election. Fifty-six percent of the voters nationwide favored Jackson, and he collected 178 of 261 electoral votes, sweeping every state south of the Potomac and west of New Jersey. Once in power, however, the Jacksonians soon enough confronted a predictable dilemma: how could they satisfy constituent demands for cheap lands, tariffs, and internal improvement while at the same time honoring the promises of little government, public economy, and radical neo-Antifederalism that accompanied their slogan of "Jackson and reform"? Significant blocks of the Jackson coalition stood naturally at war with each other on the tariff, the disposition of the public lands, and continuation of internal improvements. The new president was destined to preside over a Union increasingly racked by sectional jealousies and a people more inclined toward rhetorical polarization than mutual concessions and compromise.[59]

Nothing in the tenets of pure republicanism automatically suggested how to reconcile these interests and soothe irritated tempers. If anything, Jackson's promise to restore primitive self-government effectively raised the voters' expectations that the voice of the people, once heard, would be obeyed by their servants in office. Early gestures of local rebellion appeared across the West, where states

ke Illinois, Indiana, and Mississippi laid claim unilaterally to the public lands
nside their borders, preempting Congress's authority over the national domain.
o the South, free-trade extremists led by Vice President Calhoun, pressed their
elentless attack on the tariff. Internal improvement could not escape these
ontradictory pressures, in part because tariffs and public lands generated the
evenues for future aid to roads and canals. More to the point, the shameless
ursuit of narrow sectional interests—immodestly stripped of any shroud of
common interest" and accompanied by threats of nullification—refocused the
ignificance of the constitutional question: was this a nation or a mere confedera-
ion, and did the government in Washington have real work to do?[60]

Jackson himself was a cipher as he took up the reins of power. Not quite the
arbarian his enemies portrayed, neither was he all the things projected upon
im by voters and spoilsmen eager to join in displacing the Washington estab-
shment. Although he promised stringent reforms designed to insure the integ-
ity of future elections and prevent manipulations of the federal patronage, once
ossessed of authority Jackson seemed content with wholesale removals from
ffice and the most naked example to date of rewarding the party faithful with
overnment places. On the great issues of the day candidate Jackson had been the
oul of ambiguity, and observers eagerly scrutinized his First Annual Message to
Congress in December 1829 for clues to the coming agenda. In that message
ackson affirmed his belief in protective tariffs, observing that the 1828 schedule
ad proved neither "so injurious" as planters pretended nor as "beneficial" as
manufacturers hoped. Free trade might be ideal, but the "selfish legislation of
ther nations" compelled us to adopt protective regulations. Entranced by the
rospect of presiding over the final payment of the national debt, Jackson urged
he application of all possible resources to that end, followed by a downward
djustment of the tariff and retrenchment of federal spending. On internal im-
rovements—anathema to Virginia radicals and southern free traders but eagerly
desired by his western supporters—he played his cards very tentatively. Pointing
o the "difficulties" that had "heretofore attended appropriations" for internal
mprovement, and those certain to arise "whenever power over such subjects may
e exercised by the General Government," Jackson hoped for a plan that would
reconcile the diversified interests of the States and strengthen the bonds which
unite them." Perhaps a distribution of the surplus federal revenue to the states
ccording to representation would be the "safe, just, and federal" solution? If not,
 constitutional amendment was in order to silence this perennial source of
ontroversy.[61]

The Twenty-first Congress responded with violently sectional debates over
money and the public lands. In the House, Jonathan Hunt of Vermont introduced a distribution resolution virtually identical to Jackson's, ostensibly to stop
"unequal legislation" for internal improvements. It was met by a firestorm of

protests from the West. Proportional distribution, cried the frontier, transferre
the West's only capital stock to the states that already absorbed most of th
federal revenue. Bitter accusations from the West drew flanking attacks fro
South Carolina and Georgia (states that fancied themselves the most abused i
the Union), claiming that distribution was really a ploy to perpetuate the hate
tariff. South Carolina's William D. Martin called for an "accounting" of all th
land grants made to the West so that deductions could be made before an
patrimony was divided, and John Test of Indiana angrily demanded a parall
tally of "the useless millions" spent on the Capitol building, the White Hous
and the navy. Missouri's lone representative, Spencer Pettis, condemned dis
tribution as "intended to check the growth" of the western states: "We have ha
American Systems—anti-slavery systems—and systems, the Lord knows wha
and now we are to have an anti-emigration system to cripple the West."[62]

This bitterness was matched and exceeded in the Senate by the brawling four
month debate over Samuel Foot's resolution to prohibit the sale of new publi
lands until the millions of acres already available cleared the market. Thoma
Hart Benton of Missouri seized the occasion to detail a plot (entirely fanciful) b
which unreconstructed Federalists in New England wickedly conspired to jac
up the tariff and close off the West, the better to enslave their poorest class c
factory operatives—"a most complex scheme of injustice, which taxes the Sout
to injure the West, to pauperize the poor of the North." Robert Y. Hayne o
South Carolina, solicitous of all outbursts against power in Washington, em
braced Benton's exposé and praised the fabled "penny-or-a-peppercorn" policie
of old colonial regimes, before steering attention back to the parallel subjectio
of the South. "We stand," he complained, "towards the United States in th
relation of Ireland to England. The fruits of our labor are drawn from us to
enrich other and more favored sections of the Union." Seething as this tissue o
falsehoods took shape, Daniel Webster finally rose to deny that the East had eve
"shown an illiberal policy towards the West." It was South Carolina, not Nev
England, that pursued exclusively sectional agenda, blocking all manner of roads
canals, and other generous policies with its strict construction, anticonsolidatio
doctrines. And it was Hayne's South Carolina colleague (and Calhoun's acolyte
George McDuffie who had led an earlier bitter assault on the western states—
whose 1825 speech Webster gleefully quoted at length to the Senate.[63]

Such intemperate exchanges, separated by mind-numbing, days-lon
speeches—mostly bereft of constructive insights, calculated to infuriate but neve
to accommodate the opposition—marked the entire first session of the Twenty
first Congress. A majority continued to support internal improvement. On
major initiative for a national road from Buffalo to New Orleans failed in th
House, but stock subscriptions prevailed in behalf of the Louisville & Portlan
Canal and the Maysville and Washington Turnpikes, in addition to a miscella

eous package of river and harbor improvements. Connecting the Ohio River with Lexington, Kentucky, and comprising (said its friends) a link in a great chain of north-south communications, the Maysville Road bill drew familiar objections from predictable sources. Thomas Foster of Georgia said the road was local, not national. Polk agreed and charged internal improvers with supporting all things indiscriminately. Traversing Henry Clay country, the Maysville Road naturally attracted partisan attacks, and these objections emanated mostly from well-known enemies of federal public works. Comfortable majorities passed the bill with little expectation that time was running out on the American System. Clay himself rejoiced at the news: after the loss of the Buffalo road, "some assertion of the power of Internal improvement . . . seemed necessary." Although there was talk that Jackson resented internal improvement, Secretary of State Martin Van Buren had urged the president to say nothing until a notoriously local bill came through and then shock Congress into submission. Thus Clay and others were caught by surprise when Jackson struck down the Maysville Road.[64]

Widely assumed to be the product of Van Buren's pen (Van Buren claimed as much in his *Autobiography*), Jackson's Maysville veto nevertheless contained vital clues about how Jackson understood the deteriorating political culture that surrounded him. Acknowledging a limited power in Congress to appropriate money for *national* roads and canals (but no power to construct them in the states), Jackson failed the Maysville project for being of a "purely local character." Further admitting the elusive nature of the distinction between local and national projects, Jackson suggested it was not "expedient" to continue with the present approach to internal improvements without first delimiting the system by means of a clarifying amendment. Behind this conviction lay a growing concern for the unequal impact and political turmoil surrounding public works as well as protective tariffs. Fixated on retrenchment and economy, Jackson hated appropriations that swelled the federal budget. Unwilling to evaluate whole programs in light of each other (the American System idea), he insisted that each policy (the bank, tariffs, internal improvements) must operate fairly on all the states and pass the constitutional test on its own merits alone. All Americans, he thought, were "friends" of internal improvements, but "none certainly" were "so degenerate" as to prefer "their local interest to the principles of the Union." If so, the world had "but little to hope from the example of free government."[65]

Taken at face value, Jackson's veto of the Maysville Road reflected legitimate doubts about the progress of internal improvements since the end of the Monroe administration. Whatever good it was doing, the American System was not producing harmony and political happiness. No plan or system of national works (called for in the General Survey Act) had ever been adopted by Congress, and the logrolling system that grew up in its place seemed capable of infinite expansion. Appropriations did not flow equally to the states—*could not* do so if the

object was to aid works of national significance, because such projects were nc
equally distributed among the twenty-four states. Efforts to balance the scon
inevitably exposed lawmakers to charges of pandering for votes; refusal to do s
convicted them of partiality. Those who did not share Clay's satisfaction with th
cumulative effect of all developmental policies found states' rights radicals eage
to convert them to a neo-Antifederalist view of the Union. In the Maysville vetc
Jackson seemed to be searching for an alternative national position, less consol
idationist than Clay's American System yet less disintegrative than Calhoun
new doctrine of nullification. On its face Jackson's argument echoed Madison'
concerns in 1817: both presidents feared the corrupting implications of a scrambl
for funds in a national democratic legislature. The temptation for congressmen
to gratify ever more numerous demands from their constituents seemed to Jack
son virtually to guarantee overspending, requiring finally direct taxes to pay fo
extravagant internal improvements.[66]

Of course, nobody took Jackson's veto at face value: how could they? Politica
insult appeared to be its primary purpose. The only project dear to Henry Clay'
constituents had been deemed too local while other appropriations no less con-
stricted found presidential favor. "The hand of the 'great magician' [Van Buren
was visible in every line," shouted William Stanbery when the House receivec
the message. "There was nothing candid, nothing open, nothing honest in it.
"From the stump" it was declared, cried Joseph Vance "that General Jackson wa
the firm, steady, and consistent friend of internal improvement." Davy Crocke
claimed it drove him from the party: "I am still a Jackson man, but Genera
Jackson is not; he has become a Van Buren man." Henry Clay, already deeply
involved in the presidential contest for 1832, saw the veto as a major error by out-
of-touch Jacksonians. "We ought not to lose the advantages," Clay enthused
"which late acts of the admon [sic] have given to us." Campaigning happily on
the integrated virtues of the American System, Clay accused Jackson of violating
the people's trust and abdicating power in the face of angry minorities. Men who
hated Clay or internal improvements heard the veto no less as a political manifesto. John Randolph reportedly toasted the news: "it falls upon the ears like the
music of other days." Philip Barbour, still Virginia's leading neo-Antifederalist in
Congress, praised the veto as destroying a system that could only end in "deep
disgust on one side" and "corruption on the other." "How much, then, do we owe
to him, who averts this gangrene from our body politic?"[67]

In December 1830 Jackson enlarged the scope of his discretionary negative and
expanded his comments on how the government should function. "The successful operation of the federal system can only be preserved," he proclaimed, "by
confining it to the few and simple . . . objects for which it was designed."
Therefore, he intended to resist any doubtful exercise of power. (The first two
victims were stock subscriptions to chartered corporations and certain lighthouse

ppropriations, neither of which had been challenged before.) Critics complained that such negatives merely interposed the president's will for that of
lected representatives in Congress, but Jackson insisted that "the great body of
he people" were with him. The test of all virtue could be found in "the approba-
ion of the people," and Jackson felt himself uniquely in touch with this highest
orm of republican authority. The people would sustain him—or they could vote
him out of office. Assuming himself to be the last defender of the Constitution,
ackson proclaimed that "sustaining the State sovereignties" and "preserving the
greatest attainable harmony between them" constituted the "true faith." To those
ends every action of the government now must be directed. Here was the ground
of his objection to internal improvements: Congress simply stirred up the natural
ivalries among the states by making unequal disbursements for roads and canals.
The resulting "combinations and angry contentions" worked "baleful influences"
on legislation in Congress and wrecked the harmony of the Union. It was "beyond the power of man," he concluded, to make a government "operate with
precise equality upon the States." Nor should every state "expect to shape the
measures of the General Government to suit its own particular interests." What
Jackson wanted was a retreat from grand systems of policy, distribution of the
surplus federal revenue, and a plan of retrenchment that promised to "keep the
movements of the Federal Government within the sphere intended" by the framers. Such a plan he pledged "would receive from me a cordial and firm support."[68]

Jackson's message blended novel claims for his role as republican oracle with a
keen recognition that continued disharmony truly threatened the nation. Fights
over roads and canals threatened to destroy "mutual concession and reciprocal
forbearance," without which the Union could not go on. Effectively, Jackson's
strategy for binding up the Union by *retreating* from systems of policy exactly
contradicted improvers' efforts. Even Jackson's friends found the sentiments
harder to implement than to applaud, and the president got no such plan for distribution or retrenchment from the second session of the Twenty-first Congress.
The committee charged with the distribution question, chaired by Tennessee
Congressman James K. Polk, concluded that no scheme of distribution could be
devised that was "wholly free from objection." The Committee on Roads and
Canals arrived at a contrary conclusion, reporting that (Jackson's opposition
notwithstanding) majorities of congressmen "coming fresh from among" the
people manifested "unrelaxed zeal in favor of promoting their country's prosperity by national improvements." To prove it, Congress sent the president another package bill comprising all sorts of internal improvements—House members voting well over two-to-one in favor.[69]

Since the Maysville veto in May of 1830 Jackson stood exposed as an enemy of
national internal improvements, and long-suffering anticonsolidationists, especially from the South Atlantic states, rolled out their batteries of opposition with

renewed hope and confidence. Watching these developments from "retirement at Ashland, Henry Clay saw a presidential campaign shaping up that pitted more clearly than ever before his vision of a rising, integrated nation against the dyspeptic doctrines of Virginia neo-Antifederalists, South Carolina nullifiers, land-hungry western demagogues, and shameless spoilsmen everywhere. Convinced that the Jackson camp contained the seeds of its own destruction, Clay could not imagine that the people approved of Jackson's wholesale removals, his imperious temperament, or his frontal attack on the American System. At the same time, the success of Jackson men in local elections (especially in his home state, Kentucky) inflamed Clay's desire to stop this dangerous pretender before the people became hopelessly deceived. Jackson's goal, in the words of one of Clay's correspondents, was to "strip the General Government of most of its powers, to bring it back to a Confederation of *Sovereign* States," by throttling the Court, repealing tariffs, stopping internal improvements, and killing the Bank of the United States. In a counterstrategy around which he built the campaign for 1832, Clay reached for the center, retaining the interlocking systems including the bank, internal improvements, and the principle of tariff protection, but inviting such modifications in any or all of them as were required to restore harmony. So inclined, Clay took up his seat in the Senate in December 1831 and began to fashion his own version of the plan for peace and reconciliation Andrew Jackson called for with growing impatience.[70]

As the Twenty-second Congress gathered, southern free traders pressed hard to destroy tariff protection and western interests demanded the gradual reduction of the price of public lands, if not their outright cession to the states in which they lay. Hoping always to quiet the political waters, Jackson himself had abandoned protection, recommending tariffs for revenue only, and he was grasping for some scheme of land reform aimed at selling off the national domain as quickly as possible to actual settlers. Treasury Secretary Louis McLane offered to sell the remaining land to the states and distribute the "aggregate price" among the states, but westerners howled against any solution that transferred money into eastern hands. Clay's great hope was to quiet South Carolina with a gradual reduction of tariff rates without conceding protection in theory (or appearing to yield to threats of disunion), and to co-opt Benton's land reform radicals with a scheme of proportional distribution, generously tilted in a western direction, that simultaneously funded internal improvements, preserved the national domain, and put an end to the logrolling game in Congress.[71]

Hoping to trap the presidential hopeful, Jacksonian senators saddled Clay's Committee on Manufactures with these two explosive issues. Turning the tables, Clay reported back solutions of his own that seized enough middle ground to appear conciliatory. Citing with approval statistics marking the phenomenal growth of the West, Clay observed that land sales required no "fresh stimulus."

Reduced prices would only excite speculation, drag down the market value of private lands, and depopulate Ohio, Kentucky, and Tennessee—western states from which the majority of new emigrants presently moved. The existing land system worked, Clay concluded, and all that remained to be done was to gratify the needs of the West for capital improvements and of the East for their reasonable share of the common treasure. For this he proposed a 10 percent kickback to new states in addition to the 5 percent road money already set aside; the balance would be divided among all the states according to the federal ratio (after deducting additional grants to Missouri, Alabama, Illinois, and Indiana, bringing each state to a half-million acres). With this money the states could press on with internal improvements (or pay down debts already incurred for the same), improve education, or facilitate the colonization of free blacks outside the country, as each saw fit.[72]

Clay's bill was a brilliant package that aborted both Benton's graduation scheme and the land-grabbing cession idea while funneling large sums into western state treasuries for developmental purposes. Loaded with western advantages, the deal nevertheless threw annual sums of cash at the older states that sometimes exceeded their current budgets. Calling the bluff of his longtime enemies, Clay disavowed any intention to collect even "a cent of duty" for the purpose of internal improvement, and his bill distributed control to the states (which Jacksonians insisted knew best how to improve the country). Furthermore, it coupled his cherished objective of colonization with the existing nationalist agenda of central banking, tariff protection, and internal improvement. Not *the* plan desired by extremists in either wing of the Jackson party, Clay's deal nevertheless constituted at least *one* plausible route to harmony and reconciliation. If blocked by Jacksonians in Congress in 1832, Clay believed it would anchor a winning platform for the presidential canvass to be concluded later that year.[73]

The biggest thing wrong, of course, with Clay's bill was the fact that it came from Henry Clay. Combining reduced protective tariffs with a distribution of public land revenues, Clay's proposal duplicated exactly James Madison's recommendations when Van Buren asked that elder statesman how to untie the Gordian knot of internal improvement policy. But Jackson's unforgiving ego and the Jacksonians' thirst for office now prevented them from embracing anything that smacked of positive governance—or had been touched by Henry Clay. In a spontaneous outburst Thomas Hart Benton found Clay's principles "so strange and so mischievous" that he had to attack at once. The leading objection was that Clay's bill might satisfy western interests without gratifying Benton's preference for lower, graduated land prices. The new states were to be "enticed by a Slice from their own lands," Benton ranted: like desperate cannibals, they would be fed from their own substance "and then torn limb from limb." Failing to suppress the report and prevent its printed circulation, Clay's enemies finally committed the bill (on a casting vote by Vice President Calhoun) to the Public Lands Committee, whose counterreport repeated every possible objection to the existing land system and its high minimum price, the injustice of distribution, and the illegitimacy of federal initiatives. In open debate in late June (at the end of an exhausting session) Clay and Benton squared off again, exchanging bitter, personal charges of demagoguery (against Benton) and sectional treason (against Clay). Longtime enemies of federal control now complained (astonishingly) that states would squander the fruits of distribution on local and "disjointed" projects. Indiana, Illinois, and Missouri (for example) might construct separate railroads that did not connect at their borders, which "if made by the General Government . . . would be a direct and connected whole, of general utility to the whole nation, and worthy of its high design and cost." When this rhetorical cannonade finally ceased, the Senate passed Clay's distribution bill 26 to 18.[74]

The House adjourned without acting on distribution, but not for lack of interest in internal improvements. From the beginning of the session anti-improvers announced a desire to settle forever the "question of national internal improvements," yet one by one members of the popular chamber added to a $30,000 package of improvements until, at $1.2 million, it scandalized James K. Polk and reminded North Carolina's Thomas Hall of a "pile of logs" rolled up by the "log rollers"—they ought to set fire and burn it! This "demoniacal system" of internal improvement, Hall concluded, struck "more directly at the vitals of the sovereignty of the States" than that "canker of our peace and harmony, the tariff itself." Nevertheless, the House passed this well-fatted barrel of pork, 99 to 75, the Senate agreed, and Jackson gave his silent assent (although Clay later heard that Jackson intended to "suspend the execution" of parts of this bill to which he objected). Apparently nobody wished to go home empty-handed in the closing months of the 1832 presidential canvass.[75]

Internal improvement did not command center stage in this final session before the presidential election; tariff reform and Jackson's attack on the United States Bank generated far more heat and light and set the terms of the final battle between Jackson and Clay. Still, taken together it seemed to Clay that Jackson's lack of support for popular federal programs, his attack on the bank, tariffs, and internal improvements, his party's manipulation of patronage, the arbitrariness of the Maysville veto in light of his shameless support for election-year pork, his apparent subservience to the strident voices of southern and western extremists within the ruling coalition—all of this surely exposed Jackson as a demagogue, a hypocrite, and an altogether dangerous man. "He has put a pick axe at the base of every pillar that supports every department and every valuable institution in the Country," Clay complained in May 1832, and "all who value their Government" had better put "their shoulders together to sustain its endangered columns." Listening closely only to his friends (and hopelessly distracted by technical probems resulting from the third-party efforts of the Anti-Masons), Clay could not imagine that Old Hickory's conduct did not outrage American voters. As the results of local fall elections began to trickle in, his spirits darkened, and by mid-November a second Jackson landslide had destroyed his hopes altogether. "The dark cloud which had been so long suspended over our devoted Country," mused the gloomy campaigner, "instead of being dispelled, as we had fondly hoped it would be, has become more dense, more menacing more alarming. Whether we shall ever see light, and law and liberty again, is very questionable."[76]

Jackson's second victory opened the "nullification winter," for Clay one of the darkest periods he ever spent in Washington. In November, as the final electoral results were being tallied, South Carolina passed its Ordinance of Nullification—outlawing the collection of federal customs—and the long-threatened struggle between Jackson and the southern free-trade radicals came to a head. On 10 December 1832 Jackson ordered the nullifiers to desist: the United States was a "government, not a league," and nullification was nothing less than treason. At the same time the president reiterated his advice to Congress that the federal arm be withdrawn from all but its original purposes: "preserving the peace, affording an uniform currency, maintaining the inviolability of contracts, diffusing intelligence, and discharging unfelt its other superintending functions." To that end he demanded no more internal improvements (and the sale of all stock in projects already started), an end to tariff protection, and the sale of public lands at cost, the sooner to deprive Congress of a resource so "dangerous to the harmony and union of the States." Belligerent enough in response to disobedience, Jackson seemed eager to abandon any course of positive action that stimulated "discontent and jealousy."[77]

Humiliated once again at the polls, Henry Clay found himself in December in the Senate, a critical player in a desperate crisis brought on (he believed) by extremists in the states and the temper and venality of a military hero better loved by the people than himself. Jackson, Clay lamented, had uprooted everything gained since the adoption of the Constitution: "What single principle is fixed? The Bank? No. Internal Improvements! No. The Tariff, No. Who is to interpret the Constitution? No. We are as much afloat at sea as the day when the Constitution went into operation." Nothing was certain except "that the *will* of Andw. Jackson is to govern." Now that infamous will was set against a treasonous movement in South Carolina, and Clay feared a violent collision and certain repudiation of his cherished policies. Always the broker, Clay stepped into the impasse, hoping he could get a better deal than Jackson from the nullifiers (and maybe some credit for averting disaster).[78]

What Clay offered was a compromise tariff that slowly scaled back duties over the next nine years and lifted protection altogether in 1842. The American System was "in the greatest danger," and his goal in relaxing the system was to "preserve the manufacturing interest" while at the same time "tranquilizing" the country. Coupled with the so-called force bill that Jackson requested (and Clay supported) to punish the scofflaws in South Carolina, Clay's bill offered nullifiers a way to retreat with honor without shocking industrial capitalists by a sudden exposure to free trade. If Congress would make "a fair experiment" with tariff reduction, and pass as well his distribution bill, they would have settled, he believed, "two (if not three) of the great questions" that "agitated" the country: the tariff, public lands, and internal improvement. Distribution was the key to lasting harmony: pass it and "what State will then be disposed to go out of the confederacy, and sacrifice the great advantages administered by this Government?" But that was precisely the objection raised by Clay's adversaries. The bill created an interest that tied the states to the federal government. It arrived in the Senate, fulminated Benton, "with money in every clause, to pay its way through, as the souls of the damned arrived on the banks of the river Styx, with money in hand to pay their passage into hell." Grand schemes of policy could not "bind up all the wounds" of the Union, added Alexander Buckner (also from Missouri); their "binding efficacy" was gone. In a maddening gesture, Calhoun stepped down from the chair to condemn Clay's effort to "denationalize the public funds." The high priest of nullification (and former leading internal improver) now demanded a constitutional amendment so that the wealth of the nation could be spent directly on the great interregional "arteries of inter-communication." But the Senate backed Clay 24 to 20, and the House, at 11:00 P.M., 1 March, concurred by a generous margin of 96 to 40.[79]

"Yesterday was perhaps the most important Congressional day that ever occurred," Clay wrote James Barbour with relief; the force bill, the tariff, and the distribution bill all three passed that day as the session expired. His pleasure, alas, was short-lived: Jackson signed the first two but "pocket-vetoed" the distribution bill for continuing a policy he strongly disapproved. (The following December, he explained that "a more direct road to consolidation" could not be devised, and he ordered instead Benton's graduation plan with eventual cession of unsold lands to the states in which they lay.) Astonished by Jackson's disregard for "the Legislative authority" and by the people's willingness to "applaud whatever he does," Clay thought that the stage had been set for "a dissolution of the Union," to which there was "less aversion now than could be wished by those who love their Country."[80]

The despondency of that summer passed, and Clay returned to press his distribution scheme—and his vision of activist government—for many more years to come. More surprisingly, Jacksonian congresses continued to appropriate money for internal improvements at a steadily rising rate (roughly two and a half times the Adams administration's record): Jackson spent almost as much in 1836–37 (while his heir-apparent, Van Buren, was running for the presidency) as Adams in four full years (see Table 4). Yet Van Buren was not entirely wrong when he

TABLE 4. Federal Expenditures for Internal Improvement, 1826–1829 (Adams) and 1830–1837 (Jackson)

Year	Rivers and Harbors	Roads and Canals	Lighthouses, etc.	Stock Subscription	Total
1826	$87,049.00	$562,987.00	$188,941.00	$100,000.00	$940,803.00
1827	130,019.00	351,964.00	305,918.00		789,728.00
1828	187,505.00	401,183.00	253,728.00	1,000,000.00	1,844,244.00
1829	524,127.00	782,120.00	277,274.00	1,085,000.00	2,670,350.00
Total	928,700.00	2,098,254.00	1,025,861.00	2,185,000.00	6,237,815.00
1830	$573,779.00	$638,888.00	$233,113.00		$1,447,610.00
1831	652,213.00	362,607.00	320,719.00		1,337,370.00
1832	538,079.00	694,849.00	256,642.00		1,491,402.00
1833	703,941.00	1,053,264.00	313,810.00		2,072,848.00
1834	507,790.00	866,561.00	414,009.00		1,790,194.00
1835	568,791.00	1,233,158.00	476,920.00		2,280,704.00
1836	869,302.00	1,217,726.00	770,276.00		2,859,140.00
1837	1,361,794.00	944,259.00	594,627.00		2,902,517.00
Total	5,775,689.00	7,011,312.00	3,380,116.00		16,167,117.00

Source: U.S. Congress, *Statement of Appropriations and Expenditures for Public Buildings, Rivers and Harbors, Forts, Arsenals, Armories, and Other Public Works from March 4, 1789 to June 30, 1882,* 47th Cong., 1st sess., S. Doc. VII: 1992. For stock subscriptions, see Nelson, "Presidential Influence," appendix A. Nelson does not include value of land grants.

claimed that Jackson's vetoes in 1830 and 1833 effectively "banished" internal improvements from the national legislative docket. For nearly two decades nothing was done except under a shroud of Jacksonian disavowal. When distribution finally came in 1836 it was not Clay's bill but a makeshift scheme of Calhoun's to "deposit" with the states (as a loan) the surplus overflowing the federal treasury. Even this Jackson signed reluctantly, and candidate Van Buren campaigned openly in 1836 against any further distribution for the purpose of internal improvement. In the end, the Jacksonians seemed more determined to break up consolidated government than to bind up the nation or to harmonize the sectional interests in the Union. Promises of freedom and prosperity without constraining institutions, national programs, or legislative policies better suited the desires of a people who feared for any reason the exercise of power in Washington.[81]

It had been the central conviction of Adams and Clay and their National Republican supporters that only energetic systems of interlocking policy could bind the republic together as it entered the market revolution. Positive actions, they

believed, were required to guide development and mitigate disruptive consequences, and the national government—standing above all particular local advantages—alone seemed competent to negotiate and execute such policies. The
Jacksonians rose to power by denouncing Adams and Clay as corrupt, illegitimate governors and attacking their programs as well. Where the American
System promised a prosperous future based on capitalist development, market
integration, and a rising, complex edifice of policy and institutions, the Jacksonians promised the simple extension of the familiar habits of planting, selling,
and carving out frontier farms. To defeat the National Republicans, Jacksonians
resurrected the revolutionary impulse to reject empire and reclaim provincial
autonomy. When this renewal of liberating sentiments produced an outburst of
dangerously competitive sectional demands, for free trade in the South and free
land in the West, Jackson led a retreat from the exercise of governance. Convinced that the use of all doubtful powers inexorably endangered the Union,
Jackson steered the political machinery back toward the neo-Antifederalist conceptions long proffered by radical Virginians as the antidote to powerful forces
they could not control from home. Although in the 1830s Clay's National Republicans took up their ancestors' appellation "Whig" in an effort to associate
themselves with radical resistance to the arbitrary rule of the tyrant, "King Andrew" Jackson, it was the Jacksonians who truly rekindled rebellion against the
maturing hand of a "metropolitan" government at the center of the American
empire.

Had a straight-line projection of 1830s-style yeoman's capitalism been sustain-
able into the future, the Jacksonian solution might have served the country well;
but the capitalist system that was driving the market revolution favored industrial
development and complex structures with or without the guiding hand of government. By withdrawing the government from policy making, Jacksonians empowered markets, perhaps by default, both in politics and enterprise, as arbiters
of conflict in American society. Supposedly natural, self-regulating, cheap, virtually invisible, incorruptible, and superficially democratic, free markets for the
exchange of goods and services (or for the votes of ordinary citizens) held out
the promise of appropriate outcomes to every clash of interests or ideas. More
tempting was the fact that, while Clay's negotiated systems required each party to
concede from time to time the contrary interests of others, Jackson's alternative
of liberal democracy flattered the hope of the marketplace (and the gaming
table), that with luck one might win and win and never make concessions to
anyone.

By the end of the Jackson administration two things were equally apparent:
Americans still wanted and needed internal improvements on a monumental
scale, but they would not support a consolidated national government intentionally mounting or directing such projects. Nourished by the federal money

and land grants disbursed under Adams and Clay—and reinforced by significant infusions of cash slipped past Jackson's vetoes in appropriations for miscellaneous rivers, harbors, and internal improvements—political and economic leaders in the states once more put their shoulders to the wheels of progress in a second burst of state-level initiatives that quickly filled the space left by Jackson's retreat from national action. The result, for another brief period, was that a decentralized approach might be satisfactory after all. Only with the widespread failure of state systems in the wake of the panic of 1837 would private capitalists finally come forward to accept the role Jacksonians had offered them, as architects of the nation's economic infrastructure.

6

State Initiatives Again

JACKSONIAN HOSTILITY to *national* public works threw the initiative for internal improvements back to state authorities, who were not altogether unwilling to embrace a decentralized approach. For many state leaders, the retreat from the integrated systems of Adams and Clay enhanced opportunities for local improvers to gain a competitive edge over their neighbors and secure prosperity for their own constituents without having to deal with the frustrations and compromises inherent in national legislation. To some extent the scramble for preferment that helped destroy the congressional consensus found impetus in this state-centered competition. After all, most Americans in the Jackson years seemed content to identify with state more than national prospects. With technical help and generous federal "seed capital" already in hand (thanks to the American System initiatives before 1830 and backhanded appropriations thereafter), local improvers found themselves in better positions than they had been ten years before. At least until the panic of 1837, voters in many states enthusiastically embraced ambitious internal improvement systems of their own.

New York, of course, set the pace for state-centered improvers. What had seemed like a terrible risk turned into a tremendous bonanza by 1825, as revenues from the Erie Canal poured into the New York State treasury, financing an extensive network of additional canals and relieving other tax burdens. Private wealth seemed to spring from the banks of the waterway, and the economic transformation of upstate New York (for good or ill) became the wonder of progress-minded Americans everywhere. New York's success seemed overwhelming in the middle 1820s, but the relative failure of other efforts in Pennsylvania, Maryland, and Virginia (not to mention New York's later overextended system) could not yet clearly be seen. In fact, between 1825 and 1835 canals were making New York fantastically rich. It was equally true before 1840 that railroads remained experimental (and demonstrably inadequate), and that private investors unassisted by government were everywhere unequal to the task of creating these magnificent transportation improvements.[1] Viewed in the context of recent events, Jacksonian friends of internal improvement in the early 1830s could believe that the withdrawal of national support did not endanger but actually improved the chances for local development. Therefore, it was not in resignation but in hope that boosters in the states took up the burden thrown off by Jackson and Van Buren and pursued undaunted their state-level dreams of competitive internal improvement.

The decentralized approach to internal improvement at this crucial juncture, however, contributed much to the failure of these competing state-centered programs. First, too many projects were started at once. A dozen separate governments and countless private corporations sprang into action, commissioning engineers, borrowing money, hiring laborers, and buying supplies—all of which, being scarce, increased dramatically in price. Rather than discouraging additional ventures, such market pressures tended to exaggerate people's urgent desire to act now before scarce resources were exhausted and the malleable landscape was transformed irrecoverably. The result was an outbreak of "canal fever," a reckless enthusiasm for public works that seems in retrospect to contradict prudence and reason. Because we know that panic and depression ended this boom, and that the railroads ultimately displaced canals, we easily fault this generation for its shortness of vision and optimistic assumptions. The examples that follow, however, serve to illustrate how earnest improvers wrestled with the best information they possessed in a rapidly evolving political culture to meet the needs of a demanding public clamoring for growth and opportunity.

Ohio: Successful Reiteration

Not the threat but the promise of the Erie Canal stirred men's desires in frontier Ohio. If Clinton's "Big Ditch" proved successful, a similar canal from Lake Erie to the Ohio River would open a complete waterborne circuit from the Atlantic to the Gulf of Mexico. As early as January 1819, Ohio Governor Ethan Allen Brown had urged his legislature to hire an experienced engineer to study the "grand project of internal navigation." A Cincinnati attorney with experience in local public office, Brown took the lead in promoting a statewide system of "veins and arteries to the body politic," designed to foster vigorous growth in his frontier state. Together with Cincinnati businessman Micajah T. Williams and Cleveland entrepreneur Alfred Kelley, Brown spent the next seven years ardently promoting public canals as Ohio's most logical and necessary response to New York's daring public works commitment.[2]

Nobody doubted, of course, that an Ohio Canal would stand close in importance to Erie in the national circulation of goods and people. But just at that moment the panic of 1819 was closing banks and wrecking many of Ohio's leading fortunes. More seriously, local jealousies and narrow, short-term perspectives—the same prejudices that spoiled internal improvement systems on the national level—equally plagued state promoters who sought taxing authority for the construction of roads and canals. An Ohio canal obviously benefited the state and the region, but which lake port, which Ohio River town, and which interior communities should be favored by such an extraordinary facility? Before 1820 settlement had spread across Ohio from the river toward the north and west. Canal construction was bound to favor one of several fledgling lake ports and spark "boom" conditions in undeveloped counties through which the waterway must pass. At least three possible valleys—the Cuyahoga-Tuscarawas (east), the Sandusky (central), and the Maumee (west)—led away from Lake Erie to summits in upland Ohio. Three more—the Muskingum (east), Scioto (central), and Miami (west)—gave access to the Ohio River. Merchants and speculators ached with desire (or burned with resentment) whenever particular routes were discussed (see Map 4). Technical evaluations eventually discredited those routes that lacked adequate water at the summit levels; but within the range of possibilities, location decisions were hotly contested. Underdeveloped and capital-starved, Ohio lacked the New Yorkers' deep pockets, so any mistake was bound to be more punishing. Finally Cincinnati, the Buckeye State's leading commercial metropolis, worried that canals to Lake Erie might distract attention and resources from public works at the Falls of the Ohio near Louisville, upon which the growth of the Queen City's river trade depended.[3]

Into these crosscurrents waded Governor Brown. Believing a canal could be built for something like $3 million, he proposed in 1820 asking Congress to "sell" (payments and interest deferred ten years) 4 million acres of Indian land, which the state might then resell to finance canal construction. Congress refused, and the depression-plagued Ohio Assembly risked nothing beyond an 1821 authorization of $20,000 toward a survey at the Louisville falls. Finally, in 1822 a House committee headed by Micajah T. Williams reported that New York's maturing example virtually compelled Ohio to proceed with its own canal. If not, a chartered corporation might leap at this opportunity, Williams argued, and why "sacrifice" the "best interests of the country by placing so fair and rich a harvest" in the hands of greedy capitalists? The state should keep control, in fact, the world owed much to New Yorkers "for their practical refutation of the doctrine which has so long prevailed, that the public could not accomplish works of this kind so cheap as a corporation." The Ohio Assembly responded by directing commissioners to hire an engineer and examine the possible routes. At last things were moving in Ohio, and Governor Brown (now United States Senator Brown) fired off letters to DeWitt Clinton asking if Ohio could secure the requisite financing in New York. With money markets still recovering in 1822 from the panic of 1819, Clinton was not optimistic about the loan; but he did send James Geddes, his leading engineer, to examine the Ohio terrain.[4]

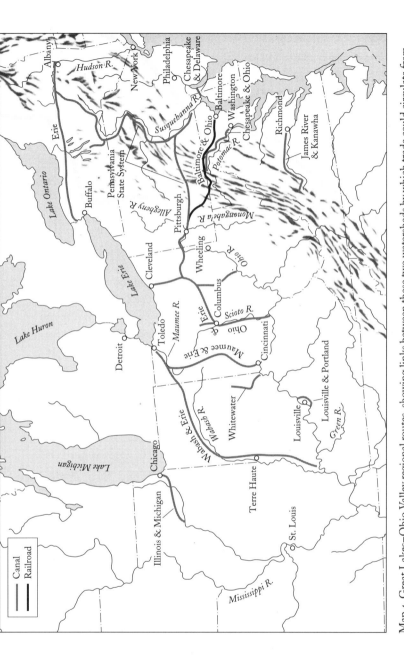

Map 4. Great Lakes–Ohio Valley regional routes, showing links between these two watersheds by which trade could circulate from the Atlantic, via the Erie Canal, Pennsylvania Main Line, or Potomac route to the Ohio-Mississippi river system and the outlet at

By the appointment of the now-famous Geddes for the first round of surveys, Ohio Governor Allen Trimble hoped to secure advice that was "above suspicion of partiality" toward any one of the proposed routes. Political support for *any* state project would depend on gratifying local interests—or convincing them that routes not chosen were technically unattractive. In January 1823, after a year of preliminary surveys, the commissioners reported three practicable routes but asked for more time and money to prepare reliable estimates. Casting about for capital resources, they suggested that Ohio seek permission from Congress to sell the state's school lands (promising to fund schools later with canal revenues), or an outright donation of land, or authority to purchase Indian reservations. Meanwhile, they gained power to solicit right-of-way donations from local private landholders, which allowed the two "acting commissioners," Micajah Williams and Alfred Kelley, to include in their technical assessment of different routes the "generosity" of local proprietors. In a second report one year later, the commissioners reluctantly concluded that it was "*extremely* doubtful" that a connection could be made between the Scioto and Miami Valleys, effectively killing the long diagonal route by which they had hoped to join the interests of Cincinnati with those of central and northeastern Ohio. Similarly, they rejected for "want of water" the popular central line through Columbus and continuing up the Sandusky Valley. What emerged as the preferred route was a shallow S-shaped canal from Cleveland up the Cuyahoga and Tuscarawas Rivers to the headwaters of the Muskingum, across the Walnut-Licking summit to the Scioto, and down the latter to the Ohio at Portsmouth. In an effort not to alienate Cincinnati completely, the board recommended a second short canal up the Miami to Dayton, which could be extended toward the Maumee and Lake Erie when future development required. Appended to the report were letters from Clinton and New York bankers assuring that Ohio could borrow $2 to $3 million with ease in New York or Europe.[5]

If local interests could be brought into line, the Ohio Canal now seemed perfectly feasible. New York's experience continued to inform the Ohio promoters: compared with the Empire State's obstacles, Ohio's "dwindle into comparative insignificance." The Ohio canal commissioners lobbied hard for a positive commitment. Canal promotions required, they argued, only credit, water, labor, local materials, and potential for economic growth. Ohio possessed all of these in abundance. Reflecting the confidence in public works that was cresting in 1824, they insisted that "every great work of this kind, in which the welfare of the people is so deeply concerned, should be under the control of the government, and not of a private company." The legislature ordered surveyors back to the field to prepare detailed estimates, while political and economic interests prepared for what was probably the final contest over whether and where to begin the Ohio canal system. It was a question, proclaimed the *Cincinnati Gazette*, "of greatly more importance to us . . . than who shall be President."[6]

Significant opposition came not from enemies of internal improvement but from the partisans of routes not selected, especially friends of the condemned Sandusky route and residents of southeastern Ohio. When the lawmakers convened in December 1824, Governor Jeremiah Morrow urged them to accept whatever recommendations the commissioners laid before them and to revise state taxes to service the anticipated debt. The commissioners' report came out 10 January 1825, calling for an Ohio Canal along the Scioto-Muskingum route and a Miami Canal from Cincinnati to Dayton, undertaken as public enterprises in the hands of the canal commissioners, financed by general obligation bonds administered by separate canal fund commissioners, and backed by state taxes and a sinking fund. To quiet noisy opposition from disappointed local interests, lawmakers adopted an ad valorem tax designed to service the debt with the windfall gains of landholders nearest these transportation lines; it also passed out strategic aid to state roads. Enacted into law on 4 February 1825, the commissioners' report set the stage for the first major public works program by a western state.[7]

The first Ohio loan of $400,000 was taken by a New York banking house that bid 97.5 for 5 percent bonds—quite a good yield despite negative publicity generated by disappointed sections seeking to undermine Ohio's credibility and defeat the loan. With money in hand, the canal commissioners laid down their final routes, collected rights-of-way, wrote their technical specifications, and began letting contracts for the northern (Cleveland) section of the Ohio Canal and the southern (Cincinnati) section of the Miami Canal. Employing a multitude of small independent contractors, many of them local farmers and businessmen (a standard strategy for American public works), the Ohio commissioners quickly pumped this borrowed capital into their cash-starved frontier economy, magnifying its immediate impact. At first woodcutters, shovelers, and teamsters were not hard to hire; but for scarce hydraulic engineers and crews skilled at building locks and dams, Ohio had to compete with projects in New York, Pennsylvania, Maryland, and Virginia. The quickening pace of internal improvements all over the United States soon drove up wages and prices. Still, Ohio's 6 percent bonds were selling at 101 in 1826 and 107 in 1827, so the commissioners pressed on confidently. Thirty-eight miles of the Ohio Canal from Cleveland to Akron was opened 4 July 1827, and about forty miles of the Miami began operating in November, accomplishments that encouraged canallers, investors, and taxpayers alike. In 1828 John C. Calhoun pronounced it "almost a miracle that a state in its infancy should . . . successfully execute so great a work." That same spring Congress approved a half-million-acre land grant to Ohio that would secure another large loan and two small ones before 1832 when construction was completed.[8]

Originally Ohio had intended to build as cheap a canal as possible, but the success of the early loans encouraged the commissioners to substitute stone for wood and make other changes that produced for them a finer canal at an ad-

vanced cost. Other popular changes, such as side cuts and feeders to accommodate local communities, also drove up final costs. Wages for common labor
quickly rose from $5 to $10 per month (plus board) by 1827, $16 in 1829, and $18 in
1832. Floods ruined partly finished works in early 1832; seasonal fevers and the
1832 outbreak of Asiatic cholera interrupted progress; and engineering mistakes
necessitated changes in the original design. Still, the two finished canals came in
at roughly one-third above the estimates and can be considered, among comparable efforts, as entirely successful. According to historian Harry Scheiber, careful attention to detail by commissioners Kelley and Williams (who resisted most
of the temptations to expand the project or divert resources into short-term
speculations) proved critical to Ohio's success.[9]

Despite earnest warnings from Commissioner Kelley not to "overload the
system with new projects," the opening of each new segment of these first two
Ohio canals only intensified popular demands for expanded service and an equal
distribution of state developmental investments. Public investment in transportation improvements quickly acquired the character of a political right, and one
Democratic newspaper in 1833 warned "all wise Legislators" not to cramp the
state's growth by opposing new public works. Bitter local rivalries and strategic
jockeying for advantage, exacerbated by the partisan rhetoric of now-ascendant
Jacksonians, sparked increasingly nasty conflicts among members of the Ohio
General Assembly. Sandusky interests demanded a railroad and hoped to block
the extension of the Miami Canal to Lake Erie. Merchants at Dayton, who
enjoyed a break in trade at the head of navigation on the Miami Canal, shifted
their support to a railroad that would perpetuate their role as a transshipment
point. Upper Miami and Maumee Valley interests howled when their erstwhile
Dayton friends embraced such a "selfish policy," forgetting "their obligations."
The 1828 federal land grant specifically required the extension of the Miami
Canal, and an 1827 grant to Indiana for the Wabash & Erie Canal further
obligated Ohio to develop the waters of the far northwest corner of the state. In
the opposite direction, Hocking Valley interests tapped the Ohio Canal with the
Lancaster Lateral Canal, and Muskingham Valley residents demanded (and got)
side cuts to Dresden and then to Zanesville. Pennsylvania investors urged east-
west connections with the Ohio Canal via the Mahoning River and a Sandy
River–Beaver Creek route. Nobody in politics opposed the principle of state aid
to such public works, but neither did anybody speak any longer for a balanced
state program. Competitive localism and private desire overwhelmed prudence
and the "broad view," fostering a widespread belief that equalization of the
benefits fell upon lawmakers as part of their "duty, upon the principle of equal
rights." As Governor Joseph Vance put it in 1838, "every principle of justice"
required expansion of the system until every section was placed "on an equality"
with those already favored.[10]

Because of this sense of entitlement to public investment, plus a revenue

The Miami Canal crossing the Miami River north of Cincinnati, Ohio. From *The Ladies'*
Repository (1842). Courtesy Ohio Historical Society.

stream from successful canals that by 1835 exceeded interest charges by $47,000,
the Ohio Assembly was besieged with demands for canals, roads, and railways.
In 1836 additional legislation massively expanded the state canal system to include the extension of the Miami to a junction with the Wabash & Erie, a Muskingum River improvement program, the Walhonding Canal, and the Hocking
Valley Canal. Still the pressure continued: the canal commissioners reported in
1837 that "nothing short of the extension of canal navigation to every considerable
district of the State will satisfy the public will, which justly claims that the
benefits conferred shall be coextensive with the burthens imposed." Spurred on
by the distribution of the federal surplus—$2.7 million to Ohio the first year—the
1837 assembly passed an open-ended "Loan Law" that promised state subscriptions of up to one-third of the capital of railroads and canals and one-half the
capital of turnpike roads to any corporation that could raise the balance from
private subscriptions. The canal board intended to limit total outlays to $1 mil-
lion per year to avoid inflating wages and prices, and authorities expected the
whole expanded network to cost about $4 million; but this marriage of democ-
racy and public enterprise soon spun out of control, whipped by the twin forces
of popular demand and booming markets.[11]

Prudence had marked the first efforts of Ohio's canal commissioners, but
unreasonable demands from local promoters generated pressures after 1836 that
nobody could resist successfully. Marietta and Zanesville, neither one on the
main line of the Ohio Canal, demanded larger locks for Ohio River steamboats
and flatboats—to compensate, they said, for their "losses." A little farther upstream, near the junction with the Ohio Canal, Dresden clamored for equal

treatment, until the whole of this branch route had been rebuilt to larger specifications than the main line itself! Lake Erie villages at the mouth of the Maumee River engaged in such ugly competition for the outlet of the Wabash & Erie Canal that the commissioners agreed to build *three* separate termini, each with identical facilities to be constructed simultaneously. Costs skyrocketed as change orders piled up: the Hocking Valley slackwater navigation became a full-fledged canal at three times the estimate; the Muskingum project accepted such shoddy work that half a million had to be spent in redesign and repair before 1841; the Wabash & Erie, estimated at $900,000, actually cost $3 million largely due to adoption of a giant sixty-foot prism (half again bigger than the standard forty-foot Ohio Canal) and the pointless triplication of lake port facilities; the Miami extension linking the original Dayton Canal with the interstate Wabash & Erie chose a fifty-foot prism and a steeper fall that quickly exhausted available water and necessitated building two additional (and expensive) reservoirs.[12]

In each of these miscalculations, political pressure nullified engineering wisdom as boosters threatened to withdraw support for the system unless their particular demands were met. In 1837 the collapse of worldwide credit markets quickly drove up the price of borrowed money, yet political jockeying in Ohio continued. The so-called Loan Law that year virtually required the state to match with high-priced money anything private capitalists invested in local turnpikes, canals, and railroad promotions, regardless of who they served or how intelligently they had been conceived. The Ohio Railroad provided a shocking example of the kind of booster fraud this scheme rewarded: for an improbable pile-supported line along the shore of Lake Erie private investors "paid" for their shares with conditional land deeds (no cash), forcing the Board of Public Works to pour a quarter-million dollars in good money into sandbanks they knew would never stand. Other railroads garnered similar sums only to fail and deed back to the state worthless stock and wilderness construction sites of little practical value. Turnpike subsidies proved more effective, but the vast majority of such new roads served the vicinity of Cincinnati. By 1840 the Ohio General Assembly stopped this hemorrhage of funds into mixed transportation enterprises, and in 1842 they repealed the Loan Law altogether, but the program had driven the state debt higher by well over $3 million.[13]

Remarkably, considering the onset of the panic of 1837 and the painful depression that endured from 1839 through 1842, Ohio continued to sell bonds and never missed a payment on its burgeoning state debt throughout this reckless expansion. In the decade after 1836 Ohio spent $13 million on canals and aid to transportation companies while keeping up interest payments that totaled (by 1842) $800,000 per year. When bond markets collapsed after 1839, the canal fund commissioners raised money for interest with high-priced, short-term loans (one of them unauthorized and nearly repudiated later by the legislature). Thanks to the cooperation of in-state banks, and a syndicate of New York buyers who took a large 1843 bond issue, the commissioners did not default, the canals were not abandoned, and Ohio's credit recovered in 1843 with the return of economic growth. Nevertheless, the potential for public bankruptcy and the imposition of new direct taxes frightened voters, who leveled blame in various directions (depending on their faith in Democrats or Whigs) and soon repudiated not their debts but their enthusiasm for public works. Lawmakers denounced the "unnatural alliance" of public and private enterprise represented by the Loan Law—now called the "Plunder Law"—and refused all new requests for public works as well. By 1851 a new Ohio Constitution prohibited state borrowing, and the political wisdom of the day had turned decidedly against public enterprise. Despite their enviable credit record, their enjoyment of some of the best transport facilities in the Union, the remarkable integrity of their public works commissioners, and their own greedy complicity in reckless expansion and the state's brush with insolvency, Ohio voters and taxpayers seized upon the liberal critique of public works that swept the country in the wake of the failure of so many other local programs. After 1850 Ohio candidates for office embraced what long had been Virginia's answer to the challenge of state internal improvements: that public works were inherently wasteful and inevitably corrupt.[14]

Indiana: Bitter Disappointments

With needs more urgent and opportunities no less compelling, frontier Indiana felt the pressure for internal improvements mounting from every quarter. Recently admitted to the Union in 1816, and peopled mostly along the banks of the Ohio and the lower Wabash and Whitewater Rivers, the entire future of the Hoosier State depended on improved access to domestic markets. But Hoosiers commanded no investment capital and scarcely could raise through taxation the sum required to operate their rudimentary government. Lying naturally in the path of westering pioneers, Indiana nevertheless competed for settlers with better-developed Ohio and with sections of Illinois, Kentucky, Missouri, and even lakeside Michigan that enjoyed better water transportation. The very progress of regional transportation breakthroughs—the arrival of steamboats on the western rivers, the promised extension of the National Road, or the opening of the New York and Ohio canals—stimulated urgent desires in frontier states to develop connecting facilities and penetrate local interiors to make their particular unsold lands more attractive than those of their neighbors. The result was a spiraling dilemma in which the needs of a state like Indiana for internal improvements mounted in inverse proportion to available local resources. Only heroic efforts and public-spirited commitment would develop these fledgling commonwealths, yet the popularity of Jacksonian rhetoric (promising to shield the people from burdensome government) fostered among the pioneers a jealous regard for self-interest that discouraged risk in behalf of the common good. After a decade's hesitation, Indiana finally launched an ambitious program of improvements that crashed disastrously within a few years. The story of how the Hoosiers came to adopt their fateful "Mammoth System," and how they recoiled from the subsequent disaster, illustrates another of the ways antebellum Americans lost their faith in public works and turned instead toward the Smithian promise of self-regulating, liberal markets.

Indiana's debate about internal improvement dated back to 1818, when Governor Jonathan Jennings reminded his assembled lawmakers that "inducements to industry and enterprise" enhanced the value of the soil while removing those "jealousies of local interest" that so often brought "undignified results to our republican institutions." Steeped in the intuitive democracy of frontier politics, Jennings nevertheless embraced principles of energetic government shared by nationalistic Republicans such as Madison, Clay, and John Quincy Adams: "The powers of our government are expressly drawn from the people to promote the welfare of all," and to "promote the general happiness and security of the people." To such ends he urged the assembly to use the "3 percent fund" (federal kickbacks on public lands sold in Indiana) to "lay the foundations of a system of internal improvement coextensive with the state."[15] Unfortunately, as the panic of 1819 brought the postwar boom to an end, the infant state of Indiana sank quickly in a quagmire of private and public debts. By the end of 1821 Jennings reported obligations of $40,000, annual revenue from taxes of $13,000 (in depreciated state currency), and estimated expense for 1822 at "something like 20,000 dollars." While the pioneers staggered under private debts, and without markets for low-priced produce, the state promised to raise their taxes, not to benefit the future but to pay off shortfalls from the past. Jawboning frantically, Jennings declared that his people, once "truly acquainted" with the embarrassment of their treasury, would shoulder appropriate taxes. But he knew this was highly unlikely, that among his constituents "public utility" was often discussed but "private interest alone pursued." With virtually no internal resources, Hoosiers soon were grasping at whatever straws of outside capital assistance they could find.[16]

The availability of assistance from Congress for the Wabash & Erie Canal set the agenda for internal improvements in Indiana when the effects of the panic subsided. Long familiar to French and Indian fur traders, the Wabash and Maumee Rivers came within a few miles of cutting a natural route through the Old Northwest linking Lake Erie with the Ohio River. This Wabash-Maumee corridor—like the fabled Potomac, the James River–Kanawha, and the Hudson-Mohawk routes—stood out (frequently in tandem with the Illinois-Michigan portage) as a natural advantage that begged for national improvement. Regional ambitions in Indiana thus dovetailed with the interests of internal improvers in Washington (such as Henry Clay and the young John C. Calhoun), who hoped to establish a national system of trunk lines on which local governments and private interests might elaborate the more detailed transportation network. In December 1823 Indiana governor William Hendricks pressed the Indiana General Assembly to seek congressional assistance for connecting the Wabash and Maumee Rivers. Congress responded with the minuscule grant of a ninety-foot right-of-way for twenty-five miles (which the state refused), and a select committee of the Indiana House concluded that the excavation of channels in the lower Wabash (paid from the 3 percent fund) would satisfy the present need for navigation.[17]

In January 1825 John Ewing of Vincennes prepared for the Indiana Senate a treatise that sketched out the beginnings of a "grand design" for statewide internal improvements to be anchored by the Wabash-Maumee route, undertaken directly by the state, and aided by congressional land grants, "under the auspices of that glorious system of internal improvement already commenced by the general government." Certain "difficulties" remained—the proposed Wabash Canal ran through lands belonging to Miami and Potawatomi Indians, and such improvements depended on "resources beyond our own means"—but happily it was "a beneficent attribute of the general power" in Washington to "grant the aid" Indiana required. Gradually political leaders in Indiana seized upon this vision of transforming their largely hypothetical sovereign domain into a thriving and integrated state by means of federal aid for a system of internal improvements. Despite their penchant for primitive democracy and radical rhetoric, the people of frontier states found the logic of Clay's American System sufficiently compelling not to insist on states' rights at the expense of federal beneficence. Locale and naked self-interest marked their factions more than principled convictions. Affiliated with national politics only by personal connections and influence, most Hoosier politicians sought advantages for themselves and their constituents when they thought about national affairs. Nearly all of them embraced the tariff, cheap land, and federal aid for internal improvements as central to any equitable national policy. When, for example, the Jackson movement swept through the nation just after Congress passed the canal grant, worried Hoosier lawmakers demanded assurances that Old Hickory supported their canal. One Indiana congressman's circular letter to his constituents on the first day of Jackson's presidency documents how little western voters understood where their new hero would take them: "should the present administration pursue the policy of the past, on the subject of Internal Improvement and the Tariff, all who really went for measures, more than for men, will rejoice in the prosperity of the country, no matter who administers its affairs."[18]

Governor Hendricks, elected to the U.S. Senate in 1825, together with Senator ames Noble and former governor, now congressman Jonathan Jennings—the founding triumvirate of Indiana politics—advocated Indiana's cause in the ever more treacherous swirl of politics in Washington. On 2 March 1827 a suitable land grant finally was offered for the Wabash & Erie Canal: one-half of five sections on either side of the proposed canal, alternate sections in a strip 5 miles wide and 160 miles long—over 527,000 acres in all. The Hoosier delegation was gleeful, but back home in Indiana the rejoicing was not universal. Most people lived in the lower reaches of the Wabash and Whitewater Valleys, a hundred miles or more from the site of this canal. Nor was the capital city, Indianapolis (still a muddy, pioneer's camp to which the government had moved just two years before), much closer. More urgent projects—canals around the Falls of the Ohio and up the Whitewater River, clearing the lower Wabash, and building innumerable highways—still waited for public expenditures. Many saw the Wabash & Erie Canal as the speculative hobby of Fort Wayne Indian agent John Tipton (who stood to gain a fortune in Indian lands). Few people relished the idea of encumbering the state's energy and scarce resources with a project in the northern wilderness, while the vast majority of voters and taxpayers stayed quite literally stuck in the mud of southern Indiana's roads and rivers. Yet here was an enormous grant of capital (paired with a similar grant to Illinois and likely to be matched by donations to Ohio and Michigan) that the infant state dared not ignore. To claim the land, Indiana must begin the canal within five years and commit to finishing in twenty; this requirement set the schedule for Indiana's subsequent movement toward a system of public works.[19]

Never again, said Governor James Brown Ray in December 1827, would the state control "such extensive and valuable resources, for prosecuting a grand system of internal improvement" that he hoped some day—like New York's—would produce a steady revenue and "relieve our fellow citizens from taxation." The challenge lay in keeping rival interests in the state in line long enough to get a system up and running. In January 1828 the legislature accepted the grant, authorized surveying of the canal, and impaneled three commissioners (carefully balanced geographically) to oversee the enterprise. No appropriation was made beyond a pittance for surveying equipment. Tipton and his friends set to work negotiating Indian removals, laying out new counties, and marking for plunder the resources of the upper Wabash Valley. Friends of experimental railway technology (including Governor Ray) produced a crosswind by advocating railroads instead of canals. Partisans of Andrew Jackson postured in an effort to keep the federal aid that they craved from inadvertently helping the Adams reelection campaign. Some Hoosiers, led by Ewing, sought to preserve the value of these capital lands by selling stock, selling land on credit, issuing scrip, and accumulating interest while construction progressed. Eager to privatize the windfall, others like Tipton pushed for early cash sales behind a screen of rhetoric flattering the common man. Taxpayers feared (not without reason) that sharks of some description would pledge the credit of the state, plunder the grant, and leave the people to pay for the canal.[20]

The devil, as always, lay in these details, and year after year sectional interests, land speculators, would-be bankers, and party builders combined in different blocks to prevent any positive action. Negotiations sputtered with Ohio over support for that section of canal lying in the Buckeye State. Boosters fished for support with additional plans—such as a cross-state canal connecting the Wabash and the Ohio via the White River at Indianapolis—that promised to extend the benefits (and certainly the costs) of internal improvement. In 1829 a U.S. Army engineer produced the first reliable estimates, and in the fall of 1830 the first canal lands were thrown on the market. Results were disappointing (driven down in part by speculators' rumors) and sales were stopped; but time was running out. Railroad enthusiasts made another troublesome bid in 1831, bragging up the cheapness and speed of their technology, begging permission from Congress to build railroads instead of a canal, and trying to dismiss the existing canal commissioners. Everyone condemned rival schemes as sure to increase taxes, while the friends and enemies of Andrew Jackson now took advantage of the local debates to air their thoughts on the American System and the Maysville veto.[21]

The Sixteenth General Assembly, facing a deadline of 2 March 1832, finally passed a bill empowering a new Board of Canal Fund Commissioners to borrow money against future land sales and authorizing the existing board to let the first contracts for construction. The new governor, Noah Noble, elected in 1831 as a canal promoter on a promise to apply "all grants . . . faithfully and economically" to the "objects designated," was delighted. Privately a "Clay man" but not yet publicly at odds with the Jacksonians, Noble set to work developing support for a network of "lateral roads and canals" to fill out the system. Having risen on the ever-shifting winds of Indiana's personal politics, Noble hoped to bestow upon his state the framework of its future prosperity—and in the process maybe rescue the American System, Henry Clay's presidential aspirations, and his own chance for a term in the Senate.[22]

Working closely with Senator John Tipton, still a Jacksonian *and* an improver, Noble labored to bring order to the clamorous demands that necessarily rose to prominence now that the Wabash & Erie Canal was begun. Friends of the Whitewater, White, and lower Wabash Rivers could not longer be put off. Some kind of central or crosscut canal was required to link natural watersheds with a central hub at Indianapolis. Direct taxation would not be tolerated by the people, so Noble introduced the idea of borrowing money for internal improvement. In 1833 he urged a small loan, believing that "both duty and interest" demanded "preparatory measures for facilitating our exports and imports." John Ewing (now in Congress) worried that a loan without a plan would generate funds to be "distributed uselessly, as the 3 pr. ct. once was." In his bid for reelection in 1834 Noble named the White and Wabash Rivers and five state roads to illustrate the scope of a statewide system, only to be castigated by his Jacksonian opponent for "entirely" ignoring other interests in the state.[23] Safely reelected, Noble finally threw down the gauntlet in December 1834. No good reason remained "why we should longer hesitate to follow the successful examples of other States." With little more resources than their public credit, New York, Pennsylvania, and Ohio had commenced their public works. The money borrowed immediately bene-fited local people "by being thrown into circulation in payment for labor, mate-rials, and subsistence." Furthermore, "so soon as the works were completed, the people and the States were repaid many fold by the increased demands and higher prices for their produce; by activity imparted to every branch of industry, and by the enhancement of the landed property of the country." Warming to his task, Noble lectured the general assembly:

> The Treasury of a well managed Government, is the pockets of the people, in which something should be placed by wise legislation, before much is required. To borrow money at a fair rate of interest, and expend it upon some well selected objects of paramount public utility, will not embarrass the Government or impoverish the people, but on the contrary, will enrich both. . . . This is not mere speculation; it is theory based upon reason and abundantly verified by facts and experience.

The time had come, Noble concluded, to name a board of public works and endorse such projects as "were capable of being extended and connected with each other upon some general plan" to subserve the "interests of the people."[24]

Stirring rhetoric notwithstanding, it took more than a year to get the "Mam-moth Internal Improvement Bill" through the interest-ridden Indiana legisla-ture. Advocates battled on behalf of rival schemes—some for a program of loans to corporations (like the one Ohio later adopted), others for a tristate trunk-line railroad from Maumee Bay to the falls of the Illinois River, still others for a general system including the Whitewater Canal, a Central Canal, and various roads or railroads. Citing their studied preference for canals over railroads and public works over private corporations, the House Committee on Canals and Internal Improvement reported a bill in January 1835 to provide for completing the Wabash & Erie and commencing "a general system." Immediately fights broke out for the inclusion of additional pet routes, and the bill eventually collapsed under the combined weight of its enemies and "friends." The Wabash & Erie made steady progress in 1835, despite verbal salvos from Tipton (who saw every diversion as a threat to his own canal-based fortune) and actual warfare in July between rival bands of Irish navvies. Meanwhile engineering reports piled

up confirming the potential of a half-dozen projects, and the voters swore to elec
only improvers to the General Assembly. Wabash & Erie commissioner David
Burr published a pamphlet explaining once more why a large state debt was :
blessing in disguise, and legislative leaders worked out a strategy that finall
resulted in success. In January 1836 Fountain County's Thomas J. Evans intro
duced a general system and the canal party resolutely beat back all amendment
until its carefully packaged bill passed both houses by comfortable margins
There was a slight Jacksonian color to the opposition language, but about half th
Democrats (in an assembly dominated by the new Whig Party) supported th
bill, and negative votes better correlated with disappointed places than with part
preference.[25]

Included in Indiana's so-called Mammoth System were the Whitewater Ca
nal (down the southeastern margin of the state), a Central Canal (from a mid
point on the Wabash & Erie through Indianapolis and down the White River to
the southwestern city of Evansville), an extension of the Wabash & Erie (to
Terre Haute on the western edge, then cutting in to connect with the Centra
below Indianapolis), a railroad from the capital to the Ohio River town of
Madison (a route where no waterway was possible), removal of obstructions in
the lower Wabash River, a macadamized replacement for the old Vincennes post
road, and surveys for two additional roads, canals, or railroads. The estimated
cost of the package was $10 million, which commissioners were authorized to
borrow at once (for twenty-five years at 5 percent) and obligated to expend on al
projects simultaneously. To secure this new debt Indiana pledged the works i
intended to build along with all future rents, tolls, and profits. Public celebration
broke out across the state, and editors battled each other with hyperbole to
document suffusions of popular "joy." Indianapolis businessman Calvin Fletcher
recorded that some members of the General Assembly got drunk, but tha
detracted little from his own euphoria: "This grand system will exalt Indiana
among the nations of the earth. I have a strong desire to live to see the completion
of this system."[26]

The vast majority of Hoosiers shared Fletcher's desire to see the system flourish, even if they disagreed on routes or technical particulars. Once it was "explained" that the debt could be secured by the public works themselves without
encumbering future tax revenues, principled opposition virtually disappeared
Full of confidence the Indiana Board of Internal Improvements met 7 March
1836 and began laying out the work. It sent out a flock of engineers to finalize
routes and answer questions of practicability left open by the legislation. Guided
by the recommendations of these expensive experts, the commissioners let contracts worth almost $2.5 million for work at widely scattered sites, including both
ends and the middle of the ambitious Central Canal. Just who was to blame for
the "all-at-once" strategy would be argued hotly in years ahead, but whether to

ratify the lawmakers, constituents, or contractors—or, as it *said*, to prevent driving up local wages—the board distributed its borrowings as democratically as possible. For skeptics the board developed ten-year illustrations of accumulating debt and the means to service it, using three different assumptions about the rising value of real estate (and including the interest due from deposits of federal surplus monies that were promised under Calhoun's recent bill). Finally, given the pressure of the times on prices and interest rates, the board wondered if it would not be wise to borrow at once as much as was needed to complete the program and avoid paying premiums for money four or five years hence?[27]

Little did Hoosier improvers know that the game was crashing around them. Critics of "the system" popped up like mushrooms, but every objection was so tainted with demands for different or additional construction that naysayers really only look savvy in the light of disasters yet to come. Finding the eastern markets glutted with public securities, Indiana's fund commissioners left Isaac Coe in New York to dispose of the paper, which he soon started selling on credit at quickly rising discounts (to firms from which he then accepted stock and private commissions). By the time international markets collapsed in the spring of 1837, the Indianapolis Sunday-school-teacher-turned-broker had sold nearly 4 million in bonds (some at nominal premiums) against which the state was to draw on accounts with the tottering Cohens Brothers of Baltimore and the Morris Canal and Banking Company of Jersey City. The Cohens failed early, but Coe funneled millions more through the Morris Company, which that firm used to prop up its own failing business before folding its tent and sailing for England with one more trunk full of signed Hoosier bonds). Thus began a nightmare of financial ineptitude, fraud, and confusion that might have led Indiana into bankruptcy regardless of mistakes made at home.[28]

But Hoosiers at home were not shy about plundering their brave new adventure in public investment. Men pressed the governor for seats on the canal board as payment for political support (one office seeker admitting there were "many" more qualified but none more "zealous" than himself). Disappointed sections of the state challenged all appointments and expenditures, looking for evidence of favoritism. Engineers' reports that contradicted local hopes (such as the recommendation *against* a railroad from Jeffersonville to Lafayette) attracted fierce objections and counterassessments.[29] To maximize the impact of borrowed money (or maybe just to speed up their favorite projects), some members of the 1836–37 General Assembly urged "classification" and a halt to those works least likely to produce early revenue. Distrusting the motives of the "classifiers," others used the same guise to reintroduce "important" routes thrown out of the original bill. Disappointed interests charged engineers and members of the board with finalizing routes to the advantage of influential landowners. Some contractors padded their bids; others begged for relief when their costs ran too high. Local specula-

tors drove up the price of shovels, wagons, mules, and especially lands near th
routes of improvement. Negotiations to purchase mill seats along the canals we
met with stony refusals or exorbitant demands from private owners, convincin
the commissioners that "water power created by our canals at the public expense
must remain "unemployed" or else be seized by eminent domain. The price o
labor rose so abruptly, diverting so many hands from agriculture, that the boar
delayed letting new contracts in 1837 and begged local husbandmen not to abar
don their natural calling for wages on the public works. Worried friends of th
Mammoth System urged their fellow citizens to forbear the temptations o
transient advantages: "each, as in a lottery, trusting to his good fortune to secu
the prize, forgetting the certain loss which must ensue in the general result." B
the possibility of failure only seemed to heighten the desire to profit quickly.[30]

Trouble only multiplied after 1837. True, the Wabash & Erie opened betwee
Logansport and Fort Wayne, but traffic found no outlet to the east (Lake Erie) o
south (Ohio River) for many more years to come. The Whitewater Canal t
Brookville progressed nicely, but flood damage and technical failures continue
to plague that endeavor. By 1838 the Madison Railroad ran successfully to Ver
non—about a quarter of its intended length—but the 400-foot bluff at Madiso
still prevented through traffic to the riverbank, and the entire appropriatio
intended for the line had been spent already. Even as funds began to run shor
the board let new contracts, and recriminations started to fly.[31] Critics (includin
Chief Engineer Jesse Williams) faulted the board for scattering contracts all ov
the state, and many now blamed the geographical partiality of the nine actin
commissioners. The "true cause of complaint," wrote the board in its own de
fense, was "the startling amount of disbursements," and that sprang from th
*"extensiveness of the system and the inherent qualities of the compromise . . . upo
which it was predicated."* If poverty now required a different approach, it shoul
be the legislature, not the board, that determined "what works shall have prece
dence" over others. Their frustration boiling over, the commissioners taunte
their critics: "And when the knife is applied to the system for the present, and th
work done, will the parties to the compromise be better satisfied than at presen
and magnanimously bear, without a murmur, the general pressure of taxation?"

Preferring not to wield that knife directly, the Indiana General Assembly i
1839 sacked the nine-member panel and gave a new board of three commis
sioners an impossible mandate: reduce and *"concentrate"* expenditures to finish a
once "a portion of the works," while taking no steps that would "jeopardize th
final completion" of the original Mammoth System. With existing debts ap
proaching $7 million (and the governor wondering why so little cash was avail
able for paying labor and interest), the engineers called for infusions of at leas
$1.5 million more per year for the next eleven years (for a total system estimate o
$23 million) and projected annual interest shortfalls averaging $300,000 begin

Madison, Indiana, from the south in 1846, showing the great bluffs that separated Indiana's Ohio River towns from the interior of the state. Madison finally breached this barrier with a steep railroad cut powered by stationary engines and later a cogwheel locomotive. From a Madison and Indianapolis Railroad Co. map. Courtesy Indiana State Library.

ning immediately. The law limited spending to $1.5 million per year, but outstanding contracts already exceeded $3 million, and legislation required perseverance on at least some projects while appearing to prohibit the cancellation of existing contracts. While the new board wrestled with this contradiction, the Morris Company failed, still owing the state $2.5 million; one by one Isaac Coe's clients followed suit, and Indiana soon found itself unable to draw as much as $4 million of its borrowed money. By the end of summer 1839 the state owed its contractors (who in turn owed their laborers) $700,000, and unpaid interest exceeded the entire state annual revenue. The board ordered work suspended. Fearing a popular tilt toward repudiation, the commissioners reminded the lawmakers of their own role in designing the system of internal improvement and begged them to protect at least the "faith and credit" of the state.[33]

Confronted with imminent bankruptcy, Indiana lawmakers ranted against spendthrift government and rising taxes, refusing to do anything responsible about the emergency. Investigations in both houses of the General Assembly began to expose the loose (and dishonest) transactions of Isaac Coe and his successor, Milton Stapp—both of whom, it was urged, should be indicted. Former governor Noah Noble, now head of the new Board of Internal Improvement, suffered much abuse as he labored to collect any part of the debts still owed to the state. Meanwhile, to mollify contractors, the state issued treasury notes—called "blue dogs"—that circulated locally more or less as money. To carry on the Wabash & Erie, Chief Engineer Jesse Williams issued more questionable scrip—

"white dogs"—against the value of unsold canal lands. In 1840 Samuel Bigge the last Whig governor of Indiana, hoped aloud for a resurrection of Henr Clay's old distribution scheme of 1832 and tried to pin the blame for the state embarrassment on national Democratic policies. But since Indiana Whigs ha claimed so baldly the 1836 Mammoth System as their own, Indiana Democra howled as injured innocents now that the system had exploded. When law makers in 1840–41 finally tried to raise money for interest, they could not plac bonds at even 7 percent, and higher taxes only brought in a flood of worthles paper "dogs." That July Indiana defaulted and did not pay interest again for fiv years.[34]

Democrats took control of the assembly in the fall elections, and while the never flatly repudiated Indiana's debts, these born-again Jacksonians refused t address the fact of defalcation. Governor Bigger summarized the dismal situa tion in December 1841: of a projected system 1,289 miles in length, only 281 mile were finished and operational. Over $8 million had been spent, and the lates estimates called for almost $12 million more to finish the system. The whol public debt stood at $15 million, on which interest was due of at least $615,00 annually, and whatever proceeds accrued "from tolls, water-rents, &c" he ex pected would be "absorbed in expenses and repairs for some time." The plain fac was that "we have neither under our control nor in prospect, for some time t come, the means to discharge the interest on the whole of our public debt." Tha Indiana had been victimized by "preconcerted imposition and fraud" the gover nor did not doubt, and he encouraged the further prosecution of any who "will fully violated their duty"; but it served no purpose any longer "to conceal our rea situation." Pieces of the system were offered for sale, but only the Whitewate Canal and the Madison Railroad found buyers interested in finishing and man aging the works. For four more years interest would accumulate a half-millior dollars per year, while lawmakers hoped for a better economy (and harvestec partisan advantages); still they could not find the fortitude to settle with thei creditors. Trolling for votes in 1843, Democratic gubernatorial candidate Jame Whitcomb summed it up this way: "For twelve long years have the WHIG PARTY HAD possession of Indiana. They found in her virgin beauty, the pride of th Western forests . . . but they beggared her—they ruled and they ruined her—the piled a debt mountain high upon her—they crushed her energies—they sappec her credit, and they gnawed like hungry dogs at her vitals."[35]

The collapse of the Mammoth System left Indiana on the horns of a demo cratical dilemma: how to recover from a popular decision gone bad in which "the people" forgot their complicity? Elected officials in the optimistic days of 1834– 36 could not impose the kind of discipline that might have saved them from wreckage in the panic and depression—things like dedicated taxes and a sinking fund designed to guarantee payment of their interest. The architects of th

Mammoth System thought they had done well to restrict it to eight projects
selected with some eye to statewide integration. Of course, in retrospect improvers' optimism proved unwarranted, and mistakes were made—most glar-
ingly the fatal policy of scattering investments everywhere at once. But no one
could be blamed for the panic of 1837; few understood the frauds and scams laid
before them by brokers in the East; none could know that Isaac Coe would be a
thief; and precious little evidence survives of public spirit or generous forbearance on the part of private citizens in Indiana, who preyed upon the carcass
of their own grand initiative. Yet when the crisis arrived, it was the men in
charge, and not the voters, who stood condemned of recklessness and folly; and
it was years before the agents of lawful English creditors (who *paid* for bonds,
even if Indiana never got the proceeds) could persuade self-governing Hoosier
Democrats that in a modern capitalist economy they simply had to retire their
debts.

Outside forces broke the stalemate that pitted Hoosiers against their creditors.
First, in 1841 Congress agreed to augment the original Wabash & Erie land grant
with an additional 260,000 acres to aid the extension to Terre Haute. In 1843
Ohio finally opened its section of the Wabash & Erie, giving Indiana at long last
an outlet to eastern markets. That same year Congress offered a third (and the
largest) gift of land if Indiana would complete the Wabash & Erie to the Ohio
River at Evansville. Encouraged by this new evidence of tangible assets, the
long-suffering English bondholders hired Charles Butler, a New York attorney,
to press the Hoosiers for terms of settlement. Arriving in Indianapolis in December 1845, Butler was told by everyone that "*nothing*" could be done. "No man
dare take the responsibility in the Legislature," he reported; none would breathe
the words "*pay* or *tax*." Yet by alternately threatening the Hoosiers and promising
to finish their grand canal, Butler finally cajoled the General Assembly into
passing an agreement that deferred one-half the state's debt and surrendered the
canal to the bondholders. When Butler's clients—the English creditors—balked
at this first Butler bill, a second deal was hammered out in 1847, sweetened by the
new federal land grant and a complete separation of the now-private canal from
the old state debt. As a result, foreign capitalists completed the Wabash & Erie,
longtime dream of Hoosier patriot-developers, while local investors and politicians were freed up to focus their attention on railroads that eventually would
ruin the business of canals.[36]

The last act of this Hoosier melodrama came at the constitutional convention
of 1850–51, during which these chastened Jacksonians rewrote their fundamental
law to prohibit public indebtedness and sharply restrict all government initiatives. The debates reflected more demagoguery than policy analysis, but the
result was a shackled government and an enlarged field for private enterprise. To
Schuyler Colfax, a South Bend editor, Whig, and railroad promoter (soon to be a

"Radical" Republican and Grant's vice president), the moral of the internal improvement story seemed clear:

> When we look back upon the scenes of excitement through which our State has passed, when we remember that so enthusiastic were the people in favor of the mammoth system, that they would as heartily and as strongly, and overwhelmingly have voted for its adoption at the polls, as did their Representatives in the Legislature, it does seem as if now in our cooler moments, with the results of that infatuation in full view before us, we should so act as to prevent, if possible, their repetition. Let us resolve, and place it in this instrument beyond repeal, that no more State debt shall hereafter be created upon any pretext whatever.[37]

Rancorous debate erupted around the proposition that the state be barred from exercising one of the ancient attributes of sovereignty. Some praised it as a simple extension of good household economics; some condemned it as a trick by local capitalists to expose the public interest to unlimited predation. The Democratic State Central Committee wanted to require referenda and direct taxation before any debts could be incurred. One delegate wondered what would happen if a famine or "some other great calamity" prevented the collection of taxes? Some voiced old-fashioned confidence in the wisdom of the people: Would a democratic people "commit self-destruction if left to themselves"—especially now "with the warning wrecks of 1836 strewn everywhere before their eyes?" Of course they would, came the answer from strict prohibitionists, some of whom now embraced the promises of private railroad corporations with the same enthusiasm people earlier lavished on public works. Delegates gave voice to a new doctrine that flowered from the seeds of Jacksonian liberalism: "I am no enemy to public improvements.... But I believe that all works of real importance can be affected by means of individual or associated wealth and enterprise." And with that view in mind, one speaker labored "to secure" for corporations "all the facilities consistent with justice and a perfect equality of rights."[38]

Such was the deft slight of hand with which new-style capitalists by 1850 joined forces with antique Jacksonians to stop what the latter called "*plunder laws*"—public works, state banks, and mixed corporations for internal improvement. Experience had shown, ranted veterans of Jackson's Bank War, that the state had "no capacity" for business and was "always cheated and plundered," while its "agents and partners" made "vast fortunes." Embarrassed by their brush with progressive dreams, determined never to be victimized again, Hoosiers struck from their constitution "all power to contract for debt for any purpose, except in case of invasion," and turned against state public works for a century to come. Instead they chartered railways by the dozen and waited for the magic of the market revolution to bring them the prosperity they craved. In the process they played

Ruins of the Kerr Lock on the Wabash & Erie Canal, Lagro, Indiana. Careful observers of the landscape can find abundant evidence of canal-era installations revealing, especially in very small towns, the centrality of canals to early hopes (often vain) for local urban development. Author photograph.

unwittingly into the hands of new private instruments, epitomized by railroad corporations, that would within a generation restructure their world and generate a "money power" the likes of which original Jacksonians could only fantasize.[39]

Theme and Variations

Indiana's disastrous experience with a state system of internal improvements illustrates a theme that can be found with variations in many American states in the 1830s. "Progress" depended on investments that private capitalists simply were not ready to make in this cash-starved American economy. Alarmist Jacksonian rhetoric notwithstanding, the "money power" before 1850 exercised more figurative than literal authority, and while bankers and capitalists may have coveted wealth and power, they did not yet command adequate sums of either one. In most of the states outside the Old South, governments took the risk instead, and they suffered the worst of the punishing consequences when the panic of 1837—a crisis fueled more by cotton and land speculations than unwise public expenditures—swept away so many different ventures. The financial wreckage and political fallout from the panic of 1837 produced a general revulsion against public works and state-owned enterprises, even in places where these had been relatively successful. Taxpayers frightened by debts and public bankruptcie joined ideological critics of state public works (some of whom believed in private sector development, while others merely opposed particular routes, projects, c programs) to proclaim the virtues of market forces and private enterprise. Bu it was not the demonstrated superiority of business corporations that recom mended the new fascination with private development, nor were the new corpo rations much less demanding of public contributions than their state-owne predecessors; rather, it was widespread evidence of public works failure that b contrast sustained the wisdom of the capitalists' new claims.

The Illinois story most resembled Indiana's during the era of state publi works. Like the Hoosier State, Illinois depended from the start on roads an canals to open its fertile prairies to permanent settlers; and like the Hoosier Illinois pioneers commanded little capital of their own. In 1822 a minuscule lan grant stirred up agitation for a canal from Lake Michigan to the Illinois Rive and local campaigns for the next fourteen years centered on this important cross state and regional connection. Illinois leaders divided sharply over the relativ merits of public works or private corporations, but a decade's failure by investor to buy stock in canal, turnpike, and railroad companies settled the question i favor of a state-owned canal with the aid of a large federal land grant (twin of th Wabash & Erie grant). Chicago and several interior cities were born of this proj ect, along with predictable jealousy and rancor in parts of the state not immedi ately served by the Illinois & Michigan Canal. Initially lawmakers fretted abou committing the credit of the state (tax dollars) to this speculative hobby of Chi cago boomers, but the ease with which the first round of canal bonds sold per suaded more cautious heads to borrow for a general state system—or watch th fruits of progress fall exclusively to friends of the canal. So it was in February 1837 just a few weeks before the panic set in, that Illinois adopted a system of railroad and river improvements no less ambitious than the Hoosier Mammoth System.[4]

Illinois voters in the 1830s ardently supported the Jackson Democrats, bu western politicians felt little discomfort in contradicting Jackson and Van Burer by their demanding federal aid for local internal improvements. Men who wounc up in the fledgling Whig Party—like Governor Joseph Duncan, who pushec hard for private corporations but ultimately signed the 1837 system bill—claimec to believe that state-owned enterprises were too prone to political corruption Advocates of rival technologies and competing cities or sections also jockeyed fo relative advantage. But nobody questioned the importance of internal improve ments or the need for the state to embark on some kind of developmental pro gram, and Illinois Democrats made some attempt to identify their program as a Van Buren measure. Democrat Thomas Carlin, a stout friend of the system elected governor in 1838, sounded the first cautionary warnings with a plea for classification and possible retrenchment, but the Illinois General Assembly which mandated work on all projects at once (even ordering that railroads be started at both ends and at midpoints simultaneously), refused to retreat as long as money could be borrowed at all. By 1839 the barrel ran dry, and taxpayers bolted at the prospect of paying actual cash for the promise of future riches. Democrats scrambled to find new assets or sources of loans, while Whig editors lobbed bombs of invective at the "grand Van Buren system" of half-built state railroads. Work stopped in 1840, the state defaulted in 1841, and in 1842 the State Bank of Illinois collapsed. With total debt over $10.6 million, annual interest due of $800,000, and revenues of just over $98,000, Illinois was bankrupt. To show for their trouble they possessed about three-quarters of a 100-mile canal, dozens of scattered sections of graded roadbed, piles of railroad iron and timber, and a single segment of functioning railroad (from Springfield to the Illinois River), on which neither state operators nor private lessees found it possible to turn a profit.[41]

Ironically, the Illinois bankruptcy sheds a more favorable light on Indiana's fiasco, at least in one particular: the adoption of railroads in the mid-1830s did not guarantee success. All of the same problems that broke Indiana's largely canal-based system crippled Illinois's system as well. A speculators' mania before the panic inflated the value of land (especially town lots, one of which was offered in Chicago for $25,000) and helped fix dollar signs in everybody's eyes. Eastern and European investors snapped up American state paper, while engineers issued surveys and estimates that proved dangerously optimistic. Railroads, like canals, were imperfectly understood and undergoing rapid technological evolution that was bound to yield losses and miscalculations. Labor and equipment shortages, engineering mistakes, relentless popular demand for all-at-once construction and expansion, and finally the crash of the international financial system brought the program down. No more—or less—unreasonable than Indiana's or Ohio's systems, the Illinois program was experimental, underfunded, and, thanks to the panic, after 1839 unfundable. Voter resistance more than corruption or folly explains the failure to classify or scale back the projects before the money disappeared. Eventually Illinois finished the canal and paid off its debts, and in the decade after 1845 most of its projected railroads were built by postpanic private corporations; but like their Indiana neighbors, these once-burned taxpayers acquired a significant prejudice against public debts and public works.

Pioneer Michigan likewise bet heavily on primitive railroads and the hope of federal aid to internal improvements. The high tide of federal support (marked by the 1827 land grants to the Wabash & Erie and Illinois & Michigan Canals) stirred boosters in frontier Detroit to start laying plans for canals or railroads between Lakes Michigan and Erie. Impatient with what seemed to them elaborate experiments in the East, many frontier interests concluded that a cheap, simple, horse-drawn railway would at least get them started on the path toward prosperity. Federal surveys identified a "central route" running west from Detroit as the most eligible for railroad construction, and the men pressing for Michigan statehood built into their vision—and their new constitution—government promotion of internal improvements (and hopes for a share of Calhoun's 1836 surplus distribution). In 1837, guided by Governor Stevens T. Mason, a committee of the first Michigan General Assembly drew up a plan for state-owned trunk lines to be augmented by private feeders. Before lawmakers were satisfied the $5 million bill had grown to include three railroads, two canals, and a dozen other projects, and carried a requirement of equal expenditures across the system. The Central got off to the quickest start, opening thirty miles of strap-iron railroad by January 1838; but then the money dried up, and local frustrations boiled over. The liberal Democrats who had engineered Michigan statehood and internal improvements were swept from power in 1839 and replaced by Whigs condemning internal improvements. But according to Robert J. Parks, sectional jealousy and partisan advantage best explain the fast-shifting alignments that followed. So resentful of their neighbors to the north were people on the Southern line that they refused to allow iron purchased for their railroad to be installed on the Central where at least cars were running and tolls were being collected.[42]

Like Illinois, early Michigan was a Democratic stronghold, but Jackson's scruples over federal aid had little impact on his supporters on the northern frontier. Neither did Virginia's "orthodox" commitment to the leadership of private corporations, a strategy more popular among western Whigs. Fear of banks and monopolistic corporations together with the lack of local capital and urgent need for roads and railroads shaped the widespread popularity of public works until the dread of taxes to service public debts drove voters to embrace an unlikely convergence of Virginia-style political economy and corporation-minded Whig ambitions. Practical experience, not ideology, drove developmental politics on the Jacksonian middle border. Before the panic of 1837 shrewd politicians rode the winds of progress wherever they could; by 1839, after the sudden reversals, whoever had been out of power tacked opportunistically into the storm at whatever angle they could. Amid the wreckage of so many state treasuries, state-chartered banks, and public works programs, private capitalists and smart politicians understandably turned (albeit sometimes grudgingly) toward the relatively untried liberal course of private enterprise.

The panic marked a turning point as well in states with much older public works programs. In 1835 Pennsylvania finally finished its so-called Main Line route and began collecting respectable tolls on a briskly rising traffic. This ungainly combination of railroads and canals, with 174 locks, three tunnels, and a unique inclined plane for lifting segmented boats over the Allegheny Ridge, had cost the commonwealth over $12 million and taken nearly a decade to complete; but in the end it worked and it anchored a statewide system of lateral canals and other public works that totaled 637 miles in 1835 and by 1842 was pushing 1,000. But collapsing financial structures after 1841 (including Nicholas Biddle's post–Bank War state-chartered Bank of the United States) prevented Pennsylvania from servicing its now staggering public debts (approaching $40 million), while falling prices and diminished trade cut into public revenues from either taxes or transportation tolls. For the first time, in 1842 the state offered creditors "interest certificates" instead of cash. Squeezed between angry voters and insistent bondholders, Pennsylvanians began to see liquidation of the system as their only way around bankruptcy. Still, theirs was not a heedless retreat: lawmakers continued to worry about monopolists gaining control of the arteries of commerce. The liquidation movement faltered after 1845, when the state's financial condition improved, and finally it succeeded in 1857 only when the closely watched and richly subsidized Pennsylvania Railroad emerged as buyer of the Main Line's property.[43]

Even in New York, where "canal fever" began, the rapid expansion of the state system of public works, fed by profits from the Erie Canal, crested in the 1830s and left the Empire State after 1837 nearly as embarrassed as its western and southern neighbors. The so-called great canal law of 1825 had authorized surveys for seventeen new lateral canals, many of which were constructed. In 1835 the state undertook to widen the Erie Canal itself from forty to seventy feet. The project had been underway just a year when the panic struck. Hard times threatened New York revenues for the first time since the early 1820s, and though an 1842 "stop and tax" law provided for payment of interest on state debts, future construction (and completion of the Erie expansion) depended on the return of surplus revenues. In the end, though, the Erie Canal recovered; traffic expanded dramatically in the 1840s and 1850s as western states finished their lines and the volume of interregional freight increased fivefold. And despite the failure of many lateral canals to repay the cost of their construction, New York's system flourished throughout the antebellum period. In fact, in this case alone it was the success of the canal, not its failure, that drew stiff competition from railroads that by 1853 had designed their consolidated, trunk-line operations precisely to steal business from the canal. In an ironic fulfillment of Indiana governor Noah Noble's theory that permanent riches would flow from timely internal improvements, most of the money that eventually flowed into America's private railroads passed through the hands of New Yorkers, who, because of their public canal, handled almost everyone's imports, exports, banking, insurance, and the fast-growing market for securities.[44]

Maryland suffered a peculiar variation of distress as friends of the Chesapeake & Ohio Canal battled the rival Baltimore & Ohio Railroad for the allegiance of voters and taxpayers throughout that small state. From its inception the great national waterway—descendant of George Washington's fabled Potomac Company, pet project of Virginia's Charles Fenton Mercer, and rare beneficiary of direct congressional assistance—the Chesapeake & Ohio enjoyed deep financial commitments from the state as well as the city of Georgetown. Local rivalries and political influence compromised engineering decisions, especially on the tidewater end of the canal, while competition from Baltimore's railroad (which shared the same valley but not the same destination) drove down revenue from tolls and stirred up resistance in Baltimore to more state aid for the public canal. By 1841 the panic and depression left Maryland "virtually insolvent." Finally completed to Cumberland in 1850 (but not beyond), the C&O never flourished as an interregional artery and repaid almost nothing to the company that built it; but it managed to drive a wedge between Baltimore and other interests in the state that complicated politics for a generation.[45]

South of the Mason-Dixon Line political dynamics arising from the presence of plantation slavery complicated and delayed the progress of state internal improvements. As a result, many southern improvers in the 1830s, especially in Virginia and the Carolinas, struggled against entrenched opposition from conservative, tax-averse, tidewater planters. In such states internal improvement issues quickly became tangled in reapportionment demands that threatened the political hegemony of large planters—and so indirectly became embroiled in questions of support for the "peculiar institution." In Virginia, for example, the 1816 Board of Public Works was allowed to invest public money only in projects already three-fifths supported by private subscriptions, effectively limiting such aid to areas least in need of assistance. Public enthusiasm for a route across the western mountains peaked in 1828 at a Charlottesville convention, where improvers tried to portray state aid as a bulwark *against* federal expenditures and thus an adjunct of states' rights orthodoxy. But new appropriations requested for the James River & Kanawha Canal were lost to combined opposition from eastern slaveholders and promoters of a rival western railroad. Simultaneous questions of constitutional reform and legislative debates over the abolition of slavery diffused energy and deflected attention from demands for either local or interregional transportation projects. In 1832 friends of the western canal accepted a charter for a new corporation that raised $5 million (this time three-fifths subscribed by the state) and pushed construction ambitiously until 1842, when the state forced the overextended company to stop and pay down its obligations. Unlike the northwestern states that were burned by grand programs in the middle 1830s, Virginia never really mounted a program of developmental public works, and its exposure to the panic and depression came filtered through mixed corporations. As a result Virginia emerged in the early 1840s still in desperate need of commercial arteries and ironically more (not less) interested in public assistance to transportation enterprises.[46]

North Carolina experienced a similar delay in developing inland navigation— also caused by planter resistance to reapportionment and potential taxation—

that left major waterways unimproved until the railroad began to show its real promise as a superior technology. Early projects, including the Dismal Swamp and Roanoke Canals, various inlets, and half a dozen river improvements met with limited success and large financial losses, while the political culture of North Carolina remained stubbornly localistic, suspicious, and antidevelopmental. An 1833 Raleigh convention found the state's condition still "highly discouraging and mortifying to her citizens," and demanded an investment law like Virginia's funded by a loan, backed up by taxes, and strictly limited to markets *inside* North Carolina. Despite its overwhelming popularity west and south of Raleigh, internal improvements failed to move the tax-averse and grossly overrepresented eastern planters, who pointed to every dollar previously lost as reason enough not to risk more. Only as a new Whig Party took advantage of the modest constitutional reforms in 1835, of the planters' distrust of Martin Van Buren in 1836, and of the imminent promise of capital assistance through the distribution of the federal surplus were internal improvers able to get much of a hearing in the North Carolina General Assembly. Building on the extraordinary early vision of university president Joseph Caldwell, whose *Numbers of Carlton* (1828) sketched out an east-west state-owned railroad from Beaufort to the Tennessee border, lawmakers started chartering railroad corporations in 1833 and after 1836 promised state aid as soon as three-fifths (later two-fifths) came in from the private sector. Although public investment in North Carolina was far from over, the canal era effectively was.[47]

Farther south and west, where plantation elites sometimes shared power more (unavoidably) with popular majorities and ambitious town-dwelling merchants, local promoters often pushed public works of internal improvement as solutions to hard times, but before the 1840s neither achievements nor losses amounted to much. South Carolina and Georgia participated minimally in the first wave of state initiatives after 1815; and the latter (largely from penury) rejected state canals for cheaper aid to local, incorporated projects, inadvertently avoiding great losses in the prerailroad era. On the cotton frontiers of Alabama and Mississippi, local boosters faced little ideological resistance but commanded neither capital nor public credit sufficient to mount significant works of improvement. Instead they focused their attention almost entirely on congressional aid or grants of land. Internal improvements in these Deep South states would blossom in the heat of the 1850s sectional crisis and help focus the passing contradiction that, in the libertarian culture of secessionists, activist government and state public works would become far more popular and necessary than they had been in the antebellum Union.[48]

Andrew Jackson's dream of decentralized internal improvements (if such *was* his dream and not just a strategy for advancement) melted in the heat of the panic of

1837 and the five-year financial crisis that followed. Old Hickory's quaint vision of development by local forces incapable of being directed, controlled, or monopolized contrary to the interests of "the people" (or their political oligarchs) collapsed as demands for larger, more integrated markets and marketing facilities first stimulated new state initiatives and then smashed them against the rocks of a business cycle not yet recognized nor understood by anybody. No "money power" caused the boom of internal improvement programs, and no illegitimate class of capitalist aristocrats plundered innocent governments in the bust that followed (although some individuals "seen" their opportunities and "took 'em"). Grassroots demands drove lawmakers everywhere to plunge into debt on behalf of their constituents: in hopes of magnificent rewards, to be sure, but also in conscious self-defense against demands from people who would not be denied their chance at winning a prize like the one on display in New York. Those that resisted temptation—primarily oligarchs (or "crackers") in southern slave states— did so not from virtue or superior wisdom but for corrupt and selfish reasons, against the demonstrated interests and wishes of majorities of common people.

The pleasing rhetoric of Jackson's moralizing fables notwithstanding, Americans demanded the market revolution long before they understood it; and while they praised Jackson for slaying a "monster bank," they simultaneously hurled themselves at the traders of bonds rather than pay taxes or invest their own savings in developing their own communities. If their political hearts thrilled to the neoclassical tones of Jackson's ancient republican litany of virtue, independence, and self-sufficiency, their economic liberty and opportunity lay in easy access to booming new markets, natural resources, bound and free labor, and profits uncontrolled by sheriffs, magistrates, or preachers. The unexpected consequence of Jackson's victory over Clay and Adams and the advocates of systematic national development was the final disconnection between policy and enterprise, at least at the national level, and the legitimization of an untried model of free competition and laissez-faire that seemed so appealing because no one imagined it could fail to yield the best possible results. The second round of state initiatives might have served to call attention to the unreliability of market forces and the potential social costs of free competition, but the lessons drawn more often cut the other way, against the wisdom of governance. With recovery in the early 1840s, American capitalists made their first bid for control of the machinery of market integration, taking advantage both of plunder gained at the expense of the states and of experiments conducted in the era of great public works. Steam railroads, now rapidly nearing modern form in the hands of new kinds of business corporations, took the lead in developmental enterprise after 1845. Free from the debts (and voters) that hobbled state authorities, men with money to invest took over internal improvements—"took them private" (as the saying goes on Wall Street today)—and quickly laid the groundwork for that national consolidation so long feared by Jacksonian ideologues.

7

Into the Railway Age

THE IMAGE OF the modern steam railroad shadows the early history of internal improvements like the ghost of Christmas yet-to-come, but throughout the 1820s and well into the 1830s railroad technology had not yet developed its winning form. Although evolving with astonishing rapidity, railroads in the 1820s still boasted fragile strap-iron rails, all kinds of roadbeds, sleepers, and crossties, and horse-drawn carriages (the animals were thought to be more practical than steam locomotion, at least for the coming generation). The first railroads ran just a few miles, typically to move heavy freight—stone or coal—to building sites, iron furnaces, or the docks of water transport systems. Limited and specialized in nature, railroads usually were pioneered by private corporations chartered to aid particular interests. Cash-strapped promoters, especially in the pioneer West, claimed that railroads were cheaper to build than canals and thus better suited to primitive regions in need of access to markets. In Pennsylvania, important railroad experiments sprang from the failure of canal engineers to conquer the Allegheny Ridge on that state's grand canal system. In Boston and Baltimore—two cities that pioneered long, interregional railways—waterborne alternatives seemed outrageously expensive or already had been taken by rival enterprises. Going into the panic of 1837, only visionary dreamers had glimpsed the real promise of "iron horse" technology that would come together so quickly in the next two decades.

In the same way that railroad hardware remained experimental, railroad operations and the private corporate business system that became so successful—and notorious—within a generation, could not have been imagined much before the 1840s. The most fanatical railroad partisans writing in the 1830s, men like D. K. Minor of the *American Railroad Journal*, could not predict the speed of trains, length of lines, size of locomotives, volume of traffic, revenues, or sums of invested capital that would characterize the industry by the time of the Civil War. Only recently had specialists begun to agree that railroad operations required a monopolistic union of the roadway and the carrier—that is, the track *and* the train—so as to blur the age-old distinction between "tolls" (charges for use of a road or canal) and "freights" or "fares" (the carrier's bill for transportation and handling). Even more than canals or public highways, integrated railroads enjoyed a tremendous potential to redefine economic networks: they might have been seen, as they often were in Europe, as natural public works best developed by the state. But growing out of private corporate ventures, and coming of age in the wake of public works wreckage after the panic of 1837, American railroads became associated in the public mind with private enterprise more than public services.

Not that "private" railroads were all that far removed from public works. Almost every line in the country demanded and received public investments in one form or another: county or municipal bonds; land for rights-of-way and depots; grants of undeveloped public lands; free stone, timber, and other materials; tariff kickbacks for imported railway iron; and, of course, the valuable franchise implicit in the charter itself. In the South, private capitalists habitually favored land and slaves over industry and commerce, so public officials pushed state investment in trunk-line railroads they hoped would be augmented by private branch lines. (Ironically while Virginia principles still celebrated private over public initiative, southerners nursed a certain preference for state public works, at least over either "*national*" projects or "*monstrous*" corporations.) When postdepression congressmen turned their attention once more to national improvement, they dreamed of railroads, not canals, through the mountains to the Pacific; but there was still no consensus for privatization and a good deal of worry about corporations. It was the railway itself, not the railway corporation, that had captured the imagination of the 1840s generation, and Americans would spend another fifteen years struggling to integrate the new technology, their mounting material ambitions, and their much-abused republican political culture into a common American destiny.

Viewed in retrospect, the national movement for internal improvement peaked in the 1830s, along with Jacksonian democracy; then together they drifted tragically toward their respective denouements in the era of the Civil War. As sectional bad feeling eroded public confidence in politics (not just over slavery but all things related, however remotely, to that peculiar institution), Americans' faith in government itself—never high—collapsed. The founders' hope of wielding power for the common good receded into memory: a distant possibility once (perhaps?) within the grasp of revolutionary statesmen, but unlikely (if not unimaginable) in the hands of their shortsighted, self-serving offspring. Public works, no matter how badly needed or nobly planned, seemed only to encourage corruption, a scramble for favors, and abuses of the taxing authority of government. The last great debates about national improvements exposed not the superiority of capitalist enterprise but this collapse of the promise of government. Unable to negotiate a political landscape shelled for two generations by states' rights radicals and seeded with land mines of sectional hostility, members of Congress who tried to embrace the Pacific railroad as the most obviously national project ever were forced to retreat (as so many states had done before them) toward the safer, more passive role of handing out public resources to incorporated parties who promised to do that which paralyzed government. True, the sectional crisis of the 1850s overwhelmed the transcontinental debates; but even without the complications of the slavery question, from the outset these proceedings were marked by a tragic reluctance, a resignation that positive action was somehow destined to be wrong. Voters north and south of the Mason-Dixon Line had come to believe that positive government had been betrayed by narrow selfish interests—whether bankers or planters, aristocrats, capitalists, politicians, "ultras," or demagogues. Government seemed at best inept; at worst it was a tool of oppression in the hands of the enemy. Either way, great designs for internal improvement lost credibility and easily fell victim to the charges of paranoid critics, that public works served only their promoters, not the nation or the people as a whole. A convergence of circumstances favored railroad corporations on the eve of the Civil War. The breakdown of politics, the perfection of railroad technology, and the novel claims of entrepreneurs that they could handle economic development without the formal partnership of sovereign governments together removed internal improvements from its central place on the national political agenda.

The Modern Steam Railroad

The Granite Railroad of Quincy, Massachusetts, holds the honor of being the first railroad in the United States. In 1827 this three-mile special-purpose installation only served to transport building stone from the quarry to the docks for delivery by ship. The second and third lines in America—the Mauch Chunk (opened 1827) and Delaware & Hudson (opened 1829)—served the same function at anthracite coal mines in eastern Pennsylvania. Among the earliest lines intended to provide general purpose transportation for all kinds of passengers and freight were the Philadelphia & Columbia (a Pennsylvania state project begun in 1828), the Camden & Amboy in New Jersey (commenced in 1830, opened 1832, affiliated with the Raritan & Delaware Canal Company), the Mohawk & Hudson in New York (chartered in 1826 but slow to raise money, opened 1832), and the Charleston & Hamburg in South Carolina (chartered 1827, commenced 1830, opened 1833). Like the coal roads that proliferated in the same years, each of these pioneer lines closed a transportation gap between well-recognized markets that were inadequately served by existing or projected canals. Often conceived as horse-powered systems and displaying a wide variety of strap-iron tracks and roadbed designs (the Philadelphia & Columbia alone tried half a dozen techniques all of which proved disappointing), these early ventures flourished mostly where canals could not be contemplated. They provided experience that set a few men dreaming of large-scale, steam-powered, integrated long lines reaching hundreds of miles and linking complex regional markets; but technology took time to mature, and throughout the 1830s prudent planners chartered dozens of two-point lines joining terminal cities less than fifty miles apart.[1]

The city of Boston, once a queen among colonial seaports, took an early interest in railroads precisely because canal development threatened to drain trade away from New England's colonial metropolis. True, the Middlesex Canal (chartered 1793) had tapped the New Hampshire countryside, but by the 1820s Providence's Blackstone Canal threatened to do the same to Boston's hinterland, while New York's Hudson River steamers captured the flood of western commerce that poured forth from the Erie Canal. In the same way that Mathew Carey pushed Philadelphia's cause in Pennsylvania, Nathan Hale and other Boston boosters cried out for internal improvements. Canals seemed unlikely to answer, especially where winter conditions promised to close their operation four or five months each year. In Massachusetts no canal or turnpike had yet repaid its investors, so conventional wisdom marked internal improvements as likely to be charges on the public treasury. Hale converted entirely to railroads because (he believed) they would be cheaper to build, profitable to run, and open all year around. As their technical record improved, he gained important supporters, including Governor Levi Lincoln, and in 1829 he prepared a detailed prospectus for a line from Boston to Albany.[2]

Early Massachusetts railroad promoters (like their canal-based public works counterparts elsewhere) insisted at first that the state really ought to build major public thoroughfares: a route from Boston to Albany should never be surrendered to a private monopoly. Visionaries first imagined railroads as closed-system point-to-point highways; they thought of a train as a ship on a voyage—something to be loaded, moved, and unloaded. In practice, however, railroad managers quickly would discover that trains produced innumerable complex transactions with multiple, overlapping "voyages" constantly entering and leaving the flow of traffic—more like water in a stream than cargo in the hold of a ship. Close students of the new technology soon agreed that proper railroads must control the operation of the trains as well as the track, especially if they used steam locomotives. Common practice had extended to turnpikes and canals a guarantee of equal access for all carriers upon payment of a toll; that this would change with railroads Hale and others intentionally obscured at first in order not to rile private teamsters and coachmen who commonly expected to be free to use the roadway themselves. Unfortunately no delicate wording or evasive explanations could overcome the fact that a cross-state railroad, even if it worked and covered its expenses, still benefited Boston and the towns along the line at the expense of rival seaports and the rest of the interior. A gathering storm of doubt and suspicion caused Hale and his friends to scale back their objective from a $3 million state project; they settled instead for a public-private venture with minority state participation. Even so, in January 1830 a solid wall of opposition in the House of Representatives buried Hale's proposal by a vote of nearly two-to-one.[3]

Thus it was in frustration (not appreciation for the corporate form) that Massachusetts' railroad pioneers turned to private corporations to pursue their transportation improvements. Massachusetts capitalists already enjoyed attractive investment opportunities in textiles, hardware, and paper manufacturing; but the failure of political consensus now threatened to postpone internal improvement, so the Boston capitalists took up the burden and begged in June 1831 for a charter to build the first leg of Hale's railroad to the Hudson, the Boston & Worcester line. Because the people generally showed so little interest in taking risks for transportation improvements, the capitalists sought protections for themselves as a price for coming forward at all. Chastened by experience with unproductive turnpikes and canals that held their owners liable for debts without limit, and familiar with the Charles River Bridge imbroglio (still raging in the courts), Boston capitalists wanted limited liability and explicit guarantees against the chartering of rival lines. Furthermore, because they faced a known majority of enemies in the Massachusetts legislature, promoters insisted on corporate freedom to set rates and rules of operation. In this way, because of its peculiar political history, the Boston & Worcester Railroad acquired landmark rights and privileges that in time would seem to define a railroad corporation. Freer than other public works to embrace innovation and solve novel technical or business problems, the directors of the Boston & Worcester set precedents for governing a railroad in behalf of private interest narrowly conceived that would not likely have evolved under public control. The result was the extraordinarily rapid development of railroad business and operating principles—and the roots of a conflict of interest that for two later generations would be known to Americans as the "railroad question."[4]

Despite all manner of misadventures (such as the disastrous location of the terminal at Boston's shallow South Cove), the Boston & Worcester completed its main line in 1835. Within a year phenomenal success, especially in passenger traffic, overwhelmed the company's cars and locomotives. As their experiment flourished, the directors of this pioneer line discovered the need to make enormous investments in rolling stock, bridges, fencing, depots, and terminal facilities, while recruiting and training personnel for scheduling and operating trains, handling passengers and freight, making repairs, and maintaining the roadway itself. Booming business yielded unforeseen problems—and produced predictable collisions. By 1838 the safety question, coupled with the promise of more traffic from connecting lines to Albany and Norwich, Connecticut, forced managers to devise a more sophisticated operating system. Having virtually no idea how to price their product or calculate the cost of services, they learned to charge "what the traffic would bear"—a principle essential to commercial viability but uniquely offensive to the mass of democratic customers. Through trial and error, by the early 1840s, the Boston & Worcester had exposed many critical problems and "invented" practical solutions that resulted in a promising model of a modern steam railroad.[5]

The immediate success of the Boston & Worcester sparked renewed interest in the longer line to Albany. Chartered in 1833 by the directors of the Worcester road, the Western Railroad Corporation raised $2 million privately in 1835 and launched a campaign for state aid to develop this link with the cash-starved interior cities. Convinced now that railroads would repay their investors, promoters of the Western managed to secure in April 1836 a $1 million state subscription from the Massachusetts legislature. Construction began in January 1837, but in April the financial panic interrupted the payment of stockholder's assessments. More public aid in the form of state bonds, backed by a mortgage on the railroad and peddled in Europe by the Baring Brothers of London, raised cash to continue construction through the depression, but not without annual visits to the legislature begging for credits to cover ever-rising expenses. By 1842, when the Western line finally opened, fully $8 million had been spent: $2 million from private subscriptions and $6 in public stock and bonds. Thus, one of the first "private" interstate long-line railroads in operation in the United States found success through a public contribution of three-quarters of its capital stock.[6]

The other great interregional pioneer railroad in the Untied States was the Baltimore & Ohio. By 1827 Baltimore's business leaders saw little choice but to plunge into railroads. Washington, D.C. boosters had gained control of the Potomac route to the West with the nationally funded Chesapeake & Ohio Canal. Pennsylvania refused to improve the Susquehanna River down to Chesapeake Bay, and Philadelphia stood ready to retain control of its interior commerce through the state's Philadelphia & Columbia Railroad and the federally funded Chesapeake & Delaware Canal. Lacking political jurisdiction over these crucial routes, Baltimore's commercial interests could act only through a private corporation and had really little choice but to build rival railroads where others controlled the waterways. This accounts for why Baltimore investors committed themselves, years before the technology had found its stride, to a railroad ten times the length of any other pioneer line in the United States.

In late February 1827, within a few days of the decision to build the Baltimore & Ohio Railroad, its promoters secured a charter granting them eminent domain, full control of railroad operations, and exemption from taxes in Maryland. Justified as necessary succor for an infant technology, these generous provisions gave the company just the protection it required to experiment in such a risky field. A week later Virginia ratified the charter, and by mid-March subscription books were opened to a fevered throng of investors. Pennsylvania refused its assent to the B&O charter, but undaunted Baltimore enthusiasts simply moved their Ohio River terminus farther south into Virginia. Soon technicians were hired and, with the aid of a dozen U.S. Army engineers, the route was explored. In April 1828 their first report gave preliminary answers to the question of how to build such a grand, long-distance thoroughfare. On 4 July 1828 the venerable Charles Carroll—Maryland's relic of the Revolution—broke ground for this most ambitious experiment in railroading.[7]

Everything had to be discovered firsthand: how to lay out a route and select appropriate grades and the radii of curves; how best to make cuts and build embankments, viaducts, and bridges; and how to design roadbeds, rails, wheels, axles, carriages, freight cars, and locomotives. Jonathan Knight, William Gibbs McNeill, and George W. Whistler set sail for England to study railroads, while Stephen Long and Caspar Wever supervised surveying and construction respectively. Legal battles ensued as the B&O fought with the Chesapeake & Ohio Canal for control of the narrow river passes between Point of Rocks and Harpers Ferry. Cost overruns appeared almost immediately (especially on masonry bridges built under Wever's direction without plans or specifications), and recriminations flew among the various "experts," distressing the directors and tearing down the harmony among the leading engineers. Nevertheless, by the end of 1829 the route had been secured as far as Point of Rocks and construction was well underway. In May 1830 Charles Carroll took the first ride aboard a horse-drawn coach thirteen miles to Ellicotts Mills.

In many ways the B&O was to American railroads what the Erie was to canals: an engineering laboratory. Trial and error on the B&O brought inventors into contact with practical problems, and their solutions often set standards and determined the particular directions in which technology continued to evolve. Laid out with horses in mind, the relatively steep grades and sharp curves on the first section of the line west of Baltimore inadvertently set the conditions experimental locomotives soon had to meet. Inventors came to Baltimore to try their hand at engine development, and in 1831 the company sponsored a contest with a prize of $4,000 that further encouraged experimental designers and resulted in the adoption, by 1832, of locomotive features that would endure for a generation.[8]

The coincidence of a railroad and canal trying to share the same narrow valley focused public attention on these two battling transportation companies throughout the decade of the 1830s. Initially favored by the Adams administration as the national realization of George Washington's Potomac Canal, and guided by longtime Virginia congressman-turned-canal president Charles Fenton Mercer, the C&O Canal enjoyed early advantages of popularity and public financing. Jacksonians, however, pulled back from national public works just as the

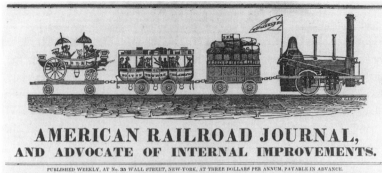

American Railroad Journal masthead, 1833. An inveterate booster of railroad technology, D. K. Minor changed his masthead often to reflect improvements in the designs of trains. Compare this somewhat fanciful portrayal of an up-to-date train in 1833 with Strickland's drawing of canal fixtures (p. 84) and the 1855 Courier & Ives print of a relatively mature-looking train in the illustration facing this one. Courtesy Purdue University Libraries.

private B&O started to captivate a new generation of improvers. In 1836 the railroad operated smoothly between Baltimore and Harpers Ferry, with a branch down to Washington City. A new bridge across the Potomac would open in 1837, and surveyors had laid out the route on up the mountain toward Cumberland. Gross receipts on the main line in 1836 totaled $281,000, expenses about $213,000; the Washington Branch yielded even more profit on somewhat less traffic. The company owned 12 locomotives and 1,100 cars, plus 233 horses and mules. In retrospect it seems as if the Jackson men were right. The private B&O seemed to verify what Jackson (and the Virginians before him) embraced as a point of ideology: that capitalists could undertake internal improvements better than the peoples' governments. That Baltimore had been forced into action by its neighbors' public works made no lasting impression on the public mind; nor did the directors of the B&O go out of their way to remind anyone that they enjoyed two critical advantages of public works, namely eminent domain and freedom from taxes. On the eve of the panic of 1837 the railroad seemed to be doing as well as the canal while costing the people nothing. But for all its apparent success, the B&O had nearly exhausted its resources before the financial crisis struck. A second decade of desperate struggle would test the company before the success of the line—and railroads in general—would be secured.[9]

During the 1830s Americans experimented with dozens of railroads, gathering in the process a wealth of technical expertise, operating principles, and managerial experience. The corporate form of organization, the heavy iron T rail, the flexible roadbed with wooden crossties, the steam locomotive, the four-wheeled truck, rudimentary systems of scheduling and control, fixtures and equipment for

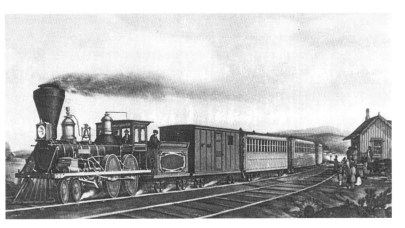

"American Express," by Courier & Ives, 1855. By the middle fifties, railroad technology had achieved a relatively familiar form that would last throughout the age of steam. What recently had seemed experimental and untested took on a dependable form so quickly after 1850 that the Civil War generation could no longer recall why canals ever had commanded respect. Courtesy John F. Stover.

handling passengers and freight, and the principle of charging what the traffic would bear—all these things appeared, took their places as components, and quickly became "standard" on the rapidly evolving American railroad. But none of it was integrated fully when the panic of 1837 slowed the progress of internal improvements throughout the United States, and much of the work of maturing and perfecting the modern steam railroad came in the decades of recovery that stood between the panic and the Civil War. During those two decades railroad corporations profited immensely from a general revulsion against public works (mostly canals) especially in states thrown into bankruptcy by spiraling debts. Lawmakers everywhere turned to corporations as buffers between the people's demands for transportation improvement and the state's responsibility for borrowing the money or doing the work. At the same time private capitalists in Europe and America took another turn in the market revolution, embracing private corporations (without the guarantees of government financing) as capable, perhaps even preferable instruments of marketplace development. The resulting privatization of internal improvements in the United States profoundly altered the relationship of government to business and transferred to the hands of capitalists most of the power to design the system that had motivated public works promoters since the founding of the republic.

The Case for Privatization

Particular histories of early American railroads substantiate the fact that most pioneer lines were built by private corporations, not by intentional choice of a "superior" form but from a failure to command the political support required for public works. In the critical decade following the completion of the Erie Canal in 1825, technical experience accumulated as readily on state-owned railroads in Pennsylvania as on the private lines springing up elsewhere. Public money flowed freely into so-called private railroads, and nobody thought the distinction between public and private necessarily defined the nature of these newest internal improvements. Only when the widespread failure of public works programs after 1837 converged with the maturing of railroad technology on those private lines most able to control their own actions would the stage be set for a marked shift in the popular conception of railroads, from public works (internal improvements) to private business ventures. The argument for private enterprise, once offered by Virginians as a strategy for thwarting public works, picked up supporters in the 1840s among these early railroad pioneers. Eventually it emerged as a new form of "wisdom" in the 1850s, especially where wounded state and local officeholders struggled to relieve themselves of staggering debts, and hungry investors saw the profits to be made from stocks and bonds of fast-growing railroad corporations.

One way to track the railroad's metamorphosis from public work to private enterprise is through reports in the popular press. Hezekiah Niles, for example, pro-improvement editor of the Baltimore newsweekly, *Niles' Register*, treated railroads as public works of internal improvement until well into the 1840s, when comments on their profitability and rising markets for their securities began to tinge reporting about railway construction and promotion. Throughout the 1830s, without surprise or comment, Niles reported state loans and guarantees and the sale of *public* stocks and bonds in behalf of private railroad ventures—even in cases like the New York & Erie Railroad, where the company appeared to be competing with the state-owned system of canals. In fact, Niles reported that New York governor William H. Seward had once opposed chartering the Erie Railroad because so influential an artery should not be given to a private corporation. But by 1839 Seward was endorsing state support for the railroad in the *common* goal of public improvement. In 1837 banker Nicholas Biddle, in a speech reported by Niles, focused his praise for new railroads on their "political" impact—that is, their tendency to unite distant parties and make the Union "worth preserving"—rather than their business prospects. In a collage of reports in 1845, Niles argued that while canal development was limited by supplies of running water, railroads could bring almost any place into the market. He also noticed the emergence of cooperative systems among the multitude of early short lines and the "artful arrangements" of tolls by which railroad managers distorted their charges in order to steal competitors' business (both portents of evils to come).[10]

D. K. Minor, founder in 1832 of the *American Railroad Journal*, tirelessly collected and distributed promotional rhetoric that similarly cast the new railroad in the traditional role improvers had assigned to roads and canals. In 1831 Charles Caldwell of Boston, in a speech at once futuristic and reminiscent of George Washington's waterworks vision, likened a railroad system centered on the nation's capital to the "blood vessels of the human body, where minor ramifications, running from the remote parts, connect themselves with others, in their course and unite in main ones, to empty their contents into the cavity of the heart." Familiar themes of development and uplift transferred without variation from the canal to the railroad literature: with railroad investment "wild" portions of Pennsylvania, it was promised, would "speedily be occupied" by "intelligent freemen . . . skilled in the arts of civilization, and refined moral and religious virtues." Echoing John C. Calhoun's original "bind the Republic" sentiments, a Massachusetts clergyman defined railroads in 1838 as "strong clamps" that were 'destined to bind together with ribs of steel the whole of this great country." Whatever the misgivings of his friend Thoreau, camped out by Walden Pond, Ralph Waldo Emerson welcomed locomotives and steamboats as "enormous shuttles" that shot "everyday across the thousand various threads of national descent and employment," binding them "fast in one web." Year after year the *American Railroad Journal* archived these predictions of political and moral improvement, language that in volume and force overwhelmed any mention of profits or private enterprise. As quickly as they became successful, railroads took their place in the public consciousness as the latest species in a genus of public works that already included roads, turnpikes, and canals.[11]

Only as the economy recovered from depression in the early 1840s did promoters and enthusiasts focus on the virtues of railroads as *private* business investments; in doing so they signaled the beginning of the first significant private-sector bid for the monumental work of internal improvement. In 1843 Minor reflected that eleven years before, when the *American Railroad Journal* started publishing, "the profitableness of railroads was not established." Now it was a fact that "well constructed railroads" constituted "the most profitable investments in the country." Other boosters denounced the "general opinion" still prevailing in 1844, that railroads did not pay, opining instead that "well located, and well managed" roads yielded "fair and constantly increasing" profits—much of which subscribers often plowed back into their companies in lieu of further assessments on their unpaid capital stock. In 1845 conservative business journalist Freeman Hunt, editor of New York's *Merchant's Magazine*, finally endorsed railroads as good investments—better than banks! That same year Niles concluded that the "fever" had returned, and the "railroad era" was "about to resume its career in this country." A few years later Henry Varnum Poor, who replaced Minor at the *American Railroad Journal* in 1849, revealed the subtle shift that was about to dislodge the railroad from its seat among public works and redeploy it as the capitalists' tool of a new conceptual era: "with no other principle than the laws of trade and the local interest of the different sections," Poor proclaimed "the Union is being fast bound together with these iron bands." All who "engaged in this work," Poor concluded, were "co-laborers together for the good of the whole." Unlike anything that came before from the pens of internal improvers, Poor's language was unmistakably Smithian; guided not by vision and public spirit but by markets and local interest, the developmental impulse had been moved from the public to the private sphere.[12]

The privatization argument got its strongest boost in those states after 183 that wrestled with debts for public works programs that were crippled (or ruined in the panic and subsequent depression. In Ohio, for example, railroads firs appeared to serve the fractional interests of routes and communities unable to command political support for a state canal. Generous provisions in 1830s railroad charters—for eminent domain, limited liability, and increasing freedom from public regulation or control—reflected a solicitous approach toward experimental private capitalists by lawmakers already committed to the hilt to a sprawling system of canals. As financial pressures squeezed the state treasury, railroad builders exploited their appeal among businessmen angered by taxation for canals that never would serve their particular towns. By the mid-1840s, these railroad enthusiasts encouraged the people's disillusionment with public work and statewide systems, begging instead for special legislation allowing local governments to aid private railroads that promised advantages to their immediate locale. Within a decade complaints about mistreatment at the hands of the capitalists produced a parallel demand for regulation in the public interest; but by then consolidation, integration, and the rising influence of out-of-state capitalists had transformed local railroads into alien enterprises with unprecedented legal autonomy. Thus by a subtle process did Ohio railroads evolve from low level feeders of the state's canal system into rival interstate arteries operated by powerful corporations capable of flouting local political authority.[13]

Indiana suffered much worse than Ohio, realizing barely half the face value of its debt and defaulting on its loans by 1841. After milking the crisis for political advantage, and finally settling with foreign creditors (who would finish and operate the Wabash & Erie Canal), Hoosier lawmakers turned to chartering railroads as safe and sure instruments of *private* development that would deliver the network first promised by the internal improvements bill. The state's firs railroad, the Madison & Indianapolis, originally part of the public works system was opened in 1847 by a private corporation. In the next decade more than a dozen local lines (mostly less than 100 miles) and one north-south trunk route— the New Albany & Salem (eventually the Monon)—laid the foundations of a wheel-and-spoke system centered on Indianapolis. Forbidden from contracting debts by its new constitution, the state's role in this development was limited to hartering corporations; meanwhile towns and counties secured permission to ncumber local taxpayers in behalf of railroad promotions and began to bid iercely against one another for the favors of speculative capitalists. Because nothing had relieved the local shortage of investment capital, Indiana corporations quickly sought investors out of state and overseas, and as the capital demands of rapidly evolving railroads increased, so did the proportion of "foreign" o Indiana ownership. By the time of the Civil War, trunk-line consolidation had hifted control if not ownership of Hoosier railroads to consortia of capitalists in New York and Boston.[14]

From the outset in the mid-1830s, the states of Illinois and Michigan had put much of their internal improvement energies and money into public railroads, with little better result than their water-working neighbors. In neither place did ufficient traffic arise from the undeveloped forests and prairies to repay elaborate nvestments, while the primitive, "expedient" (read *cheap*) lines that were started by optimistic improvers before the money ran out either performed badly or iterally collapsed under the weight of their own success. Illinois auctioned off most of its projects and focused state attention on securing a federal land grant or the Illinois Central Railroad. Michigan, not even yet a state when it launched ts public works and reeling from the effects of the depression, sold off the Central Railroad and the Southern Railroad to capitalists in Boston and New York. Here again, it was with great reluctance that voters embraced the privatization of their transportation networks. In Michigan, only the gruesome prospect of raising taxes in an economy that still lacked an infrastructure, together with he promises of absentee capitalists to pour in real money and retire the state's worthless securities in return for possession of half-built, half-ruined railroads, made the required legislation possible. Having taken the properties private, the new owners of Michigan's railroads quickly shook off the efforts of the state to regulate and control their operations and eventually integrated Michigan railoads into competing trunk lines linking Chicago with New York.[15]

Even states where internal improvement by public works had been a stirring uccess—New York is the obvious example—suffered in the late 1830s. The triumph of the Erie Canal had forced the New York legislature first to extend its ystem of waterways and then, in 1838, enlarge the original "Big Ditch." Never atisfied, local interests pressed for comparable favors and increasingly were offered railroad charters and sometimes extensions of state credit in behalf of these corporations. Declining canal revenues, due to the business depression, hreatened New York's ability to service its debts, but the danger seemed only to nflame the demands of "have-not" localities. Ironically, as public debts increased to meet the taxpayers' demands, public confidence in the government's ability to pay began to decline. From 1838 to 1842 Whig governor Seward embraced deliberate deficit spending rather than endanger the public works tradition that had

served New York so well; nevertheless, dissatisfaction with public debt and th
threat of taxation produced what historian Ray Gunn has called a "crisis c
distributive politics." The resulting 1842 "Stop and Tax" law sharply increased th
value of state stocks, while it ended state canal spending for twelve of the mos
critical years of railroad development. As they had done elsewhere, capitalist
and railroad promoters praised the laissez-faire wisdom of New York's "Radical
Democrats who, in an effort to thwart the "money power" threw open th
transport field to private interests. The very home of America's most magica
internal improvements story found itself in the mid-1840s deeply divided an
sliding steadily away from its public works tradition toward a liberal separation c
government power and private enterprise.[16]

Nearly every state that had succumbed to the internal improvement mania i
the 1830s (including southwestern states such as Louisiana and Alabama) sa
some variation of this backlash against public spending, usually resulting in th
sale of public works to private corporations and the privatization of new initia
tives. In New York and many other states, the conflicts over government deb
economic policy, and private enterprise that grew out of the depression of the lat
1830s resulted in constitutional reform and a new statement of the role of govern
ment in economic development. This is not to say internal improvement alon
was responsible for the raft of constitutional reforms that took place between 184
and 1860; but among various structural defects, strategic maneuvers, and ideo
logical differences that inspired these state conventions, developmental policie
almost always stood prominently on the list of concerns.[17]

Ironically, in Old South states where Virginia-style liberal ideology mos
effectively restricted public spending, the emergence of successful railroads stim
ulated a wave of new initiatives reflecting the old mixed-enterprise tradition an
confusing ideological affiliations at the state and federal level. (Robert Y. Hayne
for instance, the fire-eating stalwart of South Carolina radicalism, reappears i
1838 as president of a railroad with banking privileges.) In 1832, even as it returne
the James River waterworks to private hands, Virginia began borrowing mone
to invest in frontier roads, turnpikes, and railroads. By the onset of the depressio
Virginia had committed nearly $5 million, two-thirds of which had purchase
shares in private companies. The Virginia Board of Public Works became mor
of a lending than a building agency, and through the depression this body labore
successfully to meet its obligations. In 1847, when the crisis finally passed with th
commonwealth's credit still intact, Virginia began throwing public money int
railroads with unprecedented fervor: by 1860 it had loaned another $11.2 millio
to private railroad corporations and built two state-owned railroads worth $.
million more. And, while so many state constitutional conventions sharply lim
ited their governments' capacity to take on debt, the new 1852 Virginia Constitu
tion actually lengthened the term of state bonds.[18]

North Carolina experienced a more dramatic reversal of internal improvements spending, resulting, in part, from long-deferred constitutional reform. The earlier Murphey program had perished in the aftermath of the panic of 1819, and the shrill demands of western residents repeatedly failed to move conservative eastern majorities who feared taxation almost more than death. But in the 1830s the Democratic Party lost support when Andrew Jackson killed federal aid to internal improvements and forced South Carolina to collect the tariff, creating two disaffected groups that would merge (illogically) to form a viable Whig Party. Meanwhile, University of North Carolina president Joseph Caldwell introduced a plan for a state-owned central railroad, which Governor David Swain and others used in 1835 to help loosen the grip of tidewater interests on the North Carolina General Assembly and achieve at least partial reapportionment. The panic of 1837 postponed action for another twelve years, but a new incentive took root and began (portentously) to grow: not only would railroads "advance" prosperity and "strengthen" the national Union; they would make North Carolina "more respected and independent" if abolitionists ever forced a separation. Finally, in 1849 the Old North State plunged into construction of the North Carolina Railroad while subsidizing other private lines, plank roads, and navigation companies. Even though the Democrats regained control of North Carolina politics, this railroad boom lasted until secession.[19]

The resurgence of mixed enterprises and public works in the states of the Old South did not so much contradict the argument for privatization as mark those regions still underdeveloped and incapable of supporting large-scale internal improvements on the strength of private fortunes alone. Nor was the internal improvement model quite dead at the national level. Demands from the states for federal aid to internal improvements continued unabated through the administrations of Martin Van Buren, William Henry Harrison, and John Tyler. Further, prodded by demands from the South, Southwest, and the trans-Mississippi West, Congress was besieged once more with appeals for "national" projects— the South Atlantic & Mississippi Railroad, the Washington-to-New Orleans Railroad, the transcontinental or Pacific railroad—as well as the usual pork barrel of rivers-and-harbors improvements that always had escaped Jackson's hammer. Year after year Congress heard the tired arguments about the constitutionality of federal assistance, arguments by now as reflexive in Virginia and South Carolina as they were flexible and creative in Missouri, Michigan, Illinois, and Iowa— frontier strongholds of both Jacksonism and desperate need. In these years Whigs persistently failed to establish a systematic program (either the American System or the distribution of federal revenues to all the states), but the party of Jackson poured ever-larger drafts of federal largess into state and local projects under "strict-construction" principles that permitted grants of land and appropriations for "natural" (but not "artificial") rivers and harbors. In this way, at least

until 1846, Americans were able to get what internal improvements they wanted
and still cherish their orthodox principles: strict construction, states' rights, local
"popular" rule.

The Last National Debates

On 29 July 1846 James K. Polk made up his mind to veto a massive new harbour
and river bill just passed by the Twenty-ninth Congress. According to his own
lights Polk never had embraced the thinly veiled excuses by which good Democrats delivered the pork while clinging to the strict Jacksonian creed. Increasingly
buffeted by factional tensions, East-West jealousies, and the rise of a northern
antislavery or "free soil" wing, the Democratic Party had both nominated Polk
and tried to clarify its principles at the 1844 Baltimore Convention. Out of a
timeless opposition to Henry Clay and his American System had emerged at that
convention a blanket condemnation of the power "to commence or carry on a
general system of internal improvements," a rule potentially more exacting than
Jackson's or Calhoun's. (Soon enough even Jefferson and Madison were dismissed by a true believer as being "latitudinarian" about the Constitution.)[20]
Whether motivated by virtue, narrow-mindedness, or a cynical desire to do
something "safe" while juggling several other very risky gambits already on his
table, Polk by his veto reenergized the ancient Virginia strategy of contesting all
federal authority that did not serve one's immediate interest. Unfortunately for
Polk—and more so for the Democratic Party—his exercise in probity (repeated
with pride throughout his term) served only to highlight an untenable position
into which the old Democracy was backing: Polk was engineering at the time of
his veto the acquisition of California and New Mexico, which created an urgent
need for transportation in the West and brought under federal control several
new, southern routes for a Pacific railroad.[21]

If Polk's expansionist program set the stage for a contest over transcontinental
railroad projects, and if his veto invited opposition to anything that did not
accord with the interests of states' rights conservatives, the tradition of congressional land grants to the states and private contractors to assist with internal
improvements provided the constitutional platform from which the friends of
Pacific railroads hoped to launch their magnificent undertaking. Constitutional
authority had escaped Jackson's negative on the grounds that as "proprietors" of
the public lands, Congress enjoyed a right (some said a duty) to dispose of them
in ways that might enhance the value of the residue. And although such land-
grant bills invariably raised objections from proponents of "graduation" schemes
"preemption" or "homestead" bills, and a general system of distribution to include the old states, no less a critic than John C. Calhoun supported to his death
grants of alternating sections of unsold lands, so long as they bordered the route

of such internal improvements and doubled the price of adjacent federal lands. Indeed, the public record stretching back sixty years abounded with eloquence brought forth in behalf of every state and section and "falling" (as they loved to say) from the mouths of politicians of all persuasions, both for and against federal aid to public works of literally every description. In short, the field was well prepared for a raucous and sweeping review of the congressional "progress" of national improvements in all its contradictory glory.[22]

Asa Whitney, a New York merchant and Pacific railroad dreamer, was the first to lay before Congress a remarkable proposal to connect the two coasts with a railroad line. In December 1844, as the Twenty-eighth Congress gathered for its second session, Whitney forwarded a plan to build a railroad from Milwaukee on the shores of Lake Michigan to the mouth of the Columbia River. If Congress would sell him a sixty-mile-wide strip of land for sixteen cents per acre, Whitney promised to develop that land by constructing the railroad, paying as he went with the proceeds of sales of good land along the finished railroad. In twenty-five years, the road would be completed (at no taxpayer cost) and he would turn it over to the government if that's what it desired—or the road could remain the enterprise of Whitney, his "heirs and assigns." Whitney's logic was relatively simple, and it represented pretty fair understanding of political principles, geography, finance, and railroad engineering. As a private individual Whitney could purchase land and build railroads without raising constitutional objections, and if he paid for the land and gave back the railroad he could hardly be faulted for taking advantage of political favor. Beyond the Missouri River the vast majority of land he would purchase was desolate and worthless; therefore he intended to capitalize on good lands east of the dry high plains. He chose the far northern route because the land in Wisconsin and Minnesota Territory remained largely unsold, because all the major rivers at that latitude were easily bridged, and because the South Pass (in what is now western Wyoming) presented by far the best opening across the Continental Divide, with access to the Snake River and the route to Oregon.[23]

Whitney's offer struck his admirers as extraordinarily courageous and far-sighted, an example of public spirit thought extinct in Jacksonian America. Almost immediately, however, it garnered opposition from improvers everywhere south of Whitney's cold and undeveloped route. New York newspaperman George Wilkes, editor of the *Police Gazette* and self-proclaimed expert on the Oregon country, condemned the Whitney plan as a "covetous" private speculation of unprecedented magnitude and demanded instead a national public railroad whose fairness and justice "should be guaranteed by the highest authority in the country." Illinois senator Stephen A. Douglas criticized Whitney for getting ahead of settlement and proposed organizing the territory first and then granting free homesteads to settlers and alternate sections to states and territories

John C. Frémont's party approaching the Wind River Mountains. Frémont led several important U.S. Army expeditions into the mountains that separated the Great Plains from California and Oregon Territory. With the aid of publicity from his father-in-law, U.S. Senator Thomas Hart Benton, he was known for a while (not altogether fairly) as the leading authority on routes to the West. From *Report of the Exploring Expedition to the Rocky Mountains* (1845). Courtesy Purdue University Libraries.

to build public works the way they currently did. (Douglas's plan favored a route from South Pass that followed the Platte River across present-day Nebraska then more-or-less straight to Chicago.) John C. Calhoun presided over a Memphis convention in November 1845 that called for a southerly route (but proposed no plan for financing it). Thomas Hart Benton of Missouri told the Senate in 1848 that he would "never vote for giving a hundred millions of acres to any man" or go "blindfold, haphazard, into such a scheme" as Whitney's. Instead, with the interests of St. Louis foremost in his mind, he set about crafting a route that passed through his home state of Missouri. (For expertise Benton drew heavily on advice from John C. Frémont, the flamboyant army explorer thought to be most familiar with the relevant mountain passes—and, incidentally, married to Benton's daughter, Jessie.) Hydra-headed interests materialized as if called forth by the very suggestion of a railroad to the coast, and so Whitney launched in behalf of his own scheme an ambitious publicity campaign that culminated by 1848 in endorsements from over twenty states and many other private citizens conventions.[24]

While congressmen explored the possibilities for turning Whitney's idea to local advantage, the United States went to war with Mexico and seized—or "purchased"—the balance of territory west of Texas and south of Oregon. Settlers streamed into California after 1848, and with the discovery of gold that stream became a torrent. People and goods poured into bonanza markets in "Gold Rush" California, while tens of millions of bullion flowed back into the treasury of a cash-starved nation. San Francisco boomed as the entrepôt of California, and visions of Asian traders cramming that spectacular bay to disgorge their cargoes onto an American transcontinental railroad soon competed with equally fantastic schemes for diverting world trade with railroads or canals across the isthmuses of Panama and Nicaragua. South Pass remained a viable contender for a transcontinental railroad, but interests from St. Louis southward scoured their maps and explorers' notes for alternatives through or around the Rockies. Eastern capitalists, focused their ambitions on a private railroad venture across the isthmus of Panama and lobbied their representatives accordingly. Henry Varnum Poor, editor of the *American Railroad Journal*, tried unsuccessfully to arbitrate these swirling interests, while "national" conventions in St. Louis and Memphis generated formal resolutions pressing the claims of their respective cities. By 1850, when upstart California entered the Union, four or five different routes competed for public attention, linking San Diego, San Francisco, or the Columbia River with Milwaukee, Chicago, St. Louis, or Memphis—maybe even New Orleans (see Map 5). Whitney had warned Congress back in 1844 that delay would only complicate the landscape, and on that score at least his understanding was incontestable.[25]

Of course none of the advocates of different routes felt at liberty to advance them in the straightforward language of local interest or sectional advantage. The sectional balance of power in the Senate had just been destroyed by the admission of California, and "free soil" diatribes against the "slave power" coming out of the late war with Mexico left southern paranoia honed to a razor's edge. Whigs and Democrats alike stood committed to suppressing sectional political alignments, but how were they to locate and build this railroad without giving offense to somebody? By 1850 Whigs were ready to employ some kind of private corporation for any public work of such gigantic proportions, but at the first mention of the word "corporation" Democrats shrieked and trotted out the spirit of Jackson's Bank War, trussing up the Whigs as monied aristocrats, stockjobbers, and monopolists. Democrats inclined to prefer a public road to a chartered corporation ran afoul of their own hostility to national improvements as well as the gospel of government ineptitude with which they had destroyed the American System. Three western Democrats—Thomas Jefferson Rusk of Texas, Thomas Hart Benton of Missouri, and Stephen A. Douglas of Illinois—desperately hoped to locate the railroad to their local advantage, while the antique Spirit of '98 rose again in Virginia to oppose western raids on the public treasury. Passionate sectionalists in the South dared not allow the "free soil" states to control the only thoroughfare to the Pacific, whereas northerners exasperated not so much with slavery as with slavery's demands upon national politics would not abide a round-

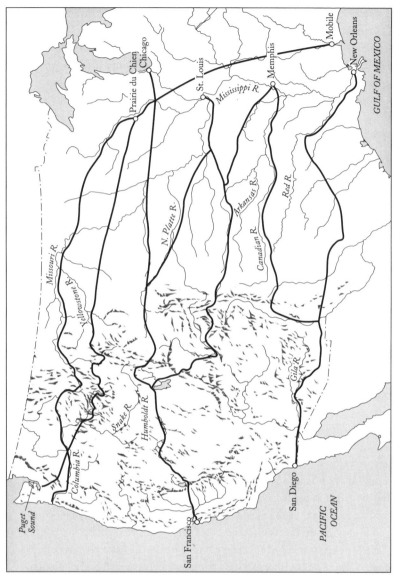

Map 5. Transcontinental Railroad routes discussed in Congress during the 1850s.

about southern route just to accommodate a paranoid "slave power." In these debates all language would be heavily freighted with bad feeling and mutual suspicions that would remain, with rare exceptions, beneath the surface of the discourse.[26]

In February 1849 Benton introduced in the Thirtieth Congress the first full-blown alternative to Whitney's plan. Taking aim at Whitney's far-northern location and building on George Wilkes's brief for a public railroad, the old Missouri senator wanted to substitute a "national central highway" from the Mississippi to the Pacific Ocean." Benton chose his words with care: *national* "because no private resources are equivalent to such a work, nor fit for it"; *central* so as to favor no section; *highway* meaning a corridor one mile wide over which could be built first a common road, then a railroad, plank roads, macadamized roads, and eventually magnetic telegraph—technologies for every taste and purse. Colonel Frémont assured him, Benton argued, that Whitney's route was "wholly impracticable," that there were better passes south of South Pass. Follow the "wild animals"—nature's "first engineers"—and a good straight route will be found from San Francisco to St. Louis, along the thirty-eighth parallel. Two or three branches might accommodate Oregon, New Mexico, and Utah; and if work began at once all along the line, the common road could be ready "next summer." Given such prospects, how could the Congress wish to make this thoroughfare "a matter for stockjobbing, a matter for sale upon the exchanges of Europe and America?" "We own the country from sea to sea," Benton concluded: "We can run a national central road through and through the whole distance, under our flag and under our laws."[27]

Meanwhile, Douglas labored to develop a strategy that would force Congress to bring the road to Chicago, his new hometown. Asking the Illinois legislature to rescind their endorsement of Whitney's plan (they did), Douglas then led a delegation to the St. Louis convention of 1849 for the purpose of upsetting Benton's well-laid plans. Because Benton's bill fixed the route in advance of the surveyor' reports, Douglas adopted the position that Congress should locate the road only *after* the engineers had studied their options. More important, good-Democrat Douglas reminded good-Democrat Benton and his Missouri friends that Congress possessed no power to make improvements in the states: therefore the national Pacific railroad must commence at the Missouri River, and Congress must use land grants to encourage "branches" to connect it with St. Louis, Chicago, or even Memphis. Because good land in Missouri was largely taken up by 1849, such land grants only could be made for an Iowa route along the forty-second parallel—leading to Chicago.[28]

An 1849 Boston meeting generated hope for a joint-stock company to build the Pacific railroad. Boston capitalist P. P. F. De Grand thought a $100 million company ($2 million private capital, the balance federal credit) could build the road in five years, working men around the clock in three shifts. Not surprisingly, however, the heirs of Andrew Jackson's 1830s Bank War were not easily moved to endorse any "monstrous" corporate solutions. In fact, Whitney's original plan had been carefully drawn to defeat tirades like Benton's against stockjobbing corporations, a fact clearly recognized by the House Committee on Roads and Canals in a favorable report to the Thirty-first Congress in 1850. As a private *but not corporate* enterprise, Whitney's bill escaped both constitutional and ideological objections. In fact, Whitney promised to charge no tolls above the cost of operations and repairs, he would issue no stock, exercise no patronage, and spend no public money.[29] Senator Benton and friends of more southerly routes claimed the Whitney line would be paralyzed by snow; but southern mountain passes reached elevations three or four thousand feet higher than South Pass, and this committee believed snow would be a greater hazard there. More proof of the virtue of Whitney's plan lay in the howling objections of "great capitalists" whose own "bubble" (the Panama railroad) it threatened to burst. In all, Whitney's bill produced a public work through private effort without raising any charge whatsoever for the original "outlay of capital." Nothing could be better.[30]

Between the constitutional scruples of some members and the bad experience of others with "reckless expenditures" in the states, the 1850 House committee could see not "the slightest chance of carrying a bill through Congress" to build a Pacific railroad "by the government." Congressmen took more pleasure in posturing for local or factional advantage than in seeking a genuine solution to the transcontinental question. For example, Missouri Democrat James Butler Bowlin claimed to draw from "hiding" in the Whitney bill some of the "mighty powers for evil" concealed there: it was a "vast scheme of speculation" that ought to fill men's minds with "absolute horror," and it chartered a corporation that would transfer to foreign investors title to "the very heart of the Republic." This was "Satan rebuking sin," scoffed J. L. Robinson of Indiana, who liked the Whitney bill precisely because it left the contractor free to choose his route and name his terminal: "It cuts loose from politicians and sections, from localities and cliques" that "defeat any law" on the subject. Robinson, a Virginia-style liberal Democrat, loathed public enterprise and sneered at the Democratic piety in which Missourians wrapped themselves as they pushed Benton's national highway, "a political monstrosity" more "gigantic and fearful" than any "undertaken by this Government." Missouri's real concern, Robinson concluded, was that the Whitney bill "does not make St. Louis . . . the metropolis of the world, nor Colonel BENTON its great manager or governor."[31]

Thus nothing could be done in 1850 or 1851. Greater enthusiasm existed at the moment for the isthmian connections through Panama, which presidents Taylor and Filmore favored (in part because they dodged the question of transcontinental route selection). California senator William Gwin begged for engineering urveys, pointing out that Benton's wild animals can climb much steeper grades han steam locomotives. Benton himself labored diligently against any isthmian r "quick" foreign solution to Pacific communications, and William Allen of)hio hysterically condemned a postal contract with the Panama Railroad: "I will ıot establish a Barbary power to levy tribute upon the commerce of two hemipheres passing over the Isthmus of Panama." But domestic political complicaions rendered the overland railroad project too problematical at least until after he next presidential election. In late 1852, however, Senate friends of the Pacific ailroad decided to try again in the short session of the Thirty-second Congress hat convened in December 1852. The previous spring various committees had oyed with the Whitney plan, a second like it in the South, a Douglas "preailroad" proposal to build a chain of military stations, with telegraphic connecions, along the emigrants' route to California, Benton's great highway, and a bill hat gave the president authority to select two routes across the territories and ake bids from private contractors. Further, a New York corporation, the Atlantic ⅹ Pacific Railroad Company ($100 million capital, Robert J. Walker and Levi Chatfield principals), offered to build a railroad if the government would give it ⅎhoice of route, land, and $30 million in bonds. Now with northern Democrat Franklin Pierce safely cued up to run for the White House, rival Democrats ⅎhought they might secure the long-deferred prize.[32]

In January 1853 Senator Gwin offered a magnificent new bill as a substitute for Douglas's emigrant-route project. Gwin proposed a southern trunk from San Francisco southeastward through Albuquerque, whence branches split off serving six different termini along the Middle Border. Based on the principle of something-for-everyone, Gwin promised over 5,000 miles of railroad paid for with 97 million acres of land (with a subsidy of $12,000 per mile in Texas, where Congress owned no land). It was assailed, in part, for being much too expensive and ambitious. Walter Brooke of Mississippi countered with a grant of land and credit to the Atlantic & Pacific corporation of New York to build along a route not specified and only with permission of any state through which it passed. Like early railroad charters in the states, Brooke's bill fixed the rates the road could charge (at less than three cents per mile) and secured to the government the right to buy back the railroad after twenty years. Still, most senators rejected any corporate solution and focused instead on the public works plans. John Parker Hale asked plaintively if colleagues could stop "guerilla warfare" and find a general bill "not filled with details" on which to "test the sense of the Senate"? But John Bell, a leading friend of the railroad, correctly responded that the details *were* the problem and nothing would do but to hammer them out now. Salmon Chase of Ohio raised the specter of sectional jealousy; orthodox Democrat Stephen Adams of Mississippi rose to "Buncombize" (Gwin's term) against internal improvements *and* corporations for home consumption; and John W.

Davis of Massachusetts lectured the Senate on the inevitability that this road must be built by a "powerful joint-stock company." The Gwin bill then was referred to a select committee of five: Bell of Tennessee, Davis of Massachusetts, Dodge of Iowa, Rusk of Texas, and Gwin.[33]

With all these objections fresh on their minds, the committee members scaled back their vision to a single road and, failing to resolve its location, took John Bell's suggestion of leaving its selection to the president and the corps of engineers. Certain of the inexpediency of trying to carry out the work with government employees, the committee looked to bids from private contractors who would actually construct and operate the railroad in exchange for land and federal bonds (not to exceed $20 million). Ten years' time was allowed for the work. The government reserved free transportation for mail, troops, and military supplies, and it authorized railroads to make convenient connections. Almost incidentally the bill gave the contractors corporate status as a necessary feature of doing business on such a monumental scale. On 2 February 1853 this new improved "Rusk bill" replaced Gwin's earlier scheme as the focus of a full-scale debate.[34]

Opposition burst from the right flank of the Democratic Party. Richard Brodhead, a Pennsylvania strict constructionist, moved to strike the whole bill and replace it with a small appropriation for surveys of the various routes. Protesting (falsely) his friendship for the bill, Brodhead saw constitutional dangers in delegating to the president such legislative duties as selecting the railroad route. James A. Bayard of Delaware espied the corporation with "fourfold the power of that corporation against which the Democratic party of the United States were at war for a series of years." Pierce would never sign it, he predicted. Jesse Bright, Indiana's leading states' rights Democrat added his "unalterable opposition" to the Rusk bill: it made the president the head of a railroad company, it built railroads inside the states, and it chartered an unconstitutional corporation. Since the Democrats railed equally against public undertaking and private corporations, Davis, a Massachusetts Whig, asked for clarification:

> We all know from our experience and observation, and we might know by reasoning *a priori*, that, if the Government undertakes, by its own immediate exercise of power, to carry on such a work . . . abuses will creep in, and that it will become a political engine necessarily. That is precisely the objection made to a corporation, yet how infinitely greater are the abuses under the management of a Government itself than those which arise under the management of any corporation whatever.[35]

Andrew Pickens Butler of South Carolina and James Murray Mason of Virginia finally leveled the ancient Democratic gospel against this, the most plausible bill yet presented for the construction of a Pacific railroad. The Rusk bill, said

J.S. Army Topographical Engineers surveying the Great Salt Lake Valley, 1849–50.
~uch scientific reconnaissance, while essential to finding routes, used surprisingly
~rimitive instruments and techniques. From Howard Stansbury, *Expedition to the Valley
f the Great Salt Lake* (1852). Courtesy Purdue University Libraries.

3utler, was an "undisguised proposition" to create the "system of internal im-
~rovements" against which the party and the states had battled for so long.
t wrongfully enlarged executive authority, gave away extravagant amounts of
~noney and land, created a monstrous corporation, and promised to transform
he "free confederacy of Republican States" into a "consolidated empire." Of
~ourse he knew that such "conservative restraint and guidance" were seen as
"stupid impediments" to the "wisdom" and "genius of YOUNG AMERICA." Still he
~eared the "irresistible" invasions of the capitalists as well as the unconstitutional
"fiat" of a "tempted majority" of the people. Two weeks week later an oracular
Mason reviewed the same ground, stating unequivocally (and more narrowly
han ever before), that Virginia always had "denied to Congress the power by any
~gency, either directly or indirectly, to construct works of internal improvement."
~alling the Rusk bill a *rape* of the Constitution," he pitied the president if the
~ill should pass: "This horde of contractors, eager for the expenditure of public
~noney, will be around him like vultures, urging him on." At the outbreak of the
Mexican War, Mason prophesied, the aging Calhoun had warned that a curtain
~ad dropped between himself and the future; but Mason now could see the
"curtain lifted" and the "opening page of the second book of American history"
~ay exposed.[36]

Such histrionics must have aggravated men who hoped to pass a railroad bill of
~ome description. John Bell asked the senators to show "in whose hands they
~hould deposit this power," if neither the president nor private corporations are

to have it? Some critics said the road was visionary, that no sensible man woul invest; others saw a shameless banquet for the capitalists. Who was right? Tru man Smith of Connecticut outlined the only three ways a Pacific railroad coul be built. All apparently agreed that if government tried "it would cost three c four times as much as it ought." Private stockholders might do better; in fact, h thought the "sagacity and shrewdness of private enterprise would be no unsaf arbiter of questions which it might be difficult to settle in the two Houses c Congress." But widespread disbelief in that view produced in the Rusk bill third alternative, the government control of a private corporation, which Smit thought an acceptable compromise. Trust the president to choose the route, for Congress insisted on it "should we not have interminable debates, and . . . the what heart-burning, what jealousies, and sectional dissentions should we nc have?"[37]

To this point the leading Democrats in favor of the railroad—Rusk, Dougla and Gwin—had let the Whigs Davis, Bell, and Smith take the lead in disputin their enemies within the Democracy, hoping quietly to hold with sheer interes those votes for which the states' rights conservatives were fishing. Finally, o 18 February Missouri Democrat Henry S. Geyer spoke briefly in defense of th bill, and Iowa Democrat Augustus Caesar Dodge, a member of the select com mittee, uncloaked the simple logic by which the bill had been constructed by it friends: "you cannot fix the termini or tour of this road in any bill, and then ge votes enough to pass it." Appealing across the decades to a patriotic vision tha predated either Jefferson's or Jackson's negativity, Dodge recited George Wash ington's commentary from 1784 of the precarious status of the western settle ments within the Union: "the touch of a feather would turn them any way." Trus the president, Dodge concluded; it is the only way to build any railroad.[38]

On 18 February a test vote on Brodhead's amendment, striking out the whol bill, failed by 22 to 34 votes, but it revealed both party (only 6 of 22 votes wer Whigs) and regional biases (all but 7 of 22 were Atlantic states) against the Rus bill. The next day, Kentucky Whig Joseph Underwood stepped over the part question and took up the old cause of the West against the "saltwater constitu tion." Did the Constitution empower coastal states to lock up their interio sisters from access to the sea? He thought not, and he argued that Congress had right, nay a duty to forge outlets for interior states—by force if the coastal state resisted. Eastern states seemed to think a limited federal government dared no exercise a power unknown to the Founding Fathers: did this bar Congress fron ever contemplating, say, hot air balloons? Finally, echoing the positive senti ments of Adams and Clay, Underwood reminded his Democratic colleagues tha if the "depravity of man" truly rendered the government incompetent to ever undertaking, then republican self-government was doomed and "its destruction could not "be hastened by a corporation such as is proposed in this bill." Vir inia's Hunter replied with frightening illustrations of how a corporation might wriggle past government restraints, warning about land speculations, stock deals, and bookkeeping tricks that would render the company infamous, unparalleled in the "annals of civilized legislation." Hunter's imagination was vivid and compelling (and nearly all that he predicted later tarnished the workings of the Union Pacific Company); by 36 to 14 senators then struck out the incorporation section. Still, what really drove the issue was not Bank War rhetoric but sectional jealousy, and those resentments boiled over as the afternoon wore on.[39]

When William DeSaussure of South Carolina moved to specify a terminus "not north of Memphis," someone called out good-humoredly "nor south of the Tennessee line." But the laughter could not conceal the bitterness. Members urged each other not to interject sectional rivalry, but Georgia's Robert Charlton insisted that the bill was sectional already: Franklin Pierce was a strict constructionist and never would approve a route that built railroads in the states. Douglas immediately denied it; one could build a southern road, he responded (disingenuously?) by getting the permission of the state through which it ran. South Carolina's Butler said notwithstanding the fact that the southern, Gila River route was best, it would not be adopted—"this road will go to the lakes." John Bell begged the South to let it pass if the South ever hoped for a road of its own; DeSaussure said get it now or all was lost. Iowa's Dodge, never one to mince words, found it fitting that a "free-soiler" (Salmon Chase) had first raised this thorny matter and a "fire-eater" (DeSaussure) now excited it. But this bill placed every city on equal ground, and Dodge would urge the president to choose, disregarding all "little, miserable, humbug amendments having their origins in local animosity or sectional discord." Just as they were ready to report the Rusk bill from Committee of the Whole to the Senate, Michigan Democrat Lewis Cass announced that he would vote for no bill allowing construction in the states, with or without permission. Cass was an old-line Democrat, a bit wooden, and plausibly driven by abstract principles. At the same time, by remembering just at that moment a core tenet of Old Republican doctrine, Cass set the stage for Illinois senator James Shields's amendment blocking the expenditure of any federal money on railroad construction in the states. Because strict-construction Democrats dared not vote against it, the Shields amendment amounted to a scalpel in Douglas's hands, allowing him to excise every route except the one to Chicago. Horrified, Rusk explained that if adopted this would "disjoint the whole bill." When it passed, 22 to 20, Gwin pronounced the bill "Destroyed." "Yes sir, destroyed," said Rusk. "Dead," offered Underwood. "Yes, sir, dead," repeated Rusk: "It will now build no road to the Pacific, and therefore it is a useless piece of paper." It being nearly suppertime, the Senate then adjourned.[40]

After a Sabbath of rest the Senate resumed its railroad debate, reconsidering the Shields amendment and adopting in its place a similar one from California's

Weller, who struggled to keep the road alive. But all friends from the Sout deserted the bill, some blaming Cass for becoming confused or Douglas fo plotting to capture the route: Bell said as much in the Senate and lashed out a well at the new, even tighter principles by which Virginia whipped the Demo cratic Party under a Baltimore Platform that apparently banned public work anywhere by any means. The game effectively was over; the delicate coalitio required to pass the Rusk bill disintegrated into sniping constituent parts. Rus and his allies could not go forward without aid to the states to build upwar of 3,000 miles of railroad in California, Texas, Arkansas, or Louisiana. Isaa Walker bitterly denounced the double standard whereby the price of public lan in Wisconsin was doubled because of improvement land grants, while Califor nia, "the youngest and one of the most brilliant sisters of the family of States (and a font of golden treasure), appeared to be getting much more. Underwoo dragged out John C. Calhoun's old 1819 "Report on Internal Improvements" an scolded the Democrats for not understanding their own ideological heroes. Fi nally, George Badger, a Whig from North Carolina, put his finger on the di lemma produced by "the principles of the Democratic party." He never "hear them without alarm," he said, for they were "brought forward" and operate "precisely to the extent, and precisely for the purpose of preventing the accom plishment of some great good for the country."[41]

Having traced the tortuous evolution of Democratic Party "doctrine" on inter nal improvements, it seems unlikely that Cass's epiphany was totally fortuitous o that Douglas's position was anything but calculated. Douglas stood on the rail road question squarely on ground prepared for him by Jefferson, Calhoun, Va Buren, and Jackson. The significant difference lies in the fact that, facing back ward for his guidance, Douglas did not see what his Democratic predecessor more reasonably *could not* see—that is, the permanent damage being done to th prospects of national popular government. Convinced the stage on which h played was the stage on which these questions *had* to be decided, Douglas did no see emerging the rival stage of private corporate enterprise that would, withi another generation, simply take governance private. And so he redealt his han in 1854, leading with the Kansas-Nebraska bill, assuming that between what h held himself and what he presumed to be the distribution of cards in other hand he could take all the tricks in turn.[42]

Consolidation: The Liberal Capitalist Paradigm

The rest of the story is familiar: how Douglas's ambition to secure the railroad la behind the Kansas-Nebraska Act, which in turn embroiled the federal part system in a self-destructive slide into extremism, paranoia, and finally war. Be cause of these entanglements the transcontinental railroad bill could not b passed until secession took the old-line southern Democrats out of Congres ltogether; then, in 1862, the residue of old Whigs and Free Soil Democrats who, like Abraham Lincoln and his vice president, Hannibal Hamlin, had been reconfigured alike as "Republicans") found it much less difficult to hammer out the details, set aside the land, and launch the two companies—the Union Pacific and Central Pacific Railroads—that would meet at last in 1869 at Promontory, Utah. But the story of internal improvements in the affairs of the early republic does not so much end at Promontory Point as on Gilded Age Wall Street and in the corporate offices of railroads in Boston, New York, Chicago, and San Francisco. The problem that a system of internal improvements always raised was the specter of consolidation; the vision that so exercised its enemies was the rise of a design that could shape, limit, and control the prospects—the liberties—of freemen in states, villages, and farmsteads across the country. Inasmuch as they became preoccupied with preventing the imposition of design at the hands of the national government, the enemies of internal improvement were entirely successful. But they did not, could not, prevent design itself from ordering the world in which Americans lived. Instead, their efforts guaranteed that design and consolidation would come from outside the halls of government: they cleared the way for the emergence of the liberal capitalist paradigm that so profoundly restructured American life in about three decades after the outbreak of Civil War.

Hardly anybody saw it all coming in the hazy light of the sectional crisis of the 850s. New York senator William H. Seward caught a glimpse of the coming future in one of his early contributions to the Pacific railroad debates, but his insights made no impression at the time. "You may make a route across this continent wherever you please," Seward argued in 1853, "there will be but two termini of that road—one in the east at New York, and the other in the West at San Francisco. And whether it goes across the continent, by the way of Whitney's route, or the Texas route, or even the Tehuantepec route, the two terminations will be at San Francisco and New York." South Carolina senator Butler asked him if he meant indirectly or directly? It mattered little, Seward answered: "commerce will fix that termination." More portentously, Seward predicted what almost nobody had yet envisioned in considering the impact of the continental railroad:

> If the road is laid in the right place, that road will stand as the road; but if it is laid in the wrong place, new parties and new corporations will begin another, and will construct it upon a better and shorter route, before this road is completed. It is idle to suppose that one road across this continent is to answer the proposed trade and communication perpetually, or for any long time. The Erie canal [*sic*] does the work of fourteen double-track railroads. And if the Erie canal does the work of fourteen double-track railroads, any man can see that one double-track railroad across this continent will not accomplish the business of this continent and of Asia.[43]

What Seward recognized (and he could hardly have known its whole impor
tance) was that the time when government decisions would mold the landscap
of commerce was fast receding in the wake of a market revolution that was jus
now transferring to the hands of private trade and enterprise the power to contrc
the wealth of nations. While most Pacific railroad advocates dreamed of the na
tion harnessing the Asian markets and riding them freely to prosperity, Sewar
seemed to understand that markets would more likely ride the nations. If ther
ever was a day when people could, by timely action, divert the flow of commerc
and industry out of its "natural" path (and there may have been, as New Yor
surely understood), that day was gone; the combined demands of market force
and ambitious entrepreneurs (both already concentrated in New York and fas
gathering in San Francisco) would not long tolerate arbitrary hurdles or ineffi
ciencies thrown up by local interests or politicians. Commanding the means o
production and distribution, and able to court favor with the people throug
rising opportunities and material prosperity, the next generation's captains o
industry would soon be able to canvass the people, not as voters but producer
and consumers, erecting a market-based "self-governing" consumer society wit
little real need for political permission or protection. On such an economic stag
the work was being done already in Seward's New York, and would spread acros
the future, with or without the legislation of the Congress; and while he did no
quite say it, Seward seemed to recognize that Congress's choice of a Pacifi
railroad route ultimately would not make or break St. Louis, Chicago, Memphis
New Orleans, the North, the South, or the West.

What was left to be decided was not whether to develop the railroads, inter
state commerce, mass markets, large corporations, or heavy industries: thes
things had taken root as a result of liberal economic convictions as old as th
Constitution and (ironically) more deeply cherished at the founding in Ol
Virginia than anywhere else in the Union. The decision remaining was merely i
and where and how the hand of government would work with private industries
producers, and consumers in ever-more integrated national markets. Almos
nobody saw it yet, and few addressed the proper questions during this last grea
debate on the subject of national internal improvement.

One voice, the antislavery radical, soon-to-be-Republican, Gerrit Smith, le
fly a remarkable exposition of what would become soon enough the Gilded Ag
doctrine of laissez-faire, in an 1854 railroad debate in the House of Representa
tives. His was a minority position, built out of radical Democratic or "Loco
foco" views from the late 1830s, and surely not recognized in 1854 for what i
suggested. Smith objected vociferously to government ownership of a conti
nental railroad; in fact, he would "far rather, that it would never be built" tha
that it be built by the hand of government. Private enterprise, Smith continued
was "abundantly adequate" to build all the railroads, and then he generalized hi

point in words that made southern libertarians such as John Taylor or Spencer Roane sound paternalistic. "It is our frequent boast, that this Republic has solved the great problem of self-government," and so it has in a restricted sense. "But what is meant by this solution?" Smith inquired. Was it meant that the people had "shown their capacity and willingness to plan and to do for themselves," that they did not need or desire "the paternal counsels and guiding hand of Government?" No, Americans had proved themselves capable of choosing their governors, but this was only the "first and lowest lesson in democracy." Still to come was the duty of the people "to grow into the Government of themselves, and not to suffer civil government to mingle itself with their affairs." Americans were quite as ready as other people to have government "regulate trade, and build asylums, and railroads, and canals." But such was the result of a long and vicious "habit of dependence," which, if not broken soon, would leave them, like the French, unable to "straighten up" and "go alone."[44]

Such a diatribe sounded foolish in the House of Representatives in 1854, yet in a short generation businessmen, employers, judges, politicians, and professors of political economy would make the claim that every intervention by the state in the affairs of business produced, in Gerritt Smith's words, "an irresistible precedent for every other gigantic work, and every other profuse expenditure at the hands of Government." Smith concluded his 1854 speech with the warning that America stood "on the brink" of the "great peril" of "encroachment by Government," and he called for the "friends of popular rights" to "take our stand against it." Right brink, wrong peril, or so it seemed to so many Americans after the war who flocked to the "popular" causes of Grangers, Antimonopolists, Greenbackers, Bimetalists, Farmers' Alliance, Single Taxers, and finally the People's, or "Populist," Party. Out of the crucible of the Civil War emerged a modern, integrated business system whose liberal creed of laissez-faire so quickly displaced the commonwealth language of republicanism that hardly anybody noticed the switch. But it was not the war so much as the habit of abusing the rhetoric, principles, and institutions of government out of which the nation had been constructed that ushered in such a rapid transformation. How else to explain how dread consolidation, when it came, was greeted with pride as the final culmination of the wisdom and experimental vision of the founders.

Designs of a New Monied Gentry

INTERNAL IMPROVEMENT almost inevitably became the issue that would complicate the promise of popular government in the new United States. Literally fixed to the ground, roads, canals, and other internal improvements were capable of altering political and economic geography: such was their express purpose. By their very nature, these tangible artifacts of positive action benefited some people more than others; in fact, every effort to conquer space and time imposed spatial hierarchy and concentrated trade and capital in ways that were potentially undemocratic. In nature (or in monarchy) such inequality might have been acceptable, but in the new self-governing United States all advantages shown and favors bestowed looked like evidence of privilege and corruption. Governments that undertook public works—at the national, state, or even local level—soon fell victim to charges of favoritism from interest groups clamoring for equal treatment. At the same time other men, hungry for office, or genuinely fearful of distant powers, found it easy to discredit such authorities, accusing them of plotting against the welfare (or liberties) of citizens close to home. Ever popular in theory, internal improvements became too treacherous for elected politicians to pursue in detail. For two generations the subject topped state and national agenda, yet no system of roads or canals—or program promoting the same— could be devised by popular governments at any level to "bind the republic together."

The failure of the campaign for national internal improvements in the early United States exposed crippling flaws in the founders' understanding of their own society and its prospects for self-government. The republican ideal posited a common or coherent "public interest," not only within each fledgling state but among the members of the Union as a whole. Of course, this common interest often was obscured by selfish private interests, temporary passions, petty grievances, or local prejudices; but properly designed representative governments, filled with wise and "disinterested" gentlemen in deliberative bodies and executive offices, were supposed to be competent to sift through competing voices and ascertain the true interest of "the people." It was imagined (especially by the leaders of the Revolution) that with the establishment of the republic an American gentry, remnants of the colonial aristocracy now distinguished partly by merit and personal success and partly by revolutionary service and sacrifice, would guide the new nation to its destiny. In fact, improvement schemes themselves were said to foster mutual good feelings and harmony of interests, kindling among the common people exactly that virtuous public spirit without which self-government was doomed. The contributions of virtuous leaders and the existence of a true commonality of interests were absolutely crucial to the republican experiment: without them the unrestrained passions and divergent interests of ordinary people presumably would tear the Union asunder. Unfortunately both proved elusive during the experiment with republicanism.[1]

For the founding generation, George Washington provided a living model of disinterested leadership. Architect of his own fortune, self-sacrificing commander of the Continental Army, "Cincinnatus" resigning his commission at the pinnacle of power, reluctant, unpaid statesman, dragged out of retirement to lead his foundering countrymen a second time, Washington stood even in his own day as a hero to the nation. Always mindful of his reputation, always struggling to set aside his interests in deference to the public good and the rarefied ideals of Enlightenment conceptions of statecraft, Washington succeeded in constructing a virtuous image that was practically unchallenged during his lifetime and quickly sanctified upon his death. Called by one biographer the "indispensable man," and often called by his contemporaries the "first man" among Americans, surely Washington personified the character and integrity Americans hoped to see in office in the republican governments.[2]

Yet even Washington could not command for long the loyalty of newly liberated Americans, nor could he legitimate the "energy in government" that he thought would be essential to the preserve of the Union—and thus liberty itself. Men like Washington, the young James Madison, John Adams, even Thomas Jefferson (the most radical among them) understood that the virtues of republican government for which they risked their fortunes and their lives included not just freedom from abuse but the privilege of being governed well. During the Confederation period, they thought they saw "specious" and "designing" men coming to power in the states—calculating men who measured their objectives by no higher mark than the demands of an interested populous. To counteract such a deterioration of government, they moved to erect a national republic specifically to gather the reigns of power back into "worthy" hands.[3] These gentry leaders tried for a generation to use that new government, along with their own wealth, prestige, and "wisdom," to promote internal improvements, to bind the Union together with golden chains of commerce and interest, friendship, political and social "intercourse." But they labored in vain, and the network of internal improvements grew without design or systematic policy direction for a century, until the railroads and large corporations began imposing order and coherence on the networks of trade and transportation.

The enduring fear of corruption, and an endlessly reusable opposition strategy that undermined positive actions favoring any party, place, or person, prevented the government of the Union from imposing such benevolent designs as many of the founders cherished. Washington himself, perhaps, embodied the heroic ideal that might have reconciled Americans to energetic rulers; but most of the monied gentry revealed soon enough a readiness to serve themselves in interested schemes and dishonest speculations. Indeed, in his zeal to locate the federal capital across from Mount Vernon and promote the Potomac gateway to the West, Washington revealed his own commitment to interest over principles, exposing the fatal flaw in all republican idealism that called for men to legislate without regard for themselves. Not yet able to imagine governance as a mere contest of interests, and lacking any term save "corruption" with which to challenge each others' designs, the statesmen of the founding generation saw no choice but to castigate their opponents not as rivals for advantage but as enemies of freedom.

Washington's dream of gentry leadership was probably elusive from the start because it built upon a faulty understanding of American conditions. Revolutionary elites in British North America flattered themselves for escaping the curse of hereditary offices and aristocratic decadence, but they still clung to a sense of prerogative, some right to govern that devolved from their wealth, experience, and station. They claimed to be constitutionally "common" and equal, and they hoped they possessed the integrity to wield power fairly in behalf of their neighbors; but close observers (John Adams, for one) worried openly about their virtue.[4] In reality American gentlemen *were* commoners, men of business as "interested" in their affairs as any members of the "lower orders," who were proscribed by their inherited political culture as unfit to hold public office. In general, such men proved unwilling to suppress self-interest in behalf of public good. They had exposed this often enough in the chaos of the Revolution and the constitution making of the founding era.[5] Soon "the people" recognized a commonality with their "betters," not of interest but of civic status and political responsibility. Accordingly they seized the opportunity to claim power and office for themselves. The resulting democratization changed the metaphors of governance forever, away from the parental or custodial images of virtual representation and toward an actual attorneyship of interests. As attorneys for the rising common man, Washington's gentry slowly lost its credibility.

Andrew Jackson played a likely, even necessary, role in America's transition from republican to democratic government. Born in the primitive Carolina backcountry and orphaned as a child during the Revolution, Jackson created his name and his fortune from scratch in the fiercely competitive environment of frontier Tennessee. Literate but hardly eloquent or lettered, violent of temperament, self-taught at military science, law, and politics, Jackson epitomized—almost in caricature—the roughhewn, self-made man that Americans of the second generation loved to think of as the model of manly virtue and integrity. Deftly resurrecting classical tropes of earlier revolutionary discourse, Jackson the "new model man" discredited all traditional marks of character—wealth, learning, experience, and sophistication—and offered himself instead as the humble successor to Cincinnatus, reincarnated as a simple servant of the people's will.[6]

In his boisterous war against the second Bank of the United States, Jackson rallied his people against a fictitious but plausible "money power" and proclaimed a great victory for popular government. His campaign against internal improvement, however (less flamboyant at the time and much neglected by historians), proved more problematic. Jackson found himself pronouncing to the people, like a parent, that they could not have what they wanted because *he* knew better what was good for them. Instinctively authoritarian, yet trapped in a rhetoric of liberty and popular rule, he could only rescue legitimacy in government by moving to withdraw the positive hand and restrict the negative hand severely. And so it was that the common man, afraid of being bullied by aristocrats and cheated by corrupt men in office, was turned toward the automatic workings of the market to find arbitration for his conflicting interests. Theoretically, markets paid no heed to heredity or breeding, respected no privilege or political connections. Only merit and the relentless interactions of supply and demand ("natural laws") rewarded or punished investors and entrepreneurs. If governments refrained from interfering in the marketplace—that is, if they appointed no monopolists, erected no "monster" bank, distributed neither "pork" nor patronage, imposed no comprehensive system of roads and canals—then free and equal persons could compete without restriction, and no one could conspire to use the people's governments to gain unfair power or control.

Ironically, a national transportation system (not of roads and canals but of railroads) emerged fairly quickly once the government left the business of internal improvement to the workings of the market. As technology matured and their networks expanded, private railroad corporations discovered in the decades that bracketed the Civil War that competition alone did not yield a rational system of transportation services. In fact, competition fostered dangerous chaos. Lacking any reasonable measure for the cost of transporting thousands of different products under widely differing conditions, railroads typically priced their services according to "what the traffic would bear." Meanwhile, high fixed costs (especially interest on borrowed money) resulting from building and equipping a railroad, forced its owners to seek all the traffic they could in order to generate revenue. Cutthroat competition resulted wherever two or more lines served the same market, driving rates below the margin of profitability. High compensatory rates charged at noncompeting points brought howls of protest from shippers claiming arbitrary discrimination and commercial injury. Efforts by managers to collaborate in order to minimize such crazy discrepancies only heightened popular hostility to railroad "combinations in restraint of trade." In fact, virtually every measure taken to integrate and rationalize railway operations (in order to realize the genuine advantages inherent in steam railroad transportation) gave the appearance of collusion by monopolistic carriers to stifle competition and gouge the public.[7]

Confronted with destructive competition, the railroads found themselves in a trap of their own devising. Railroad promoters had taken the lead in teaching the people and their governments that free competition was both natural and inerrant; but now market forces were producing a distorted system that some large shippers, dishonest managers, and Wall Street speculators exploited in the most disruptive fashion. To suppress this mischief, legitimate railroad managers (if such we can call them) labored to control ever-larger systems through mergers, acquisitions, leased lines, pools, and traffic agreements. All such consolidations were designed to give the "visible hand of management" (Chandler's term) a chance to counteract the negative impact of Smith's "invisible hand" of competition. Where effectively introduced, integration and consolidation indeed brought significant economies of scale as well as more equitable pricing, predictability in service, and the steady flow of reinvested capital that would keep railroad technology improving. But the same strategies that yielded such efficiencies also were abused for the purposes of "bulling" or "breaking" a stock, ruining a business rival, forcing a merger, building up (or tearing down) a city, or punishing a state that threatened to impose restrictions on the managers of railroad corporations. By the middle of the 1870s it was clear to everyone familiar with railway economics that some kind of order would have to be imposed on the national system, if not by government then by the managers of railroads themselves.[8]

Jay Gould grew up with the railroad system and became the most notorious Wall Street scoundrel in what was popularly called the age of the "robber barons." Born in 1836, the last year of Andrew Jackson's presidency, not an orphan like Jackson, Gould nevertheless qualifies also as a self-made man. He spent his childhood on a hardscrabble farm in the Catskills, where his father buried three wives before the lad reached the age of seven. Weak and sickly, young Jay preferred school to farming, eventually taught himself bookkeeping, surveying, some roadway engineering, and developed both a talent and a passion for speculative business. After the panic of 1857, while still in his early twenties, Jay Gould began making money by riding the updrafts and downdrafts of the volatile American markets, beginning a remarkable career as a the most hated Wall Street gambler in the postwar generation.[9]

After a brief stint in the tanning and hide trade, Gould moved into railroads

and Wall Street speculations during the Civil War. Anticipating the enormou
flow of government spending, Gould bought the almost worthless bonds of a
struggling railroad while everyone else in the market wrung their hands ove
secession. As he knew it would, wartime finance fueled almost limitless chance:
for speculation, and by 1865 Gould had acquired both cash with which to play
and a shrewd understanding of securities manipulation. Like all corporations
railroads enjoyed the right to issue stocks and bonds that traded on Wall Stree
for whatever investors would pay. Most charters limited stocks, but Gould and
others learned ways to circumvent these restrictions, such as issuing convertible
bonds. Intended to raise money for construction and operations, these securitie:
also could be used to drive stock prices up or down, or to acquire voting control o:
corporations. At the same time, the beginnings of integration among local railroad companies produced no end of contracts, leases, and purchase agreements
all of which could be capitalized on paper, then bought and sold "on the street."
By the end of the war, huge amounts of such corporate paper traded hands in
New York, representing the tremendous potential of America's railroads, o
the short-term potential for churning profits—sometimes both, and sometime:
neither.[10]

No law prevented speculation; still, clever financiers like Gould made thei
greatest killings by stretching or bending the laws that existed or inventing nev
ways to raise money that courts and lawmakers barely understood. False infor
mation, misleading reports, secret issues of stock, fabrication of records, bribery
and what we now call "insider trading" further corrupted the market, magnifying
profits for the unscrupulous and frustrating honorable businessmen. By the 1870:
Gould had proved himself master of all dirty tricks and was hated alike by
legitimate traders and rogues. Charles Francis Adams, son and grandson o
presidents, slandered Gould in print in 1870 as "a spider" who "spun huge webs
in dark corners of the market: "It is scarcely necessary to say that he had not
conception of a moral principle. In speaking of this class of men it must be fairl:
assumed at the outset that they do not and cannot understand how there can be
distinction between right and wrong in matters of speculation, so long as th
daily settlements are punctually effected." Gould was, Adams confessed, "proba
bly as honest" as other rogues, but he "was an uncommonly fine and unscrupu
lous intriguer, skilled in all the processes of stock-gambling, and passably indif
ferent to the praise or censure of society."[11]

Gould had burst on the Wall Street scene in 1867 as the underdog victor in
burlesque called the "Erie War." In 1869 he thoroughly disrupted the bullion
markets in an ill-starred "gold corner" scheme; thereafter, he savaged Mid
western railroading in his scramble to win for Erie a secure western connectior
By 1874 he had gained control of the Union Pacific, the long-dreamed-of "na
tional" transcontinental route. Secretive, dishonest, a notorious briber of judge:

and lawmakers, a ruthless competitor, considered an unscrupulous wrecker of corporations with a demonstrated willingness to sacrifice anything for short-term gain, Gould now stood in relation to the transportation system where Congress had so long been afraid to place Asa Whitney or any other agent, board, or party: in virtual control of the great national artery of trade.[12]

After almost a century of governance designed and intended to eliminate corruption, maximize liberty, and prevent accumulation of arbitrary power, especially in relation to the transportation system, a single individual—a scoundrel not elected by the people but elevated to power through fraud and deception—held the power to manipulate the transcontinental service, raise and lower rates, cut or expand service, build up or tear down cities like St. Louis, Omaha, and Kansas City. Now that it was clear and unavoidable that some kind of system would be imposed upon a national transportation network, how was it that a man like Jay Gould—and not George Washington—stood in line to be the architect of that system, finally to impose design?

Of course, Gould alone could neither make nor break the American railroad system, but he could (and did) set the tone of the industry and focus the attention of all competing railroad managers on whatever challenges Gould laid down. As long as predatory tactics could be mounted against them, other railroadmen organized their strategies around such speculative threats. In railroading, as in currency, a kind of "Say's law" developed such that bad management tended to drive out good, or (more precisely) short-term speculative gambits seemed to triumph over long-term developmental efforts.[13] In the freewheeling markets of Gilded Age America, the prizes seemed to go to the more extravagant aggressors, the more reckless innovators, the more nearly criminal competitors among a cutthroat community of entrepreneurs. More surprising still (to devotees of the Smithian model) was the fact that free competition among these titans of big business thoroughly distorted and reshaped the marketplace for ordinary merchants, farmers, mechanics, and manufacturers. As a result, their economic liberty—the very thing they were afraid of losing under a government design—seemed to disappear in a fog of laissez-faire dogma. Most alarming of all, when ordinary men and women, begging for relief, asked their popular governments to intervene, they found that those governments had been disabled by political convictions of the "common man," that government authority should not be trusted to impinge on the people's liberties.[14]

The tragedy for Americans was not that they had failed to build a national system of roads and canals, or that they lost control of the railroads to the private business sector. The tragedy lay in the subtle substitution, during the long struggle over internal improvements, of economic liberalism for political republicanism at the heart of the American experiment. Republican self-government really never got a chance to demonstrate its promise in early America because the

unfinished business from the Revolution—sectional, class, and developmenta
agendas—favored the deployment, time and again, of the radical charge of cor
ruption whenever governments took positive action. The Jacksonians' solution
combining republican rhetoric with a reliance on liberal markets for the arbitra
tion of clashing interests, ironically could not prevent the Civil War but did ushe
in the market revolution that established laissez-faire in place of the republican
commonwealth tradition. The resulting capitalist economy has paid for its as
sault on freedom and democracy with a flood of consumer benefits in which
generations since the Gilded Age usually have found adequate compensation fo
the loss of their republican birthright. But the story of internal improvements in
the early United States reveals at least the nature of that birthright and the
contrast between the designs of our new monied gentry and the dreams of the
founders, not just for liberty but also for good government.

NOTES

Introduction

1. My understanding of the founding draws heavily on Wood, *Creation*; Lienesch, *New Order for the Ages*; Wood, *Radicalism*; and Rakove, *Original Meanings*. See also McDonald, *Novus Ordo Seclorum*; Ball and Pocock, *Conceptual Change and the Constitution*; and Rahe, *Republics Ancient and Modern*. Even political theorists who tend to collapse the historical founding into a single moment of revelation acknowledge the centrality of republicanism. See Pangle, *The Spirit of Modern Republicanism*. For the contribution of Antifederalists to the founding experience, see Storing, *What the Anti-Federalists Were For*; and Cornell, *The Other Founders*.

2. See Gross, *The Minutemen and Their World*; Nash, *The Urban Crucible*; Royster, *A Revolutionary People at War*; Countryman, *The American Revolution*; and Hoffman, Tate, and Albert, *An Uncivil War*.

3. See the various essays in Beeman, Botein, and Carter, *Beyond Confederation*; also Rakove, *The Beginnings of National Politics*; Onuf, *Origins*; Morgan, *Inventing the People*; and Conley and Kaminski, *Constitution and the States*. A useful guide into these continuing conflicts is Banning, *After the Constitution*. On state constitution making, see Kruman, *Between Authority and Liberty*.

4. Considering its importance in the sources, internal improvement has generated surprisingly little historical literature. See Nelson, "Presidential Influence on the Policy of Internal Improvements"; MacGill et al., *Transportation in the United States before 1860*; Nettels, "The Mississippi Valley and the Constitution"; Albjerg, "Internal Improvements without a Policy"; Goodrich, "National Planning of Internal Improvements"; Taylor, *The Transportation Revolution*; Lively, "The American System: A Review Article"; Goodrich, *Government Promotion*; Clanin, "Internal Improvements in National Politics"; and Larson, "Bind the Republic Together." An important new contribution, Malone, *Opening the West*, offers an economist's analysis of the most complete record of antebellum federal improvement expenditures. John, *Spreading the News*, presents a detailed history of a related federal undertaking, the postal system. One unpublished classic stands at the foundation of most modern scholarship on internal improvement policy: Harrison, "The Internal Improvement Issue in the Politics of the Union."

5. Compare Hartz, *Economic Policy and Democratic Thought*; Handlin and Handlin, *Commonwealth*; McCoy, *Elusive Republic*; and Appleby, *Capitalism and a New Social Order*. An important exposition of the promise of American government is Major L. Wilson, *Space, Time, and Freedom*; see also the early chapters of Wiebe, *Opening*.

6. In addition to McCoy, *Elusive Republic*, see Scranton, *Proprietary Capitalism*; Doerflinger, *A Vigorous Spirit of Enterprise*; Nelson, *Liberty and Property*; and Matson and Onuf, *A Union of Interests*. Royster, *Harry Lee*, neatly explores the range of expectations in

a study of one disappointed revolutionary hero. For the lower-class expectations, see Gilje *The Road to Mobocracy*; and Schultz, *The Republic of Labor*.

7. The best (almost the only) treatment of internal improvement in this context is Goodrich, *Government Promotion*. See also Elazar, *The American Partnership*; Watson, *Liberty and Power*; and Feller, *The Jacksonian Promise*.

8. Two important works by Hurst set up this view of political economy: *Law and the Condition of Freedom* and *Law and Markets in United States History*. For an early treatment of Jacksonians as liberals, see Meyers, *Jacksonian Persuasion*. Horwitz advances a theory of legal instrumentalism in *Transformation of American Law*; but compare Tomlins, *Law, Labor, and Ideology*; and Novak, *The People's Welfare*. Sellers, *The Market Revolution*; Freyer, *Producers versus Capitalists*; Ashworth, *Slavery, Capitalism, and Politics*; and others advance an alternative reading of Jacksonian America in which liberal capitalism appears as a more alien force. For a review of the literature, see Gilje, *Wages of Independence*, 1–22.

9. The metamorphosis of economic thought among business leaders from the commonwealth tradition into the modern, liberal, Smithian ideal can be traced in Cochran, *Railroad Leaders*; Kirkland, *Dream and Thought*; Foner, *Free Soil, Free Labor, Free Men*; Chandler, *The Visible Hand*; Howe, *The Political Culture of the American Whigs*; Larson, *Bonds of Enterprise* (1984); and Klein, *Jay Gould*.

Chapter 1

1. George Washington to the Chevalier de Chastellux, 12 Oct. 1783, in Fitzpatrick, *Writings of George Washington*, 27:189–90.

2. Washington to Thomas Johnson, 20 July 1770, in Fitzpatrick, *Writings of George Washington*, 3:19; see generally Phelps, *George Washington and American Constitutionalism*; also Ambler, *Washington and the West*, 21–27, 136–74; and Bacon-Foster, *Potomac Route*, 3–30.

3. Harlow, *Old Towpaths*, 4; Hahn, *The Chesapeake & Ohio Canal*, 16. See Dent, "On the Archaeology of Early Canals."

4. Washington to Thomas Jefferson, 29 Mar. 1784, in Boyd et al., *Papers of Thomas Jefferson*, 7:49–51.

5. Jackson and Twohig, *Diaries of George Washington*, 6:57–68.

6. Washington to the Marquis de Lafayette, 25 July 1785, in Fitzpatrick, *Writings of George Washington*, 28:206. See Cayton, *Frontier Republic*; Onuf, *Statehood and Union*; and Perkins, *Border Life*.

7. See Ambler, *Washington and the West*, 173.

8. Washington to Henry Knox, 5 Dec. 1784, in Fitzpatrick, in *Writings of George Washington*, 28:4–5; also Washington to Jacob Read, 3 Nov. 1784, ibid., 27:486.

9. Washington to Thomas Johnson, 15 Oct. 1784, in Fitzpatrick, *Writings of George Washington*, 27:481; Washington to George William Fairfax, 30 June 1785, ibid., 28:184. See also Ferguson, *Power of the Purse*.

10. See Livingood, *Philadelphia-Baltimore Trade Rivalry*, 33–34; Hutchinson et al., *Papers of James Madison*, 8:123 (editor's note); Bacon-Foster, *Potomac Route* 42–43 (see 210–25 for the Potomac Company charter).

11. Washington to Robert Morris, 1 Feb. 1785; Washington to Lafayette, 15 Feb. 1785; Washington to Jefferson, 25 Feb. 1785, in Fitzpatrick, *Writings of George Washington*, 28:48–55, 71–81 (quotations from 55, 73, 79). See Bacon-Foster, *Potomac Route*, 44–46.

12. Washington to Thomas Johnson, 20 July 1770, in Fitzpatrick, *Writings of George Washington*, 3:18–19.

13. Washington to James Madison, 28 Dec. 1784, in Fitzpatrick, *Writings of George Washington*, 28:19; Washington to Congress, 3 Dec. 1784, in Hutchinson et al., *Papers of James Madison*, 12:478; Washington to Henry Knox, 5 Jan. 1785, in Fitzpatrick, *Writings of George Washington*, 28:24. Madison used the word "bait" in a letter to Jefferson containing a thorough account of the Potomac and James River bills, 9 Jan. 1785, in Hutchinson et al., *Papers of James Madison*, 8:224. See also Handlin and Handlin, "Origins of the American Business Corporation," 1–23.

14. Washington to Jefferson, 29 Mar. 1784, in Boyd et al., *The Papers of Thomas Jefferson*, 7:51.

15. Washington to Henry Knox, 28 Feb. 1785, in Fitzpatrick, *Writings of George Washington*, 28:93. See Onuf, *Origins*; and Rakove, *The Beginnings of National Politics*, especially 360–99.

16. Washington to Hugh Williamson, 15 Mar. 1785, Washington to Richard Henry Lee, 15 Mar. 1785; see also Washington to Barbé Marbois, 21 June 1785, Washington to Lafayette, 25 July 1785, in Fitzpatrick, *Writings of George Washington*, 28:108, 109, 169, 208.

17. Washington to James McHenry, 22 Aug. 1785, in Fitzpatrick, *Writings of George Washington*, 28:227–28, 230.

18. Washington to James Warren, 7 Oct. 1785, in Fitzpatrick, *Writings of George Washington*, 28:290–91; see vols. 28 and 29 generally. For the importance in Virginia of the Mississippi River negotiations, see Banning, "Virginia: Sectionalism."

19. Washington to Henry Lee, 5 Apr. 1786, Washington to John Jay, 18 May 1786, Washington to Jay, 1 Aug. 1786, in Fitzpatrick, *Writings of George Washington*, 28:402, 431, 501–3 (quotations); Washington to Henry Lee, 31 Oct. 1786, ibid. 29: 33–34.

20. Washington to George William Fairfax, 10 Nov. 1785, Washington to Chastellux, 18 Aug. 1786, in Fitzpatrick, *Writings of George Washington*, 28:312, 523; see Bacon-Foster, *Potomac Route*, 57–84.

21. Washington to John Jay, 10 Mar. 1787, Washington to James Madison, 31 Mar. 1786, in Fitzpatrick, *Writings of George Washington*, 29:176, 190–91; Madison to Washington, 7 Dec. 1786, Madison to Jefferson, 19 Mar. 1787, in Hutchinson et al., *Papers of James Madison*, 9:199–200, 318–20. See Freeman, *Washington*, 533–39.

22. Farrand, *Records of the Federal Convention*, 2:615–16, 620. See Collier and Collier, *Decision at Philadelphia*; Kukla, "A Spectrum of Sentiments"; and the several essays in Narrett and Goldberg, *Essays on Liberty and Federalism*; Gillispie and Lienesch, *Ratifying the Constitution*; and Conley and Kaminski, *Constitution and the States*.

23. Washington to Patrick Henry, 24 Sept. 1787, Washington to Bushrod Washington, 10 Nov. 1787, in Fitzpatrick, *Writings of George Washington*, 29:278, 312; Washington to George William Fairfax, 30 June 1785, ibid., 28:184.

24. "Proposed Address to Congress," in Fitzpatrick, *Writings of George Washington*, 30:296–308; quotations from 301. Only parts of this document survive, pages copied in Washington's hand of a seventy-three-page speech probably drafted at Mount Vernon by David Humphreys in January 1789. Fitzpatrick published what pages he could find, after the original had been suppressed, mutilated, and distributed as souvenirs by Jared Sparks in 1827, who with James Madison's blessing concluded that the sentiments could not have been Washington's. Considering that Humphreys worked in Washington's presence, that the sentiments matched much of Washington's earlier writings, that the general bothered to copy out the huge manuscript for review by his intimate friends, and finally in light of the shameless bowdlerizing of political texts that went on in the 1820s among custodians

such as Sparks, who "spoke" for the heroes of the founding, I have taken the draft to be genuine (albeit preliminary) expression of Washington's views. See the editor's note in Hutchinson et al., *Papers of James Madison*, 11:446-47; see also McCoy, *Last of the Fathers* 119-70.

25. Washington, "First Annual Message to Congress," Washington to Edward Rutledge, 5 May 1789, in Fitzpatrick, *Writings of George Washington*, 30:491-94, 309.

26. On Washington's character see James Thomas Flexnor, *Washington, the Indispensable Man*; and Wills, *Cincinnatus*.

27. Quoted in Wood, *Creation*, 131.

28. For Jefferson's lurid interpretation of New England society at the time of Shays' Rebellion, see Hatzenbuehler, "Refreshing the Tree of Liberty with the Blood of Patriots and Tyrants," 94-95.

29. See Royster, *Harry Lee*, 55-113, 169-85; also Bacon-Foster, *Potomac Route*, 85.

30. Madison to Jefferson, 20 Aug. 1784, Madison to Lafayette, 20 Mar. 1785, in Hutchinson et al., *Papers of James Madison*, 8:102, 251.

31. For Madison's part in the convention, see Banning, *Sacred Fire of Liberty*, chaps. 4-6 also Banning, *Jefferson & Madison*. Compare McCoy, *Last of the Fathers*, chap. 2, and the editor's note in Hutchinson et al., *Papers of James Madison*, 10:3-8.

32. Jefferson to Washington, 15 Mar. 1784, in Boyd et al., *Papers of Thomas Jefferson*, 7:26 Jefferson to Washington, 10 May 1789, ibid., 15:117; see also Jefferson to Madison, 8 Dec. 1784, in Hutchinson et al., *Papers of James Madison*, 8:178.

33. See editor's note in Boyd et al., *Papers of Thomas Jefferson*, 6:581-615, quotations from 584, 586; Washington to James Duane, 7 Sept. 1783, in Fitzpatrick, *Writings of George Washington*, 27:133-40. On Madison's conservatism vis-à-vis Jefferson see McCoy, *Last of the Fathers*, 58-64. See also Sneddon, "Maryland and Sectional Politics."

34. See Livingood, *Philadelphia-Baltimore Trade Rivalry*, 28.

35. "Abstract of Sundry Papers," 293-304, quotations from 298; see also Livingood, *Philadelphia-Baltimore Trade Rivalry*, 5-7; and Thomas Gilpin to Benjamin Franklin 10 Oct. 1769, in Labaree, *Papers of Benjamin Franklin*, 16:216-18.

36. *Pennsylvania Chronicle and Universal Advertiser*, 1-8 Jan. 1770; Livingood, *Philadelphia-Baltimore Trade Rivalry*, 7, 33.

37. Livingood, "The Canalization of the Lower Susquehanna," 135; Livingood, *Philadelphia-Baltimore Trade Rivalry*, 9, 31-32, 101-3.

38. Livingood, *Philadelphia-Baltimore Trade Rivalry*, 101-3, 32-33; see also Nolan, *The Schuylkill*, 276-80.

39. Livingood, *Philadelphia-Baltimore Trade Rivalry*, 103-4 (Livingood, following Rochefoucault, misprints Weston's name as Watson); Liancourt, *Travels*, 1: 28-29.

40. *American State Papers*, Class X, *Miscellaneous* 1:834-38 (quotation from 834).

41. Ibid., 837.

42. Livingood, *Philadelphia-Baltimore Trade Rivalry*, 33-34, 81-86 (quotation from 85 see also Gray, "Philadelphia and the Chesapeake and Delaware Canal," 401-6.

43. Colden's 1724 report is quoted in Whitford, *History*, 1:18; "Tacitus" [DeWitt Clinton], *Canal Policy of the State of New York*, quoted in Hosack, *Memoir of DeWitt Clinton* 280-81.

44. Colles, *Proposals for the Speedy Settlement*, 3-9. See Stevens, "Christopher Coles, the First Projector of Inland Navigation in America."

45. Colles, *Proposals for the Speedy Settlement*, 10-12.

46. Ibid., 6; George Clinton to New York Assembly, January 1791, quoted in Hosack *Memoir of DeWitt Clinton*, 286; see also Shaw, *Erie Water West*, 14-15; [New York], "An A

for Establishing and Opening Lock Navigations within this State, passed 30 March 1792," in *American State Papers*, Class X, *Miscellaneous* 1:781–87.

47. [New York General Assembly], "An Act for Establishing . . . 30 March 1792," in *American State Papers*, Class X, *Miscellaneous* 1:781–87; Whitford, *History*, 1:33.

48. *American State Papers*, Class X, *Miscellaneous* 1:765–68; Whitford, *History* 1:34–41; see Miller, "Private Enterprise," 399–403. Clinton's comment on Schuyler is quoted in Shaw, *Erie Water West*, 19.

49. For different views of New York's politics, see Countryman, *A People in Revolution*; Young, *The Democratic-Republicans of New York*; Wilentz, *Chants Democratic*; and Gunn, *The Decline of Authority*.

50. Whitford, *History*, 1:40–41; Livingood, *Philadelphia-Baltimore Trade Rivalry*, 103–4; Bacon-Foster, *Potomac Route*, 177, 185; for additional examples see MacGill et al., *Transportation in the United States before 1860* or the appendix to Gallatin, *Report*, in *American State Papers*, Class X, *Miscellaneous*, 1:753–921.

51. Elkanah Watson is quoted in Whitford, *History*, 1:39; see also Miller, "Private Enterprise," 398–400; Bacon-Foster, *Potomac Route*, 71–80.

52. Bacon-Foster, *Potomac Route*, 62–94; Whitford, *History*, 1:37–39.

53. *American State Papers*, Class X, *Miscellaneous*, 1:838–39.

54. Ibid., 1:858–59. The appendix to Gallatin's *Report* (1808) contains the single best collection of such promotional documents and scientific reports for the early period.

55. DeWitt Clinton quoted in Whitford, *History* 1:43–44.

56. For the "Whig science of politics," see Wood, *Creation*, 3–45. See also Lerner, "Commerce and Character"; and McCoy, *Elusive Republic*, 48–75.

57. For the work of the First Congress, see Bickford and Bowling, *Birth of the Nation*, especially 55–75, on the location of the federal capital. See also Bowling, "A Place to Which Tribute Is Brought"; and Sweig, "A Capital on the Potomac."

58. *Annals*, 1st Cong., 1st sess., 786–91, 835–37.

59. Ibid., 868–74, 880–81, 844, 847–48 (quotations from 871, 880).

60. Ibid., 861–80; Bowling and Veit, *Diary of William Maclay*, 140, 144–45.

61. *Annals*, 1st Cong., 1st sess., 868–909 (quotations from 868 and 909); Bowling and Veit, *Diary of William Maclay*, 141.

62. Bowling and Veit, *Diary of William Maclay*, 321. For Jefferson's original account, see "The Anas," in Ford, *Works of Thomas Jefferson*, 1:171–80. Whether Jefferson's interference actually produced the Compromise of 1790 is debated by Jacob Cooke and Kenneth Bowling, but neither scholar questions Jefferson's impression that a deal took place. See Cooke, "The Compromise of 1790"; and Bowling, "Dinner at Jefferson's."

63. See Bickford and Bowling, *Birth of the Nation*, 73–75; also Ferguson, *Power of the Purse*, 306–25; Perkins, *American Public Finance*, chaps. 10–11; McDonald, *Alexander Hamilton*, 163–261.

64. These sentiments appear throughout the appendices to Gallatin's Report, in *American State Papers*, Class X, *Miscellaneous*, 1:753–921; see also Smith, *Wealth of Nations*, 681–89, 767–68.

65. See Riesman, "Money, Credit, and Federalist Political Economy," 128–61; Appleby, *Capitalism and a New Social Order*.

66. See Wood, "Interests and Disinterestedness," 69–109.

67. George Washington, "Farewell Address," in Schlesinger, *American Presidential Elections*, 1:86–93 (quotation from 89); Philadelphia Aurora, ibid., 1:64; McCoy, *Elusive Republic*, 153; Chambers, *Political Parties in a New Nation*, 113–69 (quotation from 116).

68. Quoted in Polakoff, *Political Parties in American History*, 37.

Chapter 2

1. For a fine exposition of the contrast, see Wood, "Interests and Disinterestedness." See also Cunningham, *Jeffersonian Republicans*; Banning, *Sacred Fire of Liberty*; Banning, *Jeffersonian Persuasion*; and Sharp, *American Politics in the Early Republic*.

2. For the context of events in the Federalist decade, see Elkins and McKitrick, *The Age of Federalism*; also White, *The Federalists*.

3. For an overview of Jefferson's administration, contrast Cunningham, *Jeffersonian Republicans in Power*, with McDonald, *Presidency of Thomas Jefferson*.

4. Four modern biographies sustain all students of Thomas Jefferson: Malone, *Jefferson and His Time*; Peterson, *Jefferson*; Cunningham, *In Pursuit of Reason*; and Ellis, *American Sphinx*. A fifth body of scholarship rivals Malone's in magnitude: the editorial notes of Julian Boyd in the first 21 volumes of *The Papers of Thomas Jefferson*. I also have drawn important insights from Matthews, *Radical Politics*; and McDonald, *Presidency of Thomas Jefferson*. For a more detailed version of the argument offered here, see Larson, "Jefferson's Union and the Problem of Internal Improvements," 340–69.

5. Jefferson to John Jay, 23 Aug. 1785, in Boyd et al., *Papers of Thomas Jefferson*, 8:426; Jefferson to J. P. G. Muhlenberg, 31 Jan. 1781, ibid., 4:487; Jefferson to George Washington 15 Mar. 1784, ibid., 7:25; Washington to William Duane, 7 Sept. 1783, quoted in editor's note, ibid., 6:582. See also Cayton, *Frontier Republic*; Onuf, *Origins*; Onuf, *Statehood and Union*, 1–66; and Onuf, "Liberty, Development, and Union."

6. Jefferson to Washington, 15 Mar. 1784, in Boyd et al., *Papers of Thomas Jefferson* 7: 26–27; Jefferson to Washington, 10 May 1789, ibid., 15:117. For a particularly insightful discussion of how liberty, union, prosperity, commerce, and the West became interdependent in the minds of leading Virginia revolutionaries, see Royster, *Harry Lee*, especially 58–113.

7. Jefferson to Madison, 28 Oct. 1785, in Boyd et al., *Papers of Thomas Jefferson*, 8:682.

8. See Jefferson's draft of the Declaration of Independence, in Boyd et al., *Papers of Thomas Jefferson*, 1:429 (see generally 413–33); the editor's note and drafts of Virginia constitutions, ibid., 329–65; Jefferson to Edmund Pendleton, 26 Aug. 1776, ibid., 503–4. The intellectual tradition in which Jefferson operated is explored in Pocock, *The Machiavellian Moment*; and Wills, *Inventing America*.

9. For a narrative of Jefferson's frustrations during these years, see Peterson, *Jefferson*, 97–293; also Royster, *Harry Lee*, 189–227. Patrick Henry early played the role of nemesis later identified with Alexander Hamilton. See Jefferson to Elbridge Gerry, 11 Nov. 1784, in Boyd et al., *Papers of Thomas Jefferson*, 7:502; also Jefferson's annotations on a copy of the Articles of Confederation, ibid., 1:177–82; Jefferson to John Adams, 16 May 1777, ibid., 2:18–19. See Rakove, *Beginnings of National Politics*, especially 133–240; and Onuf, *Origins*, 3–20.

10. Jefferson to James Monroe, 17 June 1785, in Boyd et al., *Papers of Thomas Jefferson* 8:231; also Jefferson to G. K. van Hogendorp, 13 Oct. 1785, and Jefferson to David Hartley 5 Sept. 1785, ibid., 632–33, 484–85.

11. Jefferson to Madison, 16 Dec. 1786, in Boyd et al., *Papers of Thomas Jefferson*, 10:603; Madison to Jefferson, 19 Mar. 1787 (emphasis in original), and Jefferson to Madison 20 June 1787, ibid. 11:219–20, 480–81.

12. Jefferson to William Carmichael, 15 Dec. 1787, in Boyd et al., *Papers of Thomas Jefferson* 12:425–26; Jefferson to Edward Carrington, 21 Dec. 1787, and 27 May 1788; ibid. 446 and 13:208; Jefferson to Carmichael, 3 June 1788, and Jefferson to Edward Rutledge 18 July 1788, ibid., 13:232, 378; Jefferson to Richard Price, 8 Jan. 1789, ibid., 14:420; Jefferson to le Cte. De Moustier, 17 May 1788, ibid., 13:174. See Conley and Kaminski, *Constitution and the States*; and Gillespie and Lienesch, *Ratifying the Constitution*.

13. For examples of doubt, see comments on the presidency in Jefferson to Edward Carrington, 27 May 1788, in Boyd et al., *Papers of Thomas Jefferson*, 13:208–9; Jefferson to Thomas Mann Randolph, 18 Apr. 1790, ibid., 16:351; Jefferson to Monroe, 20 June 1790, and Jefferson to George Mason, 13 June 1790, ibid., 537, 493; see also a memo of Feb. 1793, explaining Jefferson's role in the compromise, in Ford, *Works of Thomas Jefferson*, 7:224–27. See also Cooke, "The Compromise of 1790," and Bowling, "Dinner at Jefferson's."

14. Jefferson memo to Washington, "Opinion of the Constitutionality of the Bill for Establishing a National Bank," 15 Feb. 1791, in Boyd et al., *Papers of Thomas Jefferson*, 19:275–80 (quotation from 276); Jefferson memo of conversation with Washington, 1 Mar. 1792, and Jefferson to Washington, 23 May 1792; ibid., 23:186–87, 535–40.

15. Jefferson to Washington, 23 May 1792, in Boyd et al., *Papers of Thomas Jefferson*, 23:535–40 (quotation from 537); see editor's note and documents, ibid., 20:718–59; and Jefferson's memo of a conversation with Washington, 10 July 1792, ibid., 24:210–11. For contrasting narratives of the collision between Jefferson and Hamilton, see Peterson, *Jefferson*, 446–78, and McDonald, *Alexander Hamilton*, 237–84. For the newspaper war, see Lienesch, "Thomas Jefferson and . . . the Origins of the Partisan Press."

16. For the framers' continued silence on their original intentions, see Knupfer, *The Union As It Is*, 1–55.

17. *Annals*, 1st Cong., 1st sess., 111, 619, 642, 659, 2160.

18. Ibid., 2nd Cong., appendix, 1350, 1356, 1453; 3rd Cong., 1st sess., 525–26; 3rd Cong., 2nd sess., 1135, 1140, 1190, 1430, 1446–47, 1471, 1502, 1510; 4th Cong., appendix, 2889, 2963, 2904; 5th Cong., appendix, 3709, 3724, 3789, 3939; 6th Cong., appendix, 1497, 1533, 1576. On coastal survey, see ibid., 3rd Cong., 2nd sess., 1249; 4th Cong., 1st sess., 149, 170; on fortifications, see 3rd Cong., 1st sess., 615–16; 4th Cong., 2nd sess., 2211–14. On coastal survey, see also Dupree, *Science in the Federal Government*, 29–33.

19. See Farrand, *Records of the Federal Convention*, 2:308; *Annals*, 1st Cong., 2nd sess., 1640–43. The best modern treatment of the postal service is John, *Spreading the News*.

20. *Annals*, 1st Cong., 2nd sess., 1640–43, 1668, 1676–86, 1712.

21. See John, *Spreading the News*, 25–63.

22. See *Annals*, 1st Cong., 2nd sess., 1677; 1st Cong., 3rd sess., 1886–87, 1890; 2nd Cong., 1st sess., 233, 238–39, 304, 283; 3rd Cong., 1st sess., 455–56.

23. For the 1794 post office law (9 May) see *Annals*, 3rd Cong, 1st sess., 1431–44. For Madison's survey bill, see ibid., 4th Cong., 1st sess., 297, 314–15. See also Chauncey Goodrich to Oliver Wolcott, 21 Feb. 1796, in Wolcott, *Memoirs*, 1:303; Joseph Habersham to Madison, 6 Apr. 1796, in Hutchinson et al., *Papers of James Madison*, 16:289–90 (for Madison's role in the 4th Congress, see editors' notes 141–50); Madison to Jefferson, 4 Apr. 1796, quoted in Harrison, "*Sic et Non*," 339.

24. Jefferson to Madison, 6 Mar. 1796, in Hutchinson et al., *Papers of James Madison*, 16:251. See also *Annals*, 4th Cong., 1st sess., 100, 104.

25. Chauncy Goodrich to Oliver Wolcott, 21 Feb. 1796, in Wolcott, *Memoirs*, 1:304; see also Harrison, "*Sic et Non*," 337–40.

26. George Washington to Congress, 7 Dec. 1796, in Richardson, *Messages and Papers* (1897), 1:194; Alexander White to Madison, 26 Sept. 1796, in Hutchinson et al., *Papers of James Madison*, 16:401–2.

27. *Annals*, 4th Cong., 1st sess., 1697–1711.

28. Madison to Jefferson, 30 Nov. 1794, in Hutchinson et al., *Papers of James Madison*, 15:396; Jefferson to Philip Mazzei, 24 Apr. 1796, in Ford, *Works of Thomas Jefferson*, 8:238–41; Jefferson to John Taylor, 1 June 1798, ibid., 430–33 (quotation from 431); see Matthews, *Radical Politics*, 1–52, 77–96.

29. Jefferson to William Branch Giles, 31 Dec. 1795; Jefferson to John Taylor, 1 June 1798, Jefferson to Taylor, 26 Nov. 1798, in Ford, *Works of Thomas Jefferson*, 8:203, 430–33, 480–81; Jefferson to Wilson C. Nicholas, 5 Sept. 1799, Jefferson to Elbridge Gerry, 26 Jan. 1799, ibid., 9:79–80, 17; Jefferson to Gideon Granger, 13 Aug. 1800, ibid., 138–41. For context, see Ketcham, *Presidents above Party*, 3–99; and Cunningham, *Jeffersonian Republicans*.

30. Jefferson to Monroe, 7 Sept. 1797, in Ford, *Works of Thomas Jefferson*, 8:340; Jefferson to Gideon Granger, 13 Aug. 1800, ibid., 9:138–40.

31. See Matthews, *Radical Politics*, 77–95, 119–26. For a defense of Hamilton's legitimacy as a republican, see Stourzh, *Alexander Hamilton and the Idea of Republican Government*.

32. Jefferson, First Inaugural Address, 4 Mar. 1801, in Ford, *Works of Thomas Jefferson*, 9:194–99 (quotation from 195); Jefferson to John Dickinson, 6 Mar. 1801, Jefferson to James Monroe, 7 Mar. 1801, Jefferson to Joseph Priestley, 21 Mar. 1801, Jefferson to Nathaniel Niles, 21 Mar. 1801, Jefferson to Thomas McKean, 24 July 1801, ibid., 9:201–4, 217–19, 221, 282–83. See Cunningham, *Jeffersonian Republicans in Power*; Cunningham, *The Process of Government under Jefferson*; White, *The Jeffersonians*; Hofstadter, *The Idea of a Party System*; and Johnstone, *Jefferson and the Presidency*.

33. Jefferson, First Annual Message, 8 Dec. 1801, in Ford, *Works of Thomas Jefferson*, 9:321–42; Jefferson to Gallatin, 1 Apr. 1802, Jefferson to Gallatin, 13 Sept. 1802, and Jefferson to Thomas Cooper, 29 Nov. 1802, ibid., 358–60, 394, 403.

34. Jefferson to Gideon Granger, 20 May 1803, Jefferson to Elbridge Gerry, 29 Mar. 1801, Jefferson to Thomas McKean, 19 Feb. 1803, Jefferson to John Bacon, 30 Apr. 1803, in Ford, *Works of Thomas Jefferson*, 9:468, 242–43, 451–52, 463–64; Jefferson to Gideon Granger, 16 Apr. 1804, ibid., 10:75–76; Jefferson to William Branch Giles, 6 Apr. 1802, ibid., 9:361–62. See also Jefferson to Gallatin, 10 Feb. 1803, ibid., 444; Jefferson to William Duane, 24 July 1803, ibid., 10:21; Jefferson to Wilson C. Nicholas, 26 Mar. 1805, ibid., 137–38. For views critical of the Jeffersonians, see Levy, *Jefferson and Civil Liberties*; Kerber, *Federalists in Dissent*; and McCormick, *Presidential Game*, especially 41–163.

35. Jefferson to Robert Livingston, 18 Apr. 1802, in Ford, *Works of Thomas Jefferson*, 9:364–68; Jefferson to John Dickinson, 9 Aug. 1803, and Jefferson's message to Congress, 17 Oct. 1803, ibid., 10:29–30, 33–44. Compare Peterson, *Jefferson*, 745–800 (especially 773–75) with Tucker and Hendrickson, *Empire of Liberty*, 108–35. See also Matson and Onuf, "Toward a Republican Empire"; and Carson, "Blank Paper of the Constitution."

36. See Jefferson, Fourth Annual Message, 8 Nov. 1804, in Ford, *Works of Thomas Jefferson*, in Ford 10:114; Jefferson to Benjamin Hawkins, 18 Feb. 1803, ibid., 9:447–48. See Tucker and Hendrickson, *Empire of Liberty*, 137–74; McCoy, *Elusive Republic*, 185–208; McDonald, *Presidency of Thomas Jefferson*, 29–73; and Horsman, *Expansion and American Indian Policy*; On the embargo, see Spivak, *Jefferson's English Crisis*.

37. A remarkable collection of manuscript petitions to the House of Representatives survives in the National Archives. See Records of the United States House of Representatives, RG 233, National Archives, Washington, D.C. (These documents remain in the official custody of the clerk of the U.S. House of Representatives and were consulted here with permission.) A few examples of these petitions can be found appended to Gallatin, *Report*, in *American State Papers*, class X, *Miscellaneous*, 1:724–920.

38. *Annals*, 7th Cong., 1st sess., 1097–1126, 1158–62; see 1349 for text of bill. Gallatin's letter to William Branch Giles, 13 Feb. 1802, is on 1100–1103.

39. Jefferson to Gallatin, 13 Oct. 1802, in Ford, *Works of Thomas Jefferson*, 9:398–99. I follow Harrison's account of the Cumberland Road and evolving administration policy. See Harrison, "Internal Improvement," 139–95.

40. *Annals*, 9th Cong., 1st sess., 22–26, 42–43, for Tracy Committee report and action.

41. Ibid., 835–40 (roll call 840). On the vote Federalists supported the bill 22 to 3; Republicans divided 37 to 38 against; individuals whose party affiliation is unclear divided 7 to 9 against. North Carolina, generally a hotbed of strict constructionism, divided 4 to 4; New York's 9 Republicans split 4 to 5 in favor, with 2 Federalists joining the majority. See Harrison, "Internal Improvement," 151–54; Harrison, "*Sic et Non*," 340–41; Madison to Monroe, 17 Dec. 1817, in Hunt, *Writings of James Madison*, 7:403–7.

42. See *Annals*, 8th Cong., 1st sess., 555; 8th Cong., 2nd sess., 11–86; 9th Cong., 1st sess., 25, 192–97, 1148–50.

43. Jefferson, Second Inaugural Address, 4 Mar. 1805, in Ford, *Works of Thomas Jefferson*, 10:130; for Madison's question, see ibid., 128n.

44. Jefferson to Gallatin, 29 May 1805, Gallatin to Jefferson, memo 16 Nov. 1806, in Adams, *Writings of Albert Gallatin*, 1:232, 319; Jefferson, Sixth Annual Message, in Ford, *Works of Thomas Jefferson*, 10:317–18.

45. Jefferson to Madison, 6 Mar. 1796, in Ford, *Works of Thomas Jefferson*, 8:226; Gallatin to Jefferson, memo 16 Nov. 1806, in Adams, *Writings of Albert Gallatin*, 1:319. See Harrison, "*Sic et Non*," 338–42.

46. Gallatin to Jefferson, memo 12 Feb. 1805, in Adams, *Writings of Albert Gallatin*, 1:228; Jefferson to Joel Barlow, 10 Dec. 1807, in Ford, *Works of Thomas Jefferson*, 10:529–30.

47. See Larson, "A Bridge, a Dam, a River"; Gray, *The National Waterway*, 1–42; Harrison, "Internal Improvement," 175–99. These debates are scattered throughout the *Annals*, 9th Cong., 1st sess.

48. *Annals*, 9th Cong., 2nd sess., 77–97. Harrison dismisses Adams's sincerity ("Internal Improvement," 195–99), but I find Adams's claim more plausible.

49. Gallatin, *Report* (1808; reprint, 1968), 7, 66–75 (quotations from 68–69); for the documentary appendix see my note 37; see Formwalt, "Benjamin Henry Latrobe." (I am indebted to Lee Formwalt and Joseph H. Harrison Jr. for alerting me to Latrobe's role in the Gallatin plan and the Porter Bill.) See also Carter, "Benjamin Henry Latrobe."

50. Gallatin, *Report*, 73–75.

51. See Harrison, "*Sic et Non*," 342–43.

52. Gallatin, *Report*, 73; Formwalt, "Benjamin Henry Latrobe," 113–28 (quotation from 117). See petitions in Records of the House of Representatives, RG 233, National Archives, filed by Congress and session.

53. Formwalt, "Benjamin Henry Latrobe," 123–28; Carter, "Benjamin Henry Latrobe," 17–21.

54. The relative unimportance of the national government was first exposed (and possibly exaggerated) in Young, *Washington Community*; see also Bogue and Marlaire, "Of Mess and Men"; and Wiebe, *Opening*. Stagg, *Mr. Madison's War*, details the breakdown of government; see also Hickey, *The War of 1812*; and Watts, *The Republic Reborn*.

55. Madison to Congress, 5 Dec. 1815 and 3 Dec. 1816, in Richardson, *Messages and Papers* (1897), 2:552–53, 561 (quotation).

56. See Stagg, *Mr. Madison's War*, 419–68; Young, *Washington Community*, 179–212; Ketcham, *Presidents above Party*, 100–123; and Wiebe, *Opening*, 7–20, 35–66. See also Skeen, "Vox Populi, Vox Dei."

57. Meriwether et al., *Papers of John C. Calhoun*, 1:367–68, 372; *Annals*, 14th Cong., 2nd sess., 296, 854. See also Hopkins et al., *Papers of Henry Clay*, 2:259; and Cumberland Road debates, *Annals*, 14th Cong., 2nd sess., 514, 1211, 1250–52, 1308.

58. *Annals*, 14th Cong., 2nd sess., 851–52.

59. Ibid., 852–58.

60. Ibid.

61. Ibid., 858.

62. Ibid., 865.

63. Ibid., 876–934 (final roll call on 934). Among Virginia Republicans, 14 of 17 oppose the bill; in New England 24 of 27 Federalists did likewise; New York overwhelming voted yea; Pennsylvania, Delaware, Maryland, the West and the rest of the South divide inconclusively.

64. Clay to Madison, 3 Mar. 1817, in Hopkins et al., *Papers of Henry Clay*, 2:322; Wiltse *John C. Calhoun*, 1:137.

65. Compare Madison to Congress, 3 Mar. 1817, with Madison to Congress, 30 Jan. 181 in Richardson, *Messages and Papers* (1897), 2:569–70, 540.

66. Ibid., 569–70.

67. Madison to Jefferson, 15 Feb. 1817, in *Letters and Other Writings of James Madison* 3:35. See Adams, *Writings of Albert Gallatin*, 2:54; Jefferson to George Ticknor, [?] Ma 1817, in Ford, *Works of Thomas Jefferson*, 12:58–59 (see also 61–63, 69, 71–73). For anothe view, see McCoy, *Last of the Fathers*, 98.

68. This explanation of the Bonus Bill veto represents an accommodation of my ow 1987 arguments with McCoy's equally compelling interpretation. Compare Larson, "Bin the Republic Together," 363–87, with McCoy, *Last of the Fathers*, 85–118.

69. Jefferson to Gallatin, 16 June 1817, in Ford, *Works of Thomas Jefferson*, 12:71–73.

Chapter 3

1. Gallatin, *Report* (1808; reprint, 1968), 75.

2. The standard survey is Taylor, *Transportation Revolution*; see also MacGill et al. *Transportation in the United States before 1860*; Goodrich, *Government Promotion*; and Shaw, *Canals for a Nation*.

3. New York State, "Report of the Commissioners appointed by the last preceding join resolution of the Senate and Assembly," 2 Mar. 1811, in New York, *Laws of the Canal*, 1:64 See Rubin, "Innovative Public Improvement," 25–47; Miller, *Enterprise of a Free People*, especially chaps. 3–6; Shaw, *Erie Water West*; Shaw, *Canals for a Nation*, 30–50; Sheriff *Artificial River*, especially chaps. 1–2. For new essays on the New York economic setting see Pencak and Wright, *New York and the Rise of American Capitalism*.

4. New York, *Laws of the Canal*, 1:68, 70–72.

5. Ibid., 80–81, 91–94. See Rubin, "Innovative Public Improvement," 47–52.

6. Rubin, "Innovative Public Improvement," 52–59.

7. "Memorial of the Citizens of New-York, in favor of a Canal Navigation between the great western Lakes and the tide-waters of the Hudson," 21 Feb. 1816, in New York, *Laws of the Canal*, 1:122–41 (quotation from 129).

8. Ibid., 140–41. For the byzantine details of New York politics, see Hanyan and Hanyan, *DeWitt Clinton and the Rise of the People's Men*; on Clinton, see also Siry, *DeWitt Clinton and the American Political Economy*; and Cornog, *The Birth of Empire*.

9. See Miller, *Enterprise of a Free People*, 77–98.

10. Ibid., 99–111. See Perkins, *American Public Finance*, 324–71.

11. See also Morison, *From Nowhere to Know-How*, 20–47; also Shaw, *Erie Water West*, chaps. 5–7. For a new look at canal diggers and construction methods, see Way, *Common Labor*.

12. See Whitford, *History*, 1:117–20.

13. Quoted in Shaw, *Erie Water West*, 184; quoted in Whitford, *History*, 1:129–30. See generally Whitford, *History*, 1:125–30.

14. Quoted in Whitford, *History*, 1:83.

15. See Albion, *Rise of New York Port*; Albion, *Square Riggers on Schedule*; Gilchrist, *Growth of the Seaport Cities*; and Pred, *Urban Growth and the Circulation of Information*.

16. See Biship, "State Works of Pennsylvania"; Livingood, *Philadelphia-Baltimore Trade Rivalry*; Hartz, *Economic Policy and Democratic Thought*; Russ, "Partnership between Public and Private"; Woolfolk, "Rival Urban Communication Schemes"; Rubin, "Imitative Public Improvement," 67–114; Rubin, "Canal or Railroad," 2–103; Rhoads, "Pennsylvania Canal"; McCullough and Leuba, *Pennsylvania Main Line*; Baer, *Canals and Railroads of the Mid-Atlantic States*; and Shaw, *Canals for a Nation*, 58–84. Two new articles by Majewski, "Who Financed the Transportation Revolution?" and "The Political Impact of Great Commercial Cities," compare financing of public works in Pennsylvania and Virginia for the antebellum period.

17. On Philadelphia's economic history, see Lindstrom, *Economic Development in the Philadelphia Region*, especially chaps. 2 and 4.

18. Gallatin, *Report*, 58, 60–61; see Myers, "The Early Turnpikes of the Susquehanna Valley," 248–59; Wood, *Turnpikes*, 11–15; Rubin, "Imitative Public Improvement," 67–68. See also Durrenberger, *Turnpikes*, chaps. 3.

19. Rowe, *Mathew Carey*, 83–97; Shelling, "Philadelphia and the Agitation in 1825"; Carlson, "Pennsylvania Improvement Society"; and Carlson, "The Pennsylvania Society for the Promotion of Internal Improvements."

20. "Fulton" [Mathew Carey], "Canal Policy—No. III," *United States Gazette*, 26 Jan. 1825; see Rubin, "Imitative Public Improvement," 70–71; Carlson, "Pennsylvania Improvement Society," 299–300; Rowe, *Mathew Carey*, 89–90; *United States Gazette*, 10 Feb. 1825.

21. *United States Gazette*, 10 Feb. 1825.

22. *United States Gazette*, 16 Dec. 1824; "Fulton" [Mathew Carey], "Canal Policy— No. I," *United States Gazette*, 16 Dec. 1824; Carey, *Brief View*, 20.

23. Nicholas Biddle to S. M. Duncan, 4 Jan. 1825, quoted in Carlson, "Pennsylvania Improvement Society," 301; see also Rowe, *Mathew Carey*, 91–93; Rubin, "Imitative Public Improvement," 72–75; "Fulton" [Mathew Carey], "Canals and Railways—No. IV," *United States Gazette*, 16 Feb. 1825; and Shelling, "Philadelphia and the Agitation in 1825," 182. William Strickland's *Report on Canals, Railways, and Roads* was published by Carey in 1826.

24. Shelling, "Philadelphia and the Agitation in 1825," 180–90; Rubin, "Imitative Public Improvement," 76–82.

25. Shelling, "Philadelphia and the Agitation in 1825," 189–203 (quotations from 191, 200, 203); Rubin, "Imitative Public Improvement," 92–98.

26. Rubin, "Imitative Public Improvement," 92–103; Shaw, *Canals for a Nation*, 66, 79–80.

27. Rubin, "Imitative Public Improvement," 104–5; Rubin, "Canal or Railroad," 59; for another assessment, see Shaw, *Canals for a Nation*, 69–71. For more construction details, see Ilisevich and Burket, "Canal through Pittsburgh."

28. Rubin, "Imitative Public Improvement," 94, 106–14 (quotation from 112).

29. Carey, *Brief View*, 11, 6–19, 22–23, 29–30.

30. See Jackson, *Chronicles of Georgetown*, 297–335; Ward, *Early Development of the Chesapeake and Ohio Canal Project*; Sanderlin, *Great National Project*, chaps. 1–5; Goodrich and Segal, "Baltimore's Aid to Railroads"; Littlefield, "Maryland Sectionalism"; Stover,

History of the Baltimore and Ohio Railroad, chaps. 1–3; Brugger, *Maryland*, chap. 5; Shaw, *Canals for a Nation*, 98–117; and Dilts, *The Great Road*, chaps. 1–6.

31. Gallatin, *Report*, 60–61; Wood, *Turnpikes*, 8–10, 19–21; Durrenberger, *Turnpikes*, 65–70.

32. Livingood, *Philadelphia-Baltimore Trade Rivalry*, 33–35; Gallatin, *Report*, 33; Baer, *Canals and Railroads of the Mid-Atlantic States*, appendix. See Browne, *Baltimore in the New Nation*, especially chaps. 4 and 6.

33. Gallatin, *Report*, 9, 13–16; Gray, *National Waterway*, 10–66.

34. Sanderlin, *Great National Project*, 31–60.

35. See Rubin, "Canal or Railroad," 63–69.

36. Ibid., 69–72, 75 (quotations from 71, emphasis in original); see also Stover, *History of the Baltimore and Ohio*, 15–27.

37. Sanderlin, *Great National Project*, 59–60; Stover, *History of the Baltimore and Ohio*, 27; Parsons, *John Quincy Adams*, 185.

38. Rubin, "Canal or Railroad," 77 (quotation, figures from 75).

39. On "mixed enterprise," see Goodrich, "Virginia System." On Virginia's early political culture, see Shade, *Democratizing the Old Dominion*, especially chaps. 1–3; also Jordan, *Political Leadership in Jefferson's Virginia*; Roeber, *Faithful Magistrates and Republican Lawyers*; Sydnor, *American Revolutionaries in the Making*.

40. See MacGill et al., *Transportation in the United States before 1860*, 264–73; Shaw, *Canals for a Nation*, 117–23; Brown, *Dismal Swamp Canal*, 31–47; Dunaway, *History*, 21–47; Hunter, "Turnpike Movement in Virginia"; Terrell, "James River Bateau"; and Rice, *The Allegheny Frontier*, chaps. 13–14. For a detailed treatment of an eighteenth-century improvement scheme, see Royster, *Fabulous History of the Dismal Swamp Company*.

41. Gallatin, *Report*, 16–18, 28–32, 61; Virginia General Assembly, *Journal of the House of Delegates, 1812–13*, 25–27, 83–89 (quotations from 87, 88).

42. Virginia General Assembly, House of Delegates, *Report of the Committee on Roads and Inland Navigation*, 27 Dec. 1816, printed in *Niles' Weekly Register* 9, supp. (1816): 149–54 (quotations from 149, 150).

43. Ibid., 150.

44. Ibid., 151–52.

45. Ibid., 152.

46. Ibid., 153–54; see Goodrich, "Virginia System," 360–64.

47. The best account of Virginia internal improvements remains the unpublished dissertation of Rice, "Internal Improvements in Virginia, 1775–1860." See also Goodrich, "Virginia System," 366–67.

48. Dunaway, *History*, 59–77, 90–91; Goodrich, "Virginia System," 366–67.

49. Goodrich, "Virginia System," 363; Virginia General Assembly, *Journal of the House of Delegates, 1817–18*, 139–41, 150–55 (quotations from 140, 152, 150); see also Dunaway, *History*, 79–91.

50. The best introduction to this colonial heritage is Ekirch, *"Poor Carolina."*

51. Quoted in ibid., xviii, 15, 29, 31. On geography, see Merrens, *Colonial North Carolina in the Eighteenth Century*. On government see Ekirch, "The North Carolina Regulators on Liberty and Corruption, 1766–1771"; and Ganyard, *The Emergence of North Carolina's Revolutionary State Government*.

52. See Greene, "Independence, Improvement, and Authority"; also Gilpatrick, *Jeffersonian Democracy*; Leffler and Newsome, *North Carolina*, chaps. 19–22; Wagstaff, *State Rights and Political Parties in North Carolina*; and Lienesch, "North Carolina: Preserving Rights."

53. William Polk to John C. Steele, 22 Nov. 1800, in Wagstaff, *Papers of John Steele*, 1:192;

William Richardson Davie to Steele, 25 Sept. 1803, ibid., 414; Saunders Donoho to Archibald D. Murphey, 26 Nov. 1807, in Hoyt, *Papers of Archibald D. Murphey*, 1:15. See Rice, "Early Development of the Roanoke Waterway."

54. From the *Raleigh Register*, 13 July 1809, quoted in Gilpatrick, *Jeffersonian Democracy*, 239. On expenditures, see Broussard, *The Southern Federalists*, 8. On Macon, see Watson, "Squire Oldway and His Friends"; Wilson, *The Congressional Career of Nathaniel Macon*; Battle, *Letters of Nathaniel Macon, John Steele, and William Barry Grove*.

55. North Carolina General Assembly, *Journal of the House of Commons, 1791*, 4; *1802*, 5–6; *1806*, 5; *1800*, 5; *1802*, 5–6; *1804*, 4–5; *1806*, 4; *1809*, 4–5; *1810*, 5. (All citations to North Carolina state documents were taken from the *Microfilm Collection of Early State Records* produced by the Library of Congress. See Jenkins, *Guide to the Microfilm Collection of Early State Records*.)

56. North Carolina General Assembly, *Journal of the House of Commons, 1806*, 5; see Morgan, *State Aid*, 3–7n; and Watson, "North Carolina and Internal Improvements."

57. "Report to the Committee on Inland Navigation," 5 Dec. 1815, in Hoyt, *Papers of Archibald D. Murphey*, 2:20–21; on Murphey, see Lerche, "The Life and Public Career of Archibald D. Murphey," especially 165–200. See also Counihan, "North Carolina, 1815–1836," 103–10.

58. "Report to the Committee on Inland Navigation," 6 Dec. 1815, in Hoyt, *Papers of Archibald D. Murphey*, 2:21–28 (quotations from 21, 26).

59. Ibid., 30n; "Report of the Committee on Inland Navigation," 9 Dec. 1816, ibid., 34–47 (quotations from 34, 44, 46); Murphey, "Memoir of Internal Improvement," ibid., 112–19; "Report of the Committee on Internal Improvement," 5 Dec. 1817, ibid., 84–85. See "Internal Improvements of North Carolina," 17–37.

60. Murphey, "Memoir," in Hoyt, *Papers of Archibald D. Murphey*, 2:103–95 (quotations from 107, 109, 184).

61. Ibid., 176–78.

62. Murphey to Thomas Ruffin, 25 Apr., 28 Mar., and 14 Aug. 1819, in Hoyt, *Papers of Archibald D. Murphey*, 1:138–39, 131, 151.

63. Murphey to Thomas Ruffin, 4 Aug., 18 Aug., 20 Dec. 1820, Murphey to [name deleted], 20 Dec. 1820, Murphy to Ruffin, 30 June, 21 July, 22 Aug. 1822, in Hoyt, *Papers of Archibald D. Murphey* 1:169, 173–74, 181–84, 244–48, 261–63.

64. See Morgan, *State Aid*, 15–22; North Carolina Board of Internal Improvement, *Report 1833*, 4.

65. North Carolina Board of Internal Improvement, *Report 1820*, v; *1821*, xx; see also *1822* and *1823*.

66. Ibid., *1824*.

67. Counihan, "North Carolina, 1815–1836," 73–79; Nathanial Macon to Bartlett Yancey, 15 Apr. 1818, in Wilson, *Congressional Career of Nathanial Macon*, 47.

68. Macon to Yancey, 15 Apr. 1818, in Wilson, "Congressional Career of Nathanial Macon," 47; see also Macon to Yancey, 8 Mar. 1818, ibid., 48–49. Alston is quoted in Watson, "'Old Rip' and New Era," 217–40 (quotation from 221).

Chapter 4

1. Richardson, *Messages and Papers*, 2:580–81. See Cunningham, *Monroe*; Ammon, *James Monroe*. Good brief introductions to the Monroe era can be found in Sellers, *Market Revolution*; Ketcham, *Presidents above Party*, chap. 7; and Dangerfield, *Era of Good Feelings*, book 2. See also Fischer, *The Revolution of American Conservatism*.

2. The best recent treatment of this critical period is Lewis, *American Union and the Problem of Neighborhood*, especially chaps. 3–5. For a quick survey, see Mayfield, *The New Nation*, especially 77–83; also Dangerfield, *Awakening*, 10–20. On the American System, see Baxter, *Henry Clay and the American System*. For the literature on economic growth and the market transformation, see Gilje, *Wages of Independence*; Sellers, *Market Revolution*, chaps. 1–6; Bruchey, *Roots of American Economic Growth*, chaps. 5–7; and North, *Economic Growth of the United States*. For politics I have relied heavily on Wiebe, *Opening*, chaps. 7–12; Heale, *The Presidential Quest*, chaps. 1–3; McCormick, *The Presidential Game*, chaps. 4–5; Wilson, *Space, Time, and Freedom*, chaps. 1–3; and McCormick, *Second American Party System*.

3. On reactionaries, see Risjord, *The Old Republicans*, especially 196–311; Jordan, *Political Leadership in Jefferson's Virginia*. For the dynamics of Virginia politics, see Shade, *Democratizing the Old Dominion*, especially chap. 3. Freehling, *The Road to Disunion*, hastens to link every conflict to the slavery question from the earliest period. For a more patient view, see Wiebe, *Opening*, chaps. 10–11. No published account has attached much significance to this early Virginia protest as a prelude to the multiple crises of 1819.

4. James Monroe, First Annual Message to Congress, in Richardson, *Messages and Papers* (1897), 2:587.

5. *Annals*, 15th Cong., 1st sess., 22–24. See Lowrey, *James Barbour*, especially chap. 5.

6. *Annals*, 15th Cong., 1st sess., 452. Committee members were Henry St. George Tucker, chair, James Tallmadge Jr., Samuel D. Ingham, Henry Randolph Storrs, Cliffton Clagett, George Robertson, and William J. Lewis.

7. Ibid., 454–60 (quotations from 454, 456, 457, 459).

8. Ibid., 1118–20.

9. Ibid., 1120–26 (quotations from 1121–22, 1126).

10. Ibid., 1139–51 (quotations from 1140, 1147).

11. Ibid., 1151–64 (quotation from 1151–52).

12. Ibid., 1164–79 (quotation from 1165, 1167, 1171). On Virginia's fear of decline, see Sutton, "Nostalgia, Pessimism, and Malaise," 41–55.

13. *Annals*, 15th Cong., 1st sess., 1164–79 (quotations from 1168, 1175, 1177, 1179, 1180).

14. Ibid., 1185–1201 (quotations from 1191–92, 1195, 1200). On the founding process and Virginia's role, see Banning, "Virginia: Sectionalism and the General Good"; Briceland, "Virginia: The Cement of Union," 201–24; also Knupfer, *The Union As It Is*, chap. 1.

15. *Annals*, 15th Cong., 1st sess., 1185–1201 (quotations from 1195, 1200).

16. See Wood, *Creation*, especially chaps. 12–13; Wood, *Radicalism*, especially chaps. 13–14; see also Morgan, *Inventing the People*, chaps. 10–11.

17. *Annals*, 15th Cong., 1st sess., 1201–17 (quotations from 1201, 1209).

18. Ibid. (quotations from 1207, 1210, 1216).

19. Ibid., 1217–22 (quotations from 1218, 1219, 1220). The liberalism of Jeffersonians is hotly contested among historians. Compare treatments in Banning, *The Jeffersonian Persuasion*; Banning, *Sacred Fire of Liberty*; Appleby, *Capitalism and a New Social Order*; Nelson, *Liberty and Property*; McCoy, *Elusive Republic*; Matthews, *Radical Politics of Thomas Jefferson*; Matthews, *If Men Were Angels*; and Kulikoff, *Agrarian Origins of American Capitalism*, especially chap. 8.

20. *Annals*, 15th Cong., 1st sess., 1224–35 (quotations from 1230, 1233). On the "Old Whig" or "country" critique of English commercial corruption, see McCoy, *Elusive Republic*, chaps. 1–3; Wood, *Creation*, 28–36; Kramnick, *Bolingbroke and His Circle*.

21. *Annals*, 15th Cong., 1st sess., 1235–49, 1268–74 (quotations from 1238, 1235, 1248, 1270). Nelson's speech was not recorded but was quoted by Mercer on 1295, 1286.

22. Ibid., 1286–1318 (quotations from 1305, 1318). See Egerton, *Charles Fenton Mercer*, especially chap. 10. Mercer quoted "Publius" (from *Federalist 16* by Hamilton) as follows: "The Government of the Union must possess all the means, and have a right to resort to all the methods of executing the powers with which it is intrusted, that are possessed and exercised by the governments of the particular States. If the interposition of the State Legislatures be necessary to give effect to a measure of the Union, they have only not to act, or to act evasively, and the measure is defeated."

23. *Annals*, 15th Cong., 1st sess., 1319–26 (quotations from 1322, 1323, 1326).

24. Ibid., 1359–80 (quotations from 1359–60, 1362, 1377–78). See book V, chap. 1, part III of Adam Smith, *Wealth of Nations*, especially 681–89.

25. *Annals*, 15th Cong., 1st sess., roll calls 1384–89. Vote totals in *Annals* do not always correspond to sum of the names given among the yeas and nays. In such cases I have used my own count of names rather than the number reported in *Annals*.

26. Hugh Nelson to Charles Everett, 2 Dec. [1817], quoted in Cunningham, *Monroe*, 47; *Annals*, 15th Cong., 1st sess., roll calls 1384–89. On the Compensation Act fiasco, see Skeen, "Vox populi, vox die," 253–74. In a feisty display of legislative independence, Henry Clay challenged a heckler in Kentucky to censure him "for the war, for the peace, or some other great act of my life, but do not quarrel with me for the mean pitiful consideration of my tavern-bills at Washington." Hopkins et al., *Papers of Henry Clay*, 2:221.

27. For a fuller illustration of this problem see Larson, "A Bridge, a Dam, a River," 351–75.

28. See Remini, *Henry Clay*, especially chaps. 5, 6, and 9. For a more sympathetic view, see Peterson, *The Great Triumvirate*, especially parts 1–2. See also Wiebe, *Opening*. For the portrait of Monroe in antique small clothes, see Dangerfield, *Awakening*, 22.

29. See Hopkins et al., *Papers of Henry Clay*, 2:204, 218, 219, 311, 121, 452.

30. Ibid., 463, 459.

31. Richmond *Enquirer*, 20 Sept. 1815. See Ambler, *Ritchie*, 53–63. On the Richmond Junto, see Ammon, "The Richmond Junto"; Harrison, "Oligarchs and Democrats." Miller, "The Richmond Junto," qualifies much of what historians have written about the influence of this group.

32. Richmond *Enquirer*, 8 Aug. 1817; see also Ambler, *Ritchie*, 63–65.

33. Richmond *Enquirer*, 9 Mar. 1816, 4 and 9 Jan. 1817.

34. See, for example, a piece titled "Virginia—Again!" in the Richmond *Enquirer*, 19 May 1818; also see Mays, *Edmund Pendleton*, 2:332–36.

35. Miller, "John Marshall versus Spencer Roane"; Newmyer, *Supreme Court Justice*, 97–114; White, *Marshall Court*, 165–74. Roane's decision appeared in Richmond *Enquirer*, 1 Feb. 1816.

36. See Richmond *Enquirer*, 1 Feb. 1816.

37. White, *Marshall Court*, 168–72; *Martin v. Hunter's Lessee*, 1 Wheaton (U.S.) 323–62, quotations from 324–25, 326–27. In his newspaper Ritchie printed Justice Johnson's concurring opinion but nothing on Story's ruling. See Newmyer, *Supreme Court Justice*, 111; and the Richmond *Enquirer*, 13 Apr. 1816. For more on Roane, see Horsnell, *Spencer Roane*; Beach, "Spencer Roane and the Richmond Junto"; and Roane, "Roane on the National Constitution," 47–122. See also Huebner, "Consolidation of State Judicial Power."

38. *Martin v. Hunter's Lessee*, 1 Wheaton (U.S.) 362–82 (quotations from 364, 374).

39. Madison's growing dissatisfaction with the nationalists' position can be seen in various private letters in volume 3 of *Letters and Other Writings of James Madison*. See, for example, Madison to Henry St. George Tucker, 23 Dec. 1817, ibid. 3:53–54; see also 50–51, 56, 142, 143–46, 164–65, 217–25. This disaffection culminated in Madison's decision to

prepare for publication his secret notes from the 1787 Philadelphia Convention. Madison to Thomas Ritchie, 15 Sept. 1821, ibid., 228-29. Jefferson's reactions can be seen in vol. 12 of Ford, *Works of Thomas Jefferson*. See, for example, 12:71-73, 139, 165, 221, 279, 300-303, 341, 394-95. See also Ambler, *Ritchie*, 64-84; McCoy, *Last of the Fathers*, 97-118.

40. Nathaniel Macon to Bartlett Yancey, 8 Mar. 1818, in Wilson, *Congressional Career of Nathaniel Macon*, 48-49, see also 51, and a sketch of Yancey's career on 44n. See Watson, "Squire Oldway and His Friends," 105-19. For a complete demonstration of the cultural conflicts engendered by internal improvement, see Watson, *Jacksonian Politics and Community Conflict*.

41. For an excellent discussion of original intentions, see Rakove, *Original Meanings*; see also Levy, *Original Intent and the Framers' Constitution*.

42. Calhoun to John G. Jackson, 31 Mar. 1818, in Meriwether et al., *Papers of John C. Calhoun*, 2:216. For studies of Calhoun, see Wiltse, *John C. Calhoun*; Capers, *John C. Calhoun—Opportunist*; Niven, *John C. Calhoun*; and Bartlett, *John C. Calhoun*. For his army reduction plan and political style, see Fitzgerald, "Europe and the United States Defense Establishment." See also the editors' introduction to Meriwether et al., *Papers of John C. Calhoun*, 3:xix-xxiii.

43. *Annals*, 15th Cong., 1st sess., 1678-79; Calhoun to Henry Clay, 7 Jan. 1819, in Meriwether et al., *Papers of John C. Calhoun*, 3:461-73 (quotations from 462, 465, 469).

44. Adams, *Memoirs of John Quincy Adams*, 4:217-18.

45. *Annals*, 15th Cong., 2nd sess., 446-514 (quotations from 449, 450-52, 455).

46. Ibid. (quotation from 471-72). The votes are recorded on 514, 530. The act with the Trimble amendment is printed on 2476. Joseph Story to Ezekiel Bacon, 12 Mar. 1818, is quoted in Cunningham, *Monroe*, 51. Clay's exaggerated sense of his own popularity was fed by the habit of asking only his friends where he stood. In his assessment of the 1818 internal improvement votes, for example, in an open letter to supporters in the *Kentucky Gazette*, 29 May 1818, he concluded that the "successful assertion, by the House of Representatives, of the power of the general government, in that particular, authorizes us to hope that the time will shortly arrive when this great means of strengthening the union, and of advancing the power, prosperity, and wealth of our country, will be liberally employed." See Hopkins et al., *Papers of Henry Clay*, 2:572-73, also 439; and Adams, *Memoirs of John Quincy Adams*, 4:28, 62-63, 70. In summer 1819 Crawford admitted most of Congress approved of internal improvements without an amendment. William H. Crawford to James Tallmadge Jr., 12 July 1819, quoted in Dangerfield, *Awakening*, 30.

47. Thomas Jefferson to John Adams, 7 Nov. 1819, quoted in Cunningham, *Monroe*, 84. On the panic of 1819, see Rothbard, *The Panic of 1819*, especially chaps. 1-2; also Dangerfield, *Era of Good Feelings*, 175-96; and Hammond, *Banks and Politics*, chap. 10.

48. See Hammond, *Banks and Politics*, 257-62. Details are found in the report of the investigating committee, *Annals*, 15th Cong., 2nd sess., 552-74.

49. *Annals*, 15th Cong., 2nd sess., 1140-1406. The final vote is recorded on 1411-12.

50. Adams, *Memoirs of John Quincy Adams*, 4:382-83; *Annals*, 15th Cong., 2nd sess., 1283-1406 (quotation from 1406). See Clay to Langdon Cheves, 14 Nov. 1819, in Hopkins et al., *Papers of Henry Clay*, 2:721-22; see also Peterson, *Great Triumvirate*, 54-55.

51. 4 Wheaton (U.S.) 400-437 (quotations from 401, 402, 405, 406, 423). See White, *Marshall Court*, 521-24, 541-52; and Gunther, *John Marshall's Defense*, 3-4.

52. William Gouge, *Short History of Paper Money* (1833), quoted in Dangerfield, *Era of Good Feelings*, 187; Nicholas Biddle to James Monroe, 5 July 1819, quoted ibid. 182.

53. See Hammond, *Banks and Politics*, 264-68; Dangerfield, *Era of Good Feelings*, 189-90. The Ohio case finally was decided in favor of the bank, returning the money. Henry

Clay represented the Bank of the United States in this cause. See Van Burkleo, "The Paws of Banks"; Ellis, *The Jeffersonian Crisis*; Rezneck, "The Depression of 1819–1822: A Social History," 44–47; and Ambler, *Ritchie*, 74–75.

54. Gunther, *John Marshall's Defense*, 52–77 (quotations from 71, 75, 58).

55. Ibid., 12, 106–54 (quotations from 110, 134, 118). For Marshall's replies, see "A Friend of the Constitution," 30 June–15 July 1819, ibid., 155–214.

56. See Freehling, *Road to Disunion*, 144–61; see also Wilson, *Space, Time, and Freedom*, 22–48; Fehrenbacher, *South and Three Sectional Crises*, 9–23; Dangerfield, *Era of Good Feelings*, 199–245. The standard monograph on Missouri debates remains Moore, *The Missouri Controversy, 1819–1821*. For a new spin on Jefferson's reaction, see Leibiger, "Thomas Jefferson and the Missouri Crisis."

57. *Annals*, 15th Cong., 2nd sess., 1166–1214 (quotations from 1166, 1180, 1186, 1193).

58. Ibid., 1203–14 (quotations from 1204, 1205, 1206). Arbuthnot and Ambrister were two Englishmen summarily executed by Andrew Jackson during his controversial raid into Florida, which figured in the excruciating debates over the Seminole War. See Dangerfield, *Era of Good Feelings*, 122–36; Lewis, *American Union*, 105–25.

59. See Cunningham, *Monroe*, chap. 7.

60. John Adams to Thomas Jefferson, 23 Nov. 1819, quoted in ibid., 86.

61. Clay to Adam Beatty, 22 Jan. 1820, in Hopkins et al., *Papers of Henry Clay*, 2:766; Adams, *Memoirs of John Quincy Adams*, 4:524, 5:3–12 (quotations from 8, 11, 12). Adams's long paragraph on this heated exchange opens with "I told Calhoun," but he sometimes lapsed into private editorializing when making up his diary, and there are no clues as to how much of this he actually spoke out loud. See James Madison to James Monroe, 10 Feb. 1820, in *Letters and Other Writings of James Madison*, 3:164–65; Cunningham, *Monroe*, 90–98. For Ritchie on Missouri, see also Richmond *Enquirer*, 21 Dec. 1819, 20 Jan. 1820, and 10 Feb. 1820.

62. Richmond *Enquirer*, 10 Feb. 1820; Thomas Jefferson to John Holmes, 22 Apr. 1820, in Ford, *Writings of Thomas Jefferson*, 10:157–58. See Peterson, *Great Triumvirate*, 59–63; and Cunningham, *Monroe*, 95–104; Remini, *Henry Clay*, 169–92; Lightfoot, "Henry Clay and the Missouri Question"; and Leibiger, "Thomas Jefferson and the Missouri Crisis."

63. See Taylor, *Construction Construed* and *Tyranny Unmasked*. Compare Dangerfield, *Era of Good Feelings*, 175–248; Wiebe, *Opening*, 209–33; Remini, *Henry Clay*, 157–60; Peterson, *Great Triumvirate*, 47–112. On Taylor, see Shalhope, *John Taylor of Caroline*; Lenner, "John Taylor and the Origins of American Federalism"; and Dodd, "John Taylor, of Caroline." On Americans' views on the law of nations, see Onuf and Onuf, *Federal Union, Modern World*.

64. See Carey, *Addresses of the Philadelphia Society for the Promotion of National Industry*, and his more famous, *Essays on Political Economy*. On Carey's work generally, see Rowe, *Mathew Carey*.

65. Clay, Speech on the Tariff, 26 Apr. 1820; in Hopkins et al., *Papers of Henry Clay*, 2:826–45 (quotations from 828, 836–38, 845).

66. Ibid., 844; *Niles' Weekly Register*, 3 June 1820.

67. *Annals*, 16th Cong., 1st sess., 441–42. On War Department activity, see Meriwether et al., *Papers of John C. Calhoun*, 4:10–13, 100, 219–20. 294, 327, 342, 381, 411, 450, 503, 511–12, 528, 539–40, 641; 5:43–44, 169; and 8:372–73. For Congress, see *Annals*, 15th Cong., 1st sess., 33, 61, 73, 79, 116, 130, 2520, 445, 430, 1448, 1393, 1114, 592, 1672, 2537, 737, 1250, 1657–60, 1664, 2540; 16th Cong., 1st sess., 462, 569, 673, 677, 682, 694–95, 858, 1331–32, 1657–59, 2213, 2244, 2617.

68. *Annals*, 17th Cong., 1st sess., 167. See ibid., 16th Cong., 2nd sess., 144–45, 152–56, 800;

17th Cong., 1st sess., 32, 59, 127–29, 443–44, 166–67, 608–10, 1682–88. On Clay's retirement, see Remini, *Henry Clay*, 191–209.

69. *Annals*, 17th Cong., 1st sess., 1684, 1685.

70. Ibid., 127–29, 443–44, 1690–92, 1734. The text of the bill is on 1872–74.

71. James Monroe, Veto Message, 4 May 1822, in Richardson, *Messages and Papers* (1897), 2:711–12; "Views of the President of the United States on the Subject of Internal Improvements," 4 May 1822, ibid., 713–52 (quotations from 716–17).

72. Ibid., 744, 749.

73. See *Annals*, 17th Cong., 1st sess., 1874–75. Internal improvement appropriations can be followed in Hill, *Roads, Rails, and Waterways*; see also Goodrich, *Government Promotion*, chap. 2; Cunningham, *Monroe*, chap. 12.

74. *Annals*, 17th Cong., 2nd sess., 484–85 (on Maryland); 443, 547–53 (on Ohio, quotation from 549); 605–25, 700–712, 725 (on internal improvements, quotations from 605, 606, 706).

75. John C. Calhoun to Micah Sterling, 12 Oct. 1823, in Meriwether et al., *Papers of John C. Calhoun*, 8:311; Monroe, Seventh Annual Message, in Richards, *Messages and Papers* (1897), 2:785–88 (quotation from 785). See Remini, *Henry Clay*, 193–220. See Clay to Peter B. Porter, 12 June 1823, Thomas Hart Benton to Clay, 23 July 1823, George McClure to Clay, 23 July 1823, Clay to Charles Hammond, 121 Aug. 1823, in Hopkins et al., *Papers of Henry Clay*, 3:433–34, 460–63, 472.

76. *Annals*, 18th Cong., 1st sess., 990–1064, 1217–1470 (quotations from 838, 996, 1056, 1057, 1062, 1217, 1225, 1231–32, 1264–66). On Clay's presidential preoccupation, see Clay to Charles Hammond, 3 Jan. 1824, Clay to Francis T. Brooke, 22 Jan. 1824, Clay to Peter B. Porter, 25 Jan. 1824, John E. Hall to Clay, 27 Jan, 1824, Clay to Porter, 31 Jan. 1824, Clay to Richard Bache, 17 Feb. 1824, in Hopkins et al., *Papers of Henry Clay*, 3:561, 603, 614–15, 629–30, 645.

77. *Annals*, 18th Cong., 1st sess., 1263.

78. Ibid., 1233, 1264, 1298, 1307–8.

79. See also John C. Calhoun to Virgil Maxcy, 17 Sept. 1823, in Meriwether et al., *Papers of John C. Calhoun*, 8:271, where Calhoun claims that he and Clay alone support internal improvements, and that of the two he can bring in the South, which Clay cannot.

80. Ibid., 1338–39, 1412, 1345.

81. Ibid., 1383–85, 1387–88.

82. Ibid., 1266, 1451.

83. Ibid., 534–66 (quotations from 559).

84. Report of the Board of Engineers of the United States, Dec. 3, 1824, in Meriwether et al., *Papers of John C. Calhoun*, 9:424–29 (quotations from 424, 428).

85. Clay, Speech on the Tariff, 30 Mar. 1824, in Hopkins et al., *Papers of Henry Clay*, 3:719, 726–27, 701; Remini, *Henry Clay*, 229–31. See also Taussig, *Tariff History of the United States*, 1–78.

86. For an insightful discussion of the potential of the American System, see Wilson, *Space, Time, and Freedom*, 49–72.

Chapter 5

1. See McCormick, *Presidential Game*, especially chaps. 1–4; Heale, *Presidential Quest*, chaps. 1–2; and Ketcham, *Presidents Above Party*, chap. 7.

2. For a comprehensive introduction, see James F. Hopkins, "Election of 1824," in

Schlesinger, *History of American Presidential Elections*, 1:349–81. Other useful accounts are Hargreaves, *Presidency of John Quincy Adams*, 1–40; Heale, *Presidential Quest*, chap. 3; McCormick, *Presidential Game*, chap. 5; Parsons, *John Quincy Adams*, chap. 6; and Remini, *Andrew Jackson and the Course of American Freedom*, chap. 5.

3. See McCormick, *Presidential Game*, 107; also Cunningham, *Monroe*, chap. 13.

4. Adams, *Memoirs of John Quincy Adams*, 5:315; Lexington *Kentucky Reporter*, 21 June 1824, reprinted in Hopkins et al., *Papers of Henry Clay*, 3:778–80.

5. Howard, "Indiana Newspapers and the Presidential Election of 1824," 177–206; see also Bartlett, *John C. Calhoun*, 116–17; and McCormick, *Presidential Game*, 124–26. On use of newspapers, see Heale, *Presidential Quest*, 50. For Crawford's charge of consolidation, see Lexington *Kentucky Gazette*, 30 Dec. 1824. On Clay's chances in Virginia, see Calhoun to Robert S. Garnett, 6 June 1824, in Meriwether et al., *Papers of John C. Calhoun*, 9:139; and Francis T. Brooke to Clay, 12 July 1824, in Hopkins et al., *Papers of Henry Clay*, 3:793–94. Nagel, "The Election of 1824," provides a summary of the way newspapers tried to inform their readers.

6. Clay to Francis T. Brooke, 26 Feb. 1823, in Hopkins et al., *Papers of Henry Clay*, 3:387–88; Calhoun to Virgil Maxcy, 17 Sept. 1823, in Meriwether et al., *Papers of John C. Calhoun*, 8:271 See Daniel Call to Henry Clay, 30 June 1824, and Francis T. Brooke to Clay, 12 July 1824, in Hopkins et al., *Papers of Henry Clay*, 3:789–90, 793–94.

7. Quoted in Heale, *Presidential Quest*, 55–56; see generally 47–63. [John Henry Eaton], *Letters of Wyoming*. For important background on Eaton and Jackson's original Tennessee supporters, see Ratner, *Andrew Jackson and His Tennessee Lieutenants*; and Sellers, "Jackson Men with Feet of Clay."

8. *Letters of Wyoming*, 3–4.

9. Ibid., 89, 19, 16–17, 23, 21; see also 25–26, 77–86, 97.

10. Ibid., 10–11, 51.

11. Ibid., 63. Eaton actually invited election by the House as part of his strategy. See Hay, "The Case for Andrew Jackson in 1824"; Hay, "The Presidential Question." Hay does not seem to recognize the parroting of Eaton's rhetoric; rather, he concludes (without evidence) that letters to the papers reflected an outdoor community of opinion. Remini, *Andrew Jackson and the Course of American Freedom*, 77, follows Hay uncritically. For a more penetrating analysis of Eaton's role in this campaign, see Heale, *Presidential Quest*, 59–63.

12. McCormick, *Presidential Game*, 119–20; see Andrew Jackson to James Lanier, n.d. [c. 15 May 1824], in Bassett, *Correspondence of Andrew Jackson*, 3:253.

13. *Letters of Wyoming*, 88; Adams quoted in Hargreaves, *Presidency of John Quincy Adams*, 23; John Quincy Adams, "Letters of Publicola," in Koch and Peden, *Selected Writings*, 228–30.

14. Jackson quoted in Remini, *Andrew Jackson and the Course of American Freedom*, 98; see also Remini, *Andrew Jackson and the Course of American Empire*, 74–99; Hopkins, "Election of 1824," in Schlesinger, *History of American Presidential Elections*, 1:378–81; Feller, *Public Lands*, 62–65; and Larson, "Liberty by Design." The Clay states changing their votes were Ohio, Missouri, and Kentucky, in the last case contradicting specific instructions from the state legislature. In addition, Illinois, Louisiana, and Maryland threw their votes to Adams. Nothing in the Constitution or precedent bound the congressional delegations to vote according to the ballots in the Electoral College. Remini is correct when he states that the existence of a quid pro quo between Adams and Clay is irrelevant, but most historians erroneously agree that the popular election was somehow required by the spirit if not the letter of the Constitution. It is my contention that as much

corruption of the electoral process can be found in the dishonest representations of *The Letters of Wyoming* as in the negotiations in Congress in January 1825.

15. Adams, *Memoirs of John Quincy Adams*, 7:63 (quotation). See Adams, Inaugural Address, in Richardson, *Messages and Papers* (1897), 2:860–65.

16. John Quincy Adams, First Annual Message, in Richardson, *Messages and Papers*, (1897), 2:867–80 (quotations from 877–78). See Allen, *Diary of John Quincy Adams*, for records the young Adams's reading and his thoughts on the same. See also Howe, *Making the American Self*, chap. 3.

17. Richardson, *Messages and Papers* (1897), 2:878–80.

18. Ibid., 2:882; "Consolidation," by "An Anti-Federalist," Lexington *Kentucky Gazette*, 20 Dec. 1824, 6 and 15 Jan. 1825. (Adams was quoted by this writer as having said that the founders were not so "ineffably stupid" as to create ineffective government. Opponents hurled the phrase back at him—notably John Randolph in his warmup to the insults that resulted in Clay's duel. See Larson, "Liberty by Design," 91.

19. Richardson, *Messages and Papers* (1897), 2:882.

20. Ibid.; John Quincy Adams to George Washington Adams, 11 Sept. 1811, in Kock and Peden, *Selected Writings*, 279. See Wood, *Creation*, 391–468; also Wood, "Interests and Disinterestedness," 69–109; and Wiebe, *Opening*, 7–109.

21. John Quincy Adams to Jonathan Hampden Pleasants, 25 June 1824, quoted in Bemis, *John Quincy Adams and the Union*, 26.

22. Following a suggestion by Madison, that the State Department could not handle all its work, Adams asked Congress to create a Home Department (British terminology), which request also resulted in charges of consolidation. See John Quincy Adams to Christopher Hughes, 22 June 1818, in Ford, *Writings of John Quincy Adams*, 6:354.

23. See Lipsky, *John Quincy Adams*, 69–77, 150–66; also John Quincy Adams to James Lloyd, 1 Oct. 1822, in Ford, *Writings of John Quincy Adams*, 7:311–12.

24. Bemis, *John Quincy Adams and the Union*, 64. See Adam Smith, *Wealth of Nations*, 681, and book V generally.

25. Richmond *Enquirer*, 10 and 13 Dec. 1825; Thomas Jefferson to William Branch Giles, 26 Dec. 1825, quoted in Ketcham, *Presidents above Party*, 138. See *Niles' Weekly Register* 10 and 17 Dec. 1825; Washington *National Intelligencer*, 14 Dec. 1825.

26. John C. Calhoun, Report of the Secretary of War to the President, 3 Dec. 1824, in *Register of Debates*, 18th Cong., 2nd sess., appendix, 29–30; Calhoun to John Andrew Schulze, 8 June 1824, Calhoun to Robert Goodloe Harper, 10 June 1824, in Meriwether et al., *Papers of John C. Calhoun*, 9:147, 153; see generally 142–82 for a sampling of these requests.

27. *Register of Debates*, 18th Cong., 2nd sess., 67, 189, 216, 487, 516–18, 682. The Committee on Roads and Canals, Hemphill Chair, also brought in a draft of a plan for a system of aid to improvement companies and outlined a host of potential objectives. See Report of the Committee on Roads and Canals, ibid., appendix, 75–81. For an excellent review of internal improvement politics in context, see Feller, *Public Lands*, 39–110.

28. *Register of Debates*, 18th Cong., 2nd sess., 189–249 (quotations from 189). Jonathan Jennings of Indiana proposed fixing the route to St. Louis immediately, thereby committing the government to finishing the whole road, but his amendment did not prevail (240–42).

29. Ibid. (quotation from 245).

30. Ibid., 216–24, 285–303, 334 (quotations from 216, 224, 294, 327).

31. Ibid., 646–81, 325–26 (quotations from 680, 325–26).

32. Ibid., 290. See Feller, *Public Lands*, 63–67, including table 3.3 analyzing votes on the Cumberland Road extension in 1825.

33. *Register of Debates*, 19th Cong., 1st sess., appendix, 9–10, 16–20; Congressional Information Service, *US Serial Set Index*, 2307–09.

34. *Register of Debates*, 19th Cong., 1st sess., 2551–53, 801–2; 19th Cong., 2nd sess., 7–12; 19th Cong., 1st sess., 704 and appendix 138–39.

35. *Register of Debates*, 19th Cong., 2nd sess., 1223; see also ibid., 19th Cong., 1st sess., 29–31, 89–108, 591–97, 619, 688–98, 712–14, 1338–52, 1376–77, 1421–22, 1504–1625; 19th Cong., 2nd sess., 310–38, 376–80, 1252, 1510–12; 20th Cong., 1st sess., 453–68, 462–70, 678–92, 788–804, 809–10, 898–9, 2596–2617. Final bills are printed in the appendix. Petition traffic can easily be tracked in the *Serial Set Index*.

36. *Register of Debates*, 19th Cong., 1st sess. 90–92, 712–14; 19th Cong., 2nd sess., 311, 316–17, 377–78.

37. See *Register of Debates*, 19th Cong., 1st sess, 20–21, 717; 20th Cong., 1st sess., 634–52; 19th Cong., 2nd sess., 1221, 1225–26.

38. Ibid., 19th Cong., 2nd sess., 1233; 19th Cong., 1st sess., 362–63.

39. Ibid., 19th Cong., 2nd sess., 571–72, 643–49 (quotations from 648).

40. Ibid., 1267–83 (quotations from 1271, 1273, 1279).

41. Ibid., 20th Cong., 1st sess., 2612; 19th Cong., 2nd sess., 1285–1300 (quotation from 1300); 19th Cong., 1st sess., 1617; 19th Cong., 2nd sess., 1300–1332 (quotations from 1313).

42. Ibid., 20th Cong., 1st sess., 115–120, 608–33 (quotations from 116, 607–8, 632–33); see Robert Y. Hayne to Calhoun, 9 Feb. 1825, in Meriwether et al., *Papers of John C. Calhoun*, 9:484.

43. *Register of Debates*, 20th Cong., 1st sess., 1510–17, 2132–35, 634–52 (quotations from 1513, 2132 645, 652).

44. Ibid., 607–8, 632–33, 2580–82, 2604–10, 2627 (quotations from 2606, 2607, 2627). See also ibid., 19th Cong., 1st sess., 698.

45. Gallatin, *Report*, 75. For interpretations of rising sectionalism that focus less on partisan strategies, see Sydnor, *The Development of Southern Sectionalism*; Ellis, *The Union at Risk*, 1–40; and Feller, *Public Lands*, 111–42.

46. Calhoun to Ogden Edwards, 2 May 1823, in Meriwether et al., *Papers of John C. Calhoun*, 8:45; Calhoun to Henry Wheaton, 20 Nov. 1824, Calhoun to Robert S. Garnett, 3 July 1824, Calhoun to James Tallmadge, 20 Nov. 1824, and Calhoun to [unknown addressee], 20 Nov. 1824, ibid., 9:396, 199, 393, and 395. See Calhoun to John Pendleton Kennedy, 10 June 1823, and Calhoun to Micah Sterling, 30 Jan. 1824, ibid., 8:101, 513–14; and Calhoun to Robert S. Garnett, 6 June 1824, ibid., 9:138–39. See also editors' introduction to ibid., l–lxiii. As late as 27 Jan. 1825 Calhoun professed to his neutrality regarding the election General Jacob Brown, who then told Adams (lviii).

47. McDuffie and Ingham quoted in Hargreaves, *Presidency of John Quincy Adams*, 44; Adams manuscript diary, 2 Feb. 1825, quoted in editors' introduction in Meriwether et al., *Papers of John C. Calhoun*, 9:lvii; Calhoun to Virgil Maxcy, 18 Feb. 1825, ibid., 570; Calhoun to Joseph G. Swift, 10 Mar. 1825, ibid., 10:9–10. See editor's introduction, ibid., xxxi–xlii.

48. See editors' introduction, Meriwether et al., *Papers of John C. Calhoun*, 9:lx–lxiii and 10:xvi–xvii, xli–xlii, for a sympathetic explanation of Calhoun's hatred for Adams; for balance, see Hargreaves, *Presidency of John Quincy Adams*, 19–40.

49. Calhoun to Samuel Ingham, 10 June 1825, Calhoun to Christopher Vandeventer, 24 June 1825, Calhoun speech at Pendleton, S.C., 26 Apr. 1825, in Meriwether et al., *Papers of John C. Calhoun*, 10:28–29, 31, 17.

50. Calhoun to Christopher Vandeventer, 10 June 1825, speech at Abbeville, 27 May 1825, Calhoun to Joseph G. Swift, 2 Sept. 1825, Calhoun to Micah Sterling, 4 Feb. and 31 May 1826, Calhoun to Andrew Jackson, 4 June 1826, ibid., 10:29–30, 21–24, 40, 72–73, 107–9, 110–11. See also Hargreaves, *Presidency of John Quincy Adams*, 47–66.

51. John C. Calhoun to Micah Sterling, 20 Sept. and 16 Dec. 1826; Calhoun to Martin Van Buren, 7 July 1826; Calhoun to Levi Woodbury, 21 Sept. 1826; Calhoun to Andrew Jackson, 24 Jan. 1825; Calhoun to Littleton W. Tazewell, 1 Apr., 1 July, 25 Aug. 1827; Calhoun to John McLean, 4 Aug. 1828, in Meriwether et al., *Papers of John C. Calhoun*, 10:204, 237, 156, 205–7, 255, 282, 292–93, 300–301, 405–6. See Calhoun's remarks in the Senate, 9 Apr. 1828, reprinted ibid., 369. See also Calhoun's draft of "South Carolina Exposition" along with the South Carolina legislature's final committee report, ibid. 444–534. Finally, see Duff Green to Calhoun, 10 Aug. and 23 Sept. 1828, ibid., 411–12, 422–24.

52. *Register of Debates*, 19th Cong., 1st sess., 16–20; see Hargreaves, *Presidency of John Quincy Adams*, 147–53. Randolph's famous quote: "I was defeated, horse, foot, and dragoons—cut up—and clean broke down—by the coalition of Blifil and Black George—by the combination, unheard of till then, of the puritan with the black-leg." *Register of Debates*, 19th Cong., 1st sess., 401. On "Onslow" and "Patrick Henry," see Meriwether et al., *Papers of John C. Calhoun*, 10:92–222, and xix–xxix for editorial commentary; also John C. Calhoun to Andrew Jackson, 4 June 1826, ibid., 110.

53. Hargreaves, *Presidency of John Quincy Adams*, 165–208 (quotation from 199). See McCormick, *Presidential Game*, 154–63, on electoral reform.

54. Adams, *Memoirs of John Quincy Adams*, 8:25, 7:525; see generally 8:22–25 and 7:517–30; also Hargreaves, *Presidency of John Quincy Adams*, 48–53. Jackson had written regarding patronage: "the very moment I proscribe an individual from office on account of his political opinion, I become myself a despot." Jackson to Andrew Jackson Donelson, in Bassett, ed., *Correspondence of Andrew Jackson*, 3:246–47.

55. Quoted in Hargreaves, *Presidency of John Quincy Adams*, 178–79. See Adams, *Memoirs of John Quincy Adams*, 8:48–50.

56. Quoted in Remini, *Andrew Jackson and the Course of American Freedom*, 99, 107; see generally 100–142. See also Remini, "Election of 1828," in Schlesinger, *History of American Presidential Elections*, 1:413–36; and McCormick, *Presidential Game*, 149–53.

57. Remini, *Andrew Jackson and the Course of Freedom*, 130, 141 (quotation). Newspapers friendly to Adams tried to focus attention on the leading role in the Jackson camp of McDuffie, Calhoun, and the ardent enemies of the American System, but these efforts seemed less effective than Jacksonian attention to corruption and pure republicanism. See, for example, "Both Sides, or The Real State of Parties," in the Indianapolis *Indiana Journal*, 5 June 1828. For evidence of Jackson pretending to support the American System, see Sidney Breese to Henry Clay, 25 May 1828, and "Junius," Lexington *Kentucky Gazette*, 6 June 1828, reprinted in Hopkins et al., *Papers of Henry Clay*, 7:299, 332–33.

58. Jackson to John McNairy, 6 Sept. 1823, in Bassett, *Correspondence of Andrew Jackson*, 3:207.

59. Remini, "Election of 1828," in Schlesinger, *History of American Presidential Elections*, 1:433–34. See McCormick, *Presidential Game*, 154. Voter turnout was twice that of 1824, but it was lowest (30 percent) where Jackson ran unopposed and highest (70 percent) where the contest was close as in New Hampshire, New York, Ohio, and Kentucky.

60. Feller, *Public Lands*, 105–18. See Ellis, *Union at Risk*, 13–40; also Freehling, *Prelude to Civil War*. In the spring of 1829 Clay mentioned rumors of a South-West alliance trading public lands for tariff reduction. Clay to Charles Hammond, 27 May 1829, in

Hopkins et al., *Papers of Henry Clay*, 8:59–60. Meyers, *Jacksonian Persuasion*, stressed the liberalism of the Jacksonians.

61. Andrew Jackson, First Annual Message, in Richardson, *Messages and Papers* (1897), 3:1014–15; see also Jackson's First Inaugural Address, ibid., 3:1000.

62. *Register of Debates*, 21st Cong., 1st sess., 477–540 (quotations from 502, 479, 489, 494, 530). See Feller, *Public Lands*, 111–42.

63. Feller, *Public Lands*, 24, 32, 33, 35, 41.

64. *Register of Debates*, 21st Cong., 1st sess., 820–42 (quotations from 831, 433–34); Clay to George Corbin Washington, 17 May 1830, Clay to Adam Beatty, 8 June 1830, in Hopkins et al., *Papers of Henry Clay*, 8:209, 220.

65. Jackson, Maysville Veto Message, 27 May 1830, in Richardson, *Messages and Papers* (1897), 3:1046–56 (quotations from 1050, 1054).

66. See Van Buren's account in Fitzpatrick, *Autobiography of Martin Van Buren*, 2:312–38.

67. *Register of Debates*, 21st Cong., 1st sess., 1140–41, 1145; 21st Cong., 2nd sess., 789; Randolph quoted in Fitzpatrick, *Autobiography of Martin Van Buren*, 2:326; see Clay to Thomas Speed, 25 June 1830, in Hopkins et al., *Papers of Henry Clay*, 8:230, also 225, 237–39; Clay speech at Cincinnati, 3 Aug. 1830, in Colton, *Life, Correspondence, and Speeches*, 5:409–15.

68. Jackson, Second Annual Message, 6 Dec. 1830, in Richardson, *Messages and Papers* (1897), 3:1071–80 (quotations from 1072, 1074–77, 1079, 1080). A rough draft of this material in Van Buren's hand can be found in *Papers of Martin Van Buren*, microfilm ed. I am indebted to Dan Feller for this reference.

69. Andrew Jackson, Second Annual Message, 6 Dec. 1830, in Richardson, *Messages and Papers* (1897), 3:1079; see *Register of Debates*, 21st Cong., 2nd sess., 555–58 (quotation from 558). For the Distribution Report, see ibid., appendix, ixxxvi–xcii; for the Roads and Canals Report, see ibid., appendix xxv–xlii (quotation from xlii). Votes on the internal improvement bill are at ibid., 334, 759, 789.

70. Henry Clay to James F. Conover, 1 May 1830, and Josiah S. Johnston to Henry Clay, 12 Jan. 1831, in Hopkins et al., *Papers of Henry Clay* 8:200, 320. For summary of campaign strategy, see Clay to Johnston, 23 July 1831, ibid., 8:374–76; see vol. 8 generally for Clay's sense of Jackson and the requirements of the campaign. See also an important speech at Cincinnati, 3 Aug. 1830, in Colton, *Life, Correspondence, and Speeches*, 5:392–415.

71. Louis McLane, Treasurer's Report, December 1831, in *Register of Debates*, 22nd Cong., 1st sess., appendix, 29–39; also Jackson, Third Annual Message, in Richardson, *Messages and Papers* (1897), 3:1117–21.

72. See Clay's committee report, *Register of Debates*, 22nd Cong., 1st sess., appendix, 112–17. See Clay's speech on the tariff in Colton, *Life, Correspondence, and Speeches*, 5:416–28. Feller's account is excellent in *Public Lands*, 142–71.

73. See Henry Clay to George Corbin Washington, 24 July 1831, in Hopkins et al., *Papers of Henry Clay*, 8:377–78; Clay reiterated his opposition to taxes in a speech to the Senate 11 Jan. 1832; see *Register of Debates*, 22nd Cong., 1st sess., 69.

74. James Madison to Martin Van Buren, quoted in Fitzpatrick, *Autobiography of Martin Van Buren*, 2:334; see *Register of Debates*, 22nd Cong., 1st sess., 785–89, 870–72, 903–7, 1096–1174 (quotations from 785, 903, 1171); also ibid., appendix, 118–26.

75. *Register of Debates*, 22nd Cong., 1st sess., 1438–41 (quotation from 1439); 3058–75 (quotations from 3067–68, 3074); also Clay to Frances T. Brooke, 5 Aug. 1832, in Hopkins et al., *Papers of Henry Clay*, 8:559. About the same time as the distribution argument, the bank veto hit the papers. See ibid., 552–53.

76. Clay to Ambrose Spencer, 12 May 1832, James Brown to Clay, 5 Nov. 1832, and Clay to Charles Hammond, 17 Nov. 1832, in Hopkins et al., *Papers of Henry Clay*, 8:512, 595, 599; see generally 548–93 for Clay's correspondence during the final months of campaign.

77. Jackson, Proclamation, 10 Dec. 1832, in Richardson, *Messages and Papers* (1897), 3:1203–19 (quotation from 1211); Fourth Annual Message, ibid., 1154–66 (quotations from 1162, 1163, 1161). Ellis, *Union at Risk*, gives a fully detailed account of the proclamation (74–101) and the balance of the crisis (101–98).

78. Clay to Frances T. Brooke, 17 Jan. 1833, in Hopkins et al., *Papers of Henry Clay*, 8:613.

79. Quotation from Clay, Speech in the Senate, 12 Feb. 1833, in Colton, *Life, Correspondence, and Speeches*, 5:555, 557, 563, 540; see *Register of Debates*, 22nd Cong., 2nd sess., 77, 219, 88, 234–35; passage in Senate, 235, in the House 1920–21; see Hopkins et al., *Papers of Henry Clay*, 8:609–10, for legislative history.

80. Clay to James Barbour, 2 Mar. 1833, and Clay to Frances T. Brooke, 2 Aug. 1833, in Hopkins et al., *Papers of Henry Clay*, 8:629, 661–62; Jackson, Fifth Annual Message, 4 Dec. 1833, in Richardson, *Messages and Papers* (1897), 3:1275–88 (quotation from 1286).

81. Fitzpatrick, *Autobiography of Martin Van Buren*, 2:337; see Feller, *Public Lands*, 172–88. Historians continue to debate the character of mature Jacksonian politics. Compare, for example, Watson, *Andrew Jackson versus Henry Clay*; Feller, *Jackson Promise*; Holt, *Political Parties and Political Development*; Watson, *Liberty and Power*: Kohl, *Politics of Individualism*; Remini, *Andrew Jackson and the Course of American Democracy*; and Formisano, *Transformation of Political Culture*.

Chapter 6

1. See Sheriff, *Artificial River*, chaps. 3, 5, and 6; Gunn, *The Decline of Authority*, chap. 4; Shaw, *Erie Water West*, chaps. 13–15; Miller, *Enterprise of a Free People*, chaps. 7–10. See also Shaw, "Canal Era in the Old Northwest."

2. Ethan Allen Brown to the Ohio General Assembly, quoted in Still, "Ethan Allen Brown," 24; Columbus [Ohio] *Gazette*, 14 Jan. 1819, quoted ibid. The standard work on Ohio canals is Scheiber, *Ohio Canal Era*. The following summary draws heavily from Scheiber's work as well as the articles cited.

3. See Scheiber, *Ohio Canal Era*, 7–30. See also Scheiber, "Alfred Kelley and the Ohio Business Elite"; Scheiber, "Ohio Canal Movement"; and Scheiber, "Entrepreneurship and Western Development." See also Farrell, "Internal-Improvement Projects in Southwestern Ohio"; and George, "The Miami Canal."

4. Ohio General Assembly, House Committee Report, 3 Jan. 1822, in Kilbourn, *Public Documents*, 25–26; see Still, "Ethan Allen Brown," 35–37.

5. Allen Trimble to Ohio General Assembly, 5 Dec. 1822, in Kilbourn, *Public Documents*, 31; Report of the Board of Canal Commissioners to the General Assembly of Ohio, 3 Jan. 1823, ibid., 31; Supplementary Report of Canal Commissioners, 13 Jan. 1823, ibid., 52; Report of the Board of Canal Commissioners to the General Assembly of Ohio, 21 Jan. 1824, ibid., 54–79 (quotation from 54); Alfred Kelley to Ethan Allen Brown, 23 Feb. 1824, quoted in Scheiber, "Ohio Canal Movement," 245. See Kilbourn, *Public Documents*, 84–96, on borrowing money.

6. Report of the Canal Commissioners 21 Jan. 1824, in Kilbourn, *Public Documents*, 74–75; *Cincinnati Gazette*, 5 Oct. 1824, quoted in Scheiber, "Ohio Canal Movement," 247, see also 248–53.

7. Scheiber, "Ohio Canal Movement," 248–53.

8. John C. Calhoun to Ethan Allen Brown, 28 Jan. 1828, quoted in Scheiber, *Ohio Canal Era*, 79; see generally 37–51. For the contracting system, see Way, *Common Labor*, chap. 2. See also Teagarden, "Builders of the Ohio Canal."

9. Scheiber, *Ohio Canal Era*, 53–79.

10. Canal Commissioners Report for 1827, quoted in Scheiber, *Ohio Canal Era*, 66; Columbus *Western Hemisphere*, 9 Dec. 1833, quoted ibid., 93; see generally ibid., 89–104 (quotations 91, 92).

11. Scheiber, *Ohio Canal Era*, 108–20.

12. Ibid., 121–25.

13. Ibid., 125–33.

14. Ibid. 140–77 (quotations from 173).

15. Jonathan Jennings, Annual Message, 9 Dec. 1818, in Esarey, *Messages and Papers of Jennings, Boon, and Hendricks*, 66–68; Jennings, Second Inaugural Address, 8 Dec. 1819, ibid., 81–82. The Indiana story is best told in Carmony, *Indiana, 1816–1850*, chaps. 4–6. See also Fatout, *Indiana Canals*; Esarey, *History of Indiana*, chap. 16; and Esarey, "Internal Improvements in Early Indiana."

16. Jennings, open letters to Corydon *Gazette*, 25 Oct. 1821, 1 Nov. 1821, 8 Nov. 1821, *Messages and Papers of Jennings, Boon, and Hendricks*, 152–63 (figures from 154, quotation from 160–61).

17. William Hendricks, Annual Message, 2 Dec. 1823, in Indiana General Assembly, *Journal of the House of Representatives* (1823–24): 13–14. The memorial was introduced and passed in one sitting, 16 Dec. (see 85); committee report and resolutions are on 198–203.

18. Indiana General Assembly, *Journal of the Senate* (1824–25): 168–75; (1827–28): 225–27, 255–56. See William Hendricks, Circular, 5 Mar. 1829, in Esarey, *Messages and Papers of Jennings, Boon, and Hendricks*, 391; see generally 329–435 for Hendricks's evolution into the Jackson era. On personal politics, see Leonard, "Personal Politics in Indiana." A series of resolutions in Indiana General Assembly, *Journal of the Senate* (1827–28): 12, 61–65, shows the efforts of a majority to endorse the tariff and internal improvements and the effort of the minority to distinguish its opposition to Adams's party tricks from their genuine warm feeling for protection and internal improvement.

19. See Fatout, *Indiana Canals*, 1–40. An extraordinary source for these political maneuverings is the correspondence in Robertson and Riker, John Tipton Papers.

20. James Brown Ray, quoted in Fatout, *Indiana Canals*, 40; Wabash & Erie Canal Bill, 5 Jan. 1828, in *Laws of the State of Indiana, 12th Session* (1828), 10–12.

21. Indiana General Assembly, *Journal of the Senate* (1829–30): 84, 122–23; (1830–31): 184, 200, 224–28, 369–72, 494–99; (1831–32): 178–79, 321–23, 340–42, and 399–401.

22. Wabash & Erie Canal Bill, 9 Jan. 1832, in *Laws of the State of Indiana, 16th Session* (1832), 3–8; Noah Noble, *Campaign Message*, 10 May 1831, in Riker and Thornbrough, *Messages and Papers . . . of Noah Noble*, 56; Noble, *Inaugural Address*, 7 Dec. 1831, ibid., 62–64. On personal politics, see S. W. Parker to Noble, 22 Jan. 1831, 26 Feb. 1831, E. M. Huntington to Noble, 27 Aug. 1831, Jos. H. Benham to Noble, 5 Sept. 1831, in Noah Noble Manuscripts, Indiana State Library, Indianapolis. See also Ratliff Boon in the *Indiana Democrat*, 17 Dec. 1832, accusing Noble of turning traitor. Tipton's original support is in Tipton to Noble, 7 Sept. 1829, although he later turned against Noble (Noah Noble Manuscripts, Indiana State Library).

23. Noah Noble, *Annual Message*, 3 Dec. 1833, in Riker and Thornbrough, *Messages and Papers . . . of Noah Noble*, 204–5; see John Ewing to Noble, 18 Jan. 1834, ibid., 221, and 242–72 generally for the campaign.

24. Noah Noble, Annual Message, 2 Dec. 1834, ibid., 319–20.

25. Indiana General Assembly, *Journal of the House of Representatives* (1834–35): 60, 183–87, 203–5; 344–52, 375–447; (1835–36): 221–32, 302–12. See also *Journal of the Senate* (1835–36): 436–45.

26. Fatout, *Indiana Canals*, 74; Thornbrough, *Diary of Calvin Fletcher*, 1:299, 302–3.

27. Report of the State Board of Internal Improvements, 17 Dec. 1836, in Indiana General Assembly, Documents (1836–37), 3–15 (quotations from 3, 11); Report of the State Board of Internal Improvement, 7 Jan. 1837, in Indiana General Assembly, *Documents* (1836–37), 3–16.

28. Report of the Canal Fund Commissioners, 16 Dec. 1837, in Indiana General Assembly, *Documents* (1837–38), 1–3; Report of the Canal Fund Commissioners (13 Dec. 1837), ibid., 1–5; see Fatout, *Indiana Canals*, 76–92.

29. Amos Clark to Noah Noble, 12 Jan. 1836, Noah Noble Manuscripts, Indiana Historical Society, Indianapolis; Report of State Board of Internal Improvement (1836), 11; Report of the Board of Internal Improvement, 15 Dec. 1837, in Indiana General Assembly, *Documents* (1837–38), 3–14; Indiana General Assembly, *Journal of the Senate* (1836–37): 329–37 (quotations from 331, 332); Indiana General Assembly, *Journal of the House of Representatives* (1836–37): 251–52.

30. Indiana General Assembly, *Journal of the Senate* (1836–37): 329–37 (quotations from 331, 332); Indiana General Assembly, *Journal of the House of Representatives* (1836–37): 251–52; Report of State Board of Internal Improvement (1836), 11; Report of the Board of Internal Improvement, 15 Dec. 1837, in Indiana General Assembly, *Documents* (1837–38), 4–12.

31. Report of the State Board of Internal Improvement, 21 Dec. 1838, in Indiana General Assembly, *Documents* (1838–39), 104–11.

32. Ibid. (quotations from 109–10).

33. Report of the Chief Engineer in Relation to the Future Liabilities and Resources of the State as Connected with the System of Internal Improvement, 12 Jan. 1839, in Indiana General Assembly, *Documents* (1838–39), 303–19. Report of the Board of Internal Improvement (1839), in Indiana General Assembly, *Documents* (1839–40), 13–30 (quotation 29).

34. Samuel Bigger, Annual Message, 9 Dec. 1840, in Thornbrough, *Messages and Papers . . . of Samuel Bigger*, 110–28; see also introduction by Gayle Thornbrough for a good account of the situation.

35. Samuel Bigger, Annual Message, 7 Dec. 1841, in ibid., 315–42 (quotations from 318, 319, 322, 329); James Whitcomb quoted in Barnhart and Carmony, *Indiana from Frontier to Industrial Commonwealth*, 1:396; see Newcomer, "History of the Indiana Internal Improvement Bonds"; Fatout, *Indiana Canals*, chaps. 7–8; and Carmony, *Indiana*, chap. 6. The exact total of the state debt varies from one account to the next because the Wabash & Erie Canal debt, backed by congressional land grants, was counted (or not) in various ways by different reports. The $15 million figure from the governor's 1841 message is supposedly all-inclusive.

36. Charles Butler quoted in Gray, "The Canal Era in Indiana," 124. Gray's article contains a good summary of the Butler bills and the resolution of the state debts.

37. Indiana, *Debates and Proceedings: 1850*, 1:653.

38. Ibid., 656–88 (quotations from 656, 677–78); Democratic Platform of 8 Jan. 1849, quoted in Kettleborough, *Constitution Making in Indiana*, 1:194. See also Smith, *Schuyler Colfax*, especially 15–45.

39. Indiana, *Debates and Proceedings*, 673; see Daniels, "The Village at the End of the Road"; Bogle, "Railroad Building in Indiana"; Simons and Parker, *Railroads of Indiana*, chap. 1.

40. See Krenkel, *Illinois Internal Improvements*, especially 1–75. The land grant came in 1827 but Illinois got a five-year extension in 1832 and permission to consider a railroad instead. As late as 1836 sensible men thought canals more certain than railroads, more durable and closer to perfection.

41. Ibid. (quotation from 158).

42. See Parks, *Democracy's Railroads*, especially 72–87; see also Larson, *Bonds of Enterprise*, 31–34.

43. Hartz, *Economic Policy and Democratic Thought*, 142–80. Shaw, *Canals for a Nation*, 72–80, has a good discussion of the success and merits of the Pennsylvania system (both economic and political).

44. Shaw, *Canals for a Nation*, 45–49; also Gunn, *Decline of Authority*, 144–69.

45. Shaw, *Canals for a Nation*, 98–108 (quotation from 107).

46. Ibid., 113–17; also Rice, "Internal Improvements in Virginia," especially chaps. 6, 9, and 10; Hodges, "Pro-Governmentalism in Virginia"; Goodrich, "Virginia System"; Turner, "Early Virginia Railroad Entrepreneurs"; and Noe, *Southwest Virginia's Railroad*, chaps. 1–4.

47. Journal of the Internal Improvement Convention which met at Raleigh, 4 July 1833, quotation from 7; also [Joseph Caldwell], *The Numbers of Carlton*. See Watson, "North Carolina and Internal Improvements"; Counihan, "North Carolina Constitutional Convention of 1835"; Weaver, *Internal Improvements in North Carolina Previous to 1860*, 16–22, 76–94; Trelease, *The North Carolina Railroad*, chap. 1; Trelease, "The Passive Voice"; Jeffrey, *State Parties and National Politics*, chaps. 3–8; Kruman, *Parties and Politics in North Carolina*, especially chap. 3.

48. See Thornton, *Politics and Power in a Slave Society*; Dupre, *Transforming the Cotton Frontier*; Morgan, "Philip Phillips and Internal Improvements"; Shaw, *Canals for a Nation*, 122–24; Martin, *Internal Improvements in Alabama*. See also Summers, *Plundering Generation*.

Chapter 7

1. Gerstner, *Early American Railroads*, 295, 611–12, 625–26, 561–78, 518–27, 128–43, 710–15. See this extraordinary book for details on all the early lines. For the dreamers, see Ward, *Railroads and the Character of America*, chaps. 1–7. For a comparative study of German and American development, see Colleen A. Dunlavy, *Politics and Industrialization*.

2. Kirkland, *Men, Cities and Transportation*, 1: chaps. 1–4; Salsbury, *The State, the Investor, and the Railroad*, chaps. 1–2; see also Larson, *Bonds of Enterprise*, chap. 2.

3. Salsbury, *The State, the Investor and the Railroad*, 31–40.

4. Ibid., 41–92; see also Chandler, *The Visible Hand*, 79–121.

5. Salsbury, *The State, the Investor and the Railroad*, 93–132.

6. Ibid., 155.

7. This account is drawn from Dilts, *Great Road*, chaps. 4–6; see also Stover, *History of the Baltimore and Ohio*, chaps. 1–3.

8. See Dilts, *Great Road*, 97. Stover, *History of the Baltimore and Ohio*, 45, quotes railroad journalist D. K. Minor calling the B&O the "Railroad University of the United States."

9. See Stover, *History of the Baltimore and Ohio*, 33–45.

10. See *Niles' Weekly Register* 52 (Aug. 1837): 358; also 50 (Mar. 1836): 1; 50 (Mar. 1836): 49, 50 (June 1836): 247; 50 (July 1836): 330; and 57 (Oct. 1839): 88. See also Gunn, *Decline of Authority*, chaps. 4–5.

11. Quotations from Ward, *Railroads and the Character of America*, 18, 61, 26, 38.

12. *Niles' Weekly Register* 64 (June 1843): 211; 66 (Aug. 1844): 389; 69 (Nov. 1845): 205; *Merchant's Magazine* (New York) 12 (1845): 158, 323–24;. Henry Varnum Poor, 10 Mar. 1848 quoted in Ward, *Railroads and the Character of America*, 25; see ibid., 8–9.

13. See Scheiber, *Ohio Canal Era*, chap. 11.

14. See Gray, "Canal Era in Indiana," 113–34; Stover, "Iron Roads in the Old North west"; Bogle, "Railroad Building in Indiana"; Stover, *Iron Road to the West*.

15. Krenkel, *Illinois Internal Improvements*, chap. 9; Parks, *Democracy's Railroads*, chap 10; Larson, *Bonds of Enterprise*, 31–52. See also Johnson and Supple, *Boston Capitalists and Western Railroads*.

16. Gunn, *Decline of Authority*, 159–73.

17. Ibid. See Holt, *Political Crisis of the 1850s*, 101–38; Thornton, *Politics and Power in a Slave Society*; *Niles' Weekly Register* 65 (Jan. 1844): 342.

18. See *Niles' Weekly Register* 55 (Sept. 1838): 40; Rice, "Internal Improvements in Vir ginia," chap. 6 (sums are from 192, 207, constitution from 210–11); see also chaps. 9–10 on railroad development in Virginia; and Noe, *Southwest Virginia's Railroad*, especially chaps 1–4.

19. Quoted in Watson, "'Old Rip' and the New Era," 223; see Lefler and Newsome *North Carolina*, 342–79; Pegg, *Whig Party in North Carolina*; Jeffrey, *State Parties and National Politics*, chaps. 8–10; Kruman, *Parties and Politics in North Carolina*, chaps. 1–3 See also Trelease, *The North Carolina Railroad*, chap. 1.

20. For the Baltimore Platform, see Charles E. Sellers, "Election of 1844," in Schle singer, *History of American Presidential Elections*, 1:799. On "latitudinarian" views, se Speech of Congressman J. A. McDougall, 29 May 1854, quoting an unnamed Virginia colleague, in *Congressional Globe*, 33rd Cong., 1st sess., appendix, 863. For Polk's veto message, 3 Aug. 1846, see Richardson, *Messages and Papers* (1899), 4:460–66.

21. See Quaife, *Diary of James K. Polk*, 1:288–89; 2:54–66, 171; 3:116, 166–69, 179, 244–49; 4:35, 52–52, 60–66, 139–40, 363–64. For context, see Morrison, *Slavery and the America West*, chap. 3. Chicago's convention to protest Polk's veto is described in Einhorn, *Property Rules*, 68–75 (thanks to Richard John for this reference).

22. See Michigan land grant debates in *Congressional Globe*, 29th Cong., 1st sess., 742 47, 751–52; 29th Cong., 2nd sess., 112–13. Another review of opinions is laid out in th Illinois Central land grant debates, ibid., 30th Cong., 1st sess., appendix, 534–37. Othe land grant debates are scattered throughout the *Congressional Globe*, each session into th 1850s.

23. My account follows an old but excellent and thorough study, Russell, *Improvement of Communication with the Pacific Coast*, especially 8–13. Whitney asked for half the strip of land—5 miles by 60 miles—for each 10 miles of road constructed on the first 800 miles of the route, after which the whole 10-mile strip would not pay the cost of construction and he would draw on the halves reserved along the eastern section. U.S. Serial Set, 30th Cong., 1st Sess., House of Representatives, *Report No. 733*, 19–26; also 31st Cong., 1st sess House of Representatives, *Report No. 140*, which reprints in appendices the whole se quence of Whitney's memorials from 1845 to 1848 as well as dozens of endorsements from state legislatures and public meetings. For Whitney, see also Loomis, "Asa Whitney Father of Pacific Railroads."

24. Wilkes, *Proposal for a National Rail-Road*, 62, 59; Russell, *Improvement of Communication*, 12–16; see U.S. Serial Set, 29th Cong., 1st sess., House of Representatives, *Report No. 773*; *Report No. 466*; *Congressional Globe*, 30th Cong., 1st sess., 1011. See also Brown, "Asa Whitney and His Pacific Railroad Publicity Campaign."

25. Russell, *Improvement of Communication*, 46–47; see U.S. Serial Set, 29th Cong., 1st sess., House of Representatives, *Report No. 773*; *Report No. 466*; 31st Cong., 1st sess., House of Representatives, *Report No. 140*.

26. The political breakdown can be followed in Morrison, *Slavery and the West*, chaps. 5–7. See also Nichols, *Disruption of American Democracy*; and Potter, *The Impending Crisis*.

27. *Congressional Globe*, 30th Cong., 2nd sess., 470–74, 381–82; see also 31st Cong., 2nd sess., 47–50, where Benton reintroduces his bill.

28. Russell, *Improvement of Communication*, 47–50.

29. Ibid., 48; U.S. Serial Set, 31st Cong., 1st sess., House of Representatives, *Report No. 140*, 1–16 (quotations from 4, 10, 11).

30. *Report No. 140*, 10–11.

31. *Congressional Globe*, 31st Cong., 1st sess., 333–35.

32. Russell, *Improvement of Communication*, 52–60, 95–96; *Congressional Globe*, 31st Cong., 2nd sess., 132, and appendix, 7; 30th Cong., 2nd sess., 49–52, 59.

33. Russell, *Improvement of Communication*, 95–109; *Congressional Globe*, 32nd Cong., 2nd sess., 125–27, 319, 339–43 (quotations from 318, 342, 343).

34. Russell, *Improvement of Communication* 101; see *Congressional Globe*, 32nd Cong., 2nd sess., 469–70 for the new bill.

35. *Congressional Globe*, 30th Cong., 2nd sess., 471–503 (quotations from 473, 503).

36. Ibid., 676–78, and appendix, 177–81.

37. *Congressional Globe*, 32nd Cong., 2nd sess., appendix, 221–29, 212–16.

38. Ibid., appendix, 186–87, 234–39 (Washington quotation from 238).

39. Ibid., 676–704; 676 for the vote on the Brodhead amendment. Regional bias is even stronger if you discount two yes votes from Wisconsin, whose delegation is protesting the terms of its own grant from the previous year that doubled the price of reserve lands. A vote to recommit the bill to Roads and Canals Committee failed 18 to 33; see 680, 699, 701, 703.

40. Ibid. 708–15 (vote from 715). See Russell, *Improvement of Communication* 102–3. Cass's only modern biography, Klunder, *Lewis Cass*, sheds no light on Cass's action at this juncture.

41. *Congressional Globe*, 32nd Cong., 2nd sess., 767–75.

42. For Douglas, see Johannsen, *Stephen A. Douglas*, 374–400; also Potter, *Impending Crisis*, chaps. 7–8.

43. *Congressional Globe*, 32nd Cong., 2nd sess., 765–66.

44. Ibid., 33rd Cong., 1st sess., appendix, 825–27.

Epilogue

1. My understanding of the founders' accomplishment rests firmly on Wood, *Creation*. For the contrasts between "disinterested" gentlemen and "interested" politicians, see Wood, "Interests and Disinterestedness." For refinements of Wood's original portrait of the founding see McDonald, *Novus Ordo Seclorum*; Lienesch, *New Order for the Ages*; Wood, *Radicalism*; Banning, *Sacred Fire of Liberty*; and Rakove, *Original Meanings*.

2. See Flexner, *Washington, the Indispensable Man*; Morgan, *The Meaning of Indepen-*

dence; Wills, *Cincinnatus*; Jones, *George Washington*; Ferling, *First of Men*; and Kaminski and McCaughan, *A Great and Good Man*.

3. Wood, quoting John Dickinson, affixed the label to this struggle: "the worthy against the licentious." See Wood, *Creation*, 475 and chap. 12 generally.

4. Ibid., chap. 14, explains Adams. See also Shaw, *Character of John Adams*; Ellis, *Passionate Sage*. For more evidence of a disbelief in public virtue, see McCoy, *Elusive Republic*, chap. 2.

5. See Royster, *A Revolutionary People at War*; Carp, *To Starve the Army at Pleasure*.

6. For Jackson's character, see Remini, *Andrew Jackson and the Course of American Empire*.

7. See Chandler, *Visible Hand*, especially chaps. 3–4. See also Benson, *Merchants, Farmers & Railroads*; Miller, *Railroads and the Granger Laws*; Larson, *Bonds of Enterprise*; and Cronon, *Nature's Metropolis*.

8. See Martin, "The Troubled Subject of Railroad Regulation."

9. The only decent biography is Klein, *Jay Gould*.

10. See Werner and Smith, *Wall Street*; and Davis and Cull, *International Capital Markets and American Economic Growth*.

11. Adams, "The New York Gold Conspiracy," in *Chapters of Erie*, 103–4. The essay originally appeared in the *Westminster Review*, Oct., 1870; also Summers, *Era of Good Stealings*.

12. For a sympathetic view, see Klein, *Jay Gould*; compare the more judgmental treatment in Grodinsky, *Jay Gould*; and the most colorful in Adams, *Chapters of Erie*.

13. See Cochran, *Railroad Leaders*; and Johnson and Supple, *Boston Capitalists and Western Railroads*.

14. For struggles to control railroad rate making, see Miller, *Railroads and the Granger Laws*; Benson, *Merchants, Farmers, & Railroads*; Larson, *Bonds of Enterprise*, chaps. 5–7. For widely divergent views on the impact and effectiveness of regulation, see Kolko, *Railroads and Regulation*; and Martin, *Enterprise Denied*.

BIBLIOGRAPHY

Manuscripts

Indianapolis, Ind.
   Indiana Historical Society
      Noah Noble Manuscripts
   Indiana State Library
      Noah Noble Manuscripts
Washington, D.C.
   National Archives and Records Service
      Record Group 233: Records of the United States House of Representatives

Congressional Debates

Annals of Congress (1789–1824). Washington, D.C.: Gales and Seaton, 1834–56.
Congressional Globe (1833–73). Washington, D.C.: Office of the Congressional Globe, 1833–73.
Register of Debates (1824–37). Washington, D.C.: Gales and Seaton, 1834–37.

Periodicals and Newspapers

Enquirer (Richmond)
Indiana Democrat (Indianapolis)
Indiana Journal (Indianapolis)
Kentucky Gazette (Lexington)
Merchant's Magazine (New York)
National Intelligencer (Washington, D.C.)
Niles' Weekly Register (Baltimore)
North American Review (Boston)
Pennsylvania Chronicle and Universal Advertiser (Philadelphia)
United States Gazette (Philadelphia)

Government Records

Indiana. *Debates and Proceedings of the Convention for the Revision of the Constitution of the State of Indiana.* 2 vols. Indianapolis: A. H. Brown, Printer, 1850.
——. General Assembly. *Documents* (by year).
——. *Journal of the House of Representatives* (by year).
——. *Journal of the Senate* (by year).

——. *Laws of the State of Indiana* (by year).

Library of Congress. *Records of the States of the United States of America*. Ed. William Sumner Jenkins. Washington, D.C.: Library of Congress, 1949. Microform.

New York. General Assembly. *Laws of the State of New York in Relation to the Erie and Champlain Canals*. 2 vols. Albany: E. and E. Hosford, Printers, 1825.

North Carolina. Board of Internal Improvement. *Report* (by year).

——. General Assembly. *Journal of the House of Commons* (by year).

U.S. Congress. *American State Papers: Documents, Legislative and Executive*. 38 vols. Class X, *Miscellaneous*. 2 vols. Washington, D.C.: Gales and Seaton, 1832–61.

——. *Statement of Appropriations and Expenditures for Public Buildings, Rivers and Harbors, Forts, Arsenals, Armories, and Other Public Works from March 4, 1789 to June 30, 1882*. 47th Cong., 1st sess. S. Doc. VII:1992. Washington, D.C.: Government Printing Office, 1886.

U.S. Serial Set. 29th Cong., 1st sess. House of Representatives, *Report No. 773*. 1846.

——. 29th Cong., 1st sess. House of Representatives, *Report No. 466*. 1846.

——. 30th Cong., 1st sess. House of Representatives, *Report No. 733*. 1848.

——. 31st Cong., 1st sess. House of Representatives, *Report No. 140*. 1850.

Virginia. General Assembly. *Journal of the House of Delegates* (by year).

Other Printed Primary Sources

"Abstract of Sundry Papers and Proposals for Improving the Inland Navigation of Pennsylvania and Maryland. . . ." *Transactions of the American Philosophical Society* 1 (1769–70): 293–304.

Adams, John, and John Quincy Adams. *The Selected Writings of John and John Quincy Adams*. Ed. Adrienne Koch and William Peden. New York: Alfred A. Knopf, 1946.

Adams, John Quincy. *The Diary of John Quincy Adams*. Ed. David Grayson Allen et al. 2 vols. Cambridge, Mass.: Harvard University Press, 1981.

——. *Memoirs of John Quincy Adams, Comprising Portions of His Diary from 1795 to 1848*. Ed. Charles Francis Adams. 12 vols. Philadelphia: J. B. Lippincott, 1874–77.

——. *Report of the Secretary of State upon Weights and Measures*. Ed. and with foreword by A. Hunter Dupree. New York: Arno Press, 1980.

——. "Ten Unpublished Letters of John Quincy Adams, 1796–1837." Ed. Edward H. Tatum Jr. *Huntington Library Quarterly* 5 (1941): 369–85.

——. *Writings of John Quincy Adams*. Ed. Worthington Chauncy Ford. 7 vols. New York: Macmillan, 1913–17.

Battle, Kemp, ed. "Letters of Nathaniel Macon, John Steele and William Barry Grove, with Sketches and Notes by Kemp P. Battle." James Sprunt Historical Monograph, no. 3. Chapel Hill: University of North Carolina Press, 1902.

Bigger, Samuel. *Messages and Papers Relating to the Administration of Samuel Bigger, Governor of Indiana, 1840–1843*. Ed. Gayle Thornbrough. Indianapolis: Indiana Historical Bureau, 1964.

Bowling, Kenneth R., and Helen Veit, eds. *Documentary History of the First Federal Congress*. Vol. 10, *The Diary of William Maclay and Other Notes on Senate Debates*. Baltimore: Johns Hopkins University Press, 1988.

[Caldwell, Joseph]. *The Numbers of Carlton, Addressed to the People of North Carolina, on a Central Rail-Road through the State*. New York: G. Long, 1828.

Calhoun, John C. *The Papers of John C. Calhoun*. Ed. Robert L. Meriwether, W. Edwin

Hemphill, and Clyde N. Wilson. 16 vols. to date. Columbia: University of South Carolina Press, 1959–.

Carey, Mathew. *Addresses of the Philadelphia Society for the Promotion of National Industry.* Philadelphia: M. Carey & Son, 1819.

———. *Brief View of the System of Internal Improvement of the State of Pennsylvania.* Philadelphia: Lydia R. Bailey, 1831.

———. *Essays on Political Economy.* Philadelphia: H. Carey and I. Lea, 1822.

Clay, Henry. *The Papers of Henry Clay.* Ed. James F. Hopkins, Mary M. W. Hargreaves, and Robert Seager II. 11 vols. Lexington: University of Kentucky Press, 1959–92.

Colles, Christopher. *Proposals for the Speedy Settlement of the Waste and Unappropriated Lands on the Western Frontiers of the State of New York, and for the Improvement of the Inland Navigation between Albany and Oswego.* New York: Samuel Louden, 1785.

Colton, Calvin. *The Life, Correspondence, and Speeches of Henry Clay.* 6 vols. New York: A. S. Barnes, 1857.

Congressional Information Service. *CIS US Serial Set Index.* Washington, D.C.: Congressional Information Service, 1975.

Douglas, Stephen A. *The Letters of Stephen A. Douglas.* Ed. Robert W. Johannsen. Urbana: University of Illinois Press, 1961.

[Eaton, John Henry.] *The Letters of Wyoming to the People of the United States, on the Presidential Election, and in Favor of Andrew Jackson. Originally published in the Columbian Observer.* Philadelphia: S. Simpson & J. Conrad, 1824.

Esarey, Logan, ed. *Messages and Papers of Jonathan Jennings, Ratliff Boon, [and] William Hendricks, 1816–1825.* Indianapolis: Indian Historical Commission, 1924.

Farrand, Max, ed. *Records of the Federal Convention of 1787.* 1911. Rev. ed. 4 vols. New Haven: Yale University Press, 1966.

Federalist. Ed. Jacob E. Cooke. Middletown, Conn.: Wesleyan University Press, 1961.

Fletcher, Calvin. *The Diary of Calvin Fletcher.* Ed. Gayle Thornbrough. 9 vols. Indianapolis: Indiana Historical Society, 1972–81.

Franklin, Benjamin. *The Papers of Benjamin Franklin.* Ed. Benjamin W. Labaree. 27 vols. to date. New Haven: Yale University Press, 1959–.

Frémont, John Charles. *Report of the Exploring Expedition to the Rocky Mountains in the Year 1842: and to Oregon and North California in the years 1843–44.* Washington, D.C.: Blair and Rives, Printers, 1845.

Gallatin, Albert. *Report of the Secretary of the Treasury on the Subject of Public Roads and Canals.* In *American State Papers,* Class X, *Miscellaneous,* 1:753–921.

———. *Report of the Secretary of the Treasury on the Subject of Public Roads and Canals.* 1808; reprint, New York: Augustus M. Kelly, Publishers, 1968.

———. *The Writings of Albert Gallatin.* Ed. Henry Adams. 3 vols. 1879; reprint, New York: Antiquarian Press, 1960.

Gerstner, Franz Anton Ritter von. *Die innern Communicationen.* 1842–43. Translated as *Early American Railroads.* Ed. Frederick C. Gamst, trans. David J. Diephouse and John C. Decker. Stanford: Stanford University Press, 1997.

Gilpin, Joshua. "Journal of a Tour from Philadelphia thro the Western Counties of Pennsylvania in the Months of September and October, 1809" (parts 1 & 2). *Pennsylvania Magazine of History and Biography* 50 (1926): 64–78, 163–78.

Hosack, David. *Memoir of DeWitt Clinton: with an Appendix, Containing Numerous Documents, Illustrative of the Principal Events of His Life.* New York: J. Seymour, 1829.

"Internal Improvements of North Carolina." *North American Review* (Boston) 12 (1821): 17–37.

Jackson, Andrew. *The Correspondence of Andrew Jackson.* Ed. John Spencer Bassett. 7 vols. Washington, D.C.: Carnegie Institution, 1926–35.

Jefferson, Thomas. *The Papers of Thomas Jefferson.* Ed. Julian P. Boyd, Charles T. Cullen, and John Catanzariti. 27 vols. to date. Princeton: Princeton University Press, 1950–.

———. *The Works of Thomas Jefferson.* Ed. Paul Leicester Ford. 12 vols. New York: G. P. Putnam's Sons, 1905.

Kilbourn, John. *Public Documents, Concerning the Ohio Canals, Which are to Connect Lake Erie with the Ohio River, Comprising a Complete Official History of these Great Works of Internal Improvement.* Columbus: Olmsted, Bailhache & Camron, Printers, 1828.

Liancourt, Duc de la Rochefoucault. *Travels through the United States of North America . . . in the Years 1795, 1796, and 1797.* 2nd ed. 4 vols. London: R. Phillips, 1800.

Madison, James. *Letters and Other Writings of James Madison (Published by Order of Congress).* 4 vols. New York: R. Worthington, 1884.

———. *The Papers of James Madison.* Ed. William T. Hutchinson, William M. E. Rachal, Robert A. Rutland, Charles F. Hobson, J. C. A. Stagg, David Mattern, Jeanne Kerr Cress, and Susan Holbrook Perdue. 17 vols. to date. Chicago and Charlottesville: University of Chicago Press and University Press of Virginia, 1962–.

———. *The Writings of James Madison.* Ed. Gaillard Hunt. 9 vols. New York : G. P. Putnam's Sons, 1900–10.

Murphey, Archibald D. *The Papers of Archibald D. Murphey.* Ed. William Henry Hoyt. 2 vols. Raleigh: North Carolina Historical Commission, 1914.

Noble, Noah. *Messages and Papers Relating to the Administration of Noah Noble, Governor of Indiana, 1831–1837.* Ed. Dorothy Riker and Gayle Thornbrough. Indianapolis: Indiana Historical Bureau, 1958.

Pendleton, Edmund. *The Letters and Papers of Edmund Pendleton, 1734–1803.* Ed. David John Mays. 2 vols. Charlottesville: University Press of Virginia, 1967.

Polk, James K. *The Diary of James K. Polk during His Presidency, 1845–1849.* Ed. Milo Milton Quaife. 4 vols. 1910; reprint, New York: Kraus Reprint, 1970.

Richardson, James D., ed. *A Compilation of the Messages and Papers of the Presidents, 1789–1897.* 10 vols. Washington, D.C.: By the Authority of Congress, 1899.

———, ed. *A Compilation of the Messages and Papers of the Presidents, 1789–1897.* 10 vols. New York: Bureau of National Literature, 1897.

Ritchie, Thomas. "Ritchie Letters." Ed. Charles Ambler. *John P. Branch Historical Papers of Randolph-Macon College* 4 (1916): 372–418.

———. "Unpublished Letters of Thomas Ritchie." *John P. Branch Historical Papers of Randolph-Macon College* 3 (1911): 199–252.

Roane, Spencer. "Roane Correspondence." *John P. Branch Historical Papers of Randolph-Macon College* 2 (1905): 123–42.

———. "Roane on the National Constitution." *John P. Branch Historical Papers of Randolph-Macon College* 2 (1905): 47–122.

Smith, Adam. *An Inquiry into the Nature and Causes of the Wealth of Nations.* Ed. Edwin Cannan. 1776; reprint, New York: Modern Library, 1937.

Stansbury, Howard. *An Expedition to the Valley of the Great Salt Lake of Utah: Including a Description of its Geography, Natural History and Minerals, and an Analysis of its Waters; with an Authentic Account of the Mormon Settlement.* Philadelphia: Lippincott, Grambo, 1852.

Steele, John. *The Papers of John Steele.* Ed. H. M. Wagstaff. 2 vols. Raleigh: North Carolina Historical Commission, 1924.

Strickland, William. *Report on Canals, Railways, Roads, and Other Subjects, made to The Pennsylvania Society for the Promotion of Internal Improvement.* Philadelphia: H. C. Carey & I. Lea, 1826.

Taylor, John. *Construction Construed and Constitutions Vindicated.* 1820; reprint, New York: Da Capo Press, 1970.

——. "Letters of John Taylor, of Caroline County, Virginia." Ed. William E. Dodd. *John P. Branch Historical Papers of Randolph-Macon College* 2 (1906): 252–353.

——. "Of Principles and Men: The Correspondence of John Taylor of Caroline with Wilson Cary Nicholas, 1806–1808." Ed. David N. Mayer. *Virginia Magazine of History and Biography* 96 (1988): 345–88.

——. *Tyranny Unmasked.* Ed. F. Thornton Miller. 1822; reprint, Indianapolis: Liberty Fund, 1992.

Tipton, John. *The John Tipton Papers.* Ed. Nellie Armstrong Robertson and Dorothy Riker. 3 vols. Indianapolis: Indiana Historical Bureau, 1942.

Van Buren, Martin. *The Autobiography of Martin Van Buren.* Ed. John C. Fitzpatrick. *Annual Report of the American Historical Association for the Year 1918.* 2 vols. Washington, D.C.: Government Printing Office, 1920.

——. *Papers of Martin Van Buren.* Washington, D.C.: Library of Congress, 1960. Microfilm.

Washington, George. *The Diaries of George Washington.* Ed. Donald Jackson and Dorothy Twohig. 6 vols. Charlottesville: University Press of Virginia, 1976–79.

——. *The Writings of George Washington.* Ed. John C. Fitzpatrick. 39 vols. Washington, D.C.: Government Printing Office, 1931–44.

Wilkes, George. *Proposal for a National Rail-Road to the Pacific Ocean.* New York: Daniel Adee, Printer, 1847.

Wilson, Edwin Mood, ed. *The Congressional Career of Nathaniel Macon.* James Sprunt Historical Monographs, no. 2. Chapel Hill: University of North Carolina Press, 1900.

Wolcott, Oliver. *Memoirs of Administrations of Washington and John Adams.* Ed. George Gibbs. 2 vols. New York: Privately printed [W. Van Norden, Printer], 1846.

Books and Articles

Adams, Charles Francis. "The New York Gold Conspiracy." In Adams, *Chapters of Erie and Other Essays,* 100–34. Boston: James R. Osgood, 1871.

Albion, Robert G. *The Rise of New York Port, 1815–1860.* 1939; reprint, Boston: Northeastern University Press, 1984.

——. *Square Riggers on Schedule: The New York Sailing Packets to England, France, and the Cotton Ports.* Princeton: Princeton University Press, 1938.

Albjerg, Victor L. "Internal Improvements without a Policy (1789–1861)." *Indiana Magazine of History* 28 (1932): 168–79.

Alvarez, Eugene. *Travel on Southern Antebellum Railroads, 1828–1860.* University: University of Alabama Press, 1974.

Ambler, Charles H. *George Washington and the West.* Chapel Hill: University of North Carolina Press, 1936.

——. *Thomas Ritchie: A Study in Virginia Politics.* Richmond: Bell Book & Stationery, 1913.

Ammon, Harry. *James Monroe: The Quest for National Identity*. Charlottesville: University Press of Virginia, 1990.

———. "The Richmond Junto, 1800–1824." *Virginia Magazine of History and Biography* 61 (1953): 395–418.

Appleby, Joyce. *Capitalism and a New Social Order: The Republican Vision of the 1790s*. New York: New York University Press, 1984.

Ashworth, John. *Slavery, Capitalism, and Politics in the Antebellum Republic*. Vol. 1, *Commerce and Compromise, 1820–1850*. New York: Cambridge University Press, 1995.

Bacon-Foster, Corra. *Early Chapters in the Development of the Potomac Route to the West*. 1912; reprint, New York: Burt Franklin, 1971.

Baer, Christopher T. *Canals and Railroads of the Mid-Atlantic States, 1800–1860*. Wilmington, Del.: Regional Economic History Research Center, 1981.

Ball, Terence, and J. G. A. Pocock, eds. *Conceptual Change and the Constitution*. Lawrence: University Press of Kansas, 1988.

Banning, Lance. *After the Constitution: Party Conflict in the New Republic*. Belmont, Calif.: Wadsworth Publishing, 1989.

———. *Jefferson & Madison: Three Conversations from the Founding*. Madison: Madison House, 1995.

———. *The Jeffersonian Persuasion: The Evolution of a Party Ideology*. Ithaca: Cornell University Press, 1978.

———. *The Sacred Fire of Liberty: James Madison and the Founding of the Federal Republic*. Ithaca: Cornell University Press, 1995.

———. "1787 and 1776: Patrick Henry, James Madison, the Constitution and the Revolution." In *Toward a More Perfect Union: Six Essays on the Constitution*, ed. Neil L. York, 59–89. Salt Lake City: Brigham Young University Press, 1988.

———. "Virginia: Sectionalism and the General Good." In *Ratifying the Constitution*, ed. Michael Allen Gillispie and Michael Lienesch, 261–99. Lawrence: University of Kansas Press, 1989.

Barker, Charles R. "The Stony Part of Schuylkill, Its Navigation, Fisheries, Fords and Ferries." *Pennsylvania Magazine of History and Biography* 50 (1926): 344–66.

Barnhart, John D., and Donald F. Carmony. *Indiana from Frontier to Industrial Commonwealth*. 2 vols. New York: Lewis Historical Publishing Company, 1954.

Bartlett, Irving H. *John C. Calhoun: A Biography*. New York: W. W. Norton, 1993.

Baxter, Maurice. *Henry Clay and the American System*. Lexington: University of Kentucky Press, 1996.

Beach, Rex. "Spencer Roane and the Richmond Junto." *William and Mary Quarterly*, 2nd ser., 22 (1942): 1–17.

Beeman, Richard, Stephen Botein, and Edward C. Carter II, eds. *Beyond Confederation: Origins of the Constitution and American National Identity*. Chapel Hill: University of North Carolina Press, 1987.

Bemis, Samuel Flagg. *John Quincy Adams and the Union*. 1956; reprint, Westport: Greenwood Press, 1965.

Benson, Lee. *Merchants, Farmers & Railroads; Railroad Regulation and New York Politics, 1850–1887*. Cambridge, Mass.: Harvard University Press, 1955.

Bickford, Charlene Bangs, and Kenneth R. Bowling. *Birth of the Nation: The First Federal Congress, 1789–1791*. Washington, D.C.: First Federal Congress Project, 1989.

Bishop, Avard Longley. "The State Works of Pennsylvania." *Transactions of the Connecticut Academy of Arts and Sciences* 13 (1907–8): 149–297.

Bogle, Victor M. "Railroad Building in Indiana, 1850–1855." *Indiana Magazine of History* 58 (1962): 211–32.

Bogue, Allan, and Mark P. Marlaire. "Of Mess and Men: The Boardinghouse and Congressional Voting, 1821–1842." *American Journal of Political Science* 19 (1975): 207–30.

Bowling, Kenneth R. "Dinner at Jefferson's: A Note on Jacob E. Cooke's 'The Compromise of 1790.'" *William and Mary Quarterly*, 3rd ser., 28 (1971): 629–48.

———. "'A Place to Which Tribute Is Brought': The Contest for the Federal Capital in 1783." *Prologue* 8 (1976): 129–39.

Briceland, Alan V. "Virginia: The Cement of Union." In *The Constitution and the States: The Role of the Original Thirteen in the Framing and Adoption of the Federal Constitution*, ed. Patrick T. Conley and John P. Kaminski, 201–24. Madison, Wis.: Madison House, 1988.

Broussard, James H. *The Southern Federalists, 1800–1816*. Baton Rouge: Louisiana State University Press, 1978.

Brown, Alexander Crosby. *The Dismal Swamp Canal*. Chesapeake, Va.: Norfolk County Historical Society, 1967.

Brown, Margaret L. "Asa Whitney and His Pacific Railroad Publicity Campaign." *Mississippi Valley Historical Review* 20 (1933): 209–24.

Browne, Gary L. *Baltimore in the New Nation*. Chapel Hill: University of North Carolina Press, 1980.

Bruchey, Stuart. *The Roots of American Economic Growth, 1607–1861*. New York: Harper & Row, 1965.

Brugger, Robert J. *Maryland: A Middle Temperament*. Baltimore: Johns Hopkins University Press for the Maryland Historical Society, 1988.

Capers, Gerald M. *John C. Calhoun—Opportunist: A Reappraisal*. Gainesville: University of Florida Press, 1960.

Carlson, Robert E. "The Pennsylvania Improvement Society and Its Promotion of Canals and Railroads, 1824–1826." *Pennsylvania History* 31 (1964): 295–310.

Carlson, W. Bernard. "The Pennsylvania Society for the Promotion of Internal Improvements: A Case Study in the Political Uses of Technological Knowledge, 1824–1826." *Canal History and Technology Proceedings* 7 (1988): 175–205.

Carmony, Donald F. *Indiana, 1816–1850: The Pioneer Era*. Indianapolis: Indiana Historical Bureau and Indiana Historical Society, 1998.

Carp, E. Wayne. *To Starve the Army at Pleasure: Continental Army Administration and American Political Culture, 1775–1783*. Chapel Hill: University of North Carolina Press, 1984.

Carson, David A. "Blank Paper of the Constitution: The Louisiana Purchase Debates." *Historian* 54 (1992): 477–90.

———. "That Ground Called Quiddism: John Randolph's War with the Jefferson Administration." *Journal of American Studies* 20 (1986): 71–91.

Carter, Edward C., II. "Benjamin Henry Latrobe and Public Works: Professionalism, Private Interest, and Public Policy in the Age of Jefferson." *Public Works History* 3 (1976): 1–29.

Cayton, Andrew R. L. *Frontier Indiana*. Bloomington: Indiana University Press, 1996.

———. *Frontier Republic: Ideology and Politics in the Ohio Country*. Kent, Ohio: Kent State University Press, 1986.

Chambers, William Nisbet. *Political Parties in a New Nation: The American Experience, 1776–1809*. New York: Oxford University Press, 1963.

Chandler, Alfred D., Jr. *The Visible Hand: The Managerial Revolution in American Business*. Cambridge, Mass.: Belknap Press, 1977.

Clanin, Douglas E. "Internal Improvements in National Politics, 1816–1830." In *Transportation and the Early Nation: Papers Presented at an Indiana American Revolution Bicentennial Symposium*, 30–60. Indianapolis: Indiana Historical Society, 1982.

Cochran, Thomas C. *Railroad Leaders, 1845–1890: The Business Mind in Action*. Cambridge, Mass.: Harvard University Press, 1953.

Cole, Donald B. *Martin Van Buren and the American Political System*. Princeton: Princeton University Press, 1984.

Collier, Christopher, and James Lincoln Collier. *Decision at Philadelphia*. New York: Ballantine Books, 1986.

Conley, Patrick T., and John P. Kaminski, eds. *The Constitution and the States: The Role of the Original Thirteen in the Framing and Adoption of the Federal Constitution*. Madison, Wis.: Madison House, 1988.

Cooke, Jacob E. "The Compromise of 1790." *William and Mary Quarterly*, 3rd ser., 27 (1970): 523–45.

Cornell, Saul. *The Other Founders: Anti-Federalism and the Dissenting Tradition in America, 1788–1828*. Chapel Hill: University of North Carolina Press, 1999.

Cornog, Evan. *The Birth of Empire: DeWitt Clinton and the American Experience, 1769–1828*. New York: Oxford University Press, 1998.

Counihan, Harold J. "The North Carolina Constitutional Convention of 1835: A Study of Jacksonian Democracy." *North Carolina Historical Review* 47 (1969): 335–64.

———. "North Carolina, 1815–1836: State and Local Perspectives on the Age of Jackson." Ph.D. diss., University of North Carolina, 1971.

Countryman, Edward. *The American Revolution*. New York: Hill & Wang, 1985.

———. *A People in Revolution: The American Revolution and Political Society in New York, 1760–1790*. Baltimore: Johns Hopkins University Press, 1981.

Cronon, William. *Nature's Metropolis: Chicago and the Great West*. New York: W. W. Norton, 1991.

Cunningham, Noble E., Jr. *In Pursuit of Reason: The Life of Thomas Jefferson*. Baton Rouge: Louisiana State University Press, 1987.

———. *The Jeffersonian Republicans: The Formation of Party Organization, 1789–1801*. Chapel Hill: University of North Carolina, 1957.

———. *The Jeffersonian Republicans in Power; Party Operations, 1801–1809*. Chapel Hill: University of North Carolina Press, 1963.

———. *The Presidency of James Monroe*. Lawrence: University Press of Kansas, 1996.

———. *The Process of Government under Jefferson*. Princeton: Princeton University Press, 1978.

Dangerfield, George. *The Awakening of American Nationalism, 1815–1828*. New York: Harper & Row, 1965.

———. *The Era of Good Feelings*. New York: Harcourt, Brace, & World, 1952.

Daniels, Wylie J. "The Village at the End of the Road: A Chapter in Early Indiana Railroad History." *Indiana Historical Society Publications* 13 (1938): 13–112.

Davis, Lance E., and Robert J. Cull. *International Capital Markets and American Economic Growth, 1820–1914*. New York: Cambridge University Press, 1994.

Dent, Richard J. "On the Archaeology of Early Canals: Research on the Potowmack Canal in Great Falls, Virginia." *Historical Archaeology* 20 (1986): 50–62.

Dilts, James D. *The Great Road: The Building of the Baltimore and Ohio, the Nation's First Railroad*. Stanford: Stanford University Press, 1993.

Dodd, William E. "Chief Justice John Marshall and Virginia, 1813–1821." *American Historical Review* 12 (1906–7): 776–87.

———. "John Taylor, of Caroline, Prophet of Secession." *John P. Branch Historical Papers of Randolph-Macon College* 2 (1906): 214–52.

Doerflinger, Thomas M. *A Vigorous Spirit of Enterprise: Merchants and Economic Development in Revolutionary Philadelphia*. Chapel Hill: University of North Carolina Press, 1986.

Dunaway, Wayland Fuller. *History of the James River and Kanawha Company*. Columbia Studies in History, Economics and Public Law, vol. 305, no. 236. New York: Columbia University Press, 1922.

Dunlavy, Colleen A. *Politics and Industrialization: Early Railroads in the United States and Prussia*. Princeton: Princeton University Press, 1994.

Dupre, Daniel S. *Transforming the Cotton Frontier: Madison County, Alabama, 1800–1840*. Baton Rouge: Louisiana State University Press, 1997.

Dupree, A. Hunter. *Science in the Federal Government: A History of Policies and Activities to 1940*. Cambridge, Mass.: Harvard University Press, 1957.

Durrenberger, Joseph Austin. *Turnpikes: A Study of the Toll Road Movement in the Middle Atlantic States and Maryland*. Valdosta, Ga.: n.p., 1931.

Egerton, Douglas R. *Charles Fenton Mercer and the Trial of National Conservatism*. Jackson: University Press of Mississippi, 1989.

Einhorn, Robin L. *Property Rules: Political Economy in Chicago, 1833–1872*. Chicago: University of Chicago Press, 1991.

Ekirch, A. Roger. "The North Carolina Regulators on Liberty and Corruption, 1766–1771." *Perspectives in American History* 11 (1977–78): 199–258.

———. "*Poor Carolina*": *Politics and Society in Colonial North Carolina*. Chapel Hill: University of North Carolina Press, 1981.

Elazar, Daniel. *The American Partnership: Intergovernmental Cooperation in the Nineteenth-Century United States*. Chicago: University of Chicago Press, 1962.

Elkins, Stanley, and Eric McKitrick. *The Age of Federalism*. New York: Oxford University Press, 1993.

Ellis, Joseph J. *American Sphinx: The Character of Thomas Jefferson*. New York: Alfred A. Knopf, 1997.

———. *Passionate Sage: The Character and Legacy of John Adams*. New York: W. W. Norton, 1993.

Ellis, Richard E. *The Jeffersonian Crisis: Courts and Politics in the Young Republic*. New York: Oxford University Press, 1971.

———. *The Union at Risk: Jacksonian Democracy, States' Rights, and the Nullification Crisis*. New York: Oxford University Press, 1987.

Esarey, Logan. *History of Indiana from Its Exploration to 1850*. 1915; reprint, Indianapolis: Hoosier Heritage Press, 1970.

———. "Internal Improvements in Early Indiana." *Indiana Historical Society Publications* 5 (1912): 3–158.

Eubanks, Cecil L. "New York: Federalism and the Political Economy of Union." In *Ratifying the Constitution*, ed. Michael Allen Gillespie and Michael Lienesch, 300–340. Lawrence: University Press of Kansas, 1989.

Farrell, Richard T. "Internal-Improvement Projects in Southwestern Ohio, 1815–1834." *Ohio History* 80 (1971): 4–23.

Fatout, Paul. *Indiana Canals*. West Lafayette, Ind.: Purdue University Press, 1972.

Fehrenbacher, Don E. *The South and Three Sectional Crises*. Baton Rouge: Louisiana State University Press, 1980.

Feller, Daniel. *The Jacksonian Promise: America, 1815–1840*. Baltimore: Johns Hopkins University Press, 1995.

———. *The Public Lands in Jacksonian Politics*. Madison: University of Wisconsin Press, 1984.

Ferguson, E. James. *The Power of the Purse: A History of American Public Finance, 1776–1790*. Chapel Hill: University of North Carolina Press, 1961.

Ferling, John E. *The First of Men: A Life of George Washington*. Knoxville: University of Tennessee Press, 1988.

Fischer, David Hackett. *The Revolution of American Conservatism: The Federalist Party in the Era of Jeffersonian Democracy*. New York: Harper & Row, 1965.

Fitzgerald, Michael. "Europe and the United States Defense Establishment: American Military Policy and Strategy, 1815–1821." Ph.D. diss., Purdue University, 1990.

Flexner, James Thomas. *Washington, the Indispensable Man*. Boston: Little, Brown, 1974.

Foner, Eric. *Free Soil, Free Labor, Free Men: The Ideology of the Republican Party before the Civil War*. New York: Oxford University Press, 1970.

Ford, Lacy K. "Republican Ideology in a Slave Society: The Political Economy of John C. Calhoun." *Journal of Southern History* 54 (1988): 405–24.

Formisano, Ronald P. *The Transformation of Political Culture: Massachusetts Parties, 1790s–1840s*. New York: Oxford University Press, 1983.

Formwalt, Lee W. "Benjamin Henry Latrobe and the Revival of the Gallatin Plan of 1808." *Pennsylvania History* 48 (1981): 99–128.

Fox, Stephen C. "The Bank Wars, the Idea of 'Party,' and the Division of the Electorate in Jacksonian Ohio." *Ohio History* 85 (1979): 253–76.

Freehling, William W. *Prelude to Civil War: The Nullification Controversy in South Carolina, 1816–1836*. New York: Harper & Row, 1966.

———. *The Road to Disunion: Secessionists at Bay*. New York: Oxford University Press, 1990.

Freeman, Douglas Southall. *Washington*. Abridged by Richard Harwell. 1948; abr. ed. New York: Charles Scribner's Sons, 1968.

Freyer, Tony A. *Producers versus Capitalists: Constitutional Conflict in Antebellum America*. Charlottesville: University Press of Virginia, 1994.

Ganyard, Robert L. *The Emergence of North Carolina's Revolutionary State Government*. Raleigh: North Carolina Bicentennial Commission, 1978.

George, John J., Jr. "The Miami Canal." *Ohio Archaeological and Historical Publications* 36 (1927): 92–115.

Gieck, Jack. *A Photo Album of Ohio's Canal Era, 1825–1913*. Rev. ed. Kent, Ohio: Kent State University Press, 1988.

Gilchrist, David. *The Growth of the Seaport Cities, 1790–1825*. Charlottesville: University Press of Virginia, 1967.

Gilje, Paul A. *The Road to Mobocracy: Popular Disorder in New York City, 1763–1834*. Chapel Hill: University of North Carolina Press, 1987.

——, ed. *Wages of Independence: Capitalism in the Early American Republic*. Madison, Wis.: Madison House, 1997.

Gillespie, Michael, and Michael Lienesch, eds. *Ratifying the Constitution*. Lawrence: University Press of Kansas, 1989.

Gilpatrick, Delbert H. *Jeffersonian Democracy in North Carolina, 1789–1861*. New York: Columbia University Press, 1931.

Goodrich, Carter. *Government Promotion of American Canals and Railroads, 1800–1890*. New York: Columbia University Press, 1960.

——. "National Planning of Internal Improvements." *Political Science Quarterly* 63 (1948): 16–44.

——. "The Virginia System of Mixed Enterprise: A Study of State Planning of Internal Improvements." *Political Science Quarterly* 64 (1949): 355–87.

Goodrich, Carter, ed. *Canals and American Economic Development*. New York: Columbia University Press, 1961.

Goodrich, Carter, and Harvey Segal. "Baltimore's Aid to Railroads: A Study in the Municipal Planning of Internal Improvements." *Journal of Economic History* 13 (1953): 2–35.

Gray, Ralph D. "The Canal Era in Indiana." In *Transportation and the Early Nation: Papers Presented at an Indiana American Revolution Bicentennial Symposium*, 113–34. Indianapolis: Indiana Historical Society, 1982.

——. *The National Waterway: A History of the Chesapeake and Delaware Canal, 1769–1965*. Urbana: University of Illinois Press, 1967.

——. "Philadelphia and the Chesapeake and Delaware Canal, 1769–1823." *Pennsylvania Magazine of History and Biography* 84 (1960): 401–6.

Greene, Jack P. "Independence, Improvement, and Authority: Toward a Framework for Understanding the Histories of the Southern Backcountry during the Era of the American Revolution." In *An Uncivil War: The Southern Backcountry during the American Revolution*, ed. Ronald Hoffman, Thad W. Tate, and Peter J. Albert, 3–36. Charlottesville: University Press of Virginia for the United States Capitol Historical Society, 1985.

Grodinsky, Julius. *Jay Gould: His Business Career, 1867–1892*. Philadelphia: University of Pennsylvania Press, 1957.

Gross, Robert A. *The Minutemen and Their World*. New York: Hill & Wang, 1976.

Gunn, L. Ray. *The Decline of Authority: Public Economic Policy and Political Development in New York, 1800–1860*. Ithaca: Cornell University Press, 1988.

Gunther, Gerald, ed. *John Marshall's Defense of* McCulloch *v* Maryland. Stanford: Stanford University Press, 1969.

Hahn, Thomas F. *The Chesapeake & Ohio Canal: Pathway to the Nation's Capital*. Metuchen, N.J.: Scarecrow Press, 1984.

Hammond, Bray. *Banks and Politics in America from the Revolution to the Civil War*. Princeton: Princeton University Press, 1957.

Handlin, Oscar, and Mary Flug Handlin. *Commonwealth: A Study of the Role of Government in the American Economy: Massachusetts, 1774–1861*. Cambridge, Mass.: Harvard University Press, 1969.

——. "Origins of the American Business Corporation." *Journal of Economic History* 5 (1945): 1–23.

Hanyan, Craig, and Mary Hanyan. "De Witt Clinton and the People's Men: Leadership and Purpose in an Early American Reform Movement, 1822–1826." *Mid-America* 73 (1991): 87–114.

———. *DeWitt Clinton and the Rise of the People's Men.* Montreal and Kingston: McGill–Queens University Press, 1996.

Hargreaves, Mary W. M. *The Presidency of John Quincy Adams.* Lawrence: University Press of Kansas, 1985.

Harlow, Alvin F. *Old Towpaths: The Story of the American Canal Era.* New York: D. Appleton, 1926.

Harrison, Joseph H., Jr. "The Internal Improvement Issue in the Politics of the Union, 1783–1825." Ph.D. diss., University of Virginia, 1954.

———. "Oligarchs and Democrats, the Richmond Junto." *Virginia Magazine of History and Biography* 78 (1970): 184–98.

———. "*Sic et Non:* Thomas Jefferson and Internal Improvement." *Journal of the Early Republic* 7 (1987): 335–49.

Hartz, Louis. *Economic Policy and Democratic Thought in Pennsylvania, 1776–1860.* Cambridge, Mass.: Harvard University Press, 1948.

Hatzenbuehler, Ronald L. "'Refreshing the Tree of Liberty with the Blood of Patriots and Tyrants': Thomas Jefferson and the Origins of the U.S. Constitution." In *Essays on Liberty and Federalism: The Shaping of the U.S. Constitution,* ed. David E. Narrett and Joyce S. Goldberg, 88–104. College Station: Texas A&M University Press, 1988.

Hay, Robert P. "The Case for Andrew Jackson in 1824: Eaton's *Wyoming Letter.*" *Tennessee Historical Quarterly* 29 (1970): 139–51.

———. "'The Presidential Question': Letters to Southern Editors, 1823–24." *Tennessee Historical Quarterly* 31 (1972): 170–86.

Heale, M. J. *The Presidential Quest: Candidates and Images in American Political Culture, 1787–1852.* London: Longman, 1982.

Hickey, Donald R. *The War of 1812: A Forgotten Conflict.* Urbana: University of Illinois Press, 1989.

Hill, Forest G. *Roads, Rails, and Waterways: The Army Engineers and Early Transportation.* Norman: University of Oklahoma Press, 1957.

Hodges, Wiley E. "Pro-Governmentalism in Virginia, 1789–1836: A Programmatic Liberal Pattern in the Political Heritage." *Journal of Politics* 25 (1963): 333–60.

Hoffman, Ronald, and Peter J. Albert, eds. *Launching the "Extended Republic": The Federalist Era.* Charlottesville: University Press of Virginia for United States Capitol Historical Society, 1996.

Hoffman, Ronald, Thad W. Tate, and Peter J. Albert, eds. *An Uncivil War: The Southern Backcountry during the American Revolution.* Charlottesville: University Press of Virginia for the United States Capitol Historical Society, 1985.

Hoffman, William S. "The Downfall of the Democrats: The Reaction of North Carolinians to Jacksonian Land Policy." *North Carolina Historical Review* 33:1 (1956): 166–80.

Hofstadter, Richard. *The Idea of a Party System: The Rise of Legitimate Opposition in the United States, 1780–1840.* Berkeley: University of California Press, 1969.

Holt, Michael F. *The Political Crisis of the 1850s.* New York: W. W. Norton, 1978.

———. *Political Parties and American Political Development: From the Age of Jackson to the Age of Lincoln.* Baton Rouge: Louisiana State University Press, 1992.

Horsman, Reginald. *Expansion and American Indian Policy, 1783–1812.* East Lansing: Michigan State University Press, 1967.

Horsnell, Margaret E. *Spencer Roane: Judicial Advocate of Jeffersonian Principles*. New York: Garland, 1986.

Horwitz, Morton. *The Transformation of American Law, 1780–1860*. Cambridge, Mass.: Harvard University Press, 1977.

Howard, Thomas W. "Indiana Newspapers and the Presidential Election of 1824." *Indiana Magazine of History* 63 (1967): 177–206.

Howe, Daniel Walker. *The Political Culture of the American Whigs*. Chicago: University of Chicago Press, 1979.

———. "The Political Psychology of *The Federalist*." *William and Mary Quarterly*, 3rd ser., 44 (1987): 485–90.

———. *Making the American Self: Jonathan Edwards to Abraham Lincoln*. Cambridge, Mass.: Harvard University Press, 1997.

Huebner, Timothy S. "The Consolidation of State Judicial Power." *Virginia Magazine of History and Biography* 102 (1994): 47–72.

Hunter, Robert F. "The Turnpike Movement in Virginia, 1816–1860." *Virginia Magazine of History and Biography* 69 (1961): 278–89.

Hurst, James Willard. *Law and the Condition of Freedom in the Nineteenth Century United States*. Madison: University of Wisconsin Press, 1956.

———. *Law and Markets in United States History: Different Modes of Bargaining among Interests*. Madison: University of Wisconsin Press, 1982.

Hurt, R. Douglas. *The Ohio Frontier: Crucible of the Old Northwest, 1720–1830*. Bloomington: Indiana University Press, 1996.

Ilisevich, Robert D., and Carl K. Burket Jr. "The Canal through Pittsburgh: Its Development and Physical Character." *Western Pennsylvania Historical Magazine* 68 (1985): 351–71.

Jackson, Carlton. "The Internal Improvement Vetoes of Andrew Jackson." *Tennessee Historical Quarterly* 25 (1966): 261–79.

Jackson, Richard P. *The Chronicles of Georgetown, D.C. from 1751–1878*. Washington, D.C.: R. O. Polkinhorn, Printer, 1878.

Jeffrey, Thomas E. "Internal Improvements and Political Parties in Antebellum North Carolina, 1836–1860." *North Carolina Historical Review* 55 (1978): 111–56.

———. "National Issues, Local Interests, and the Transformation of Antebellum North Carolina Politics." *Journal of Southern History* 50 (1984): 43–74.

———. *State Parties and National Politics: North Carolina, 1815–1861*. Athens: University of Georgia Press, 1989.

———. "'Thunder from the Mountains': Thomas Lanier Clingman and the End of Whig Supremacy in North Carolina." *North Carolina Historical Review* 56 (1979): 366–95.

Jenkins, William Sumner, ed. *Guide to the Microfilm Collection of Early State Records*. Washington, D.C.: Library of Congress, 1951.

Johannsen, Robert W. *The Frontier, the Union, and Stephen A. Douglas*. Urbana: University of Illinois Press, 1980.

———. *Stephen A. Douglas*. New York: Oxford University Press, 1973.

John, Richard. *Spreading the News: The American Postal System from Franklin to Morse*. Cambridge, Mass.: Harvard University Press, 1995.

Johnson, Arthur M., and Barry E. Supple. *Boston Capitalists and Western Railroads; A Study in the Nineteenth-Century Railroad Investment Process*. Cambridge, Mass.: Harvard University Press, 1967.

Johnstone, Robert M., Jr. *Jefferson and the Presidency: Leadership in the Young Republic.* Ithaca: Cornell University Press, 1978.

Jones, Robert F. *George Washington.* New York: Fordham University Press, 1986.

Jordan, Daniel P. *Political Leadership in Jefferson's Virginia.* Charlottesville: University Press of Virginia, 1983.

Kaminski, John P., and Jill Adair McCaughan, eds. *A Great and Good Man : George Washington in the Eyes of His Contemporaries.* Madison, Wis.: Madison House, 1989.

Kerber, Linda K. *Federalists in Dissent: Imagery and Ideology in Jeffersonian America.* Ithaca: Cornell University Press, 1970.

Ketcham, Ralph. *Presidents above Party: The First American Presidency.* Chapel Hill: University of North Carolina Press, 1984.

Kettleborough, Charles, ed. *Constitution Making in Indiana.* Indianapolis: Indiana Historical Commission, 1916.

Kirkland, Edward C. *Dream and Thought in the American Business Community, 1860–1900.* Ithaca: Cornell University Press, 1956.

———. *Men, Cities and Transportation: A Study in New England History, 1820–1900.* 2 vols. Cambridge, Mass.: Harvard University Press, 1948.

Klein, Maury. *The Life and Legend of Jay Gould.* Baltimore: Johns Hopkins University Press, 1986.

Klunder, Willard Carl. *Lewis Cass and the Politics of Moderation.* Kent, Ohio: Kent State University, 1996.

Knupfer, Peter B. *The Union As It Is: Constitutional Unionism and Sectional Compromise, 1787–1861.* Chapel Hill: University of North Carolina Press, 1991.

Kohl, Lawrence Frederick. *The Politics of Individualism: Parties and the American Character in the Jacksonian Era.* New York: Oxford University Press, 1989.

Kolko, Gabriel. *Railroads and Regulation, 1877–1916.* Princeton: Princeton University Press, 1965.

Kramnick, Isaac. *Bolingbroke and His Circle: The Politics of Nostalgia in the Age of Walpole.* Cambridge, Mass.: Harvard University Press, 1968.

Krenkel, John H. *Illinois Internal Improvements, 1818–1848.* Cedar Rapids, Iowa: Torch Press, 1958.

Kruman, Marc W. *Between Authority and Liberty: State Constitution Making in Revolutionary America.* Chapel Hill: University of North Carolina Press, 1997.

———. *Parties and Politics in North Carolina, 1836–1865.* Baton Rouge: Louisiana State University Press, 1983.

Kukla, Jon. "A Spectrum of Sentiments: Virginia's Federalists, Antifederalists, and 'Federalists Who Are for Amendments,' 1787–1788." *Virginia Magazine of History and Biography* 96 (1988): 277–96.

Kulikoff, Allan. *The Agrarian Origins of American Capitalism.* Charlottesville: University Press of Virginia, 1992.

Larson, John Lauritz. " 'Bind the Republic Together': The National Union and the Struggle for a System of Internal Improvements." *Journal of American History* 74 (1987): 363–87.

———. *Bonds of Enterprise: John Murray Forbes and Western Development in America's Railway Age.* Boston: Division of Research, Harvard Business School, 1984.

———. "A Bridge, a Dam, a River: Liberty and Innovation in the Early Republic." *Journal of the Early Republic* 7 (1987): 351–75.

———. "Jefferson's Union and the Problem of Internal Improvements." In *Jeffersonian Legacies*, ed. Peter S. Onuf, 340–69. Charlottesville: University Press of Virginia, 1993.

———. "Liberty by Design: Freedom, Planning, and John Quincy Adams's 'American System.'" In *The State and Economic Knowledge: Reflections on the American and British Experience*, ed. Barry E. Supple and Mary O. Furner, 73–102. Cambridge: Cambridge University Press for the Woodrow Wilson Center, 1990.

———. "'Wisdom Enough to Improve Them': Government, Liberty, and Inland Waterways in the Rising American Empire." In *Launching the "Extended Republic": The Federalist Era*, ed. Ronald Hoffman and Peter J. Albert, 223–48. Charlottesville: University Press of Virginia for the United States Capitol Historical Society, 1996.

Lefler, Hugh T., and Albert R. Newsome. *North Carolina: The History of a Southern State*. 2nd ed. Chapel Hill: University of North Carolina Press, 1963.

Leibiger, Stuart. "Thomas Jefferson and the Missouri Crisis: An Alternative Interpretation." *Journal of the Early Republic* 17 (1997): 121–30.

Lenner, Andrew C. "John Taylor and the Origins of American Federalism." *Journal of the Early Republic* 17 (1997): 399–423.

Leonard, Adam A. "Personal Politics in Indiana, 1816–1840." *Indiana Magazine of History* 19 (1923): 1–281.

Lerche, Margaret Evans. "The Life and Public Career of Archibald D. Murphey." Ph.D. diss., University of North Carolina, 1948.

Lerner, Ralph. "Commerce and Character: The Anglo-American as New-Model Man." *William and Mary Quarterly*, 3rd ser., 36 (1979): 3–26.

Levy, Leonard W. *Jefferson and Civil Liberties: The Darker Side*. Cambridge, Mass.: Harvard University Press, 1963.

———. *Original Intent and the Framers' Constitution*. New York: Macmillan, 1988.

Lewis, James E., Jr. *The American Union and the Problem of Neighborhood: The United States and the Collapse of the Spanish Empire, 1783–1829*. Chapel Hill: University of North Carolina Press, 1998.

Lienesch, Michael. *New Order for the Ages: Time, the Constitution, and the Making of Modern America*. Princeton: Princeton University Press, 1988.

———. "North Carolina: Preserving Rights." In *Ratifying the Constitution*, ed. Michael Allen Gillespie and Michael Lienesch, 343–67. Lawrence: University Press of Kansas, 1989.

———. "Thomas Jefferson and . . . the Origins of the Partisan Press." In *Jeffersonian Legacies*, ed. Peter S. Onuf, 316–39. Charlottesville: University Press of Virginia, 1993.

Lightfoot, Alfred. "Henry Clay and the Missouri Question, 1819–1821." *Missouri Historical Review* 61 (1967): 143–65.

Lindstrom, Diane. *Economic Development in the Philadelphia Region, 1810–1850*. New York: Columbia University Press, 1978.

Lipsky, George A. *John Quincy Adams: His Theory and Ideas*. New York: Thomas Y. Crowell, 1950.

Littlefield, Douglas R. "Maryland Sectionalism and the Development of the Potomac Route to the West, 1768–1826." *Maryland Historian* 14 (1983): 31–52.

Lively, Robert A. "The American System: A Review Article." *Business History Review* 29 (1955): 81–95.

Livingood, James W. "The Canalization of the Lower Susquehanna." *Pennsylvania History* 8 (1941): 131–47.

———. *The Philadelphia-Baltimore Trade Rivalry, 1780–1860*. Harrisburg, Pa.: Pennsylvania Historical and Museum Commission, 1947.

Loomis, Nelson H. "Asa Whitney: Father of Pacific Railroads." *Proceedings of the Mississippi Valley Historical Association* 6 (1912–13): 166–75.

Lowrey, Charles D. *James Barbour, a Jeffersonian Republican*. University: University of
    Alabama Press, 1984.
MacGill, Caroline E., et al. *History of Transportation in the United States before 1860*. 1917;
    reprint, New York: Peter Smith, 1948.
Maizlish, Stephen E. *The Triumph of Sectionalism: The Transformation of Ohio Politics,
    1844–1856*. Kent, Ohio: Kent State University Press, 1983.
Majewski, John. "The Political Impact of Great Commercial Cities: State Investment in
    Antebellum Pennsylvania and Virginia." *Journal of Interdisciplinary History* 28 (1997):
    1–26.
——. "Who Financed the Transportation Revolution? Regional Divergence and Internal
    Improvements in Antebellum Pennsylvania and Virginia." *Journal of Economic History*
    56 (1996): 763–88.
Malone, Dumas. *Jefferson and His Time*. 6 vols. Boston: Little, Brown, 1948–81.
Malone, Laurence J. *Opening the West: Federal Internal Improvements before 1860*.
    Westport, Conn.: Greenwood Press, 1998.
Martin, Albro. *Enterprise Denied: Origins of the Decline of American Railroads, 1897–1917*.
    New York: Columbia University Press, 1971.
——. "The Troubled Subject of Railroad Regulation in the Gilded Age, a Reappraisal."
    Journal of American History 6 (1974–75): 339–71.
Martin, William Elejius. *Internal Improvements in Alabama*. Johns Hopkins University
    Studies in Historical and Political Science, ser. 20:4. Baltimore: Johns Hopkins
    University Press, 1902.
Matson, Cathy D., and Peter S. Onuf. "Toward a Republican Empire: Interest and
    Ideology in Revolutionary America." *American Quarterly* 37 (1985): 496–531.
——. *A Union of Interests: Political and Economic Thought in Revolutionary America*.
    Lawrence: University Press of Kansas, 1990.
Matthews, Richard K. *If Men Were Angels: James Madison and the Heartless Empire of
    Reason*. Lawrence: University Press of Kansas, 1995.
——. *The Radical Politics of Thomas Jefferson: A Revisionist View*. Lawrence: University
    Press of Kansas, 1984.
Mayfield, John. *The New Nation, 1800–1845*. Rev. ed. New York: Hill and Wang, 1982.
Mays, David John. *Edmund Pendleton, 1721–1803: A Biography*. 2 vols. Cambridge, Mass.:
    Harvard University Press, 1952.
McCormick, Richard P. *The Presidential Game: The Origins of American Presidential
    Politics*. New York: Oxford University Press, 1982.
——. *The Second American Party System: Party Formation in the Jacksonian Era*. New York:
    W. W. Norton, 1966.
McCoy, Drew R. *The Elusive Republic: Political Economy in Jeffersonian America*. Chapel
    Hill: University of North Carolina Press, 1980.
——. *The Last of the Fathers: James Madison and the Republican Legacy*. New York:
    Cambridge University Press, 1989.
McCullough, Robert, and Walter Leuba. *The Pennsylvania Main Line Canal*. York, Pa.:
    American Canal and Transportation Center, 1973.
McDonald, Forrest. *Alexander Hamilton: A Biography*. New York: W. W. Norton, 1979.
——. *Novus Ordo Seclorum: The Intellectual Origins of the Constitution*. Lawrence:
    University Press of Kansas, 1985.
——. *The Presidency of Thomas Jefferson*. Lawrence: University Press of Kansas, 1976.
Merrens, Harry Roy. *Colonial North Carolina in the Eighteenth Century: A Study in
    Historical Geography*. Chapel Hill: University of North Carolina Press, 1964.

Meyers, Marvin. *The Jacksonian Persuasion Politics and Belief.* Stanford: Stanford University Press, 1957.

Miller, F. Thornton. "John Marshall versus Spencer Roane: A Reevaluation of *Martin* v. *Hunter's Lessee.*" *Virginia Magazine of History and Biography* 96 (1988): 297–314.

———. "The Richmond Junto: The Secret All-Powerful Club—or Myth." *Virginia Magazine of History and Biography* 99 (1991): 63–80.

Miller, George H. *Railroads and the Granger Laws.* Madison: University of Wisconsin Press, 1971.

Miller, Nathan. *The Enterprise of a Free People: Aspects of Economic Development in New York State during the Canal Period, 1792–1838.* Ithaca: Cornell University Press, 1962.

———. "Private Enterprise in Inland Navigation: The Mohawk Route Prior to the Erie Canal." *New York History* 31 (1950): 398–413.

Moore, Glover. *The Missouri Controversy, 1819–1821.* Lexington: University of Kentucky Press, 1953.

Morgan, David T. "Philip Phillips and Internal Improvements in Mid-Nineteenth-Century Alabama." *Alabama Review* 34 (1981): 83–93.

Morgan, Edmund S. *Inventing the People: The Rise of Popular Sovereignty in England and America.* New York: W. W. Norton, 1988.

———. *The Meaning of Independence: John Adams, George Washington, Thomas Jefferson.* Charlottesville: University Press of Virginia, 1976.

Morgan, J. Allen. *State Aid to Transportation in North Carolina.* N.p: N.p., 1911.

Morison, Elting E. *From Nowhere to Know-How.* New York: Basic Books, 1974.

Morrison, Michael A. *Slavery and the American West: The Eclipse of Manifest Destiny and the Coming of the Civil War.* Chapel Hill: University of North Carolina Press, 1997.

Murrin, John. "1787: The Invention of American Federalism." In *Essays on Liberty and Federalism: The Shaping of the U.S. Constitution,* ed. David E. Narrett and Joyce S. Goldberg, 20–47. College Station: Texas A&M University Press, 1988.

Mushkat, Jerome, and Joseph G. Rayback. *Martin Van Buren: Law, Politics, and the Shaping of Republican Ideology.* DeKalb: Northern Illinois University Press, 1987.

Myers, Richmond E. "The Early Turnpikes of the Susquehanna Valley." *Pennsylvania History* 21 (1954): 248–59.

Nagel, Paul C. "The Election of 1824: A Reconsideration Based on Newspaper Opinion." *Journal of Southern History* 26 (1960): 315–29.

Narrett, David E. "A Zeal for Liberty: The Anti-Federalist Case against the Constitution in New York." In *Essays on Liberty and Federalism: The Shaping of the U.S. Constitution,* ed. David E. Narrett and Joyce S. Goldberg, 48–87. College Station: Texas A&M University Press, 1988.

Narrett, David E., and Joyce S. Goldberg, eds. *Essays on Liberty and Federalism: The Shaping of the U.S. Constitution.* College Station: Texas A&M University Press, 1988.

Nash, Gary B. *The Urban Crucible: Social Change, Political Consciousness, and The Origins of the American Revolution.* Cambridge, Mass.: Harvard University Press, 1979.

Nelson, E. C. "Presidential Influence on the Policy of Internal Improvements." *Iowa Journal of History and Politics* 4 (1906): 3–69.

Nelson, John R., Jr. *Liberty and Property: Political Economy and Policymaking in the New Nation, 1789–1812.* Baltimore: Johns Hopkins University Press, 1987.

Nettels, Curtis. "The Mississippi Valley and the Constitution, 1815–29." *Mississippi Valley Historical Review* 11 (1924–25): 332–37.

Newcomer, Lee. "A History of the Indiana Internal Improvement Bonds." *Indiana Magazine of History* 30 (1936): 106–15.

Newmyer, R. Kent. *Supreme Court Justice Joseph Story: Statesman of the Old Republic.* Chapel Hill: University of North Carolina Press, 1985.

Nichols, Roy F. *The Disruption of American Democracy.* 1948; reprint, New York: Collier, 1962.

Niven, John. *John C. Calhoun and the Price of Union: A Biography.* Baton Rouge: Louisiana State University Press, 1988.

Noe, Kenneth W. *Southwest Virginia's Railroad: Modernization and the Sectional Crisis.* Urbana: University of Illinois Press, 1994.

Nolan, J. Bennett. *The Schuylkill.* New Brunswick, N.J.: Rutgers University Press, 1951.

North, Douglass C. *The Economic Growth of the United States, 1790–1860.* Englewood Cliffs, N.J.: Prentice-Hall, 1961.

Novak, William J. *The People's Welfare: Law and Regulation in Nineteenth-Century America.* Chapel Hill: University of North Carolina Press, 1996.

Onuf, Peter S. "Liberty, Development, and Union: Visions of the West in the 1780s." *William and Mary Quarterly,* 3rd ser., 43 (1986): 179–213.

———. *The Origins of the Federal Republic: Jurisdictional Controversies in the United States, 1775–1787.* Philadelphia: University of Pennsylvania Press, 1983.

———. *Statehood and Union: A History of the Northwest Ordinance.* Bloomington: Indiana University Press, 1987.

———, ed. *Jeffersonian Legacies.* Charlottesville: University Press of Virginia, 1993.

Onuf, Peter S., and Nicholas Onuf. *Federal Union, Modern World: The Law of Nations in an Age of Revolutions, 1776–1814.* Madison, Wis.: Madison House, 1993.

Pangle, Thomas. *The Spirit of Modern Republicanism: The Moral Vision of the American Founders and the Philosophy of Locke.* Chicago: University of Chicago Press, 1988.

Parks, Robert J. *Democracy's Railroads: Public Enterprise in Jacksonian Michigan.* Port Washington, N.Y.: Kennikat Press, 1972.

Parsons, Lynn Hudson. *John Quincy Adams.* Madison, Wis.: Madison House, 1998.

Pegg, Herbert Dale. *The Whig Party in North Carolina.* Chapel Hill, N.C.: Colonial Press, 1968.

Pencak, William, and Conrad Edick Wright, eds. *New York and the Rise of American Capitalism: Economic Development and the Social and Political History of an American State, 1780–1870.* New York: New-York Historical Society, 1989.

Perkins, Edwin J. *American Public Finance and Financial Services, 1700–1815.* Columbus: Ohio State University Press, 1994.

Perkins, Elizabeth. *Border Life: Experience and Memory in the Revolutionary Ohio Valley.* Chapel Hill: University of North Carolina, 1998.

Peterson, Merrill D. *The Great Triumvirate: Webster, Clay, and Calhoun.* New York: Oxford University Press, 1987.

———. *Thomas Jefferson and the New Nation: A Biography.* New York: Oxford University Press, 1970.

Phelps, Glenn A. *George Washington and American Constitutionalism.* Lawrence: University Press of Kansas, 1993.

Pocock, J. G. A. *The Machiavellian Moment: Florentine Political Thought and the Atlantic Republic Tradition.* Princeton: Princeton University Press, 1975.

Polakoff, Keith Ian. *Political Parties in American History.* New York: John Wiley & Sons, 1981.

Potter, David M. *The Impending Crisis, 1848–1861.* New York: Harper & Row, 1976.

Pred, Allan R. *Urban Growth and the Circulation of Information: The United States System of Cities, 1790–1840.* Cambridge, Mass.: Harvard University Press, 1973.

Rahe, Paul. *Republics Ancient and Modern: Classical Republicanism and the American Revolution*. Chapel Hill: University of North Carolina Press, 1992.

Rakove, Jack N. *The Beginnings of National Politics: An Interpretive History of the Continental Congress*. New York: Alfred A. Knopf, 1979.

———. *Original Meanings: Politics and Ideas in the Making of the Constitution*. New York: Alfred A. Knopf, 1996.

Ratcliffe, Donald J. "Politics in Jacksonian Ohio: Reflections on the Ethnocultural Interpretation." *Ohio History* 88 (1979): 5–36.

Ratner, Lorman A. *Andrew Jackson and His Tennessee Lieutenants: A Study in Political Culture*. Westport, Conn.: Greenwood Press, 1997.

Remini, Robert V. *Andrew Jackson and the Course of American Democracy, 1833–1845*. New York: Harper & Row, 1984.

———. *Andrew Jackson and the Course of American Empire, 1767–1821*. New York: Harper & Row, 1977.

———. *Andrew Jackson and the Course of American Freedom, 1822–1832*. New York: Harper & Row, 1981.

———. *Henry Clay: Statesman for the Union*. New York: W. W. Norton, 1991.

———. *Henry Clay: Statesman of the Old Republic*. New York: W. W. Norton, 1991.

———. *Martin Van Buren and the Making of the Democratic Party*. New York: Columbia University Press, 1951.

Rezneck, Samuel. "The Depression of 1819–1822: A Social History." *American Historical Review* 39 (1933): 28–47.

Rhoads, Willard R. "The Pennsylvania Canal." *Western Pennsylvania Historical Magazine* 43 (1960): 203–38.

Rice, Otis K. *The Allegheny Frontier: West Virginia Beginnings, 1730–1830*. Lexington: University Press of Kentucky, 1970.

Rice, Philip M. "The Early Development of the Roanoke Waterways—A Study in Interstate Relations." *North Carolina Historical Review* 31 (1954): 50–74.

———. "Internal Improvements in Virginia, 1775–1860." Ph.D. diss., University of North Carolina, 1948.

Riesman, Janet. "Money, Credit, and Federalist Political Economy." In *Beyond Confederation: Origins of the Constitution and American National Identity*, ed. Richard Beeman, Stephen Botein, and Edward C. Carter II, 128–61. Chapel Hill: University of North Carolina Press, 1987.

Risjord, Norman K. *The Old Republicans: Southern Conservatism in the Age of Jefferson*. New York: Columbia University Press, 1965.

Roeber, A. G. *Faithful Magistrates and Republican Lawyers: Creators of Virginia's Legal Culture, 1680–1810*. Chapel Hill: University of North Carolina Press, 1981.

Rothbard, Murray N. *The Panic of 1819: Reactions and Policies*. New York: Columbia University Press, 1962.

Rowe, Kenneth Wyer. *Mathew Carey: A Study in American Economic Development*. Johns Hopkins University Studies in Historical and Political Science, ser. 51:4. Baltimore: Johns Hopkins University Press, 1933.

Royster, Charles. *The Fabulous History of the Dismal Swamp Company: A Story of George Washington's Times*. New York: Alfred A. Knopf, 1999.

———. *Light-Horse Harry Lee and the Legacy of the American Revolution*. New York: Alfred A. Knopf, 1981.

———. *A Revolutionary People at War: The Continental Army and American Character, 1775–1783*. Chapel Hill: University of North Carolina Press, 1979.

Rubin, Julius. "Canal or Railroad: Imitation and Innovation in the Response to the Erie Canal in Philadelphia, Baltimore, and Boston." *Transactions of the American Philosophical Society*, n.s., 51 (1961): 2–103.

———. "An Imitative Public Improvement: The Pennsylvania Main Line." In *Canals and American Economic Development*, ed. Carter Goodrich, 67–114. New York: Columbia University Press, 1961.

———. "An Innovative Public Improvement: The Erie Canal." In *Canals and American Economic Development*, ed. Carter Goodrich, 15–66. New York: Columbia University Press, 1961.

Russ, William A., Jr. "The Partnership between Public and Private Initiative in the History of Pennsylvania." *Pennsylvania History* 20 (1953): 1–21.

Russell, Robert R. *Improvement of Communication with the Pacific Coast as an Issue in American Politics, 1783–1864*. Cedar Rapids, Iowa: Torch Press, 1948.

Salsbury, Stephen. *The State, the Investor, and the Railroad: The Boston & Albany, 1825–1867*. Cambridge, Mass.: Harvard University Press, 1967.

Sanderlin, Walter S. "The Expanding Horizons of the Schuylkill Navigation Company, 1815–1870." *Pennsylvania History* 36 (1969): 174–91.

———. *The Great National Project: A History of the Chesapeake and Ohio Canal*. Baltimore: Johns Hopkins University Press, 1946.

Scheiber, Harry N. "Alfred Kelley and the Ohio Business Elite, 1822–1859." *Ohio History* 87 (1978): 365–92.

———. "Entrepreneurship and Western Development: The Case of Micajah T. Williams." *Business History Review* 37 (1963): 345–68.

———. *Ohio Canal Era: A Case Study of Government and the Economy, 1820–1861*. Athens: Ohio University Press, 1969.

———. "The Ohio Canal Movement, 1820–1825." *Ohio Historical Quarterly* 69 (1960): 231–56.

———. "The Pennsylvania & Ohio Canal: Transport Innovation, Mixed Enterprise, and Urban Commercial Rivalry, 1825–1861." *Old Northwest* 6 (1980): 105–35.

———. "State Policy and the Public Domain: The Ohio Canal Lands." *Journal of Economic History* 25 (1965): 86–113.

———. "Urban Rivalry and Internal Improvements in the Old Northwest, 1820–1860." *Ohio History* 71 (1962): 227–92.

Schlesinger, Arthur M., Jr., ed. *History of American Presidential Elections, 1789–1968*. 4 vols. New York: Chelsea House, 1971.

Schultz, Ronald. *The Republic of Labor: Philadelphia Artisans and the Politics of Class, 1720–1830*. New York: Oxford University Press, 1993.

Scranton, Philip. *Proprietary Capitalism: The Textile Manufacture at Philadelphia, 1800–1885*. New York: Cambridge University Press, 1983.

Seager, Robert, II. "Henry Clay and the Politics of Compromise and Non-Compromise." *Register of the Kentucky Historical Society* 85 (1987): 1–28.

Sellers, Charles G., Jr. "Jackson Men with Feet of Clay." *American Historical Review* 62 (1957): 537–51.

———. *The Market Revolution: Jacksonian America, 1815–1846*. New York: Oxford University Press, 1991.

Shade, William G. *Democratizing the Old Dominion: Virginia and the Second Party System, 1824–1861*. Charlottesville: University Press of Virginia, 1996.

Shalhope, Robert. *John Taylor of Caroline: Pastoral Republican*. Columbia: University of South Carolina Press, 1980.

Sharp, James Roger. *American Politics in the Early Republic: The New Nation in Crisis.* New Haven: Yale University Press, 1993.

Shaw, Peter. *The Character of John Adams.* Chapel Hill: University of North Carolina Press, 1976.

Shaw, Ronald E. "The Canal Era in the Old Northwest." In *Transportation and the Early Nation: Papers Presented at an Indiana American Revolution Bicentennial Symposium,* 89–112. Indianapolis: Indiana Historical Society, 1982.

———. *Canals for a Nation, 1790–1860.* Lexington: University Press of Kentucky, 1990.

———. *Erie Water West: A History of the Erie Canal.* Lexington: University of Kentucky Press, 1966.

Shelling, Richard I. "Philadelphia and the Agitation in 1825 for the Pennsylvania Canal." *Pennsylvania Magazine of History and Biography* 62 (1938): 175–204.

Sheriff, Carol. *The Artificial River: The Erie Canal and the Paradox of Progress, 1817–1862.* New York: Hill & Wang, 1996.

Simons, Richard S., and Francis Parker. *Railroads of Indiana.* Bloomington: Indiana University Press, 1997.

Siry, Stephen E. *DeWitt Clinton and the American Political Economy: Sectionalism, Politics, and Republican Ideology, 1787–1828.* New York: Peter Lang, 1990.

Skeen, C. Edward. "'Vox Populi, Vox Dei': The Compensation Act of 1816 and the Rise of Popular Politics." *Journal of the Early Republic* 6 (1986): 253–74.

Smith, Edwin J. "Spencer Roane." *John P. Branch Historical Papers of Randolph-Macon College* 2 (1905): 4–33.

Smith, Willard H. *Schuyler Colfax: The Changing Fortunes of a Political Idol.* Indianapolis: Indiana Historical Bureau, 1952.

Sneddon, Leonard J. "Maryland and Sectional Politics: Canal Building in the Federalist Era." *Maryland Historian* 6 (1975): 79–84.

Sorin, Gerald. *The New York Abolitionists: A Case Study of Political Radicalism.* Westport, Conn.: Greenwood Press, 1971.

Southerland, Henry deLeon, Jr. "The Federal Road, Gateway to Alabama, 1806–1836." *Alabama Review* 39 (1986): 96–109.

Southerland, Henry deLeon, Jr., and Jerry Elijah Brown. *The Federal Road through Georgia, the Creek Nation, and Alabama, 1806–1836.* Tuscaloosa: University of Alabama Press, 1989.

Spivak, Burton. *Jefferson's English Crisis: Commerce, Embargo, and the Republican Revolution.* Charlottesville: University Press of Virginia, 1979.

Stagg, J.C.A. *Mr. Madison's War: Politics, Diplomacy, and Warfare in the Early American Republic, 1783–1830.* Princeton: Princeton University Press, 1983.

Stevens, John Austin. "Christopher Coles, the First Projector of Inland Navigation in America." *Magazine of American History* 2 (1878): 340–48.

Still, John A. "Ethan Allen Brown and Ohio's Canal System." *Ohio Historical Quarterly* 66 (1957): 22–56.

Stone, Richard Gabriel. *Hezekiah Niles as an Economist.* Johns Hopkins University Studies in Historical and Political Science, ser. 51:4. Baltimore: Johns Hopkins University Press, 1933.

Storing, Herbert J. *What the Anti-Federalists Were For?* Vol. 1 of *The Complete Anti-Federalist,* ed. Herbert J. Storing, with the assistance of Murray Dry. Chicago: University of Chicago Press, 1981.

Stourzh, Gerald R. *Alexander Hamilton and the Idea of Republican Government.* Stanford: Stanford University Press, 1970.

Stover, John F. *History of the Baltimore and Ohio Railroad*. West Lafayette, Ind.: Purdue University Press, 1987.

———. *Iron Road to the West: American Railroads in the 1850s*. New York: Columbia University Press, 1978.

———. "Iron Roads in the Old Northwest: The Railroads and the Growing Nation." In *Transportation and the Early Nation: Papers Presented at an Indiana American Revolution Bicentennial Symposium*, 135–56. Indianapolis: Indiana Historical Society, 1982.

Summers, Mark W. *The Era of Good Stealings*. New York: Oxford University Press, 1993.

———. *The Plundering Generation: Corruption and the Crisis of the Union, 1849–1861*. New York: Oxford University Press, 1987.

Sutton, Robert P. "Nostalgia, Pessimism, and Malaise: The Doomed Aristocrat in Late-Jeffersonian Virginia." *Virginia Magazine of History and Biography* 76 (1968): 41–55.

Sweig, Donald. "A Capital on the Potomac." *Virginia Magazine of History and Biography* 87 (1979): 74–104.

Sydnor, Charles. *American Revolutionaries in the Making: Political Practices in Washington's Virginia*. New York: Free Press, 1952.

———. *The Development of Southern Sectionalism, 1819–1848*. Baton Rouge: Louisiana State University Press, 1948.

Taussig, F. W. *Tariff History of the United States*. 1892; reprint, New York: Johnson Reprint, 1966.

Taylor, George Rogers. *The Transportation Revolution, 1815–1860*. New York: Rinehart, 1951.

Teagarden, Ernest M. "Builders of the Ohio Canal, 1825–1832." *Inland Seas* 19 (1968): 94–103.

Terrell, Bruce G. "The James River Bateau: Nautical Commerce in Piedmont Virginia." *Virginia Cavalcade* 38 (1989): 180–91.

Thornton, J. Mills, III. *Politics and Power in a Slave Society: Alabama, 1800–1860*. Baton Rouge: Louisiana State University Press, 1978.

Tomlins, Christopher L. *Law, Labor, and Ideology in the Early American Republic*. New York: Cambridge University Press, 1993.

Trelease, Allen W. *The North Carolina Railroad*. Chapel Hill: University of North Carolina Press, 1991.

———. "The Passive Voice: The State and the North Carolina Railroad, 1849–1871." *North Carolina Historical Review* 61 (1984): 174–204.

Tucker, Robert W., and David C Hendrickson. *Empire of Liberty: The Statecraft of Thomas Jefferson*. New York: Oxford University Press, 1990.

Turner, Charles W. "Early Virginia Railroad Entrepreneurs and Personnel." *Virginia Magazine of History and Biography* 58 (1950): 325–34.

Van Burkleo, Sandra F. "'The Paws of Banks': The Origins and Significance of Kentucky's Decision to Tax Federal Bankers, 1818–1820." *Journal of the Early Republic* 9 (1989): 457–87.

Wagstaff, Henry McGilbert. *State Rights and Political Parties in North Carolina—1776–1861*. Johns Hopkins University Studies in Historical and Political Science, ser. 24:7–8. Baltimore: Johns Hopkins University Press, 1906.

Ward, George Washington. *The Early Development of the Chesapeake and Ohio Canal Project*. Johns Hopkins University Studies in Historical and Political Science, ser. 17:9–11. Baltimore: Johns Hopkins University Press, 1899.

Ward, James A. *Railroads and the Character of America, 1820–1887*. Knoxville: University of Tennessee Press, 1986.

Watson, Alan D. "North Carolina and Internal Improvements, 1783–1861." *North Carolina Historical Review* 74 (1996): 37–73.

Watson, Harry L. *Andrew Jackson versus Henry Clay: Democracy and Development in Antebellum America*. New York: Bedford Books, 1998.

——. *Jacksonian Politics and Community Conflict: The Emergence of the Second American Party System in Cumberland County, North Carolina*. Baton Rouge: Louisiana State University Press, 1981.

——. *Liberty and Power: The Politics of Jacksonian America*. New York: Hill & Wang, 1990.

——. "'Old Rip' and New Era." In *The North Carolina Experience: An Interpretive and Documentary History*, ed. Lindley S. Butler and Alan D. Watson , 217–40. Chapel Hill: University of North Carolina Press, 1984.

——. "Squire Oldway and His Friends: Opposition to Internal Improvements in Antebellum North Carolina." *North Carolina Historical Review* 54 (1977): 105–19.

Watts, Steven. *The Republic Reborn: War and the Making of Liberal America*. Baltimore: Johns Hopkins University Press, 1987.

Way, Peter. *Common Labor: Workers and the Digging of North American Canals, 1780–1860*. Baltimore: Johns Hopkins University Press, 1993.

Weaver, Charles Clinton. *Internal Improvements in North Carolina Previous to 1860*. Johns Hopkins University Studies in Historical and Political Science, ser. 21:3–4. Baltimore: Johns Hopkins University Press, 1903.

Werner, Walter, and Steven T. Smith. *Wall Street*. New York: Columbia University Press, 1991.

White, G. Edward. *The Marshall Court & Cultural Change, 1815–1835*. Abr. ed. New York: Oxford University Press, 1991.

White, Leonard D. *The Federalists: A Study in Administrative History*. New York: Macmillan, 1948.

——. *The Jeffersonians: A Study in Administrative History, 1801–1829*. New York: Macmillan, 1951.

Whitford, Noble E. *History of the Canal System of the State of New York*. 2 vols. Albany: Office of the State Engineer, 1906.

Wiebe, Robert H. *The Opening of American Society: From the Adoption of the Constitution to the Eve of Disunion*. New York: Alfred A. Knopf, 1984.

Wilentz, Sean. *Chants Democratic: New York City and the Rise of the American Working Class, 1788–1850*. New York: Oxford University Press, 1984.

Wilkes, George. *Proposal for a National Rail-Road to the Pacific Ocean*. New York: Daniel Adee, Printer, 1847.

Williams, Max R. "The Foundations of the Whig Party in North Carolina: A Synthesis and a Modest Proposal." *North Carolina Historical Review* 47 (1970): 115–29.

Willoughby, William R. "Early American Interest in Waterway Connections between the East and the West." *Indiana Magazine of History* 52 (1956): 319–42.

Wills, Garry. *Cincinnatus: George Washington and the Enlightenment*. Garden City, N.Y.: Doubleday, 1984.

——. *Inventing America: Jefferson's Declaration of Independence*. Garden City, N.Y.: Doubleday, 1978.

Wilson, Major L. *Space, Time, and Freedom: The Quest for Nationality and the Irrepressible Conflict, 1815–1861*. Westport, Conn.: Greenwood Press, 1974.

Wiltse, Charles. *John C. Calhoun.* 3 vols. Indianapolis: Bobbs-Merrill, 1944–51.

Wood, Frederic J. *Turnpikes of New England and the Evolution of the Same through England, Virginia, and Maryland.* Boston: Marshall Jones Company, 1919.

Wood, Gordon S. *The Creation of the American Republic, 1776–1787.* Chapel Hill: University of North Carolina Press, 1969.

———. "Interests and Disinterestedness in the Making of the Constitution." In *Beyond Confederation,* ed. Richard Beeman, Stephen Botein, and Edward C. Carter II, 69–109. Chapel Hill: University of North Carolina Press, 1987.

———. *The Radicalism of the American Revolution.* New York: Alfred A. Knopf, 1992.

Woolfolk, George Ruble. "Rival Urban Communication Schemes for the Possession of the Northwest Trade, 1783–1800." *Mid-America* 38 (1956): 214–32.

Young, Alfred F. *The Democratic-Republicans of New York: The Origins, 1763–1797.* Chapel Hill: University of North Carolina Press, 1967.

Young, James Sterling. *The Washington Community, 1800–1828.* New York: Columbia University Press, 1966.

Zelinsky, Wilbur. *Nation into State: The Shifting Symbolic Foundations of American Nationalism.* Chapel Hill: University of North Carolina Press, 1988.

INDEX